Civilization in the 5th Century

Frederic Ozanam

Published 2017 by Jovian Press

10 9 8 7 6 5 4 3 2 1 0 00 000 0

CONTENTS

HISTORY OF CIVILIZATION IN THE FIFTH CENTURY.

Doubtless fascinating to watch the genius of a people burst forth under a burning or an icy sky, on virgin soil, or in historic land, yield to the impress of contemporary events, and put forth its first blossoms in those epic traditions or in those familiar songs, which still retain all the uncultured perfume of nature. But beneath that popular poetry wherein the great nations of Europe have shown all the variety of their respective characters, we perceive a literature which is learned but common to all alike, and a depository of the theological, philosophical, and political doctrines which moulded for eight hundred years the education of Christendom. Let us study that common education, and consider the modern nations, no longer in that isolation to which the special historian of England or of Italy condemns himself, but in the spirit of that fruitful intercourse marked out for them by Providence, tracing the history of literature up to the Middle Age, by reascending to that obscure moment which beheld letters escaping from the collapse of the old order, and thence following it through the schools of the barbarous epoch, till the new settlement of the nations, and its egress from those schools to take modern languages in possession.

This long period extends from the fifth to the thirteenth century. Amidst the tempests of our times, and in face of the brevity of life, a powerful charm draws us to these studies. Wo seek in the history of literature for civilization, and in the story of the latter we mark human progress by the aid of Christianity. Perhaps in a period in which the bravest spirits can only see decay, a profession of the doctrine of progress is out of place; nor can one renew an old and discredited position, useless formerly as a commonplace, dangerous now-a-days as a paradox. This generous belief, or youthful illusion, if the name suits better, seems nothing better than a rash opinion, alike reproved by conscience and denied by history. The dogma of human perfectibility finds little adhesion in a discouraged society, but mayhap that very discouragement is in fault. Though often useful to humble man, it is never prudent to drive him to despair. Souls must not, as Plato says, lose their wings, and, renouncing a perfection pronounced impossible, fling themselves into pleasures of easy achievement. For there are two doctrines of progress: the first, nourished in the schools of sensualism, rehabilitates the passions, and, promising the nations an earthly paradise at the end of a flowery path, gives them only a premature hell at the end of a way of blood; whilst the second, born from and inspired by Christianity, points to progress in the victory of the spirit over the flesh, promises nothing but as prize of warfare, and pronounces the creed which carries war into the individual soul to be the only way of peace for the nations.

We must try and restore the doctrine of progress by Christianity as a comfort in these troubled days; we must justify it in refitting its own religious and philosophical principles, and cleansing it from errors which had placed it at the disposal of the most hateful aims; we must prove it by applying it to those ages which seem chosen to bely it, to an epoch of worse aspect, of misery unrivalled by our own—for we cannot join with those who accuse Providence itself in the blame they cast on the present time. Traversing rapidly the period between the fall of the Empire and the decline of the barbarian powers, where most historians have found only ruin, we shall see the renewal of the human mind, and sketch the history of light in an age of darkness, of progress in an era of decay.

Paganism had no idea of progress; rather it felt itself to lie under a law of irremediable decay. Mindful of the height whence it had fallen, Humanity knew no way to remount its steeps. The Sacred Book of the Indians declared that in primitive ages, "Justice stood firm on four feet, truth was supreme, and mortals owed to iniquity none of their good things; but as time went on, justice lost each foot in succession, and as each fell, rightly earned property diminished one quarter." Hesiod amused the Greeks by his tale of the Four Ages, the first of which saw modesty and justice fly, "leaving to mortals only devouring grief and irreparable woe." The Romans, the most sensible of men, placed in their ancestors the ideal of all wisdom; and the senators of the age of Tiberius, seated at the feet of their ancestral images, resigned themselves to deterioration in the words of Horace—

Ætas parentum, pejor avis tulit

Nos nequiores mox daturos

Progeniem vitiosiorem.

And if here or there a wonderful foreboding of the future breaks out, as in the case of Seneca, announcing in grand terms the revelation reserved by science for futurity, they were but the dawn-lights of Christianity just arising upon the earth, and gilding with its rays intellects which seemed most remote from its influence.

It is with the Gospel that the doctrine of progress appeared, not only teaching, but enforcing human perfectibility; the saying *Estote perfecti* condemns humanity to an endless advance—for its end is in eternity. And what was of precept to the individual, became the law of Society. St. Paul, comparing the Church to a mighty body, desires it to increase to a perfect maturity, and realize in its plenitude the humanity of Christ; and a Father of the Church, St. Vincent of Lerins, confirms this reading of the Sacred Text by inquiring, when he had established the immutability of Catholic dogma, " Will, then, there be no progress in the Church of Christ ? Surely there will, and in plenty; for who could be so jealous of the good of mankind, so accursed of God, as to stay that progress ? But it must be advance and not change; of necessity, with the ages and centuries, there must be an increase of intelligence, of wisdom, of knowledge, for each as for all."

The great Bossuet continued this patristic tradition, and though so hostile to innovation, believed in an advance in the faith.

" Although constant and perpetual, the Catholic unity is not without her progress; she is known in one place more thoroughly than in another, at one time more clearly, more distinctly, more universally than at another." We cannot wonder at this contrast between the sentiments of antiquity and of Christian times. Progress is an effort whereby man breaks loose from his present imperfection to seek perfection; from the real, to approach the ideal; from self-regard to that which is higher than self ; when he loves and is content with his corruption, there can be no progress. The ancients were, doubtless, aware of the divine spell of perfection; in many points they even came near to it, but perceived only under an obscure and misty figure, though it elevated souls for a time, weighed down by pagan egoism, they fell back upon self; and that mankind might come forth from itself not for a mere moment, but forever, the pure perfection of God's revelation must shine upon his soul.

The God of Christianity stands revealed as Truth, Goodness, and Beauty, drawing man to Him by faith through Truth, by hope through Beauty, by love through Goodness. Capable of grasping what is true and good, the human mind catches only a glimpse of what is beautiful. Truth we define, as the schools of old, to be the equation of the idea and the object, *Æquatio intellectus et rei.* We can express goodness, after Aristotle, still farther back, as being "the end to which all existences tend;" but beauty we cannot define, or, rather, philosophers exhaust themselves in attempts which fail to become classical. Plato pronounces it to be the splendour of the truth; according to Augustine, Beauty is unity, order, harmony. But absolute Beauty is precisely the absolute harmony of the divine attributes; lying so little within our cognizance that we fail to reconcile the liberty of God with His eternal necessity, or His justice with His mercy. Thus these mysterious concords elude whilst they charm us, and perfect beauty is ever longed for and never present.

According to Christianity, man lives a double life of nature and grace. In the supernatural order, truth revealed to faith forms dogma; good embraced by man becomes morality; beauty glanced at by hope inspires worship: though everything seems immovable, yet, even here, according to Vincent of Lerins, the law of progress claims obedience. Dogma is changeless, but faith is an active power: *Fides quoerens intellectum.* Preserving truth, it meditates and comments upon it, and from the Credo which a child's memory may hold evolves the Summa of St. Thomas. Precepts are fixed, but their practice is multifarious: the Sermon on the Mount contained all the inspiration of Christian love, but ages were required to draw from it the monasteries, schools, and hospitals which civilized and covered Europe. Worship lastly is unchangeable in its fundamental idea of sacrifice: and a little bread and wine sufficed for the Martyr's liturgy in the dungeon, but untiring hope inspires man to draw nearer to that Divine beauty which cannot be gazed on face to face on earth—it brings in aid everything which seems to point to heaven, as flowers, fire, or incense; gives to stone its flight, and causes its cathedral spires to soar aloft, whilst it bears prayer on its double wings of poetry and music, higher than the churches or their towers. But it reaches only a point infinitely below its aspiration, and thence springs the melancholy which is breathed forth from the hymns of our great festivals; therefore the devout man feels the weariness of the world stealing upon him at the end of our sacred rites, and says with St. Paul, *Cupio dissolvi,* "I desire to be dissolved and be with Christ," the constant cry of the soul which pines for a larger sphere; whilst Christianity represents her saints advancing from light to light, and the bliss of the life to come as an eternal progress.

The supernatural order rules, enlightens, and fertilizes the order of nature. Philosophy is nourished by dogma; the laws of religion afford a basis to political institutions, and worship produces architects and poets; yet the natural order, although subordinate, remains distinct, with reason, however insufficient, as a light peculiar to itself, manifesting truth, beauty, and goodness in social organization, and through the arts. Science begins in faith and finds therein her principle of progress, for there is a natural faith which is the very foundation of reason, and gives science a group of undemonstrable truths as a point of departure. Faith is necessary to science, and Descartes, wishing to rebuild the edifice of human knowledge, allowed himself the single certitude, *Cogito ergo sum.* At the same time faith starts science on a boundless course by giving it the idea of the infinite, from which pitiless and tormenting thought, the human mind, condemned to despise that it knows, to rush with passion into the unknown, will never he delivered until, arrived at the end of Nature, it finds God. In the second place, love becomes the principle of progress in social institutions. This order rests on two virtues, justice and charity; but justice involves love as necessary to that recognition of the right of another which narrows our own right and restrains our freedom of action. And justice has its limits, but charity has none: pressed by the command to do to others the good desired for one's self, which is infinite, the lover of mankind will never feel that he has done enough for his fellows till he has spent his life in sacrifice, and died, declaring, "Iain au unprofitable servant." Lastly, hope is the principle of progress in art. We know how perfect beauty flies at the pursuit of the human imagination, and no one has explained more vividly than St. Augustine the agony of the soul before that eternal flight of the eternally desired ideal.

" For my own part, my expression nearly always displeases me, for I long for the better one which in thought I believe that I possess; the idea illumines my mind with the rapidity of the lightning flash, but not so language: it is slow and halting, and whilst it is unfolding itself, thought has retired into its mysterious obscurity."

His complaint is common to all who seek for a beauty they have imaged, and are high-souled enough to confess that they have never found; it was that of the dying Virgil bequeathing his " Æneid " to the flames, of Tasso inconsolable over the defects of his " Jerusalem; " but still hope, stronger than the acknowledged impotence of these mighty minds, regains a hold on their successors, and brings them back to the interrupted task; she inspires the generations of architects and painters who build after the Parthenon, the Coliseum, and Notre Dame de Paris have been reared, or paint Christs and Madonnas before time has effaced the colours of Giotto and Raphael, or those still more hardy poets who dare to advance upon a world that yet rings with the measures of Homer or of Virgil. It is true that such inimitable examples trouble them at the outset, making them hesitate like Dante at the threshold of his poetic pilgrimage to Hell; but hope drives them on, and if more than once on his shadowy course the poet feels his knees tremble and his heart quail, hope revives him, and pointing to Beatrice, his ideal smiling upon him from on high, forces his steps to their goal. If it is thus that Christian philosophy understands the law of progress, the question remains whether it is a moral or necessary law, whether it bears resistance or demands obedience? History seems to answer that it is necessary and perforce obeyed, less visibly so in times of heathenism, when darkened dogma lent but a feeble light to the progress of the mind, but distinctly when Christianity had placed religious certainty like a pillar of fire at the vanguard of humanity.

The course of ages affords no grander spectacle than that of mankind taking nature in possession through science; it has been traced by M. von Humboldt with an inspired hand, albeit with that of a septuagenarian, — and we may add two features, namely, that man, in gaining creation, is reducing into possession both himself and his God. We behold the Ægyptian race contracted at first in the Nile valley, the desert on either side setting its limit to their habitable world; then raising their eyes to those stars whose revolutions brought back the overflow of the sacred stream, they marvelled at their ordered courses, counted them, noted their rising and setting, till the ignorant people bound to a corner of the earth gained knowledge of the sky. The Phoenicians appeared, armed with astronomy and calculation, braved not only the seas which washed their shores, but the Atlantic to the Irish coasts, whence their ships brought tin, and the world opened to their mariners her Western side. Greece again turned her mind to the East, whence danger had come to her with Darius and Xerxes—where Alexander, that bold youth, or rather faithful servant of civilization, was to find empire and double in a few years the Grecian world: but her Aristotle was to carve out for her a vaster and more lasting dominion, by laying hands on the invisible as well as the visible, and by giving laws alike to Nature and to Thought. Sages in many generations continued his work; Eratosthenes measured the earth; Hipparchus mapped out the heavens; humanity became self-regarding—philosophers studied man in his essence, historians in his deeds. Herodotus affixed to his tale of the Median wars the history of Egypt and of Persia, and Diodorus Siculus pushed his research to the remotest nations of the north. Rome added little indeed to these discoveries, but she traversed the known world throughout, pierced roads over it, rendered it available to men, *Perrius orb is;* the nations approached— incapable of mutual love, circumstance compelled them to mutual knowledge, and in the " Germania" of Tacitus was written the history of the future. That ancient science had only an imperfect knowledge of God; Plato, who made the nearest approach to the Father of all things, did not conceive Him to be a Sole, Free, or Creating Power, but opposed to Him an Eternal Matter. Paganism threw a shadow likewise over nature and humanity; as the majority of minds shrank from exploring the secrets of a physical world peopled by their imagination with jealous divinities, so historians could do little justice to races sprung from hostile gods, destined some to rule, others to obey. Progress would have stopped had not Christianity appeared to chase away the superstitious awe which environed nature, and restore mankind to itself in unity of origin and of destiny.

With Christianity appeared conquerors destined to leave the Eagles of Rome in their rear. In the seventh century Byzantine monks buried themselves in the steppes of Central Asia, and crossed the great wall of China. Six centuries later monks also carried Papal mandates to the Khan of Tartary, and showed to Genoese and Venetian merchants the road to Pekin. Following on their track, Marco Polo traversed the Celestial Empire, and preceded by two centuries the Portuguese mariners to the isles of Sunda. In another region, Irish monks, impelled by the missionary fervour that burnt in their cloisters, ventured upon the Western Ocean, touched in 795 the frozen shores of Iceland, and, pursuing their pilgrimage towards the unknown land, were cast by the wind on the coast of America. When in the eleventh century the Norsemen landed in Greenland, they learned from the Esquimaux that to the south of their country, beyond the bay of Chesapeake, "white men might he seen clothed in long white robes, who marched singing and bearing banners." And yet those cloisters, whence issued the explorers of the globe, were devoted to divine culture, and gave birth to the scholastic theology which, starting from the idea of God, spread over the individual and society a light unknown to antiquity, so that those controversies, so often charged with over-subtlety, held minds in suspense for five hundred years, and were the discipline of modern reason.

The Middle Age was a better servant to the moral than the physical sciences; yet a word from Roger Bacon and the inexact calculations of Marco Polo impelled Columbus on the way to the New World; his faith was the better part of his genius—its obstinacy repaired the error of his conjectures, and in reward God gave him, as he said, the Keys of Ocean, the power of breaking the close-riveted fetters of the sea. An entire creation unfolded itself with the new earth; the tributes of plants and of animals multiplied; and when, some years later, the vessels of Magellan effected the voyage round the globe, man found himself master of his home. Science, too, landed at the ports of China and India, forced their impenetrable society, brought to light their sacred writings, their epopees and histories, and the moment approached in which she was to cause the hieroglyphics of Thebes and the inscriptions of Persepolis to speak.

And whilst man was conquering his earth, lest he should find a moment of repose Copernicus opened out immensity by breaking up the factitious heavens of Ptolemy; the stars fled back from the puny distance awarded them by the calculations of the old astronomy, but the telescope brought them back, and observation grouped them under simpler and more learned laws.

Earth itself seemed to fade in presence of those masses of heavenly bodies sown like islands in an ocean of light. But man grows greater in realizing his nothingness, and miserable are they who think such a vision is apt to estrange him from God, as if their expectations had been duped, and they had hoped to find Him seated, as the ancients fabled, on a throne of matter; for whatever carries man away from the visible and finite, brings him perforce nearer to the Being pronounced by the faith to be infinite and invisible, and as in David's times the stars were telling of the glory of the Creator, so to Kepler and to Newton they sang no other song. If thus the law of progress drags all human intelligence in its train, society cannot remain unmoved. In the great empires of the East, where an all-powerful authority crushed the will, there could be no progress because there was no contest. Liberty called the nations of Ionian Greece to action, made and unmade potentates as unsteady as the gods of Olympus; but there also progress had little power, because the principle of order was wanting. The two necessary constituents were confronted in Rome; one strong in the majesty of the patrician order, the other energizing in plebeian perseverance, they were bound to meet in conflict: but the struggle was ordered by rule, and from it proceeded that Roman law which was the greatest effort of antiquity to realize on earth the idea of justice. But admirable as its system was for regulating contracts, it was ill at ease in dealing with persons. It sanctioned slavery; and without speaking of the state of the wife and child, mere domestic chattels whom the family-father could slay or sell, established—such was its idea of justice—a class of men without God, or family, or law, or duty, or conscience. Cicero mentioned the word charity *(caritas)*, but, far from its reality, dared not condemn the gladiatorial conflicts. Pliny the Younger openly praised them, and Trajan, best of Roman princes, gave an hundred and twenty-three holidays, on which ten thousand combatants slaughtered each other for the pastime of the world's most polished race. We, in fact, dare not thoroughly realize all the horrors of that pagan society which mingled with the most refined mental pleasures the deepest glut of blood and lust.

It was the task of Christianity to revive in souls, and infuse into institutions, two sentiments without which neither charity nor justice can exist—respect for liberty and for human life. Not at one blow, but little by little, the Gospel reconquered freedom for man. It destroyed the very standing ground of slavery by giving the slave the conscience which made him no longer a thing but a person, and endowed him with duties and rights, while following centuries worked out its ruin by the favour shown to enfranchisement, and the transformation of personal servitude into villenage, till a constitution of Pope Alexander III. declared slavery no longer existent in the Christian society. Lapse of time, as well as genius and courage, were also wanted to re-establish respect for life. Christianity might have thought its labour half achieved when the laws of its emperors punished the murder of new-born infants, and suppressed gladiatorial shows; but then the barbarians bore down from their forests their twin-craving for gold and carnage—people armed itself against people, city against city, castle against castle, and the distracted Church was forced to throw herself between the combatants, protesting her hatred of blood, *ecclesia abhorret a sanguine*, while the barbarous instinct still burst forth amid crusades, and ran riot at the Sicilian Vespers. Such were the forces she had to contend with to prevent slaughter; and it was her work also to preserve life, to cherish the exposed infant, the useless and infirm burdens rejected by faithless society, but held in honour by Christianity. It seemed still harder to keep alive progress in Art; for what could be achieved after the ancients, or how could simplicity and grandeur be pushed beyond the limits they had reached ? Yet such beauty, if inimitable, is also inspiring, and leaves in the soul a desire, a passion of reproduction. Although the human mind could never surpass the works of antiquity, it could add monument to monument, and increase the adornment of its earthly abiding place. Beneath the Rome of the Caesars, of marble and gold—become, as Virgil says, the most beautiful of objects—was dug the subterranean city of the Christians; and the chapels hollowed out in these vaults by obscure and tardy progress were one day to pierce the earth, soar higher than the temples and theatres of Paganism, and in St. Peter's and St. Mary Major give to the ruins of Forum and Coliseum a living beauty. And yet if the ancient art possessed a special power of rendering the finite and visible with purity of form, calm of attitude, and truth of movement, it had not the gift of reproducing what was infinite and invisible. Who but admires the basreliefs with which Phidias adorned the frieze of the Parthenon—their simplicity of gesture, their vigour and grace of form; and yet in the quarrels of the Lapithae and Centaurs, we wonder at the calm on the features of the combatants, slaying without passion or dying without despair, as if art was straining to express some heroic ideal, inaccessible to human feeling. A contemporary witness, however, undeceives us by betraying the impotence of that Grecian art, which could give to stone life but not expression. Xenophon has shown us

Socrates loving to visit artists, and aid them with his advice, and how one day, on a visit to the painter Parrhasius, the following conversation took place:—

Socrates.—" Is not painting the art of reproducing what one sees ? You imitate with colour the depths and heights, light and shadow, softness and hardness, culture and rudeness, freshness and decay; but, still, that which is the most lovable, which most wins our confidence and kindles our longings, dost thou copy that, or must we look upon it as inimitable ? "

Parrhasius.—" How can it be represented, since it has neither proportion nor colour, and cannot, in short, be grasped by vision ? "

Socrates.—" But does not one mark in the expression now friendship, now dislike ? "

Parrhasius.—"Doubtless one does so."

Socrates.—" Surely, then, such passions should be shown in the expression of the eye, for pride, modesty, prudence, vivacity, meanness, all manifest themselves in the face, as in the gait, attitude, or gesture."

The same Christian presentiment which revealed to Socrates the nothingness of the false gods, and the perversity of the heathen morality, laid bare the want in Greek art. Christianity gave to the meanest of its faithful the sense of things which could not be seen nor measured; and the labourer of the Catacombs, adorning, in the lantern's flicker, and under the dread of persecution, the tombs of the martyrs, represented Christ, the Virgin, the Apostles, or Christians at prayer, with rude execution and faulty proportion, but with the light of heaven in their eyes. A consciousness of eternity animated these paintings; it passed into the frescoes which in the barbarous epoch adorned the churches of Rome and Ravenna, so that the whole progress of Italian painting from the thirteenth to the fifteenth centuries was absorbed in kindling Christian beauty of expression beneath the surface loveliness of the ancient forms.

Thirdly, classic art bore a character of unity. One sole form of civilization, the Graeco-Latin, was known to antiquity, and beyond its light there was nothing but barbarism. Cultured society glutted itself with that very barbarism in the form of slaves unable to participate in its mental delights. Art was but the pleasure of a minority. Whilst the wealthy Roman, retained by official duty at York or at Seleucia, had Propertius and Virgil read aloud to him under a portico which recalled his mother city, the Briton or Parthian was profoundly ignorant of his master's favourite authors. Christianity shed its inspiration over every nation which received it; revived the old idioms of the East, and enriched them with the beauties of her Greek, Syrian, Coptic, or Armenian liturgies; it burst forth in the Western languages, flowing as in five mighty rivers through the literature of Italy, France, Spain, Germany, and England. And thus two advantages accrued to the modern world: on the one hand, beauty, preserving its one type, found new and infinite manifestations in the genius, passion, and language of so many different races; on the other, mental pleasures were diffused, and art achieved its aim of educating not a few but the many, of delighting not the happy but the toilworn and suffering, and so shedding, as it were, a heavenly light on the intolerable weariness of life.

Thus mankind seems inevitably drawn towards a perfection never to be wholly compassed, but to which each succeeding age brings it nearer: a necessity which has scared many wise minds, and raised two objections against the doctrine of progress. Some repel it for its arrogance in supposing the men of each generation better than their forefathers, and thus bringing past time and tradition into contempt; others, as tending to fatalism, for if the last age must be best, as there are some in which virtue and genius were certainly darkened, progress is reduced to the simple uninterrupted increase of material benefit. But these difficulties vanish before the distinction between man the individual and mankind. God did not create mankind without an eternal plan, which, being sustained by His Infinite Power, cannot remain void of effect. The will which moves the stars rules also the inarch of civilization; humanity accomplishes its necessary destiny, but, being composed of free persons, with an element of liberty, so that error and crime find their place in its course, and we behold centuries which do not advance, but even recede—days of illness, and years of wandering. Who can say that the wretched carvings which degrade the Arch of Constantine excel the metopes of the Parthenon ? or that the France of Charles VI. was more powerful than that of Philip Augustus or St. Louis? We may go farther, and pronounce the fourteenth century with its Hundred Years' War, the sixteenth with its anarchy in the conscience and absolutism on the throne, the eighteenth with its license of mind and morals, frenzies of modern society—some recovery of which was seen in the wondrous outbreak of 1789, which, although turned from its proper course, brought back the nations to the Christian tradition of public right. In such times of disorder, God leaves individuals masters of their actions, but, keeping His hand on society, suffers it not to collapse, but waits till, arrived at a certain point, it can be brought back, as by a by-path, in darkness and pain, to the perfection of which it had been forgetful. So mankind never entirely and irremediably errs; the light burns somewhere which is to go to the front of the straying generation and bring it along in its wake. When the Gospel failed in the East, it dawned on the races of the North; and when the schools of Italy closed before the Lombard invasion, the literary passion was kindled in the depths of Irish monasteries. Sometimes progress, interrupted in politics, finds scope in art; and wearied art commits to science the guidance of the human intellect. If, as under Lous XIV., public spirit is silent, the voices of orators and poets attest that thought is not rocked to sleep. If, in our own age, eloquence and poetry seem to have fallen from the height to which the seventeenth century had Rome them, scientific genius has mounted no less high, and the times of Ampère, Cuvier, and Humboldt are not open to the charge of stagnation.

But while humanity works out its inevitable destiny, the individual remains free, able to resist the cogent but not necessary law of progress, the interior impulse or the example of society, which draws him to a higher aim. And two qualities there are, namely, inspiration and virtue, which are personal, and do not yield to the direction of a period. The "Divine Comedy" surpassed the "Iliad" by all the superiority of the Christian faith; but Dante was not more inspired than Homer. Leibnitz knew infinitely more than Aristotle, but was his thought more intense? The heroism of the early Christians was not surpassed by that of the missioners of the barbarous epoch, and these again have found rivals in those intrepid priests of our day who court martyrdom in the public places of Tonquin or the Corea. The great souls of the Middle Age, St. Louis, St. Francis, St. Thomas Aquinas, loved God and man with as much passion, and served justice and truth with as much perseverance, as the noblest characters of the seventeenth century. Time, or increasing light and softening manners, only brings knowledge within reach, makes virtue of easier attainment, and adds to the debt of gratitude which accrues to us with the heritage of our forefathers; and thus the doctrine which is accused of despising the past, brings all the future, as it were, forth from its recesses, recognizes no progress for new ages without the tradition of those which went before, and destroys also both arrogance and fatalism, in seeing in the march of progress the history not of man alone, but of God, respecting man's liberty, working out His purpose by man's free hands, unrecognized by His creatures, and often in spite of their plans.

So far is such a view from favouring Materialism, that it has rallied round it the greatest Christian spiritualists, such as Chateaubriand and Ballanche, to speak of the dead, and M. de Bonald, who recognizes " in these very revolutions, these scandals of the world, the means in the hands of the Supreme Governor of bringing to perfection the constitution of society." We might rather incur the reproach of pushing our respect for spirit to the neglect of matter, of forgetting the useful beneath the true, the good, and the beautiful, and in our consideration of science, social institutions, and the arts, passing over the industry which is so dear to our contemporaries. For industry must not be despised, when, in subordination to higher things, it brings light to the study of nature, inspires public good, and corrects the grossness of matter by purity of form. When science, art, and public spirit throw thus upon industry their triple ray, it becomes instinct with life, and is of true service to mental progress—a sight afforded by those Italian republics which were as resolved to compass immortality as to amass wealth, as bold in their monuments as in their navigation. But if the development of the industrial principle overwhelms and arrests instead of humbly waiting upon intellectual progress, society is degraded, and falls for a season into the way of decline.

We have hitherto treated of progress with facility by choosing those great historical spaces in which it is easy to select events, and group them at will. We must now reduce ourselves to a narrower sphere, and treat of an epoch which seems entirely to militate against our theory—the period from the fall of the Western Empire to the end of the thirteenth century, the moment which it is customary to hail as the reawakening of the human mind. Had only one good principle been implanted in man, progress would have been but its calm and regular development; but as there are two principles in him, perfection and corruption, corresponding to civilization and barbarism in society, progress becomes a struggle with consequent alternations of victory and defeat. Every great era of history takes its departure from ruin, and ends in a conquest. The first period upon which we enter opens with the most stupendous of all catastrophes, that of the Roman Empire. We can hardly realize the majesty of that dominion which secured by its laws the peace of the world, by its schools the education of the nations, and adorned its provinces by covering them with a crowd of roads, aqueducts, and cities. Doubtless Roman avarice find cruelty caused these benefits to be dearly purchased, but the opinion the prostrate races had formed of their ruler was so high that the crash of her fall struck terror into the hearts, not only of consulars in the peaceful seclusion of their villas, or of philosophers and *literati* fascinated by a civilization to which the human mind had devoted all its light, but even to the Christians and the very recluses of the Desert. They were forced to expect the approach of the day of doom in witnessing the fall of an order which alone, according to Tertullian, warded off the consummation of time. At the news of that night of fear, in which Alaric entered Rome with fire and sword, St. Jerome shuddered in the depth of his Bethlehem solitude, and exclaimed, "A terrible, rumour reaches us from the West, telling of Rome besieged, bought for gold, besieged again, life and property perishing together; my voice falters, sobs stifle the words I dictate, for she is a captive, that City which enthralled the world."

Quis cladem illius noctis, quis funera fando

Explicet, aut possit lacrymis aequare dolorem?

But the catastrophe which terrified the whole world afforded no astonishment to St. Augustine. Whether his great genius was less bound by an antique patriotism, or whether love had raised it to calmer heights, he was able to measure with a firmer glance the portentous events around him. Amidst the pagan fury which charged upon the Church the disasters of the Empire, he wrote his "City of God," in which, deducing from the origin of Time the destinies of Rome and the world, he marked with luminous pen the outlines of that Christian law of progress which we have feebly sketched. At the beginning, he wrote, two principles of love built two cities: the love of self, in contempt of God, reared the city of the world; the love of God, scorning self, raised the heavenly city. The earthly republic was visible, as in Babylon or Rome, and was doomed to perish; the unearthly state was invisible, and though for a time confounded with the worldly commonwealth, could not share in its ruin. The growth was continuous, from the patriarchal family, through Israel, to the Christian Church; persecution gave it increase, heresy distinctness, torment fortitude; its course on earth was as a week of labour; its Sabbath was to be spent in Heaven, in no sterile and dreamy repose, but in the everlasting energy of a loving intelligence. The sequel justified the forebodings of St. Augustine; upon the ruins of the vanquished empire Christian civilization arose as a conqueror, excelling in its depth, and the difficulty and scope of its task, all the conquests of old.

Christianity firstly took for her object the conquest of the conscience; and of this Rome had never dreamed. In laying the hands of her legions on subject provinces, and that of her proconsuls on their populations, she had never troubled herself with souls and their immortal destinies. She disciplined the barbarians, and did better service by instructing them, but never thought of converting them; her Paganism made conscience a slave to deified passions, and conversion involved the government of carnal impulse by a purified reason. But Christianity held for nothing the mere possession of soil, and the enforced submission of nations; it claimed dominion over the intellect and the will, and announced to brutalized minds, which knew only of murderous and lustful divinities, a spiritual dogma; to men of violence it had to give a law of mercy and pardon; to immolators of human victims to propose a worship comprised in prayer, preaching, and a bloodless oblation. Nor did the novelty of these doctrines touch hearts perforce, neither could the subtle persuasion of her priests triumph easily over the ignorant; for we see Rathbod, Duke of Frisia, when, hesitating under the arguments of St. Wulfram, he had caused the equivalent for the Walhalla of his ancestors to be proposed to him, declaring that, for his part, he would rather rejoin his forefathers than go with a crowd of beggars to inhabit the Christian heaven.

But the conquest of mind could be effected by mind only, and force of arms, far from serving, could hardly avoid compromising, the cause, as was often the case. Instruments were wanted in which mental power could alone appear; and by such feeble and despised means as women, slaves, and the sick, was the conversion of the barbarians accomplished. It was effected by Clotilda among the Franks, Theodolinda among the Lombards, Patrick was found working in Ireland, and, lastly, two men, absent from the sphere of action, who put no foot on the hostile soil, directed from the heart of Italy the conquest of the North. The one, St. Benedict, in his desert at Monte Cassino, formed the monastic host, and armed them with obedience and toil; the spirit with which he inspired them, at once charitable and sensible, full of intrepidity and perseverance, impelled them to the heart of Germany, to the recesses of Scandinavia, where they cut down with the forests the superstitions which they enshrined. The other, St. Gregory, though hardly able, during his twelve years' pontificate, to leave his couch of suffering for three hours each day, organized the invasion of civilization upon barbarism, reformed the Frankish Churches, and reconciled to Catholicism the Lombardic and Yisigothic Arians.

Lastly, Rome, with her admirable sagacity, had been content with a limited empire; but the Church, with greater confidence, desired a boundless rule. From the cliffs of Britain, Roman generals had discerned and coveted the Irish shores. Doubtless Probus, when he had ravaged Germany up to the Elbe, dreamt of its reduction to a province. The prudence of the Senate had arrested these schemes of aggrandizement, but Christianity disdained its counsels of prudence. A young Gaul named Patrícius, kidnapped by Irish pirates, and sold on their island, succeeded in escaping, and having regained Gaul, buried himself in the monastery of Lerins. Some years later he appeared in Ireland as papal emissary, and in his turn reduced his captors to the light and golden yoke of the Gospel. At the end of thirty-three years Ireland was converted, and gave to the Faith a race capable of the extremes of labour and devotion. The evangelization of Germany cost more labour, and three hundred years of preaching and martyrdom were wanted to gain the old Roman stations on the Rhine and the Danube; and then inch by inch to grasp Thuringia, Franconia, and Frisia. Every age the Christian colonies were multiplied; they were buried in nameless solitudes, to perish age by age under a wave of Paganism, devoted alike to its false gods and to national independence. The struggle lasted till St. Boniface, after constituting at last the ecclesiastical province of Germany, died in Frisia, pardoning his barbarous murderers. The Roman had known how to die, and that had Rome him on to the conquest of half the world; but the Christian alone could die without revenge, and this power gained for him the whole.

Such being the progress of Christian conquest in the Merovingian period, let us examine its results. What at once strikes us in them is the fact that the Church, though loving the barbarians to the point of dying for them, and even by their hands, did not detach herself from the old civilization, which she preserved by breathing her spirit into its ruins; and in this again the supernatural order sustained the natural order, and gave it life.

Dogma firstly was the salvation of science. Whereas the pagan myth had loved darkness, had shrouded itself in mysteries and initiations, and shrunk from discussion, Christian doctrine loved the open light, preached on the housetops, and provoked controversy. St. Augustine said, "When the intelligence has found God, it still goes in search of Him," and added, finally, " *Intellectum ralde ama*"—Love understanding; and so, as revelation stood in need of intelligence, philosophy began again. It was open to the Church to commit the writings of the pagan philosophers to the flames, or to have suffered the barbarians to destroy them; yet she guarded them, and set her monks, as to a holy task, to copy the writings of Seneca and of Cicero. St. Augustine brought Plato into the schools under his bishop's robe. Boethius opened the door to Aristotle by translating the introduction of Porphyry, which became the text-book of philosophic teaching. The Franks, Irish, and Anglo-Saxons, the children of pirates and ravagers of towns, grew pale over the problem as to the real or only mental existence of genus and species, the question which carried in embryo the whole quarrel between Realists and Nominalists, the Scholasticism of the Middle Age, and, to speak more exactly, the philosophy of all time.

Secondly, the religious law saved social institutions: it was a Christian opinion that God had let a reflex of His justice shine out in Roman law, which was also believed to present a marvellous agreement with the Mosaic institutions; and this idea was the origin of a compilation published towards the end of the fifth century, " Collatio legum Mosaicarum et Romanarum."

The Church preserved Roman law, gathered from it the wisest dispositions in the body of the law ecclesiastical, and put it forth as the common law of the clergy and of Roman subjects under barbarian control. She taught it to the barbarians themselves, as evidenced by the Lombardic, and, more especially, the Visigothic code. But of all of the political works to which the clergy of the time applied its hand, the consecration of royalty was the greatest. Born in the forests of Germany, fenced by a profoundly heathen tradition, and full of bloodthirsty instincts, Christianity threw upon it the toga of the Roman magistrate, and taught it to rule by justice rather than by force. Later, to complete its purification, the Church restored to it the consecration of the kings of Israel, desiring to mould the warrior chiefs into shepherds of the people, who by a gentle sway would temper the reign of justice with charity.

Thirdly, Christian worship saved art. When the religion emerged from the Catacombs and built its churches, its first model was the Basilica, the tribunal of the magistrates—the most august object that antiquity could show. It proceeded to cover their walls with mosaic, the lines of which, if they do not recall its harmony and just proportion, often rival the simple grandeur of Grecian art. The bishops and civilizing monks of France and England drew to their side the most perfect artists of Italy to build basilicas after the ancient form, and to animate them by fresco and glass-painting. To these churches, already instinct with life, voice was to be given; their chants were to rise as one sound, that the concert of the lips might symbolize the union of souls. Schools of church music were accordingly opened, deriving their form and rule from that of St. John Lateran; but music, the seventh of the liberal arts according to the ancients, presupposes the knowledge of the rest, and it was not reached till the dusty ways of the *trivium* and *quadrivium* had been followed to their end. And as melody could not be divorced from poetry, so the doors of the ecclesiastical school could hardly be closed on the poets. Indeed they had already effected an entrance, quoted as they were on every page by St. Basil, St. Augustine, and St. Jerome. Some sterner spirits did try to stop Virgil upon the threshold; but others, more accommodating, pointed out that the sweet singer of Mantua had announced the advent of Messiah, so Virgil passed in with the Fourth Eclogue in his hands, and brought all the classic poets in his train.

But it was but part of the task of the Church to have preserved antiquity. She was also bound to collect the fertile elements which existed in the chaos of barbarism; for there is no ignorance, however thick, which is not streaked by some light; no violence so undisciplined as not to acknowledge some law; no manners so trifling as not to be redeemed by some ray of inspiration. Christianity developed in the Germans that balance of intellect which a false philosophy had never warped. It stamped upon their manners and hallowed in their laws the two fine feelings of respect for the dignity of man and the weakness of woman. In the warrior-songs wherewith this unlettered race celebrated the deeds of their ancestors, there is more inspiration to be felt than in all the declamations of the Latin Decline. The Church shrank from breaking the harp of Gaulish bard or Scandinavian scald; she only purified it by adding another chord for the praise of God and of His saints, and the family joys which Christ had blessed. The last effort of the labour which steeped the world of barbarism with civilization, and brought from the barbarians new life for the world of civilization, was seen in Charlemagne.

A second era opens upon us here with a ruin, and that of a Christian power, and at first sight nothing could seem more disastrous; for no empire has ever appeared better founded in itself, or more necessary to society, than that of Charlemagne. That great man had not received in vain the title of Advocate of the Church; for he protected her by his sword from outward assault, and caused her canons to be respected within the fold. He revived the universal monarchy of the Caesars, and united the pacified nations by his beneficent policy. The school was raised in the palace, and the learned crowded round the conqueror who had laid might under tribute to mind. But so grand an order was not destined to a long continuance, and Charlemagne himself before his death had to lament its decay. Thirty years after his death, the great organism of his empire broke into three parts at the treaty of Verdun. The Norman torrent rolled upon it, rushing up the Weser, the Rhine, the Seine, and the Loire; the pirate bands ascended the rivers, sacked the cloisters, and cast into the same fire rich copies of the Bible and manuscript copies of Aristotle and Virgil. At the same time the Hungarians, dragging with them the Slavonic tribes, invaded Germany, Burgundy, and Italy. Brothers of the Huns, they passed over Europe like a tempest, and the herbage, trampled by their cavalry, did not bud anew. At sight of so much misery, the world thought herself lost, and again imagined herself to be touching the end of time. The deacon Florus, at Lyons, sang thus of the fears of his contemporaries:—

"Mountains and hills, woods and streams, and ye, oh deep dales, weep for the race of the Franks! A mighty race flourished under a brilliant dynasty. There was but one king, one nation. Its children lived in peace and its foes in fear; the zeal of its bishops was emulous in giving their people holy canons in frequent councils. Its young men learnt to know the holy books; the hearts of its children drank deep of the fount of learning. Happy, indeed, had it known its felicity, was the empire which had Rome for her citadel, the bearer of the keys of heaven for her founder; but now this majesty has fallen from its lofty height, and is spurned by the feet of all. Ah! who does not recognize the fulfilment of that Gospel prophecy, ' When the

Son of Man cometh, think ye that He will find upon earth a remnant of His Faith?' "

But when all seemed lost, salvation was imminent. Providence loves such surprises, and shows thereby the power of its government and the impotence of our own. Suddenly that very people who had seemed unloosed for the Church's destruction, became its regenerators and guardians. The German invasions had not sufficiently renovated Roman Europe. The north-west corner of France and the south of Italy had felt too little that fertilizing influence which alone can restore an exhausted soil. The Normans poured over these regions like a deluge, but as one which brings life. From the blazing ruins of the monasteries, monks, escaping the massacre, went forth, preached to the pirates, and often converted them. The Normans entered into Christian civilization, and brought to it their genius for maritime enterprise; for government, as shown by the conquest of England; for architecture, to be exhibited in Sicily, in the gilded basilicas of Palermo and Monreale, or in Normandy itself, by the abbey towers and spires which line the Seine banks from its mouth to Paris, and make it a fit avenue of monuments for a royal people. A little later the Hungarians and Sclaves fell, still stained with blood,

at the feet of St. Adalbert, and the scourges of God became his willing and intelligent servants. They brought to the Church the aid of their invincible swords, covered its Eastern side from Byzantine corruption and Moslem invasion, and thus at last assured the independence of the West.

Moreover, that dismemberment of the Empire which drew groans from Florus the deacon, prepared remotely for the emancipation of the modern nations. France, Germany, and Italy arose, though it is true that the disruption of the monarchy, when pushed to an extreme, ended in the feudal subdivisions. The vices of the feudal system are well known, but it had at least the virtue of attaching men to the soil who were devoted to a nomad life and greedy of adventure. It held them by the double bond of property and sovereignty. Mere property in the soil would not alone have restrained the descendant of the barbarians, preferring by far movable wealth, gold, splendid weapons, and herds of cattle. But when the lord became at once proprietor and sovereign, master alike of the fief and of its inhabitants, his pride was moved, he learned to love his land and his men and to fight in their defence. The Church saw that this habit of drawing the sword for others raised the character, she recognized in feudal devotion a remedy for the evils of the system and proposed an heroic ideal to that warlike society in chivalry, the armed service of God and of the weak. As feudalism divided mankind by the subdivision of territory and the inequality of right, so chivalry united it by brotherhood in arms and equality in duty.

Thus Christendom expanded, and slowly elaborated an organization compatible with her great principle.

But how could leisure for thought he found in that age of iron, and who was forthcoming to save the title-deeds of the human intellect, when the monks had but time to lay the relics of the saints on their shoulders in their flight from death ?—for many a chronicle breaks off at the Norman invasion, and many churches refer to that epoch the loss of their charters and of their legends. Two islands of the West had escaped the sovereignty of Charlemagne—wonder as we may how Great Britain and Ireland, enfeebled as they were by intestine war, could have avoided absorption into an empire which reached from the mouth of the Rhine to that of the Tiber, from the Elbe to the Theiss. But it was needful that amid the decay of the Carlovingian dominion a less troubled society should afford a refuge to science and literature, and during the eleventh century the monasteries of

Ireland continued to support a whole people of theologians, men of letters and skilled in dialectic. From time to time their surplus population flowed over on to the coast of France, where, according to a contemporary, a troop of philosophers were seen to arrive. Amidst the nameless stood John Scotus Erigena, notorious to the point of scandal, bold to temerity, erudite enough to revive the doctrines of Alexandria, but halting upon the very brink of Pantheism, soon enough to exercise an incontestable influence over the mystics of the Middle Age. England on her side, watching from afar the fall of the Carlovingian dynasty, inaugurated the reign of Alfred the Great; the heroic youth reconquered the kingdom of his fathers, and with the hands that had expelled the Danes, reopened the schools. At the age of thirty-six he placed himself under a master to learn Latin, translated the pastoral of St. Gregory for the use of the clergy, the " Consolatio " of Boethius and the histories of Orosius and Bede for public instruction, "trembling," as he said, " at the thought of the penalties which the powerful and the learned would incur in this world and the next if they have neither known how to taste wisdom themselves nor to give it to others to enjoy."

Whilst these lights were shining in the north, Germany was also preserving the sacred fire, in the three monasteries of New Corbey, Fulda, and St. Gall. These powerful abbeys, protected from the barbarians by strong walls, by public respect against rapacious princes, embraced schools, libraries, and studios for copyists, painters, and sculptors. Look at St. Gall, where we may almost feel a first breath from the Revival: its inmates are not confined to transcribing pagan authors under obedience, or collecting the Latin Muses with troubled and remorseful curiosity. The ancients are not merely honoured there, but loved with that intelligence which gives back to the past its life: its monks engaged in learned discussions, argued against all comers on grammar or on poetry, and even gave their opinion in Chapter in verses from the "Æneid." Latin literature hardly sufficed for the appetite of these recluses: they aspired to penetrate into Greek antiquity, and did so under the guidance of a woman. The chronicle of St. Gall has preserved the graceful tale, which in no way detracts from the gravity of monastic manners. It relates how the Princess Hedwige, affianced in her youth to the Emperor of the East, had learnt Greek. On the rupture of their engagement Hedwige gave her hand to a landgrave of Suabia, who soon left her a widow, free to live in prayer and study. She took up her residence near the abbey, and caused herself to be instructed by an old monk in all the learning of the time. One day the old man was accompanied by a young novice, and on the landgravine inquiring what whim had brought the child, the latter replied that though scarcely a Latin he wished to become a Greek—

Esse velim graecus cum vix sit, Domna, Latinus.

The verse was bad, but its author was pretty and docile. Hedwige made him sit at her feet, and gave him as a first lesson an anthem from the Byzantine liturgy; and continued her care for him till he understood the language of St. John Chrysostom, and was able to teach it to others. By this noble hand Greek literature was restored to St. Gall, and Hedwige, pleased with the lessons she had given and received, loaded the learned abbey with gifts, the most remarkable among which was an alb of marvellous workmanship, embroidered with the nuptials of Mercury and Philologia.

Thus literature did not entirely perish, though it languished in Italy, Spain, and France, the Latin countries. But even there teaching was continuous, and its most famous inheritor was one who belonged to those three countries by birth, by education, and by fortune, Gerbert, the monk of Aurillac, who was taught, not, as has been thought, by the Arabs of Cordova, but at the episcopal school of Visch, in Catalonia, and subsequently Rome aloft by the admiration of his contemporaries to the very chair of St. Peter. His illustrious name alone sufficiently acquits Southern Europe of the charge of barbarism, and dispenses us from a mention of the less famous workmen who laboured with silent perseverance to keep unbroken the chain of tradition. Assuredly tradition, without which progress is impossible, must be guarded, but it must also be enlarged. As antiquity possessed no forms of sufficient variety or life for the genius of the new era, modern languages were to arise. Alfred, master of Latin at the age of thirty-six, was at home at twelve in the war-songs of the Anglo-Saxons; by writing it in prose and forcing it to translate the firmness and precision of ancient thought, he fixed that most poetical and therefore most indefinite of idioms. The monks of St. Gall at the same time made it their task to pass into that Teutonic dialect—the rude accents of which the Emperor Julian had compared to the cry of the vulture—not only the hymns of the Church but the Categories of Aristotle, and the Encyclopaedia of Martianus Capella. Though the growth of the Neo-Latin languages was more gradual, yet from the ninth century downwards the traces of their existence were multiplied. The Council of Tours prescribed preaching in the vernacular, and we have proof that it was obeyed in a recently discovered homily, the date of which cannot bo later than the year 1000. Its syntax is barbarous, and presents a confused mixture of French and Latin words; yet from the chaos in which this old preacher struggled was to proceed the language of Bossuet.

The cause of civilization was to conquer, but only after running the greatest risk, especially from the condition of the Church, then degraded at Rome by the profanation of the Holy See, and invaded in every part by feudal customs, which changed bishoprics into fiefs, and bishops into vassals. Salvation was, however, to spring from the Church, and out of the quarter in which the spiritual life had sought refuge, for it was the monastic reform of Cluny which decided the destiny of the world. A French monk named Odo, a student of Paris, had buried his learning and his virtues in a monastery, situated four leagues from Mâcon, in the depths of a silent valley, only troubled from time to time by the shouts of hunters and the baying of their hounds. He introduced a severe rule, which, however, did not exclude the literary passion or artistic culture, and which, by its intrinsic force, brought under the government of Cluny a number of religious houses in France, in Italy, and in England. Unity in the hierarchy, in administration, and in discipline was thus established in these monasteries, ready to extend thence into the general Christian society when the time arrived. The day soon came; it was the Christmas Day of the year 1048. The Bishop Bruno, nominated by the Emperor Henry III. to fill the chair of St. Peter, happened on his way to Italy to visit the Abbey of Cluny; when there an Italian monk named Hildebrand, the son of a carpenter, drawn to Cluny some years before through zeal for reformation, dared to present himself to the new Pontiff, and tell him that an emperor's nomination could confer no right in the spiritual kingdom of Christ: he adjured him to proceed to Rome, throw off his empty title, and restore to clergy and people their liberty of election. Bruno, to his great credit, listened, desired to take him with him, and on his arrival in Rome placed himself at the discretion of the clergy and the people. He was chosen pope, and Hildebrand, from his position beside the pontifical throne, already gave evidence of what his future course was to be under the name of Gregory the Seventh.

Gregory VII. inaugurated a new period which began by a reverse. At the outset that great pontiff is seen by the mere force of his word to reduce the sensual and bloodthirsty Henry IV. to seek penitence and pardon at the Castle of Canossa, and then it indeed appeared that barbarism had been conquered, and that Europe was willing to submit to the laws of a theocracy, which risked the loss of temporal power, but was destined to revive spiritual life throughout the world. But some years later the same emperor took Rome, enthroned an Antipope in the Vatican, and force again coerced conscience, whilst Gregory VII. uttered at Salerno his dying words, " I have loved righteousness and hated iniquity, and therefore I die in exile." More terrible than ever seemed the catastrophe in which, not an empire alone, but that principle which alone could give empires vigour, was perishing; yet this time Christians did not look for the world's immediate extinction, and one of the bishops in attendance on the dying Pope answered him, " My Lord, you cannot die in exile, for God has given you the earth for a possession and its nations for an inheritance."

And, indeed, from the tomb of Gregory VII. proceeded that medieval progress which is too well known, too incontestable, too much enlightened by modern science, to make more than a sketch of its principal features necessary. The strife between the hierarchy and the empire continued more formidably as the rival powers found more illustrious champions—on the one side Frederic I. and Frederic II., as great in the field as in the council chamber, on the other the Popes

Alexander III., Innocent III., Innocent IV., consummate politicians and heroic priests. After two centuries of warfare, the vanquished empire renounced its usurpations on the spiritual order; the Popes, in aiming at aggrandizing the Church, had achieved her freedom; the two powers separated—force returned to its own province, and the rights of conscience were saved. At the same time the Papacy executed another design of Gregory VII. It gathered into one the nations of the West, long given up to ceaseless conflicts, without justice and barren of result, and poured them over the East. There, if fight they must, they might wage a sacred war, justified by a most holy cause, and with the victory of right and liberty as its result and reward. The nations, Rome far away from that powerful German empire and its usurped dominion over them, freed themselves from vassalage and regained their autonomy. Foucher, of Chartres, pictures the crusaders, whether German, French, or English, living together on terms of brotherly equality. The modern nations gained their spurs in Palestine, and to the visible unity of the empire succeeded the moral unity of the Christian commonwealth.

And feudalism succumbed to the same blow. Under the banner of the cross the middle class fought with the same title as the nobles, that of soldiers of Christ; they gained the same indulgences, and if they fell, equally with them earned the martyr's palm. The merchants of Genoa and of Venice planted the scaling-ladder on the walls of Saracen towns, and led the assault with as firm a hand and as fierce a bearing as the barons of France. In vain did feudalism create in the Holy Land her principalities and her marquisates. She returned thence in her agony, returned to find in Europe a triple contest to maintain; against the Church, which reproved private war; against royalty spreading its jurisdiction daily to the prejudice of seignorial rights; and, lastly, against the nascent power of the commonalty. The Commonwealths of Italy, allied to the Papacy by a community of peril, were bound to espouse its cause, and the first example is seen in the republic of Milan, whose glorious history is well known. In 1046 a noble named Gui had obtained by bribery the archbishopric of that city, and was maintained in it by a corrupted clergy and a tyrannical aristocracy. Two schoolmasters, the priest Landulf and the deacon Ariald, undertook to relieve the profaned see of St. Ambrose, so banding together, first their own pupils, and then gradually the bulk of the populace, they bound them in solemn league against the simoniacal and incontinent clergy. Rome roused herself at the sound of the dispute, and Peter Damiani, charged as Papal Legate with the reform of the Church of Milan, heard the complaints of the people, and obliged the archbishop and his clergy to sign a public condemnation of concubinage and simony. But their engagement was soon trampled underfoot, and Ariald died at the hands of his enemies, but left an heir of his design in the warrior Harlembert, who was beloved by the multitude and powerful by his eloquence as well as by his prowess. He was declared the champion of the Church, received from the Pope the gonfalon of St. Peter, rallied the discouraged party of reform, bound it by a new oath, and sustained an obstinate war against the nobility, whom he expelled from the city, and at length died in triumph in repelling an assault, fighting at the head of his men with the standard of St. Peter in his hand. But the reigning Pope was Gregory VII., and he consummated the work of the deacon and the knight. Simony and concubinage were conquered, the nobility reduced to a mere share in the government, and the commonalty of Milan gained that strong plebeian organization which for two hundred years was the support of popes and the dismay of emperors.

Whilst the cities of Lombardy and Tuscany formed themselves into republics, and treated on equal terms with monarchs, the communal spirit had passed the Alps, the Rhine, and the Pyrenees. After the admirable work of Augustin Thierry, there is no need for us to show how the spirit of liberty revivified the reminiscences of the Roman municipality or the traditions of the German guild; if it did not succeed in rendering the cities paramount, it made them sharers in sovereignty. Their deputies took part in States General, and the Christian principle of natural equality produced equality in the political order.

In the midst of this strife and agitation, literature found ample place, and filled it with special distinction. It is not true that literature only loves peace; she loves war, too, when civilizing in its results—when the sword is drawn in the cause of intellect, and when not interests but contrary principles are encountered; when minds, divided between those principles, are bound to exercise the power of choice and consequently of thought. The ages of Pindar and of Augustus sprang from Salamis and Pharsalia; the quarrel over investitures awoke the scholastic philosophy; and Gregory VII. wished not only for a chaste but also for a learned clergy. At a council at Rome, in 1078, he renewed the canons which instituted in each episcopal see chairs for instruction in the liberal arts. It is not easy, as some have imagined, to enslave a people by putting it under priestly guidance. Wherever a priest has stood, the succeeding generation will find a theologian; in the third the theologian will bring forth a philosopher, who in his turn will produce a publicist, and the publicist will bring liberty. Those who know little of the Middle Age will only see in it one long night, during which priests are keeping watch over troops of slaves; yet one of these slandered priests was called Anselm, and he was troubled with the desire of finding the shortest proof of the existence of God. The thought alone sufficed to make him a great metaphysician, to bring him disciples, to rouse up opponents, and plunge the Christian mind into the controversy which was to range Abelard against Bernard, and drive many an intellect to the last excess of temerity. Amidst, but rising above, the tempest, appear the two Angels of the Schools, St. Thomas Aquinas and St. Bonaventura, charged with the task, if death had not checked it, of laying the last stone to the edifice of Christian dogma and mysticism respectively. These two Saints did not dread enervating theology by recognizing philosophy as a distinct science, nor profess that haughty contempt for reason which has been lately too much affected. From the heights of eternal truth they did not despise the wants of their time, but embraced them with a disinterested view; and St. Thomas wrote on the origin of laws, on the legitimate share of democracy in political constitutions, on tyranny and insurrection, pages which have startled a later age by their boldness. Never was thought more free than in the supposed era of its bondage, and, as if liberty alone was little, she had power. Her universities were endowed by Pope and Emperor; she possessed laws, magistracies, and a studious but turbulent people. An historian of the epoch gave Christendom three capitals—Rome, the seat of the Hierarchy; Aix-la-Chapelle, the seat of Empire; and Paris, the seat of Learning. Life flowed in full tide through the learned literature, but it did not gush less aboundingly, and flourished with greater grace and freedom, in the vulgar tongues. It brought forth from them two kinds of poetry, one common to all the Western nations, though ripening earliest on its native soil of France, which sang of the heroes who are the type of chivalric life, and that respect for women which is its charm; the other the national lay which is proper to each people, and records its individual genius and tradition. Germany had her *Nibelungen-lied*, still steeped in barbarous colouring and pagan association; in it we behold long cavalcades riding through nameless forests, bloodstained banquets, the children of light at issue with those of darkness, and the hero-conqueror of the Dragon perishing for the sake of an accursed treasure and an abandoned woman. The mists of the North lent their shadows to these sombre fictions, but the Southern sunshine gave warmth and colour to the epic of the Cid. Spain in its essence lived in this hero, the terror of infidels but a rebel to his king—religious, but with so proud a piety that the Almighty Himself is said to have treated him with distinction, and warned him, through St. Peter, of his departure from the world.

Italy chose a still better part, and found inspiration in holiness. The land which Gregory had ploughed produced from its furrows a double harvest of Saints and of artists; here St. Anselm, St. Francis, St. Thomas, and St. Bonaventura, with a number of tender and ardent souls clustered around their greater intellects; there a whole generation of architects and painters, who, with Giotto at their head, formed rank at the tomb of St. Francis; the bond uniting faith and genius was never more visible, and the national poem of Italy was naturally counted a sacred epopee. Thus did Dante think, and from his meditations proceeded that patriotic and theologic poem, written for a country whose passions it stirred—for the Christian world, whose Belief it glorified—for the Middle Age, whose crimes, virtues, and learning it pictured—for modern times, which it surpasses in the grandeur of its presentiments; a poem that rang with the groans of earth and the hymns of heaven.

. . . . Poema sacro

A cui ha posto man cielo e terra.

It is also our duty to discuss the growth of industry and material prosperity, the humbler tasks which are imposed upon the majority. We may say that in many ways the Middle Age preserved, expanded, and increased the material wealth of the ancient world. We have seen already how the crusades gave back to the Latins all those ways of commerce which had of old been opened on the side of the Levant; how apostolic zeal impelled men beyond these and to the very extremity of Asia; we have beheld the monks reaping the tradition of Roman agriculture, reconquering foot by foot, by spontaneous toil, lands which the indolence of slaves had left waste, and carrying the precepts of the Georgics to the banks of the We ser and the Elbe. We must point also to the ancient cities saved from the fury of the barbarians or rising again from their ashes, thanks to the courage of their bishops or the respectful immunities which surrounded the reliquaries of their saints, as well as to the new cities multiplying around the abbeys; for, like all civilizing influences, the Church loved to build. But it was not as Rome built, for Christianity has, so to speak, changed the aspect of towns as well as the manners of men: of old every soul was turned outwards—a man lived in the public place, or in the richly decorated *atrium*, where he received his clients; the rest of his house was neglected, and the narrow chambers opening on the peristyle were good enough for his women, children, and slaves. But Christianity turned the heart of man towards inner joys, pointed out happiness at the domestic hearth, and made him embellish the place in which he passed his life with his wife and family; thence came the splendid woodwork and tapestry, the richly carved furniture, in which lay the pride of our ancestors. At first sight the modern towns seem far inferior to the cities of old. The ancients built small temples, it is true, but their amphitheatres were immense, their baths stupendous, their porticoes and colonnades without number. The Christian city was grouped humbly round the cathedral on which every effort had been expended; if there was any other public building it would be the town-hall, the school, or the hospital. The ancients built for pleasure, and in that department we must despair of rivalry: our towns are built for work, for sorrow, and for prayer,

and it is in the knowledge of these that the eternal superiority of Christian times consists.

We may finish here with Dante, the worthy follower of Charlemagne, and of Gregory VII., coming as a conqueror to inaugurate a new era of progress, by his own defeat to point to a new epoch of ruin. For the great poet who carried on to the Middle Age the legacy of his triumphant thought, was also great in his failure, exiled from his country, which denied him sepulture, and destined to be followed by that fourteenth century which was to see the fall of the Italian republics, France in the flames of war, and the schools in decline. But neither this dreary age nor any other could prevail against the design of God and the vocation of humanity.

We have traversed a space of eight hundred years, a considerable portion of human destiny, and have encountered three epochs, each commencing with a season of decline: but each decline veiled a progress, assured by Christianity, to be worked out obscurely and silently as if beneath the surface, till it came to the light of day, and burst forth in a juster economy of society, in a brighter flash of intellect. We have reached the term of the Middle Age, but must beware of supposing that humanity had but to descend, even but one short slope, before reascending to higher altitudes, which would not yet be the last. We have given full credit to the Middle Age, and may now avow what was wanting to that period so full of heroism, but also instinct with pagan associations and savage passions. From these came perils to the faith, which never had to enter upon conflicts more terrible, disordered manners, mad impulses of the flesh, lust for blood, and all that caused saints, preachers, and contemporary moralists to despair. As severe judges, they acknowledged the vices of their epoch, and many even ignored the very good which they themselves produced. The scandals which deceived them show us that the Middle Age did not fully achieve Christian civilization, and from the error of these great souls, we may learn, amidst our own deterioration, not to deny an invisible progress. Fallen upon evil days, we must remember that the Faith in progress has traversed darker times, and like Æneas to his despairing comrades, let us say that we have passed so many trials that God will also end our present probation,—

O passi graviora, dabit Deus bis quoque finem!

THE FIFTH CENTURY.

Before entering upon a study of the barbarous epoch, we must know in what the wealth of the human mind consisted at the moment of the invasions; how much of it was to perish in that great catastrophe, as an empty ornament buried in the grave of antiquity; and how much was to survive as the heritage of the modern nations. We shall start from the death of Theodosius at the dawn of the fifth century, and, leaving aside the East as exercising but a remote influence on the period, confine ourselves to the destinies of humanity as worked out in the provinces of the West.

At the moment when all civilization seemed doomed to extinction, we find two forms of it, one pagan, the other Christian, confronting each other with their respective doctrines, laws, and literature, disputing for the possession of the fresh races who were pressing upon the threshold of the Empire. Paganism, indeed, had taken no speedy flight before the laws of the Christian emperors and the progress of philosophy. At the close of the sixty years during which the edicts of Constantius, renewed by Theodosius, had been pressing hard upon the superstitions of idolatry, in the West at least the temples were still open, and the sacrificial flames still unextinguished. When Honorius came to Rome in 404 for the celebration of his sixth consulate, the shrines of Jove, of Concord, and of Minerva still crowned the Capitol, and the statues of the old deities on their pediments were still presiding over the Eternal City. Votive altars covered with inscriptions testified that the blood of bulls and goats had not ceased to flow, and to the middle of the fifth century the sacred fowls were fed whose presages governed Rome and the World. The pagan festivals and their appropriate games were still marked in the calendars. We hardly realize antiquity in its nature-worship, which, amidst the songs of poets and the apologies of sages, resulted in the celebration of the two great mysteries of life by religious prostitution and human sacrifice, or how in the theatre and amphitheatre dedicated as temples to Bacchus and Sol, the gods were honoured by mysterious rites, comprising nameless horrors which outraged the plainest laws of modesty, or by the mutual massacre of myriads of gladiators rushing to death amidst the applause of earth's most polished race. It was lust and bloodshed which in despite of imperial edicts kept the crowd spell-bound at the altars of their idols.

Philosophy had done no more towards redeeming the higher minds of the ruling class, the heirs of the old senatorial families. The prodigious labours of the Alexandrian philosophers, however admirable for erudition, subtlety, and boldness, had only tended to revive Paganism, by lending to the worship which the Roman aristocracy could only defend as a State institution the gloss of a refined interpretation. The old system was to fall by the hand of Christianity, before the spiritual weapons of controversy and charity, preaching and martyrdom. We shall glance at the learned discussions in which St. Augustine exhausted his zeal and eloquence to attract the choice intellect of a Volusian, a Longinian, or a Licentius, but will mark more closely the rise of that instruction which was devoted to the ignorant and the insignificant, to whom Paganism had never preached, enter the families in which war, as it were, was levied against some idolatrous parent till he was brought a happy captive to the waters of Baptism, and listen to the shouts of the circus when the monk Telemachus threw himself between the fighting gladiators and died under the stones of the spectators to seal by his blood the abolition of those detestable games.

But error yielded slowly, like night leaving its mists behind. The

Pantheism of Alexandria was destined to a new birth, to carry its temerity into the very chairs of the Scholastic philosophy. In the full blaze of classic antiquity in the schools of Jamblichus, of Maximus of Ephesus, and the last pagan philosophers, flourished magic and astrology and the occult sciences, supposed to have been spawned in the darkness of the Middle Age. Moreover, the ignorant country-folk *(pagani)* shrunk from parting with a religion which appealed to their passions. The pilgrims from the North wondered in the eighth century at seeing the squares of Rome still profaned by pagan dances. The Councils of Gaul and Spain long pursued with anathema the sacrilegious art of the diviners, and the idolatrous practices of the Calends of January. Latin superstitions joined hands with those of Germany to make a last stand against conquering Christianity. Everything pagan in character, however, did not

deserve to perish, for even in a false religion there is a meritorious craving for commerce .with Heaven, of fixing it in times and places, and under definite symbols. The Church had the faculty of appreciating this want, which is a right of human nature. She spared the evangelized nations useless violence, and reconciled art and nature to Christ by dedicating to Him the temples and festivals, flowers and perfumes, hitherto lavished on false divinities. The heretic Vigilantius was scandalized at this wise economy, but St. Jerome undertook to justify it, and in his reply we see the germ of that tender policy which inspired St. Gregory to instruct the English missioners to leave to the newly made Christians their rustic festivals, innocent banquets, and earthly joys, that they might be the more willing to taste of spiritual consolations. Thus the whole of the Church's struggle against Roman polytheism was but an apprenticeship to another conflict which she was destined to wage against the Paganism of the barbarians, and in her last efforts to convert the ancient world we foresee the genius and patience she was to display in the education of the new nations.

The preparation for the future amidst the ruins of the past, the conjunction of perishable elements with an immortal principle, which affords so strong a contrast in the history of religion, is more manifest in that of Law, which in the fifth century the emperors organized by giving force to the writings of the old jurisconsults, and codifying the decisions of Christian princes. The lawyers of the classic age had never abjured the law of the Twelve Tables, and all the efforts of the school had failed in obliterating the pagan character impressed on the constitution of the State and of the family.

The pagan doctrine was to deify the City, to make an apotheosis of public power, to render it sovereign in the conscience without any further appeal to abstract justice. The Emperor had inherited a divine right over the goods, the persons, and the souls of men. He was above the law, which was the creature of his will; as depositary of military power *(impérium)* he was master of every life, as Vicar of the rights of the Soman people he was strictly the only proprietor of the soil of the provinces, of which the natives had but a precarious possession. It was not surprising that he should extract the taxes by exhausting the one and torturing the other; and there was no excess of persecution or of exaction that did not find principles to justify it.

The iniquity of the public law had descended into that of civil life. The father, as representative of Jove, surrounded by his tutelary gods, the images of his ancestors who lent him their majesty, exercised right of life and death over his wife, could expose his children or crucify his slaves. Philosophers admired this family constitution, with its priestly and military power installed at every hearth, as a domestic empire on the model of which was framed the empire of the World.

But the violence of authority had provoked a resurrection of liberty. The human conscience, outraged in its last refuge, began a memorable resistance by opposing to the civil law that of the tribes and the praetorial edicts, the *responsa* of the jurisconsults and the constitutions of princes to the Code of the Twelve Tables, lastly succeeding in introducing into the imperial councils such firm and subtle minds as those of Gaius, Ulpian, and Papinian, who tempered the severity of the old legislation. But the struggle lasted for eight centuries, and the victory of equity could only be effected by the triumph of Christianity. A new faith was necessary to deal its death-blow to the respect for the old laws, embolden Constantine to decree the civil emancipation of woman, the penalty of death against the murderer of a son or of a slave, to elicit from Valentinian III. and Theodosius IV. the noble declaration that the prince is bound by the laws—a short speech, but marking the greatest of all political revolutions, causing the temporal power to descend to a lower but securer place, and inaugurating the constitutional principle of modern society. The Roman law, as reformed by Christian emperors, survived the crash of the empire, penetrated gradually the barbarian mind, and earned Bossuet's panegyric, "that good sense, the master of human life, reigned throughout it, and that a more beautiful application of natural equity had never been seen."

But the crown of pagan society, and its incomparable lustre, was derived from its literature. Rome doubtless knew no longer the inspiration of her great centuries, yet the reigns of Constantine and of his successors, so often accused of hastening the Decline, seemed for a space to give a new flight to the eagles, a fresh burst to the genius of Rome. Ammianus Marcellinus composed history with the dash and bluff sincerity of a soldier. Vegetius, in his " Treatise on the Military Art," gathered up the precepts of the science before it passed away to the Goths and the Franks, and the contemporaries of Symmachus rank him with Pliny in the exquisite urbanity of his correspondence, and the elegance of his panegyric. Among the poets, three may he distinguished, as worthily sustaining the old age of the Pagan Muse.

Of these Clandian stood first. Born in Egypt, he had early drunk deep at the sources of Alexandrian learning, from which the great poets of the Augustan era had drawn, and had found a stray chord of that Latin lyre broken on the day on which Lucan caused his veins to be opened. Since the " Pharsalia," Rome had heard nothing comparable to the songs which told of the disgrace of Eutropius or the victories of Stilicho. But Clandian was so steeped in pagan memories that he could only move in a cloud of fables, so to speak, out of sight of his Christian age, out of hearing of the voices of St. Ambrose and St. Augustine thundering at Milan and Hippo, not even thinking of defending the menaced altars of his gods. He was singing of the Rape of Proserpine as the cultus of the Virgin Mary was taking possession of the Temple of Ceres at Catania, and was inviting the Graces, the Nymphs, and the Hours to deck with their garlands Serena, the lovely wife of Stilicho, who in her hatred of idolatry had torn the necklace from the image of Cybele to adorn her own neck. He dared to introduce the Christian princes into Olympus, and bring upon the scene Theodosius, Jupiter's greatest foe, talking familiarly with Jove himself. Rutilius Numatianus, though also a pagan, wrote under less illusion, and with a more accurate feeling as to the spirit of his age. He was no mere poet by profession, but a statesman, a prefect of Rome, though ou leaving the city in 418 to revisit his native Gaul, then under the ravages of the barbarians, he wrote of his journey in verses so graceful as to deceive the ear into a remembrance of Ovid. The ardour of his patriotism, his passionate worship of Rome, as the greatest deity of antiquity, saved him from illusion, and raised him high above his literary contemporaries.

" Hear me, listen, O Rome, ever beauteous Queen of a world that is forever thine own: thou who art one amongst the Olympians, hearken, Mother of men and of gods; when we pray in thy temples we are not far from heaven. For thee the sun doth turn on his course, he rises upon thy domains, and in their seas doth he plunge his chariot. From so many diverse nations thou hast moulded one sole country; from that which was a world hast thou made a city (*Urbem fecisti quod prius orbis erat).* He who can count thy trophies can tell the number of the stars. Thy gleaming temples dazzle the eye. Shall I sing of the rivers, that the vaults of air bring to thee—the entire lakes that feed thy baths? Shall I tell of the forests imprisoned beneath thy ceilings, and peopled with melodious birds? Thy year is but an eternal spring, and vanquished Winter respects thy pleasures. Raise the laurel from thy brow, that the sacred foliage may bud forth anew around thy hoary head! It is thy children's tradition to hope in danger, like the stars which set but to rise again. Extend, extend thy laws, they will live through centuries become Roman perforce, and alone among things of earth dread not thou the shuttle of the Fates."

Finely and truly drawn. The old Roman magistrate, with a lawyer's insight, foresaw that Rome, betrayed by her arms, would still reign by her laws; and, pagan as it was, his faith in his country did not deceive him.

Sidonius Apollinaris was pagan neither in creed or in name, but he was in education and in habit of mind. Christian, like Ausonius, but like him reared in the schools of the grammarians and rhetoricians of Gaul, he could not construct an hexameter or hang together dactyls or spondees without stirring up every mythological association. Whether he was composing the panegyric of the Emperor Avitus, or that of Majorian after the deposition of Avitus, or that of Anthemius after the fall of Majorian, he treated always of the same deities, who were never weary of taking part in the triumph of the victor. Happily, his panegyrics failed before the complaisance of the gods, for Sidonius was converted, became a bishop, and was destined to become a saint. But though he mastered his passions he could not stifle his recollections. M. Ampère has ably shown the struggles of that mind divided between victorious faith and mythology, which still so thoroughly possessed it, that in writing to St. Patientius, Bishop of Lyons, in praise of a distribution of corn to the poor, he could find no higher congratulation possible than in calling him a second Triptolemus.

Such was the sequel of the old poetry, though Sidonius found one more disciple in the sixth century in the person of Fortunatus, and the writings of Clandian found copyists and imitators in the monasteries of the Middle Age. But antiquity was to propound a harder lesson to the ages which followed. Rome in losing genius had still retained tradition, had formed a magistracy of instruction and provided the schools of the Capitol with thirty-one professors of jurisprudence, of rhetoric, and of grammar. The youth pressed into these schools with ardour and in such numbers, that an edict of Valentinian was necessary for a sort of police regulation of the studies. Gratian had desired that the provinces should enjoy the same benefit, and that every great town should possess public chairs with rich endowments. The favour of law multiplied these laborious grammarians, who made it their profession to explain and comment, and consequently religiously to preserve the classic texts. The learned Donatus, whose lectures St. Jerome had attended, fixed the principles of Latin grammar. Macrobius, in his commentary on the dream of Scipio, and in the seven books of the "Saturnalia," brought all the memories of Alexandrian philosophy and of Greek poetry to elucidate the thought of Cicero and of Virgil. Lastly, Marcianus enveloped in a spirited and graceful allegory the seven liberal arts wherein all the learning of the ancients had just been comprised. We must not wonder that the science of antiquity could be compressed within the narrow compass of seven arts; upon that condition and under that form, the heritage of the human mind was destined to traverse the barbarous epoch, and the treatises and commentaries whose dryness we despise were to save Latin literature. The textbook of Martianus Capella was to become the classic summary of all secular instruction during the sixth and seventh centuries, to be multiplied under the pens of monks, and be translated into the first stammering utterances of the modern languages. Donatus became so popular that bis name was a synonym of grammar in the schools of the Middle Age; no student was too poor to possess a *Donatus*, and there was a Provençal grammar under the name of *Donatus Provinciális*. The Middle Age was right in attaching itself to the masters who gave it that example of toil which is more necessary than genius, for genius is but a thing of the moment; and God, who never wastes it, seems to will that the world should know how to dispense with it. Yet He never lets labour fail, but distributes it with a liberal hand, as a punishment or as a blessing, effacing the distinction between ages and between men. Genius ravishes intelligence for a brief space, raising it, indeed, above the common condition of life, but work comes to recall it from its lofty forgetfulness and reduce it to the level of mortals. When we see Dante Rome by the flight of his thought to the highest sphere of his Paradise, to the threshold of the infinite, we may well hesitate in our belief of the destined equality of all souls; but when in the intervals of his song we mark him exhausting his sweat in study, paling over the labour like the meanest scholar of his century, we take courage in finding equality re-established and humbler spirits avenged.

We see, then, that antiquity was not to be entirely buried beneath the ruins of the Roman Empire; we must now find the new principle which preserved it, how the Christianity which has been held so inimical to the old civilization laid upon it a hand which was beneficent though it might be severe, as upon the sick whom we treat with rigour and weaken but to save. The close of the fourth century still rang with the pathetic accents of the Fathers. M. Villemain has done justice to those masters of Christian eloquence in a work which can never he revised, and we must shrink from a subject which, in the words of one of old, he has made his possession forever. The East we leave aside. The West had mourned the death of St. Ambrose in 393, and St. Jerome in his seclusion in the Holy Land only acted on events through the authority of his untiring correspondence. St. Augustine remained to fill with his presence the opening years of the fifth century, and with his thought those which followed. This is not the place to relate his history, or to depict his tender but impetuous heart, or his soul tormented by its cravings after light and peace; and who, indeed, is ignorant of his career, his birth under the African sky, his education at Madaura and Carthage, his long aberration, and the Providential guidance which brought him to Milan and to the feet of St. Ambrose, the conflict of his will groaning under the strokes of grace, the voice which cried out to him, *Tolle, lege !* In the writings of this great mind we shall study that which is even greater—Christian metaphysics taking its first form, and Christianity defending itself with redoubled vigour, that it might remain what God had made it, namely, a religion, instead of being degraded by the sects to a philosophy or a mythology.

A thirst for God tormented the soul of St. Augustine like a malady depriving his day and night of their repose. This want had cast him into the assemblies of the Manichees, in which he had been promised an explanation of the origin of evil; had impelled him towards the Neoplatonic school, to learn the nature of the Supreme Goodness; and, lastly, had flung him upon his knees under the fig-tree in his garden to embrace Christianity, as he wetted the pages of St. Paul's epistles with his tears. Henceforward his life was but one long struggle towards "the Beauty, ever ancient yet ever new, which to his reproach he had begun to love so late." Shortly after his conversion, in the retreat that he had given to his tempest-tost mind under the shades of Cassiciacum, he wrote those "Soliloquies" in which he supposes his reason to demand from him the aim of his knowledge. " Two things," he replied, " namely, God and the soul." But to what notion of Him did he aspire? Did it suffice to know God as he knew Alypius, his friend? Nay; for knowledge does not alone imply a grasping by means of the senses; a seeing, touching, or feeling. But would not the theology of Plato or Plotinus satisfy his curiosity? Assuming them to be true, Augustine wished to go beyond them. But mathematical truths are perfect in their clearness. Would he not be content at knowing the attributes of God as the properties of the circle or of the triangle are known? "I agree," he replied, "that the verities of mathematics are very clear, but, from the experience of God, I expect a different happiness and a different joy."

Boldly, but with firm steps, he began his course on the road towards the knowledge of God. He determined to leave Italy—that land of temptation—and it was while he was awaiting a favourable wind at Ostia, and leaning one day with his mother from the window of their house in contemplation of the sky, that he fell into that wonderful train of thought which has been handed down by him in the ninth book of his " Confessions " :—

"We were alone, talking with infinite sweetness, forgetful of the past looking beyond the future, of what the eternal life of the blest would be. . . .

Raised towards God by the ardent aspiration of our souls, we traversed the whole sphere of things corporeal, and the sky also, in which the sun, moon, and stars spread abroad their light. And in our full admiration of thy works, O Lord, we mounted yet higher, and reached the region of the soul; then passed higher yet, to repose in that Wisdom, itself Uncreated, by whom all things were made, which has ever existed and will ever be; in whose Eternal Being is no past, present, or future. And as we spoke thus, with this thirst for the wisdom of God, for a moment, by an effort of the heart, we touched upon it, and then groaned as we left the first-fruits of our souls clinging there whilst we descended to earth at the sound of our voices." Regretfully do we abridge that wonderful narration. They are indeed happy who have had such experiences, with a mother like his; who, with her, have found their God and never again lost sight of Him.

These few words comprise the whole of his metaphysical system. In them he introduces the novelty of his doctrine as compared with that of Plato or of Aristotle, the idea of Omnipotence, which, if not unknown to antiquity, was at least contradicted by the theory of an Eternal Matter, by refusing to the Supreme Worker the privilege of producing the clay which His hands were permitted to fashion. Philosophy of old had lived upon an equivocal axiom: *Ex nihilo nihil.* To establish the counter-dogma of Creation, Augustine found it necessary to dive deep into the secrets of Nature, and thence to re-ascend to God (1) by the idea of Beauty,

as shown in his work "De Musicâ;" (2) by the idea of Goodness, as in the "De Libero Arbitrio;" (3) by the idea of Truth, as in the treatise " De Vera Religione." M. l'Abbé Maret has thrown light upon the vast work which he pursued in spite of the demands of theological controversy, amidst a people whom he was called upon to instruct and to govern, in the presence of the Donatists and before the approach of the Vandals. The

"Theodicea" of St. Augustine was, however, achieved, to be elaborated to the highest degree by St. Anselm, and finally enriched by the arrangement and additional corollaries of St. Thomas Aquinas. But the Bishop of Hippo was the acknowledged master of the generation of philosophers who filled the Middle Age with their discussions. Popular tradition gave testimony to this fact, and we read in the " Golden Legend " how a monk in ecstasy on beholding the heaven and the hosts of the elect, wondering at not seeing St. Augustine, inquired for the holy doctor. "He is higher far," it was answered; " gazing ever on the Holy Trinity, and discussing It throughout eternity."

Mysteries, indeed, failed to discourage the genius of St. Augustine. From the time in which he uttered that great speech, *Intellectum valde ama*, he became of necessity the guide of all the theologians who, like St. Anselm, were willing to put faith in quest of intelligence. *Fides quoerens intellectum*— not the idea of God alone, but the whole cycle of Christian dogma, was embraced in his meditations. No depths were too obscure for his search, no controversy too perilous for his intellect. His age was endangered by two forms of heresy; one of pagan parentage, the other the offspring of the philosophic schools. On the one hand, the Manichees were restoring the doctrines of Persia and of India, the strife of the two principles, emanation and metempsychosis—errors which had power to fascinate even nobler minds, as in the case of St. Augustine himself for so many years, to seduce the vulgar and form in Rome a powerful sect which terrified St. Leo the Great by its orgies. Four hundred years of preaching and martyrdom thus seemed fated to result in a rehabilitation of pagan fables, and Christianity to dissolve at the breath of Manes into a mere mythology.

On the other hand, the Arians, in denying Christ's divinity, the Pelagians, in suppressing grace, severed the mysterious ties which linked man to God. The supernatural element disappeared, whilst the Platonic

Demiurgus replaced the Consubstantial Word, and the Faith was reduced to the level of a philosophy. St. Augustine prevented this issue, and as his early life had been spent in struggling free from the Manichaean net, so its later years were devoted to combating Arius and Pelagius. Like all the great servants of Providence, he fought less for his own time than for posterity. The moment was approaching wherein Arianism was to enter as a conqueror through all the breaches of the Empire, in the train of the Goths, Vandals, and Lombards; and in those days of terror bishops would have had little leisure to study by the light of conflagrations the disputed questions of Nicaea, had not Augustine kept watch over them. His fifteen treatises on the Trinity comprised all the objections of the sectarians and all the arguments of the orthodox; and it was to him the victory was due in the conferences of Vienna and Toledo, when the Burgundians and Visigoths abjured their heresy. In later days, when the Manichaeism preserved in the East by the Paulicians had regained its sway in the West, when its disciples, under the names of Cathari or Albigenses, had mastered the half of Germany, of Italy, and of Southern France, and gravely imperilled Christian society, it was not the sword of Simon de Montfort which suppressed it—for fire and sword cannot conquer thought however false, (rather many noble hearts must have wavered at the sight of the violence which degraded the crusade, and was condemned by Innocent III.)—but the sound doctrine of St. Augustine, as expressed by his firm yet loving intellect, resettled their faith, and regained the Christian world for orthodoxy. In that conflict, the excesses of which we must detest, but need not to exaggerate, victory was due to truth rather than to force.

Christianity must be the soul of a society which it fashions after its own image, and in the fifth century that great work seemed near its achievement. The Papacy, fully acknowledged in its authority since the time of St. Irenaeus and Tertullian, which had presided at Nicaea, and to which the Council of Sardica had referred all episcopal judgments, found in St. Leo the Great a mind capable alike of defending its rights and understanding its duties. While the Greek mind was divided between Nestorius and Eutyches, Leo intervened with the judicious force of a lawful authority, and caused the Council of Chalcedon to save the faith in the East. His more especial task lay in preserving Western civilization, by appeasing Genseric at the very gates of Home, Probably in the person of Hosius of Cordova.—*(Tr.)*

Attila at the passage of the Mincio, and by forming the monastic legions which were to execute the designs of the Papacy. Souls worn out by vice and public misfortune were driven into seclusion by the fame of the institutions of the deserts, and the popular histories of their saints written by St. Athanasius, St. Jerome, and Cassian. The wealthy but menaced cities of Rome, Milan, and Treves still possessed amphitheatres for the pleasure of the mob, but side by side with monasteries, in which were moulded a race better able to cope with the dangers of the future. The austere men, the enemies of light, as the pagan Rutilius disdainfully calls the monks whom he found in the islands which fringed the Italian coast, were soon to be the only guardians of enlightenment. The great abbeys of Lerins, of the island of Barba, of Marmontiers, were open a century before the time of Benedict, not to introduce the religious life into the West, but to perpetuate it, in tempering its rigour.

But as Christian people could not emigrate entirely into the cloister, we must mark how the new faith gradually took possession of the lay world, and, by correcting its laws and manners, formed a more gentle society than that of St. Augustine's time, and equal to it in polish. We see in the clever letters of St. Jerome to the Roman matrons, who claimed descent from the

Gracchi and Emilii, and spent their time in learning Hebrew, speculating on the mystic words of Isaiah, and diving into every controversy of their time, to what a pitch the Church had brought female education. It formed a better estimate of the sex which antiquity had condemned to spinning wool, in hopeless ignorance of things of divine or of political interest.

St. Jerome never appeared more noble than in stooping to teach Lœta how to train her child, by putting letters of box-wood or ivory under its eyes, and rewarding its early efforts by a flower or a kiss. Of old it had been said, *Maxima debetur puero reverentia,* but the saintly doctor went further, and made Laeta's daughter the angel of her house; and it was her task to begin, when a mere baby, the conversion of her grandfather, a priest of the old gods, by springing upon his knee and singing the Alleluia, in spite of his displeasure. Christianity did not, as men say, wait for the favouring times of barbarism, to build up in darkness the power of popes and monks, but laid the foundations of its edifice in the light of day, under the jealous gaze of the pagans. The approaching invasions seemed more fraught with danger than advantage to its interests. The Canon law, whose birth we have noticed, found an obstinate resistance from the passions of the barbarians, and the Gospel had to devote more than twelve centuries to calming the violence of the conquerors, and reforming the evil instincts of their race, in restoring that clearness of intellect, that gentleness in the commerce of life, that tolerance towards the erring, and the many other virtues which throw over the society of the fifth century some of the charm of modern manners.

But Religion had not consummated her work as long as Literature resisted, and the century which saw the fall of so many altars beheld that of the Muses still surrounded by an adoring multitude. Yet Christianity shrank from condemning a veneration for the beautiful, and as it honoured the human mind and the arts it produced, so the persecution of the Apostate

Julian, in which the study of the classics had been forbidden to the faithful, was the severest of its trials. Literary history possesses no moment of greater interest than that which saw the School, with its profane traditions and texts, received into the Church. The Fathers, whose Christian austerity is our wonder, were passionate in their love for antiquity, which they covered, as it were, with their sacred vestments, and thus guaranteed to it the respect of the future. By their favour Virgil traversed the ages of iron without losing a page, and by right of his Fourth Eclogue took rank among the prophets and the sybils. St. Augustine would have blamed Paganism less if, in place of a temple to Cybele, it had raised a shrine to Plato, in which his works might have been publicly read. St. Jerome's dream is well known, and the scourging inflicted upon him by angels for having loved Cicero too well; yet his repentance was but short-lived, since he caused the monks of the Mount of Olives to pass their nights in copying the Ciceronian dialogues, and did not shrink himself from expounding the lyric and comic poets to the children of Bethlehem.

While pagan eloquence, expelled from the Forum, could find no outlet but in the lecture-halls of the rhetoricians, or in the mouths of the mendacious panegyrists of the Cœsars, a new form of oratory had founded its first chair in the Catacombs, and was drawing inspiration from the depths of the conscience. St. Ambrose organized it, and filled a chapter of his book, "De Officiis," with precepts on the art of preaching, which St. Augustine developed, not fearing, in his treatise, " De Doctrinâ Christiana," to borrow from the ancient rhetoric as much as was consistent with the

gravity of the Gospel message. We may listen, in Peter Chrysologus, Gandentius of Brescia, Maximus of Turin, to orators at once learned and popular, but their light was outshone by another preacher, who addressed himself not to some thousands of souls, but to the entire West. Amidst the confusion of the invasions, Salvian undertook the task of justifying the action of Providence. Eloquence never raised a more terrible cry than that which told from his lips the agony of the Roman world, pointing to the mockery which accompanied its fall, to its vain struggles beneath the hand of God, and His treatment of fire and sword which failed to effect its cure. *Secamur urimur non sanamur.*

The ancients, in writing history, had aimed at literary beauty, and thus loaded the narrative with ornament and declamation. The Christians only looked for truth, they wished for it in facts, and applied themselves to re-establishing order in time, which led to the dry but scrupulous chronicles of St. Jerome, of Prosper of Aquitaine, and the Spaniard Idatius. They sought for truth in the unravelling of causes, and, so to speak, made the Spirit of God to wander over the chaos of human events. The philosophy of history, so finely sketched by St. Augustine in his " City of God," was developed by the pen of Paulus Orosius. He was the first to condense the annals of the world into the formula *Divinâ providentiâ agitur mundus et homo*. His works became the type of the chronicles which multiplied in the Middle Age. Gregory of Tours could not treat of the Merovingian period without ascending to the origin of things; and Otto of Freysingen, in his fine work, " De Mutatione

Rerum," continued the chain of history to which Bossuet was to add the last and most elaborate link.

Poetry, in the last place, was destined to surrender the language which had been lavished on the false gods to the praises of Christ. When the Empress Justina was threatening to deliver over the Basilica of Milan to the Arians, St. Ambrose, with the Catholic people, passed day and night in the sacred place, and, to wile away the tediousness of the vigils, introduced the hymn-tunes which had already found a place in the Eastern Church. The sweetness of the sacred chant soon gained the ear of the West, and Christianity possessed a lyric poetry. Contemporaneously it beheld its epic take its rise in the verses of Sedulius and of Dracontius, and could even say with one of old, *Nescio quid majus nascitur Iliade.* Not that modern genius could hope to rival the matchless perfection of the Homeric forms, but because humanity thus found the true and oecumenical epopee whereof every other was but a shadow, the themes of which were the Fall, Redemption, and Judgment, which was to traverse the ages, and culminate in Dante, Milton, and Klopstock.

Moreover, in the fifth century, two Christian poets rose above the crowd. One was St. Paulinus, who laid aside the honours of his rank and fortune to dwell at the tomb of St. Felix of Nola, and who celebrated the peace of his seclusion in verses which were already quite Italian in their grace. As he depicts the basilica of the Saint blazing with taper-light, its colonnades hung with white draperies, its flower-strewn court, with the troops of devout mountaineers from the mountains of the Abruzzi bringing their sick on litters, or driving their cattle before them to receive a blessing, we might

fancy ourselves present at a pilgrimage of the Neapolitan peasantry at the present clay. The other was the Spaniard Prudentius, who, at the end of a life full of honours, and long service to his duty, devoted to God the remnants of a tuneful voice and a dashing style. Beneath a method which the authors of the golden age would not have disowned, a modern cast of thought is apparent, whether the poet is borrowing the most genial accents of our Christmastides to invite the earth to wreathe its flowers round the cradle of the Saviour, or, as in the hymn of St. Laurence, is drawing the veil with a Dantean hardiness from the Christian destinies of Rome, or, as in his reply to Symmachus, makes a prayer to Honorius for the abolition of the gladiatorial shows the peroration of his invective against Paganism:—

Nullus in urbe cadat cujus sit poena voluptas !

Jam solis contenta fens infamis arena

Nulla cruentatis homicidia ludat in armis !

It is not sufficiently known, but we perhaps may learn, how the poetical vocation of the Middle Age was sustained by those writers who filled the libraries, shared with Virgil the honours of the "Æneid," and moulded the best imaginations of the time, until the mind grew weary of the chaste beauty of a poetry that had no pages for expurgation.

Our work would be incomplete if, amongst these germs of future greatness, we should forget Christian art, which had emerged from the Catacombs to produce in the light of day the basilicas of Constantine and Theodosius, the sepulchral bas-reliefs of Rome, of Ravenna, and of Aries, and the mosaics with which Pope Sixtus III. embellished, in 433, the sanctuary of St. Mary Major. The cupola already swelled over the tomb of St. Constance, and the Latin cross extended its arms in St. Peter's and in St. Paul's. The empire was still standing, and its every type was to be found in that Romanesque and Byzantine architecture which was soon to cover with monuments the shores of the Loire, Seine, and Bhine, and which from the broken arch of its vault was to produce all the beauties of the Pointed Gothic.

We have thus traced the rise of the modern faith, of modern society, and of modern art, all of which were born before the inroad of the barbarians, and were destined to grow sometimes through their aid, sometimes in their despite. The Barbarian mission was not that of inaugurating a craving for the infinite, a respect for women, or a sad-coloured poetry. They came to break with axe and lever the edifice of pagan society, in which Christian principles were cramped; yet their blows were not so crushing as to leave no remnants of the old ramparts, in which heathenism still might lurk. We shall find that half the vices attributed to the barbarians were those of the Roman Decline, and a share of the disorders charged upon nascent Christianity must be laid to the account of antiquity. In this category must be placed the vulgar superstitions, the occult sciences, the bloody laws put in force against magic, which do but repeat the old decrees of the Caesars; the fiscal system of the Merovingian kings, which was entirely borrowed from the imperial organization; the corruption, lastly, of taste and the decomposition of language, which already prognosticated the diversity of

the new idioms. Beneath the common civilization which was destined to knit into one family all the races of the West, the national character of each struggles to the surface. In every province the Latin tongue found an obstinate resistance in native dialects, the genius of Rome in native manners. The distinctive elements in the three great Neo-Latin nations could already be recognized. Italy had statesmen in Symmachus and Leo the Great, and was soon to possess Gregory the Great, Gregory VII, and Innocent III. Spain claimed a majority among the poets, and gave them that dashing spirit which has never failed from Lucan to Lope de Vega. The " Psychomachia " of Prudentius was a prelude to the allegorical dramas, to the "Autos Sacramentales" of Calderon. Gaul, lastly, was the country of wits, of men gifted with repartee. We know the eloquence of Salvian, the play of words so dear to Sidonius Apollinaris, but that sage of the Decline was, moreover, full of the ancient heroism, when called upon to defend his episcopal see of Clermont from the assaults of the Visigoths. And these were the very features in which Cato summed up the Gallic character: *Hem milita rem et argute loqai.*

Such is the plan of our course, for it is not necessary to follow out in detail the literary history of the fifth century, but only to seek light for the obscurity of the succeeding ages. As travellers tell of rivers which lose themselves amongst rocks, to appear again at some distance from their hiding-place, so we shall ascend above the point at which the stream of tradition seems to fail, and will attempt to descend with it into the gulf, that we may be certain that the issuing stream is indeed the same. As historians have opened a certain chasm between antiquity and barbarism, so let us undertake to re-establish the unfailing communication granted by Providence in time, as well as in space; for there is no study more fascinating than that of the ties which link the ages, which give to the illustrious dead disciples century after century down the future, and thus demonstrate the victory of thought over destruction.

PAGANISM.

In the fifth century Paganism, at first sight, seemed but a ruin. It is commonly supposed that the fall of superstition was imminent before the preaching of the Gospel, and that Christians have claimed an easy miracle in the destruction of an old cult which had long tottered beneath the blows of philosophy and the popular reason. Yet eighty years after the conversion of Constantine Paganism survived, and a greater lapse of time, a stronger expenditure of effort, was required to dispossess the ancient religion of the Empire, still mistress of the soil through its temples, of society through its associations, of some higher souls by the little truth it held, of the mass by the very excess of its errors.

When the Emperor Honorius, in 404, celebrated his sixth consulate at Rome, the poet Clandian, charged with the task of doing public honour to the heir of so many Christian emperors, invited him to recognize in the temples which surrounded the imperial palace his heavenly body guard, and pointed to the sanctuary of the Tarpeian Jove which crowned the Capitol, and the sacred edifices which rose on every side toward the sky, upholding on their pediments a host of gods to

preside over the City and the World. We cannot accuse the poet of reviving in hyperbole the lustre of an extinct Paganism. Several years later a topographical survey of Rome, in numbering the monuments which the sword and fire of the Goths had spared, still counted forty-three temples and two hundred and eighty chapels. The Colossus of the Sun, a hundred feet in height, still reared its front by the side of the Flavian amphitheatre, which had reeked with many a martyr's blood. Statues of Minerva,

Hercules, and Apollo decorated the squares and cross streets, and the fountains still gushed under the invocation of the nymphs. Time had gone by filled with the spirit of Christianity, the era of St. Augustine and of St. Jerome, but in 419, under Valentinian III., Rutilius Numatianus still sang of the pagan city as mother of heroes and of gods. "Her temples," said he, "bear us nearer to heaven." It is true that imperial edicts had closed the temples and forbidden the sacrifices, but the continued renewal of these laws during fifty years shows their constant infringement. In the midst of the fifth century the sacred fowls of the Capitol were still fed, and the consuls, on entering office, demanded their auspices. The Calendar noted the pagan festivals side by side with the feasts of the Saviour and the Saints. Within the City and beyond, throughout Italy and the Gallic provinces, and even the entire Western Empire, the sacred groves were still untouched by the axe, idols were adored, altars were standing, and the pagan populace, believing alike in the eternity of their cult and of the Empire, were waiting in scornful patience till mankind grew weary of the folly of the cross.

Hitherto, indeed, the fortunes of Rome had seemed mingled with those of her gods, and from the three great eras of her history had been gradually evolved the pagan system which we remark in the fifth century. The kingly epoch had furnished the antique dogmas on which reposed the whole theology of Rome. Supreme over all things stood an immutable power, unknown and nameless; beneath were other deities known to men, but perishable in nature, Rome along towards a fatal revolution which was to destroy the universe and raise it up anew; lower still came souls, emanations of the Deity, but fallen and doomed to an expiation on earth and in hell, until they became worthy of a return to their first abode. A close commerce between the visible and invisible worlds was in consequence maintained through the media of auguries, sacrifices, and the worship paid to the Manes. Rome herself was a temple in near relation to heaven and hell, square in form, facing towards the East, according to the ancient rites. Each patrician's house was a sanctuary, wherein the ancestral images from their place of honour watched over the fortunes of their descendants. The laws of the City, hallowed by the auspices, expanded into oracles, magistracies became sacerdotal, every important act in life a religious transaction. A people so permeated with respect for their gods and their ancestors, under their eyes as was the firm conviction in council or in war, was fit for great achievements. These obscure but potent doctrines had disciplined the old Romans, and sustained the edifice of the commonwealth; as the cloacae of Tarquin, those sombre but gigantic vaults, had purified the soil of the City and supported its monuments.

Doubtless the Greek mythology modified the austerity of this primitive belief. It had, however, appeared during the most flourishing ages of the republic, with the first examples of that bold policy which was to advance by enlarging the circle of its law and of its worship, and receive into the bosom of Rome the conquered nations and their gods. The divinities of Greece followed the car of Paulus-Emilius and of Scipio to the Capitol; but though the victor descended when his hour of triumph was past, the captive gods remained to attract every art around their shrines. Sculptors and poets reared an Olympus of marble and gold in place of the deities of clay to which the old Romans had done homage. Religion lost her power over morality, but over the imagination she reigned supreme. At length the advent of the Caesars opened Rome to the worship of the East. As the respect for primitive traditions was withering away, so society, rather than remain godless, sought new idols at the world's extremity. It was in Isis and Serapis, in Mithra and his mysteries, that troubled hearts now sought repose. Vespasian and his successors have been often blamed for their

FREDERIC OZANAM

sanction to the barbarous rites which the Senate had for long contemptuously repelled, but the emperors did but renew the old policy, and as sovereign pontiffs of a city which boasted of giving peace to the world, it was their duty to reconcile all religions. They realized the ideal of polytheism, in which there was room for all the false gods, but no place for the True.

Thus was that mighty religion rooted in the history, the institutions, the very stones of Rome; and, in justice to Paganism, it had stronger ties in the souls of men, for the ancient society would never have survived so many ages had it not possessed some of those truths which the human conscience never entirely lacks. The Roman religion placed one supreme deity above all secondary causes; he was proclaimed upon his temples as very good and very great. The feciales called him to witness before hurling the dart which carried with it peace or war. The poet Plautus showed the messengers of this god visiting cities and nations to procure " written in a book the names of those who sustained wicked lawsuits by false witness, and of those who perjured themselves for money; how it is his task to be judge of appeal in badly judged causes, and if the guilty think to gain him by presents and victims, they lose at once their money and their trouble." Such language was that of a poet rather than a philosopher, but it was addressed to the mob, and gained their applause in touching, like so many nerves, the group of beliefs which lay at the root of the public conscience. It was mindful also of the dead, and had touching prayers in their behalf. " Honour the tombs, appease the souls of your fathers. The Manes ask for little: to them devotion stands in the place of rich offerings." Expiatory sacrifices for ancestors were handed down as a charge upon the inheritance from father to son, ceremonies whose power was to he felt in hell, to hasten the deliverance of souls who were undergoing purgation, and bring the day in which they were to seat themselves as its tutelary deities around the family hearth. The whole funeral liturgy bore witness to faith in a future life, to the reversibility of merits, to the solidarity of the family organization. The thought of a God and remembrance of the dead were as two rays, unkindled by philosophy but proceeding from a higher Source, with capacity of still guiding, after the lapse of ages of pagan darkness, some chosen spirits in the right way; so they throw light on the obstinate resistance offered to Christianity by some honest but timid souls, who answered, like Longinian, to the arguments of St. Augustine, that they hoped to reach God by way of the old observances, and through the virtues of antiquity.

But that small and well-meaning band judged wrongly of the religion whose doomed altars they were defending. If Paganism possessed elevating influences, so also did elements exist in Chaos. Side by side with doctrines which might have sustained life in the individual intellect and in society, a principle was working which must ever impel towards ruin the person of man and civilization itself. The evil leaven of heathenism laboured to extinguish reason in man by separating it from the supreme truth whence all its light is derived. Whereas religion is bound to strain every nerve in snatching the human soul from the distractions of sense, to give it an upward flight in raising the veils which, hang over the spiritual world, Paganism diverted it from the sphere of ideas by promising to find its god in the regions of sense. It pointed, firstly, to Him in Matter itself, whose hidden forces it bade the faithful to deify. The Romans adored the water of their fountains, stones, serpents, and the accustomed fetishes of the barbarian. Mankind till then had paid honour to an unknown power, conceived to be greater than himself; his second and more culpable error lay in adoring himself, in deifying that humanity which he recognized as weak and sinful. The priests, sculptors, and poets of Paganism borrowed for their gods not only the features but the frailties of mortals, and thence rose the fables which throned in heaven the passions of earth; thence came the whole system of idolatry hardly to be realized in the intensity of its madness. It was no calumny of Christian apologists, but the avowal of the wise ones of the old cult, that the idols were as bodies into which the powers of heaven descended when conjured by the prescribed rites; that they were held captive there by the smoke of victims, nourished by their fat smeared upon the statues, their thirst slaked when priests poured over them cupfuls of gladiatorial blood. Men of sober reason spent whole days in paying to the Jupiter of the Capitol the homage which as clients they owed to a patron— some in offering him perfumes, others in introducing visitors or declaiming comedies to him. But Rome began to crave for a more concrete God than the Capitolian Jove, and found a living and most terrible deity in the person of her Emperor. Earth could offer nothing more divine in the sense of a majesty at once recognized and obeyed, and Paganism did but push its principles to their consequence in deifying the Caesars; but reason fell to the lowest depth of degradation, and the Ægyptians grovelling before the beasts of the Nile outraged humanity less than the age of the Automnes, with its philosophers and jurisconsults rendering divine honours to the Emperor Commodus.

Again, Paganism perverted the Roman will by turning it from the supreme good by means of the two passions—fear and desire. Man craves for God, and yet dreads Him, as he fears the dead, the life to come, and all invisible things. Drawn irresistibly towards Him, he takes flight and avoids His very Name, and the fear which severs him from his last end is the chief cause of all his aberrations. At first sight, Paganism seemed a mere religion of terror, which in disfiguring the idea of God, only made Him more obscure, more threatening, more crushing to the imagination of man. Nature, which it proposed as an object of adoration, seemed but a third force, governed by no law, subject only to the tremendous caprices which revealed themselves in the lightning flash and the earthquake, or the volcanic phenomena of the Roman Campagna. Amidst the thirty thousand deities with which he had peopled the world, the Roman, far from being confident in their protection, was full of disquietude. Ovid represents the peasantry assembled before the image of Pales, and the following is the prayer which he makes them utter:—

" O goddess, appease for us the fountains and their divinities, appease the gods dispersed in the forest depths; grant that we may meet no Dryads, nor Diana surprised at the hath, nor Faunus, when towards midday he tramples the herbage of our fields."

If the bold peasants of Latium thus shrank from an encounter with wood-nymphs, it is no marvel that they adored Fever and Fear. This feeling of terror permeated the entire religion, and gave rise to numberless sinister rites, and the machinery in sight of which Lucretius might well say that fear alone had made the gods. It produced those frenzies of magic which were but a despairing effort of man to resist these cruel deities, and conquer them not by the moral merits of prayer and virtue, but by the physical force of certain acts and fixed formulas. There is no sight stranger but more instructive than of that system of incantation and senseless observance by means of which earth's wisest race sought to lay nature in fetters; but which sooner or later burst most terrible in power through its bonds, and took vengeance on man through death. As, then, death remained the ultimate ruler of the heathen world, so human sacrifice was the last effort of the pagan liturgy. It was principally by the infernal gods, by the souls of ancestors wandering pale and attenuated around their burial-place, that blood was demanded. Under Tarquin the First, children were sacrificed to Maria, the mother of the Lares. In the brightest age of the republic and of the empire, a male and female Gaul and a pair of Greeks were buried alive to avert an oracle which had promised the soil of Rome to the barbarians; the spell pronounced over the heads of the victims devoted them to the gods of hell; and Pliny, a contemporary of these cruelties, was only struck by the majesty of the ceremonial, and the force of its formulas. When Constantine, and with him Christianity, had mounted the imperial throne, the pagan priests still offered, year by year, a cup of blood to Jupiter Latialis. Vainly did the Romans forbid to their conquered nations the slaughter of which they gave the example, and in the third century human sacrifice still lingered in Africa and Arcadia, as if all the laws of civilization were powerless to stifle the brutish instincts which Paganism let loose in the depths of man's fallen nature.

But mankind, in flying from the true good, followed one which was false. The terror which drove him from God plunged man into lustful indulgence, and the religion of fear became the sanction of carnal pleasure. We must glance at the excesses of this error, if only to disabuse the minds who, repelled by the sternness of the Gospel, turn regretfully to antiquity, asking in what respect the Roman civilization was inferior to that of Christian times. Though Nature is constantly affording a spectacle of decay, she is prodigal also in the principle of life. She shows man that same power which exists in him for the perpetuation of his race and is open to be abused by him to his loss, and exhales from every pore a dangerous spell, as it were, which is liable to cause him to forget his spiritual destinies. Far from guarding man therefrom, Paganism plunged his being into the intoxications of sense, and brought him to adore the propagating principle in nature. Phidias and Praxiteles were the servants of its brilliant worship, and an obscene symbol was selected as a summary of its mysteries. The feasts of Bacchus saw it led in procession through the towns and villages of Latium, amidst ceremonies in which matrons of noble birth played their part. Songs and pantomime accompanied the rite, and robbed the women who joined in it of all excuse on the score of ignorance of its meaning; and though these infamies have been veiled by the name of symbolism, doubtless where the priests placed symbols, the populace found incentives and examples. The gods were honoured by imitation, and their adulteries served to reassure the consciences which scrupled. At length, from venerating love as the life-principle which circulated in nature, they came to deify the nameless lusts by which nature itself is outraged, and the immolation of beauty and modesty ranked as the worthiest tribute to the apotheosis of the flesh. Prostitution became a religion, and its temples at Cyprus, at Samos, and at Mount Eryx, were served by thousands of courtesans. Lust also claimed its human victims, and terror and passion, the twin scourges of the old society, drove mankind to the same abyss. Far distant from the supreme good, man had deified the two forms of evil, destruction and corruption, with a cult of which self-destruction was the essence. In the face of an error so monstrous, of a worship which outraged the intellect in sanctioning murder and feeing impurity, St. Augustine declared that Christians honoured human nature too much to suppose that she herself could have sunk so low, finding it more pious to believe that the Spirit of Evil alone had conceived such horrors, and had dishonoured man that it might enslave him.

But these abominations, calculated as they were to raise every soul against Paganism, helped to subjugate men by depraving them, and thus preserved for more than a century the dominion of which the old religion had been robbed by law. Imperial edicts had proscribed the superstitions, dispersed the priests of Cybele and the priestesses of Venus, but all the lustful and bloody features of the old cult survived in the amphitheatre. St. Cyprian had called idolatry the mother of the games, and it was needful for a religion, whose object it was to throw a divine halo over pleasure, to lay prompt hold upon the public amusements. Rome had borrowed from Etruria gladiatorial combats to appease the dead, histrionic dances to cajole the anger of heaven. The Roman people held its festivals for the gods and its ancestors, and laboured to reproduce in symbolic representation the delights of the Immortals. The races of the Circus signified the movement of the stars, the dances of the theatre the voluptuous impulses which enslave every living being. In the conflicts of the amphitheatre were depicted in miniature the struggles of humanity. The dedication of the Circus to the sun was marked by an obelisk raised in the midst of the enclosure; on the line dividing it were built three altars in honour of the Cabires; and every column and monument, as well as the post around which the chariots turned, had its tutelary god. Before the opening of the races, a procession of priests bore round the Circus images of the gods reposing on richly embroidered couches, and numbers of sacrificial acts preceded, interrupted, and followed the sports. When the napkin, falling from the hands of the magistrate, gave the signal for the charioteers, the darlings of Rome, to enter the arena, and the intoxicated and panting multitude pursued, with cries loud and long, the chariots which they favoured or scorned, divided into furious factions, and ended in coming to blows, then were the gods content, and Romulus recognized his people— his children, indeed—who had lost their world-wide dominion, who were bought and sold for money, but could still forget everything in the Circus, and find therein, according to the expression of a contemporary writer, their temple, their forum, their country, and the theme of all their hopes. The Calendar of 448 still marked fifty-eight days of public games—in that year of terror in which Genseric and Attila were awaiting in full panoply the hour appointed by Heaven.

The theatre was the domain of Venus, for when Pompey restored in marble the wooden benches on which the Romans of old had sat, he dedicated his edifice to the goddess who perturbed all nature by the power of her fascinations. It also was a temple, with a garland-crowned altar in the midst, set apart for a performance of the myths in which the gods appeared as exemplars of the deepest immorality. It was there that the mimes, youths withered from infancy, played in pantomime the loves of Jupiter or the frenzies of Pasiphae. But the prosaic common-sense of the Romans was ill-content with the pleasure of dramatic illusion; they spurned a vainly-excited emotion, so, to soothe their leisure, the ideal had to cede to reality: women were dishonoured on the stage, or, if the drama was tragic, the criminal who played the part of Atys was mutilated, or the personator of Hercules was burnt. Martial boasts of an imperial festival in which Orpheus appeared charming the mountains of Thrace with his lyre, drawing trees and rocks after him enamoured by his melody, and finally torn limb from limb by a bear, while the cries of the actor, who thus threw some life into the languor of the old tragedy, were drowned by songs and dances. Three thousand female dancers served like so many priestesses the theatres of Rome, and were kept in the city when, on the occasion of a famine, all the grammarians were expelled. The sovereign people could not do without its lovely captives; it covered them with applause and with flowers, but caused them to uncover their bodies before the image of Flora. Yet the senators on the front ranks showed no indignation, and the rhetorician Libanius wrote an apology for dancers and mimes, justifying them by the precedent of the pleasures of Olympus, and praising their continuance of the education given to the people formerly by the priest; whilst the pagan party was powerful enough to obtain a prohibition of baptizing actors, except in danger of death, lest as Christians they might escape the public pleasures of which they were the slaves.

Paganism did not afford the gods any sweeter pleasure than that of contemplating the perils of men from the depths of their own repose, so the amphitheatre had more tutelary deities than the Capitol, and Tertullian could say that more demons than men assisted at the spectacle. Diana presided at the chase, and Mars at the combats; and when the magisterial edicts had sanctioned the sports, the men who were the destined prey of the wild beasts appeared in garments sacred to Saturn, whilst the women were crowned with the fillets of Ceres, as victims in a sacrifice.! After the earth had been loaded with the corpses of gladiators in one of these popular shows, a gate of the arena opened and disclosed two personages, one bearing the attributes of Mercury struck the bodies with the end of his flame-coloured caduceus, to assure the people that the victims no longer breathed, and the other, armed with Pluto's hammer, despatched those who still survived. This apparition reminded the spectators that they were assisting at funereal games, and that the blood which was spilt was rejoicing the manes of the old Romans in their infernal dwelling-place. It was the spirit of Paganism which permeated that mighty people, as the magistrates, priests, and vestal virgins bent in applause from the height of the Podium, that they might do high honour to their ancestors, and eighty thousand spectators joined in the action with a shudder of joy. The wise offered no resistance to this brutalizing of the mass. Even Cicero, though troubled by a momentary scruple, dared not absolutely condemn practices so rife with instruction for a people of warriors; and the younger Pliny, though a man of benevolence and wisdom, congratulated Trajan on having provided "no enervating spectacle, but manly pleasures, destined to rekindle in the souls of men contempt for death and pride in a well-placed wound." Yet, as if to humiliate such bloodthirsty wisdom, the military worth of the Romans diminished as the games of cruelty were multiplied. The Republic had never witnessed the sufferings of more than fifty pairs of gladiators in a day, but five hundred figured in the games given by the Emperor Gordian; and the Goths were at the very gates of Rome as the prefects were engaged in supplying the arena and finding a sufficient number of prisoners ready to devote themselves for the pleasures of the Eternal City.

Paganism had thus, as if in a forlorn hope, taken its last stand in the public amusements. Thence it defied the eloquence of the Fathers, disputed souls with them, moulded society after its own fashion, and therein it might be known by its fruits. Pagans themselves acknowledged that the passion for the Circus hastened the decline of Rome, and that nothing of mark could be expected from a people which passed days in breathless interest over the issue of a chariot race. And how much more did the fault lie with the theatre, and what eyes could have Rome with impunity the gestures and scenes in which Rome found her recreation? Christian priests knew the result, and one of them declared that he could point to men whom the incitations of those spectacles had torn from the nuptial couch and thrown into the arms of courtesans. Yet fathers of families took their wives and daughters to witness them; nor could they see anything that the temple services had not already made familiar. But the amphitheatre was resistless in its attractions, and the greatest school ever opened for the demoralization of man. Alypius, the friend of St. Augustine, a philosopher, a man of learning, and with Christian leanings, was drawn one day, through want of moral courage, to the scenes which his better nature loathed. At first he vowed to see nothing, and closed his eyes, when suddenly, at the sound of a death-shriek, he opened and turned them upon the arena, and did not withdraw them till the end. He drank in cruelty with the sight of blood, quenched his thirst in the Fury's cup, and intoxicated his spirit with the reek of the slaughter. No longer the same man, he became like the most ardent of that barbarous crew. He shouted, and felt his veins on fire, and brought away a passion to return, no longer with those who had taken him, but with others dragged thither by himself. To such a depth of irresolution, lust, and savageness had Paganism, ever corrupting itself and man with it, reduced earth's most civilized people. Behind the popular creed stood Philosophy, which from having combated now sought to defend it, and succeeded with sufficient art to rally around the old religion the most enlightened members of Roman society. It had at the outset announced itself to be a revolt of reason against Paganism, and our respect is due to those early sages who remounted to the sources of tradition, to explain the secrets of nature, in spite of the superstitious terrors which barred their approach, and with still greater courage busied themselves in the solitudes of the conscience, still desolate from the lack of Christian enlightenment. They had sought the First Cause to which Socrates, in teaching all the Divine attributes which Creation makes known, had nearly approached. But the mere glimpse of the True God caused the thrones of the false deities to totter, and these philosophers, in exposing the foundations of the pagan society, dreaded the collapse of the whole superstructure. Loving truth insufficiently, whilst they despised humanity, they devoted their genius to rehabilitating errors which, as they said, were necessary to the peace of the world. Cicero publicly derided the augurs, but in tracing the plan of an ideal republic in his " Treatise on Law," he placed therein augurs, whose decisions were to be obeyed on pain of death. Seneca ridiculed the worship of idols, but did not shrink from drawing the conclusion that even the wise ought to practise it, and thus honour custom and truth. The Stoics justified public worship for reasons of state, and protected the current mythology by an allegorical interpretation. Nature they defended as an active principle, energizing under many forms, and which was open to veneration under many names—to be called Jupiter in the life-giving aspect, Juno in the air, Neptune in water, or Vulcan in fire—explanations which were but as preludes of the prodigious work by which the school of Alexandria was to undertake the reconciliation of the imperial religion with reason.

History has made the school of Alexandria well known, and we can trace its rise in the East, how it passed into the West and established a school at Rome, which concurred in the political restoration of Paganism set on foot by Augustus, was for three ages upheld by the Caesars, and was prolonged to the fifth century through the obstinacy of the patrician order in defending its interests and its deities. Neoplatonism appeared at Rome under Antoninus, in the person of Apuleius, a learned but superstitious and adventurous African, who had visited the schools and sanctuaries of Greece and of Etruria, and returned to travel from town to town, haranguing the people and laying claim to a combination of the wisdom of philosophers, and the piety of the initiated in the Mysteries. The Imperial City admired his eloquence, and the provinces delighted in his opinions, which had such power in Africa that St. Augustine, after the lapse of two centuries, devoted twenty-five chapters of " The City of God " to their refutation. Meanwhile the declamations of Apuleius had prepared men's minds for a teaching of greater gravity and deeper scope. Plotinus, the chief of the Alexandrian philosophers, came to Rome in 244, passed twenty-six years there, and reckoned among his auditors senators, magistrates, and matrons of noble birth, to whom this Ægyptian of half-frenzied countenance, who expressed himself in semi-barbarous Greek, seemed a messenger of the gods. A praetor was seen to lay down his fasces, dismiss his slaves, and relinquish his property, that he might abandon himself to wisdom. So rapid was the increase of his disciples, that Plotinus was bold enough to demand from the Emperor Gallian a plot of land in Campania on which he might found a city of philosophers, to be governed by the rules of Plato. Although the design failed, and the republic of sages was never constituted, yet he left behind him a host of followers, who carried his doctrines into the senate and the camp, the schools and the social life of Rome. Porphyry was the most faithful and learned of his disciples, and wrote books at Rome, in Sicily, and at Carthage, his three places of residence, which were translated into Latin, finally popularized the Neoplatonic views, and were handed down into the fifth century. Under Valentinian III., Macrobius, in the full blaze of Christianity, wrote a commentary on " Scipio's Dream," in which he found occasion to set forth the system of Plotinus as an ancient doctrine, common to the first minds of Greece and Rome, whether poets or metaphysicians, as capable of reconciling every school of thought, and justifying every fable of mythology. Such being the propagandists of Neoplatonism in the "West, it remains to note by what occult influence a philosophy intrinsically abstruse, and charged with Greek subtleties, could seduce the good sense of the Latins.

The contradiction which lay at the root of the old philosophy was the very point of the Alexandrian doctrines. Beginning with a departure from Paganism, they returned to it by long byways, charmed the reason by a promise of sublime dogmas, and satisfied the imagination by conceding all its fables. This was calculated to soothe many a spirit tormented by a double craving after faith and reason, but too weak to embrace the austere belief of the Christians. Plotinus incited a society, trembling at the earliest disasters of the Empire, which seemed to cause all pleasures of earth to slip from their grasp, to take refuge in God. It was necessary, he said, and St. Augustine praised the saying, to fly towards the spiritual abodes in which dwelt the Father and every good thing. He spared no effort, however costly, to achieve his lofty aim, and as the giants piled mountain on mountain to reach the sky, so did Plotinus labour to reach a knowledge of God by a fusion of the three great systems of Zeno, of Aristotle, and of Plato. With Zeno, he gave to the world a soul, which made of it one single existence; with Aristotle, he placed above the world an Intelligence whose sole function was self-contemplation; and, with Plato, he fixed at the summit of all things an Invisible Principle, which he called the One, or the Good. But though he named it he pronounced it indefinable, and so veiled it from the gaze of mankind. The One, the Intelligence, the World-Soul, were not three Gods, but three Hypostases of a Sole God, who proceeded from his unity to think and to act.

As the three Hypostases produced themselves in eternity, so was the World-Soul engendered in time. It gave forth space first, then the bodies destined to people space, such as the demons and the constellations, lastly men, animals, plants, and the bodies we think inanimate. But nothing in nature is really inanimate, for everything lives and thinks according to one life and one thought; for the Neoplatonists saw in the infinity of productions an emanation from the Divine Substance communicating itself without impoverishment—the sun pouring forth a wasteless light, the fountain which fed the river reseeking its source, and the whole universe aspiring to return to its primaeval unity.

Nor was the destiny of man's soul different. Contained at first in the Divine Spirit, it had lived a pure life therein, till the sight of the world of matter beneath tempted it to essay an independent existence. Detached from the Divine Parent, it fell to inhabiting bodies formed after its own image, and human life became a Fall, of which the soul could repent, and raise herself so as to pass after death into a higher sphere. But too often she comes to delight in her exile, abandons herself to the senses, and, on reaching death, is degraded to animating the bodies of brutes Or of plants, whose lives of sensuality or of stupidity she had been imitating. Thus, in proportion to her wallowing in evil, does the soul sink deeper into matter, till by a supreme effort she tears herself from the mire and begins to aspire; but, whatever may be the length of probation, its end is certain, for a time must come when good and evil alike shall find themselves confounded in the bosom of the Universal Soul.

This was assuredly a grand and elevating doctrine. When it spoke of a Supreme God, and declared Him to he One, Immaterial, and Impassible, it seemed as if nothing were left but to break the old idols. Some of these doctrines surprised Christians, who thought them to have been pilfered from the Gospel, as some, nowadays, have accused Christianity of enriching itself from the spoils of Neoplatonism. Yet, without denying that something might have been borrowed from the new religion, published two ages before, all the speculations of Alexandria had their issue in Paganism. The Principle placed by Plotinus at the summit of all things had nothing in common with the God of the Christians. They acknowledged in the First Cause perfections which brought Him near to the intellect and to the heart; he robbed his First Principle of every attribute, denied him thought and life, forbade either definition or affirmation concerning him. His god was an abstraction, which could neither be known nor loved, an illogical and immoral being—fit character for the deities of Paganism. A similar abyss separated the trinity of Plotinus from our own, in which the Unity of Nature subsists through the equality of Three Persons, whereas the philosopher destroyed the Divine One-ness in his three unequal Hypostases. In his scheme, the First Principle alone was perfect and indivisible; the second and third detached themselves from it by a sort of deterioration, and leant towards the imperfect world which they had engendered. Nor was this divided god a free agent, but produced by necessity, by the inevitable outflow of his Substance, a world as eternal as himself. The Pantheism of Plotinus deified matter and justified magic, because, as he said, the philtres and formulas of the magician tend to reawaken the attractions whereby the Universal Soul governs all things; and it sanctioned idolatry because the sculptor's chisel, in causing marble to assume a character of expression and beauty, prepares for the Supreme Soul a receptacle in which she reposes with greater satisfaction.

Such was the issue of the boldest flight of metaphysics in the old school, and its accompanying morality proceeded to the same extremities. Since it was the property of the divine nature to produce and animate everything, the human souls which it had generated could not arrest their own descent to matter. In their first fall there was no free will, and, consequently, no moral guilt. If new sins caused them to sink lower, this was but necessary to people the lower regions of the Universe, and fill the ladder of emanations to its last degrees. Evil thus became necessary, or, rather, evil only existed as a lesser good in the succession of existences that were farther and farther removed from the divine perfection which had produced and was to reabsorb them. An ultimate reception into the Unity, in utter unconsciousness of their past, was thus to be the end of both the just and of the unjust. Plotinus therefore returned, through the doctrine of Metempsychosis, to the old fables, and though severe in his personal character, disarmed morality by a suppression of the idea of individual permanence, without which a future life affords in prospect neither hope nor fear; whilst the doctrine of the emanation of the soul from the Divine Substance tended to that worst form of idolatry, the deification of man. The essence of Paganism was breathed forth in the haughty satisfaction with which the dying philosopher answered one of his disciples; "I am labouring," said he, " to disengage the divine element within me." In looking closely at the distinctive dogmas of Plotinus, his unrevealed unity, and imperfect trinity, the emanations which composed the substance of the Universe, the fall and rise of souls, we see traces of the mysteries of an old theosophy long prevalent in the East. The Etruscans had communicated it to the ancient Romans, and their descendants of the Decline might have recognized with surprise, in the writings of the Ægyptian philosopher, doctrines which formed the basis of the national religion. They saw them now clothed in eloquence, fortified by the subtleties of logic, brightened by the fires of mysticism; but the Neoplatonists gave them, besides, sufficient justification for the rest of their creed, even to its most extravagant fables. Thus Apuleius had distinguished the incorporeal deities who were incapable of passion from the daemons endowed with subtle bodies, but having souls full of human feeling; and mythology had taken refuge in the distinction. It was no longer the gods, but daemons, who loved the odours of sacrifices, whom the poets had brought upon the scene, whom Homer had, without profanation, introduced on the battlefield. Porphyry imagined thousands of explanations for the myths of Egypt and of Greece, and Macrobius made it his one aim to justify the old fables through philosophy; "for," said he, " the knowledge of things sacred is veiled; nature loves not to be surprised in her nudity. When Numenius betrayed, by a rash interpretation, the mysteries of Eleusis, we are told that the outraged goddesses appeared to him in the guise of courtesans, and accused him of having drawn them from their shrines, and made them public to the passers-by: for the gods have ever loved to reveal themselves to men, and to serve them under the fabulous features in which antiquity has presented them." The Neoplatonists were equally ingenious in rehabilitating the observances which shocked the reason or outraged nature. Plotinus, being more of a philosopher than a theologian, had only justified the old superstitious incidentally; but his disciples, impatient of the hesitating methods of philosophy, craved for a speedier commerce with heaven by means of theurgy, by sacrifices, spells, and magical arts. Jamblichus wrote a proof of the divinity of the idols, undertook the defence of Venus and Priapus, and approved the veneration of the obscene symbols. The Emperor Julian professed to reform Paganism. He could, with a word, have shorn it of its abominations, but he authorized the mutilation of the priests of Cybele, "for thus does it behove us," he said, "to honour the Mother of the Gods." The most learned plunged deepest into superstition, and men whose minds had fed on Plato and Aristotle, wasted their vigils in the hope of evoking at their will gods, daemons, and departed souls: or, assembled round a vervein-garlanded tripod, questioned fate as to the end of the emperor and his destined successor. Thus was the prophecy of St. Paul accomplished, and the heirs of that Alexandrian philosophy which professed to have gathered up the scattered lights of antiquity only restored its frenzies of vice.

In this manner was heathenism reinvigorated by the Neoplatonists, precisely as was congruous to a worn-out society, tired of doubt, incapable of faith, but a prey to every superstition which was offered to it. From the pagan aristocracy, whose views they seconded, their welcome was assured, and their school of philosophy, which had blossomed into a religious sect, became the bulwark of a political party. In fact, the senatorial families who were attached to the old creed had not followed the court to Constantinople, Milan, or Ravenna, but remained at Rome, to adorn with their patrician majesty the capital which the Caesars had repudiated. In it at least they hoped to guard the sacred hearth of the Empire, and avert the anger of the gods by their fidelity to the ancient rites. They drew to their side and covered with patronage and applause the men who defended by their learning the old interests and the old altars. By the aid of an allegorical interpretation the nobility tasted the sweetness of believing otherwise than the common people, and yet preserving the customs of their ancestors; whilst, strong in the teaching of Porphyry and Macrobius, they looked with pity ou the mad crowd who were drawn to Baptism, and cared not to conceal their contempt for the Christian rulers, to whose charge they laid all the disasters of the state. Disquieted within, hearing a threatening attitude to those without, the pagan world looked to them as champions, who, looking again to the future, were ready to support any ruler who would resume Julian's incompleted task. At court they had followers of mark enough to gain the highest dignities of the state; from the offices of the priesthood they drew a certain amount of influence and a considerable revenue; their palaces comprised whole towns, and their demesnes were provinces from which they could summon at will an army of slaves and clients; and by the public games which they provided they wielded their last weapon for kindling the passions of the people. At the opening of the fifth century, the best representation of the Roman aristocracy, the man best fitted to grace it by his eloquence and learning, was Symmachus, the prefect of Rome. His versatile genius, capable alike in the sphere of politics as in that of learning, was the wonder of his contemporaries; and men of taste, comparing his letters to those of Pliny, desired to see them written on rolls of silk. He had sung of the vine-clad volcanoes of Baiae in graceful verse, and taken a high rank among orators by right of his panegyrics, in which he had exhausted on Christian princes the language of idolatry. So active an intellect could not but live in close relation to the finest wits of the time. In his letters to Ausonius he compared him to Virgil, and the poet's reply put Symmachus side by side with Cicero. He was the chosen patron of all new lectures and declamations. One day he was observed in high spirits at having just been present at the first appearance

of the rhetorician Palladius, who had charmed the auditory by his florid eloquence; another time, when the city of Milan had applied to him for a professor of eloquence, he sent for a young African noted for his learning and genius, proposed him a subject, heard with approval, and dispatched him to Milan. The youth was Augustine, and Symmachus little knew the injury he was doing to his gods in sending such a disciple to the Bishop Ambrose. His well-founded authority in literature was enhanced by his brilliant political position. Successively governor of Lucania, proconsul of Africa, prefect of Rome, and lastly consul, as a versatile politician but pure administrator, Symmachus had become the crown of the Roman nobility, and the soul of that senate which he did not hesitate to name the best part of the human race. He beheld in it the last asylum of the doctrines to which he had devoted all his genius and all his fame. Like the patricians of old, whose example he followed, he aspired to reunite all religious and civil honours in his own person, and add the fillets of the priest to the fasces of the consul. To his post in the college of pontiffs he brought a scrupulous ardour which withered the timidity of his colleagues, and groaning over the abandonment of the sacrifices, was as eager to appease the gods by victims as to defend them by the powers of his eloquence.

This zealous pagan, so justly respected for his learning, certainly merited to be the spokesman of the cause of polytheism when it made its last public protest in demanding the restoration of the altar of victory. This altar had stood in the midst of the senate house, had given it the character of a temple, and served to recall the ancient theocratic system of law and the alliance of Rome with the gods. The Christian emperors had removed it as a scandal, and the pagan senators declared that they could no longer deliberate in a place which had been thus profaned, and shorn of the auspices of the divinity who, for twelve hundred years, had preserved the Empire. Symmachus took charge of the complaint, and showed in his protest how much faith the mind of an idolater could preserve. His eloquent plaint began and ended in scepticism, and in face of the religious differences which sundered his contemporaries, his view grew dark and uncertain.

" Every one," said he, "has his peculiar custom and rite; surely it is just to recognize one and the same divinity beneath these different forms of adoration. We contemplate the same stars, the same heaven is common to both, and we are enfolded by the same earth. What does the manner matter in which each seeks for truth ? One sole way cannot suffice for arriving at that great mystery; and yet how healthy are such disputes for the slothful."

This revealed the hidden sore of paganism, and showed that the efforts of philosophy had only issued in a declaration of the inaccessibility of truth. Yet the spirits which were too worn out for faith had force left still for persecution; and the same Symmachus, who was so uncertain about the gods, to whom the supreme reason of things was veiled by an eternal mist, who deemed religious controversy an unworthy waste of a statesman's time, hunted down with indefatigable energy a vestal who had fallen. He consulted with the imperial officers, importuned the prefect of the city and the president of the province, and took no repose until he had seen the culprit buried alive, according to the custom of his ancestors; for the bloody instincts of his creed were preserved as fresh beneath the robe of the senator and the polish of the man of culture as beneath the rags of the populace who crowded the amphitheatre. In **a.d.** 402, Symmachus desired to celebrate his son's praetorship by games, and before the time fixed had drained the provinces of their rarest products in the way of racehorses, wild beasts, comedians, and gladiators; but amidst these cares an unlooked-for calamity overtook him, which he confided in a letter to Flavian, his friend. All the philosophy of Socrates was not enough, he said, to console him for twenty-nine of the Saxon prisoners whom he had purchased for the arena having impiously strangled themselves rather than serve the pastimes of the sovereign people.

Such was the effect of heathen wisdom on a naturally upright and benevolent soul in the fifth century, that advanced age in the world's life, bright moreover with all the lights of antiquity. A contemporary historian, himself a pagan, has undertaken a general description of the aristocracy, and represents the last guardians of the traditions of Numa as no longer believing in the gods, but not daring to dine or bathe before the astrologer had assured them of the favour of the planets. The sons of those Romans who had gone forth with the eagle's flight, as it were, to conquest under the frigid or the torrid zone, thought they had rivalled the doings of Caesar if they coasted the bay of Baiae, cradled in a sumptuous bark, fanned by boys, and declaring life unbearable if a ray of sun stole through the awning spread overhead. They exposed to public gaze all the infamy of their domestic orgies, and appeared abroad surrounded by a legion of slaves, headed by a troop of youths who had been mutilated for their hideous pleasures. What respect could these voluptuaries have for their fellow-creatures? Little did they recognize the sanctity which lies in the blood and tears of men, and whilst they had only a laugh for the clever slave who skilfully killed his fellow, they condemned another to the rods who had made them wait for hot water.

Such men as these loved the creed which left their vices at peace. In despair of truth they only asked for repose in error, and St. Augustine had sounded the depth of their hearts, or rather of their passions, when he put into their mouths this language, that of materialists of every age:—" What matter to us truths which are not to be reached by human reason ? What is of importance is that the State should stand, should be rich, and, above all, tranquil. What touches us supremely is that public prosperity should serve to augment the wealth which keeps the great in splendour, the small in comfort, and, consequently, in submission. Let the laws ordain nothing irksome, forbid nothing that is agreeable; let the ruler secure his people's obedience by showing himself no gloomy censor of their morals, but the purveyor of their pleasures; let the markets teem with beautiful slaves; let the palaces he sumptuous and banquets frequent, at which every one may gorge, drink, and vomit till daybreak; everywhere let the sound of dancing be heard and joyous applause break over the benches of the theatre; let those gods be held true who have assured us such happiness; give them the worship they prefer, the games they delight in, that they may enjoy themselves with their adorers. We pray them only to make our felicity lasting, that we may have no cause for fear from plague or foe."

But the foe was at the gate, and the hour approaching in which doctrines which had been handed down from school to school, and found their place in the Roman senate, were to undergo their supreme probation before the barbarians, that the world might see what philosophic Paganism could do towards saving the Empire, or, at least, making its fall dignified. In **a.d**. 408, Alaric presented himself before Rome, and the smoke of the enemy's camp could be seen from the temple of the Capitolian Jupiter. At this pressing moment the first act of the senate, assembled in deliberation, was to put to death Serena, the widow of Stilicho and niece of Theodosius—a victim whom the gods required; for it was said that this sacrilegious Christian had once entered the Temple of Cybele and carried off the necklace from the image. Serena was strangled after the old fashion *(more majorum)*, but that last human sacrifice did not save her country. Alaric demanded all the gold, silver, and precious stones of the city, and only left the Romans their dishonoured lives; whereupon the prefect, Pompeianus, caused the Etruscan priests, who boasted of having saved the little town of Nurcia by their spells, to be summoned, and they undertook to bring down fire from heaven upon the barbarians, but on condition that public sacrifice should be offered at the public expense in presence of the senate, and with all the pomp of past ages. Such an open infringement of the imperial edicts was dreaded by the senate, and as at the same time Alaric modified his conditions, the ransom of Rome was fixed at 6,000 pounds of gold and 30,000 of silver. The patrician families charged themselves with its payment; but as the money in their treasuries did not suffice, it was necessary to seize the gold in the temples; so they robbed the gods they had been defending of their ornaments, and as the weight required was not yet forthcoming, melted down several of their images, and amongst them the statue of Valour *(Virtutis)*.

There is something truly pathetic in this catastrophe of a mighty religion; and could one forget all the error which was mingled in its teaching, all the crime which found sanction in its practice, it would be impossible to regard without emotion the believers who clung to it, motionless at the altars of their gods, showing some remnant, if not of the energy, at least of the obstinacy, of the Roman character. "We, without justifying their stubbornness, must consider the inevitable perplexity of the mind balanced between two hostile creeds, and especially now that their faith required a struggle. This was in the mind of the Fathers as, acknowledging the painful process by which souls are conquered, they exclaimed, *"Non nascuntur sed fiunt Christiani!"* "But we must not, on the other hand, by an unjust parallel, compare the ruin of the fifth century with the confusion of our own time, or place the pagan collapse in the same category with the supposed decline of Christian civilization. History does not halt to point to apparent recurrences of events, knowing that in our softness we always exaggerate the evils of the present time, and find our vanity flattered in surpassing the misfortunes of our ancestors. Civilization, it tells us, cannot perish through passions which it corrects, nor by institutions which it may modify, but by doctrines which an inflexible logic impels to their results. History points to a difference in favour of our age which may reassure the most fearful; for our Christianity does not distinguish, like the heathen philosophy, between the religion of higher minds and that of the people, nor found the peace of the world upon a system of necessary falsehood. It does not, like Plotinus, under the guise of a pantheistic principle, practically deify matter, and issue in governing nations through their interests and their pleasures *(panem et circenses),* which is pure political materialism. Christianity especially docs not profess, with Symmachus, doubt or indifference on the momentous questions of God, the soul, and futurity; but as long as it can give an answer at once supremely authoritative and supremely reasonable to these problems, nothing is really lost, for the truths of eternity do not let fall those societies in time which are of their own moulding, and the invisible is the sustaining influence of that visible civilization in which it reveals itself.

THE FALL OF PAGANISM, AND WHETHER ITS FALL WAS ENTIRE.

We have seen by what an inexorable necessity Paganism led the aristocracy of Rome to degradation, her people to barbarism, and her empire to destruction. If regenerated humanity was to subsist, the old order must perish, and it is our object now to consider the manner of its fall, and whether its extinction was complete. Paganism did not succumb, as has often been supposed, to the laws of the Emperors, nor did Constantine, when, in **a.d**. 312, he gave liberty to the Christians, desire them to turn the sword upon their foes of the old religion. A later edict, which seems entirely modern in its principle, promised to the heathens the same tolerance as was afforded to the faithful. " For," as it said, " it is one thing to engage in mental conflicts in order to conquer heaven, another to employ force to coerce conviction." Notwithstanding the instigation of the Arians, who were interested in laying violent hands upon the conscience, and certain edicts of Constantius against superstition, Paganism continued in possession of its liberties and privileges until the end of the fourth century, when the menacing attitude of its professors, and their eager rallying round any usurper, elicited a sterner legislation. Two laws of Theodosius, and four of Honorius, effected the closing of the temples, by suppressing their revenues and forbidding their sacrifices. These seemed crushing blows to idolatry, but St. Augustine attests that in Africa the idols remained standing, and that their worshippers were powerful enough to burn a church and slaughter sixty Christians. In spite of the imperial edicts, there was no case known of pagans being condemned and punished by death for the sake of religion; and the Imperial line was about to end, but polytheism was destined to survive it, as if to prove that ideas are not to be slain by the sword, and that even false doctrine is more durable than the powers of earth.

Paganism, then, perished by the two weapons of controversy and charity. The controversy on both sides was loud and free, and was prolonged in the East until a decree of Justinian closed the schools of Athens; whilst in the West Ammianus, Clandian, and Rutilius calumniated with impunity the new religion, and its saints and monks. The old cult was entrenched behind the consent of antiquity, and struggled to retain its hold over the mind by every art which was calculated to touch it, by the subtlety of philosophic interpretation, the majesty of its ritual, the charm of its mythology, whilst it enlisted every human interest and passion against the Gospel. Then, as ever, it reproached Christianity with hatred of the human race, in other words, its contempt of the world, with an avoidance of the public pleasures, and the incompatibility of its laws with the maxims and manners which had built up the greatness of Rome.

By it calamity had befallen the Empire whose frontiers had been delivered to the barbarians by the outraged gods, and heaven kept back its very rain on account of the Christians. *Pluvia desit causa Christiani.*

The Christian apologist answered with inimitable equity and vigour, refusing in the first place to condemn entirely the old civilization, acknowledging a modicum of truth in the doctrines of the philosophers, of good in the Roman legislation, and, as we shall see hereafter, preserving the literature whilst they rejected the fables of antiquity with a thorough discernment,—thus doing honour to the human mind, and teaching it to recognize the divine ray within it. Having thus rubbed off the polish of

Paganism, they presented it to the eyes of the people, naked and bloodstained, in the full horror of its impure and murderous observances; instead of the glosses which are so pleasing to our modern delicacy, instead of explaining away the crime of idolatry by acknowledging it as a necessary error, the apologists kindled conscience against a hateful worship by showing in it the work of the devil and the reflexion of hell. This system of argument, at once full of charity towards human reason, but without pity for Paganism, was presented in its entirety in the writings of St. Augustine.

The Bishop of Hippo had become the light of the universal Church; Asia and Gaul pressed him with questions; the Manichaeans, Donatists, and Pelagians left him no repose. But it was the pagan controversy which absorbed his life, overflowed into his letters, and inspired his greatest works. In **a.d**. 412, Africa was governed by Volusian, a man of noble birth, and attached to the old religion, who was drawn towards the Church by the genius of Augustine, but brought back to his superstitions by the idolatrous examples all around him. One day, as he was whiling away his leisure in conversation with some men of letters, had touched on many points of philosophy, and deplored the contradictions of the sects, the discussion turned upon Christianity. Volusian set forth his objections, and at the close, of the usual cavils against Holy Writ and the mysteries, showed the real cause of his repugnance by accusing the new religion of preaching pardon of injuries which was irreconcilable with the dignity of a warlike state, and so hastening the decline of Rome, of which the calamities produced by the rule for a century of Christian princes was sufficient evidence. A disciple of Augustine, who had taken part in this discussion, related it to his master, and implored him to answer it. He complied, and without neglecting the theological objections, mainly directed his attack to the political questions. Beginning by expressing surprise that the mildness of Christianity should give scandal to men accustomed to praise clemency with the sages of old, he denied that the faith had suppressed justice in insisting upon charity. Christ had not forbidden war, but had only desired it to be just in its cause, and merciful in its process; if the state had possessed such warriors, magistrates, or taxpayers as the Church required, the Republic would have been intact. If the Empire had been carried off by a wave of decay, yet St. Augustine could point to a period long anterior to the Christian era, and show how in the time of Jugurtha the public morals were entirely corrupted, and how Rome might have been sold if a purchaser could have been found; and then in horror at the profligacy which was sapping the core of humanity when the new faith appeared, the Bishop of Hippo exclaimed, "Thanks to the Lord our God, who has sent us against so great evils an unexampled help, for whither were we not carried, what souls would not the horrible wave of human perversity have carried off, had not the Cross been planted above us, that we might seize and hold fast to that sacred wood. For in that disorder of manners, detestable as they were, that ruin of the old discipline, it was time that an authority should come from on high to announce to us voluntary poverty, continence, benevolence, justice, and other strong and shining virtues; it was necessary not only that we might honourably order this present Life and assure a place in this earthly city, but to lead us to eternal salvation, to the all-holy Republic, to that endless nation of which we are all denizens by the title of faith, hope, and charity. Thus, as we are living as travellers on earth, we should learn to tolerate, if not strong enough to correct, those who wish to establish the Republic on. a basis of unpunished vice, when the ancient Romans had founded and aggrandized it by their virtues. If they had not that true piety towards the True God which would have conducted them to the eternal city, they kept at least a certain native righteousness which sufficed to form the city of earth, to extend and to preserve it. God wished to manifest in that glorious and opulent Empire what civil virtues could effect, even when divorced from true religion, that with the addition of the latter men might become members of a better city, which had truth for its sovereign, charity for its law, eternity for its duration."

Noble words, and yet Augustine did not aim at perfection of eloquence, according to the standard of the rhetoricians, but at convincing Volusian, whose yielding convictions only waited for the last assault. It was this hope that impelled him from the first blow of controversy to the depths of the subject, and brought forth the first idea of his " City of God." This was in 412, and the twenty-two books of that work, commenced the following year, interrupted and continued by snatches during fourteen years, were not concluded until 426. St. Augustine did but develope therein the doctrine of the above letter, which he did not exceed in eloquence; and it is thus that immortal books are born, not from the proud dream of the lover of vain-glory, nor from leisure nor solitude, but of the travail of a soul which has been flung into the struggles of its age, has sought for truth and found inspiration. We shall have occasion soon to study and analyze the " City of God," and note the commencement of a science unknown to the ancients—the philosophy of history, but we may pause for a moment now before the greatest work undertaken for the refutation of Paganism. Its plan gave the author an occasion of attacking and destroying in succession the mythological theology of the poets, the political theology of statesmen, the natural theology of the philosophers of old time; and whilst he dissipated the last scruples of the scientific, he left no pretext for repugnance on the part of men of letters. That religion which they charged with a reaction towards ignorance and barbarism gave ample evidence of rivalling by its beauty the good things of profane antiquity; for what was the elegance of Symmachus in comparison with the thunders of the apologists for

Christianity ?

Yet the new faith would not have changed the world had it appealed only to men of learning and science. This had been the crying fault of philosophy. Plato had written on the door of his school, "Let none but geometers enter here," and Porphyry, seven hundred years later, confessed that he knew of none among so many sects which could teach a way of salvation for every soul. But Christianity had found a universal path of safety: the teaching of the poor was its special novelty, and persecutors long reproached her with recruiting in the workshops or in the cottages of weavers or of fullers. At the beginning of the fifth century, the working-classes in the towns, who occupied, according to a poet, the upper floors of the houses, were almost entirely devoted to the new religion. But idolatry was still mistress of the rural districts: votive garlands still adorned the sacred trees; the traveller came across open temples in which the sacrificial embers were burning, or statues with portable altars at their feet, or encountered some haggard peasant with a tattered mantle over his shoulders and a sword in his hands, professing to be a votary of the great goddess Diana, and to reveal futurity by her aid. Yet the Church believed that these rude men, who toiled and suffered and led that pastoral life from which the Saviour had drawn His parables, were not far from the kingdom of God, so she collected labourers and shepherds into her temples, and did not disdain arguing before them as St. Paul before the Areopagus.

The homilies of St. Maximus of Turin form the chief example of this popular controversy. The inhabitants of the rugged valleys of Piedmont defended step by step the superstitions of their forefathers, and the bishop provoked the dispute by making his first onslaught, on the fatalism which attracted the souls of the indolent, by discharging them from all moral responsibility.

" If everything is fixed by destiny, why, O pagans, do you sacrifice to your idols? To what purpose those prayers, that incense, those victims, and those gifts which you lavish in your temples? That the gods may not injure us, is the answer. How can those beings who are unable to help themselves, who must be guarded by watch-dogs that robbers may not carry them off, who cannot protect themselves against spiders, rats, or worms, injure you? But, they reply, we adore the sun, the stars, and the elements. They worship fire, then, which can be quenched by a drop of water or fed by a stick of wood; they worship the thunder, as if it was not as obedient to God as the rains, the winds, and the clouds; they adore the starry sphere which the Creator has made with so marvellous an art for an ornament of beauty to the world. Lastly, the pagans reply, the gods whom we serve inhabit the heaven."

The preacher followed them into this last refuge and scourged with his satire the crimes of these divinities —Saturn devouring his children, Jupiter married to his sister, the adulteries of Mars, then he continued:—

"Is it on account of her beauty that you give Venus alone among the goddesses an abode in a planet ? What do you make up there of that shameless woman among a crowd of men? What do you say of the host of children you pagans have given to Jupiter? and if once they were born of the gods, why do we not see the same thing now? or is it that Jupiter has grown old, and Juno past childbearing ? "

We cannot wonder that this system of preaching did not shrink from bold images, familiar expressions, or from sarcasm, if it was necessary to subdue a coarse-minded audience. Christianity stooped thus to the language of the vulgar to instruct and reawaken thought in minds held incapable of reasoning, to break the bonds of superstition, and release the souls of men from the terrors which peopled nature with malevolent deities, and from the pleasures by which men repaid themselves for the horror caused by their gods. Whereas eloquence subdued the more intelligent, the grosser minds were carried away by example; the waters of baptism fell upon their brow to sanctify its sweats, and these poor people returned calmed and purified to their ploughs and their flocks, dreading no longer an encounter with Satyrs or Dryads in the depth of the forests. Yet the earth had not lost its enchantment, for at every step they could recognize the footprint of the Creator, and they laboured upon its soil as in the vineyard of the Heavenly Father. Bacchic orgies no longer profaned the manners of which Virgil had sung as pure and peaceful; Christianity had given to the men of the fields the happiness which to the poet of the " Georgics " had been only a dream. They could realize their happiness now, and love the poverty which the Gospel had blessed; self-respect was present in every hovel; and as at length the Supreme Cause of all things, the truth of which philosophers had been ignorant, had been manifested to the ignorant, they could afford to spurn their superstitious fears, inexorable fate, and the din of greedy Acheron.

The conquest of conscience, commenced by controversy, was consummated by charity. It was not a charity of that peaceful nature which knew no enemy, and dreamed only of delivering the captive, building schools and hospitals, and covering the old Roman world with its peculiar institutions, as a wounded body is swathed in bandages, but charity, as it were, in arms, attacking Paganism with the novel weapons of gentleness, forgiveness, and devotion. We must enter the recesses of those Roman families which were still divided between the old and the new belief, and see how their Christian members were skilled in laying siege to a pagan soul with tender violence, counting no time lost if it was led at last to the altar of Christ. St. Jerome shows us this very spectacle in bringing us into the house of Albinus, who was a patrician and pontiff of the old religion. His daughter, Laeta, was a Christian, and had Rome to a Christian husband the young Paula, whose education occupied Jerome in his desert retreat. The latter wrote to Laeta, " Who would have believed that the grand-daughter of the pontiff Albinus would, from a vow made at a martyr's tomb, have brought her grandfather to listen smilingly as she stammered a hymn to Christ, and that the old man should one day cherish on his knees a virgin of the Lord ? " Then he added, in touching consolation to Laeta :—

" A holy and faithful house sanctifies the one infidel who remains firm in his principles. The man who is surrounded by a troop of Christian children and grandchildren, must be already a candidate for the faith. Laeta, my most holy sister in Jesus Christ, let me say this, that you may not despair of your father's salvation."

He ended by adding advice to encouragement, and entered into and directed the last attack of the domestic plot, to which the old man's obstinacy was destined to yield.

" Let your little child, whenever she sees her grandfather, throw herself on his breast, hang on his neck, and sing him the Alleluia in spite of himself."

To such pious manœuvres, repeated doubtless in every patrician house, that proud and opiniated spirit of the old Romans, which formed the last rampart of Paganism, surely though slowly succumbed.

But kindness and consideration were naturally easy when the conversion of a parent was the aim, and a greater merit lay in preaching truth to enemies and conquering fanatical crowds by generosity. When St. Augustine took possession of his see at Hippo, the imperial laws put sword and fire at his disposal against the pagans, but he at once forbade violence, and was even unwilling that they should be forced to break the idols raised upon their lands.

" Let us begin rather," he said, " by destroying the false gods in their hearts." Once the Christians of the little town of Suffecta, forgetful of his instructions, destroyed a statue of Hercules. The pagan populace, in a fury, took up arms, and rushing upon the faithful, killed sixty of them. St. Augustine might have obtained the execution of the homicides, not only by setting the edicts of Theodosius in motion, but under the whole system of Roman law against murder and violence in arms; but he wrote to the pagans of Suffecta, reproaching them, indeed, with the shedding of innocent blood, and threatening them with the Divine justice, but refrained from summoning them before the tribunals of earth.

" If you say that the Hercules was your property, be at peace, we will restore it; stone is not wanting to us; we have metal, many kinds of marble, and workmen in abundance. Not a moment shall be lost in carving out your god, in moulding and gilding it. We will also be very careful to paint him red, that he may be able

to hear your prayers; but if we give you back your Hercules, restore to us the number of souls of which you have robbed us."

Language so full of sense, so hardy, and yet so tender, was calculated to touch men's hearts; for human nature loves that which excels it, and the doctrine of pardon towards enemies ended in gaining the world which it had at first astonished.

As the imperial edicts had no power to demolish the idols, still less could they close the arenas. Constantine, by a constitution of **a.d.** 325, promulgated in the first fervour of his conversion, had, indeed, forbidden those games of bloodshed; but the passions of the populace, stronger than law, had not only protected their pleasures, but insisted on making the princes accomplices in them, so that the victories of Theodosius still provided gladiators for the amphitheatres of Rome. Vainly did the eloquence of the Fathers ring against these bloody amusements; vainly did the poet Prudentius, in pathetic verse, press Honorius to command that death should cease to be a sport, and murder a public pleasure. But charity accomplished what no earthly power had dared commence. An Eastern monk, named Telemachus, one of those useless men, those enemies to society, as they were called, took up his staff one day and journeyed to Rome, to put down the gladiatorial combats. On the 1st of January of the year **a.d.** 404, the Roman people, piled tier upon tier on the benches of the Coliseum, were celebrating the sixth consulate of Honorius. The arena had already been reddened with the blood of several pairs of gladiators, when suddenly, in the thick of an assault of arms which held every eye fixed, and kept every mind in breathless suspense, a monk appeared, rushed forward with outstretched arms, and forced the swords asunder. At the sight, the astonished audience rose as one man, roaring in question as to what madman it could be who dared to interrupt the most sacred pleasures of the sovereign people. Then curses, threats, and finally stones, rained from every circle. Telemachus fell dead, and the combatants he had striven to part finished their bout. This blood was needed to seal the abolition of the games of blood, for the martyrdom of the monk forced the irresolution of Honorius, and an edict of the same year, which seems to have extorted obedience, suppressed the gladiatorial shows, and with them idolatry lost its chief 'support. The Coliseum remains to this day, and the mighty breach in its side symbolizes the assault of Christianity upon Roman society, which it entered only by dismantling it. To-day we must bless the ruin which it made, as on entering the old amphitheatre we discern therein only the signs of peace, plants growing, birds building their nests, children playing innocently at the foot of the wooden cross which rises in the midst as the avenger of humanity which was outraged, the redemptress of humanity which fell.

We may marvel that, before so much love and so much light, the world did not yield at once, to the entire discomfiture of Paganism. But one portion of the latter survived in spite of Christianity, and as if to keep it strung to an eternal resistance, while another remained in the very bosom of the Church which showed her wisdom in respecting the legitimate wants of man and the innocent pleasures of the nations. For Paganism has two constituent parts, the one being an absolutely false religious idea, the other the true idea of the necessary relation of man with the invisible world, and the consequent methods of fixing that relation under sensible forms in temples, festivals, and symbols. Religious thought cannot be confined to the solitary domain of contemplation, but proceeds thence to grasp space by the temples which it causes to be reared, time by the days which it keeps holy, and nature in her entirety, by selecting as emblems such things as fire, perfume, and flowers, her brightest and purest products. These truths ought not to perish, and the policy of the Church had to solve the difficulty of crushing idolatry without stifling beauty of worship. The zeal of the Fathers was displayed on every page of their writings, and they have been charged with pushing it to the point of Vandalism in demanding the destruction of the temples. But St. Augustine took a most effectual step towards obviating that passion for iconoclasm which seizes whole nations at some moment of intense public emotion, and forbade Christians to turn articles which had been devoted to the service of the false deities to their personal use. He desired that the stone, wood, and precious metals should be purified in the service of the state, or in honour of the true God, and his maxims saved many a building in Italy, Sicily, and Gaul which remains to us instinct with the genius of antiquity. The Pantheon of Agrippa became the Basilica of All the Martyrs, and in Rome alone eight pagan sanctuaries stand in our day under the invocation of a saint as protector of their ancient walls. The Temple of Mars at Florence, and that of Hercules at Milan, were converted into Baptisteries. Sicily defended for long her ancient altars; but when the Council of Ephesus had given to the veneration of the Mother of God a new and brilliant lustre, the Sicilians surrendered, and the soft touch of the Virgin opened more temples than the iron hand of the Caesars. The Mausoleum of the tyrant Phalaris was made sacred to our Lady of Mercy, and the temple of Venus, on Mount Eryx, formerly served by a college of harlots, became the Church of St. Mary of the Snows.

And if the people hankered after those lofty porticoes beneath which their fathers had prayed, still more difficult was it to rob them of those festivals which had lightened the severity of their labour, and broken in upon the monotony of their life. So Christianity hallowed in place of suppressing them, and from the end of the fourth century solemnities in honour of the martyrs took the place of those of the false gods. The bishops encouraged an admixture of sober joy with the gravity of these pilgrimages, permitted fraternal love-feasts on their celebration, and transported thus into the Church the fairs which had tempted the multitude to the worship of Bacchus and Jupiter. Yet the perseverance of the clergy failed to displace the days which custom had consecrated, and the cycle of the Christian year was forced to conform in many particulars to the pagan calendar. Thus, according to the authority of Bede, the procession of Candlemas consigned the Lupercalia to oblivion, and the Ambarvalia only yielded to the rustic pomps of the Rogations. As the peasants of Enna, in

Sicily, could not detach themselves from the joyful festivals they always held after harvest in honour of Ceres, the Feast of the Visitation was retarded on their account, and they offered on the altar of Christ the ripe wheat-ears with which they had garlanded their idols.

In fact, if Christianity prohibited the adoration of Nature, she never cursed or condemned that which constituted the visible beauty of the universe. It beheld, not only in the heathen religion, but in the public ritual, a symbolism which employed creatures as the signs of a sacred language between God and man. The seven-branched candlestick had lighted the tabernacle of Moses, the gums of Arabia had burnt on the altar, and year by year the Hebrew people had gathered palm-branches and foliage for the Feast of Tabernacles. The rites which were so common to every worship were to pass into the new religion. The poet Prudentius was already inviting Christian virgins to the tomb of St. Eulalia, and bidding them bring baskets of flowers in honour of the youthful martyr; and at the same period was the custom introduced of burning tapers before the places where the saints reposed. The priest Vigilantius cavilled at this practice, and taxed it with idolatry; but St. Jerome replied, and his clever genius embraced at once the whole scope of the question.

" You call these Christians idolaters. I deny it not, for all who believe on Christ have come from idolatry; but because we rendered this worship once to idols, must it be forbidden now to offer it to the true God ? All the churches of the East burn candles at the moment of the reading of the Gospel, not truly to dissipate the darkness, for at that hour the sun is shining with all its brightness, but as a sign of joy, in memory of those lamps which the wise virgins kept burning in honour of the Eternal Light, of which it is written, ' Thy word, O Lord, shall be a lamp unto my feet, and a light unto my paths.' "

St. Jerome summed up on this point the whole policy of the Church, whereby she achieved the conversion of the Roman world, as well as the civilization of the barbarians. Two centuries later, when the Anglo-Saxons poured in crowds to baptism, and demanded permission to burn their idols, Pope Gregory the Great moderated this zeal, and wrote to his missioners, directing them to destroy the images but to preserve the temples, and consecrate them, that the people, having acknowledged the true God, might the more readily come to worship Him in places to which they had become accustomed. He also advised them to replace the old pagan orgies by orderly banquets, in the hope that if they allowed the people some sensible gratifications, they might rise more easily to spiritual consolations.t The enemies of the Roman Church have triumphed over these passages, in which they have only seen the abomination brought into the sacred place; but we must rather admire the utterances of a religion which has penetrated into the depths of humanity, and knowing what conflicts with passion she must of necessity demand from it, shrinks from imposing needless burdens. This course has shown that true knowledge and love of human nature whereby alone it can be won.

But there was that other principle in Paganism with which the Church could not treat, which she had to attack without respite, and which on its own side offered a resistance as imperishable as the passions in which it was rooted. At first, the old religion had hoped to preserve itself intact, and spring over the period of the invasions like Æneas traversing burning Troy with the gods he had saved. Pagans counted with joy a multitude of sympathizers amongst those Goths, Franks, and Lombards who had covered the face of the Western Empire. Roman polytheism, faithful to its maxims, held out the hand to the polytheism of the barbarians, and as the Jupiter of the Capitol had admitted the strange divinities of Asia to share his throne, he could hardly reject Woden and Thor, who were compared to Mercury and Vulcan. They were, it was said, the same heavenly powers honoured under different names, and the twin cults were bound to sustain one another against the jealous God of the Christians. Thus the wave of invasion seemed to leave a sediment which revived the genius of Paganism, and in the midst of the sixth century, when Rome had passed fifty years under Gothic domination, the idolatrous party boldly attempted to reopen the Temple of Janus and restore the Palladium. So, at the opening of the seventh century, St. Gregory the Great awakened the solicitude of the Bishops of Terracina, Corsica, and Sardinia towards the pagans in their respective dioceses. About the same time, the efforts of St. Romanus and St. Eloi barely achieved the conversion of Neustria, and in the next century Austrasia was so much troubled by the corruption of the clergy and the violence of the nobles, that multitudes abandoned the Gospel and restored their idols. In truth, the two systems of Paganism were mingled, and the struggle sustained by the Church for three centuries against the deities of Rome was but an apprenticeship to the longer conflict she was destined to wage against the idols of the Germans. In that case, also, she conquered by a charity whose only term was martyrdom, and by a controversial method which carried its consideration for rude minds to the last degree. The Church treated these barbarians with the same respect as the people of Italy or of Greece, and the entire polemical system of the old apologists reappeared in the homilies of the missioners who evangelized Frisia and Thuringia. The Bishop Daniel, in expounding the proper method of discussion with the pagans of the North, renewed the arguments of St. Maximus of Turin. " You must ask them," he said, " if their gods breed still, and if not, why they had ceased to do so."

But Charlemagne was now about to appear, to assure to Christianity dominion, but not repose. Vanquished Paganism was transformed, and instead of a worship became a superstition. Yet, under the new form, it retained its essential faculty of leading men astray through their fears and their lusts. The converted races agreed to hold that their former gods were so many daemons, but upon the condition of reverencing and invoking them, and attaching an occult virtue to their images. Thus the Florentines had dedicated the Temple of Mars to St. John; but a certain awe still attached to the image of the fallen god. In the year 1215, a murder committed upon the spot brought the Guelphs and Ghibellines to blows, upon which Villani, an able historian, but one apt to be carried away by the opinions prevalent in his time, concluded "that the enemy of the human race had retained a certain power in his ancient idol, since at its feet the crime had been committed which had brought upon Florence so many evils." These malevolent phantoms were but slowly dissipated, for imaginations could not shake themselves free of a spell which had bound them for so many ages. The ancient gods still kept their place in imprecations and oaths, and to this day the Italians swear by Bacchus. Pagan associations were as firmly and still more dangerously perpetuated in the sensual festivals, with their orgies and obscene songs, which the canons of the councils held in Italy, France, and Spain did not cease to condemn. The pilgrims from the North were astonished, on visiting Rome, at seeing the calends of January celebrated by bands of musicians and dancers, who paraded the town with sacrilegious songs and exclamations which savoured of idolatry. When the Italian cities were hastening, in their newly acquired liberty, to form themselves in the image of Rome, they established consuls and wished for public games. Horse and foot races were celebrated, and the lustful memories of old time came to mingle with these recreations, and races of courtesans were given in imitation of the festivals of Flora. If the Italy of the Middle Age did not actually revive the gladiatorial conflicts, she did not renounce bloody spectacles. At Ravenna, at Orvieto, and at Sienna, custom had fixed certain days upon which two bands of their citizens took up arms and slaughtered each other for the amusement of the mob. Petrarch, in 1346, grew indignant at beholding a renewal at Naples of the butcheries of the Coliseum. He relates how, one day, he was drawn by some friends to a spot not far from the city, where he found the court, the nobility, and the multitude ranged in circles assisting at the warlike sports. Noble youths were being slaughtered there under the eyes of their fathers, their glory consisting in the coolness with which they received the death-blow; and one of them rolled in a pool of blood at the very feet of the poet. Petrarch, horror-stricken, struck spurs into his horse and fled, vowing to quit before three days were past a land which was stained with Christian blood.

If pagan instincts thus lurked in the bosom of Catholic society, we may expect to see them burst forth as soon as Paganism reappeared openly in the heresy of the Albigenses. From Bulgaria to Catalonia, from the mouths of the Rhine to the pharos of Messina, millions of men arose, fought, and died for a doctrine, the essence of which lay in replacing the austerity of Catholic dogma by a new mythology, in recognizing two eternal principles of Good and Evil, and dethroning the sole God of the Christians.* This popular heathenism surprises us in an epoch wherein the Church seemed absolute over the conscience; but, more strange still, it possessed a learned element, as if the human reason, once set free by the new faith, had fallen back into its old slavery, whilst in every age men of learning, ingenuity, and perseverance conspired to renew the traditions of the school of Alexandria, and restore error by philosophy and the occult sciences.

Up to the seventh century we can trace the pagan doctrines in the Gallo-Roman schools, which even contained men who were professedly heathen; and the writers of that epoch were still combating the false learning of those who boasted of extending the discoveries of .their predecessors, but were in reality attached to their errors. But these dying sparks were to be extinguished in the obscurity of the barbarous era. It was in the midst of the Carlovingian Revival that a theologian of depth, who had studied in the monastic schools of Ireland, John Scotus Erigena, began to profess, with force and brilliancy of exposition, a philosophy which was thoroughly imbued with the Alexandrian opinions. He tempered its excesses, indeed, by contradictions which saved his own orthodoxy, but failed to satisfy the logic of his disciples—a logic which three hundred years later impelled Amaury de Bene and David de Dinand to teach publicly the pantheistic tenets of the unity of substance, the identity of spirit and matter, and of God and nature. The Church perceived the greatness of the danger, and the new sect succumbed to the condemnations of her doctors and her councils; but these pantheistic principles, yet alive, lay hidden amongst the disciples of Averrhoes, to appear again with a more menacing attitude in the persons of Giordano Bruno and of Spinoza.

And whereas a false system of metaphysics was enticing many minds back to pagan antiquity, a greater number still were being drawn thither through those occult sciences which formed the living sore of the Middle Age. Christianity has been charged with breeding, in her favouring obscurity, astrology and magic, as well as the sanguinary legislation by which their excesses were repressed; but it is forgotten that the classic ages of the hidden sciences were the most brilliant periods of Paganism, that they flourished at Rome under Augustus, were elaborated at Alexandria, and could claim Jamblichus, Julian, and Maximus of Ephesus, the most illustrious of the Neoplatonists, amongst their neophytes. It was in vain that Origen, who had detected the secrets of the adepts, unveiled a portion of their artifices, by what illusions they caused the thunders to mutter, daemons to appear, death's-heads to speak; for the vulgar believed in the mysteries which afforded the charm of fear. But the Caesars were troubled by that divining art which boasted of having announced their advent, but also foretold their fall, and we find the astrologers suffering banishment as *mathematicians* under Tiberius, persecuted for three centuries, and finally proscribed by constitutions of Diocletian and of Maximian. It was the legislation of the pagan emperors, carried on by Valentinian and Valens, and received into the codes of Athalaric, of Liutprand, and of Charlemagne, which founded the penal laws against sorcery which prevailed in the Middle Age; and thus did the torch of the ancient wisdom kindle the piles with which the Church has been reproached.

But penal fires could effect nothing against the fascinations of the forbidden fruit. In the thirteenth century, an age when Christian civilization was in its bloom, the doctrines reappeared which tended to deify the stars, by submitting human wills to their influence. Astrology had made its peace with the law, and placed itself beside the thrones of princes, or even in the chairs of the universities; armies refused to march unless preceded by observers who would mark the height of the stars, and rule the conjunction under which camps should be traced or battle given. The Emperor Frederick the Second was surrounded by astrologers, and the republics of Italy had theirs as well, so that the rival factions disputed for heaven in addition to earth.t On the other hand, there was a renewal of the radical vice of Paganism, of the despairing struggle between man and nature, the attempt to conquer the latter, not by science or by art, but by superstitious operations and formulas; the adepts in magic renewed the idolatrous observances, not only in the secrecy of their laboratories, but in the numerous writings to which fear and curiosity afforded a circulation, in the shade of school or of cloister. Albert the Great recognized their influence, and in his summary of the processes by which those erring spirits boasted of predicting and governing the future, we may wonder at superstitions which the ancients themselves decried and repudiated; for instance, "Those abominable images which they call Babylonian, which appertain to the worship of Venus, and the figures of Belenus and of Hercules, whom they exorcise by the names of the fifty-four daemons attached to the service of the Moon: upon them they inscribe seven names in direct order to obtain a happy issue, and seven inversely to avert an unlucky event. In the first case, they incense them with aloes and balm; in the second, with resin and sandal-wood.

So much could error effect in the time of St. Louis and St. Thomas Aquinas, though theologians exhausted their arguments against the magicians and astrologers, and Dante fixed them in the lowest circle of his Hell. The occult sciences threw their spell over mankind, until they faded before the broad light of the sixteenth century. Yet Paganism did not expire with them, but continued to seethe like the lava of a volcano, terrifying the Christian world by chronic eruptions. No, Paganism could not be extinct in the hearts of men as long as a terror of God and the voluptuous influences of nature reigned therein together, nor could it be stifled in the schools as long as Pantheism held its own, and new sects rose to announce the apotheosis of humanity and the rehabilitation of the flesh. And the old error still ruled in Asia, in Africa, and in half of the islands of ocean, maintaining itself by threats and in arms, and now making martyrs at Tonquin and in China, as of old in Rome and Nicomedia : it still contends with the Church for six hundred millions of immortal souls.

A celebrated man, the object of our just regrets, but often liable to erroneous conclusions, has written, " How dogmas end." But the study we have made may teach us that dogmas do not end. Humanity has only recognized two of them, though under diverse forms—that of the true God and that of the false deities. The latter was the masters of pagan hearts and the old society, the idea of the former went forth from among the Judaean hills to enlighten Europe first, and thence, little by little, the remainder of the world. The struggle between these two dogmas is the key of history, and affords to it all its grandeur and its interest; for what can be a prouder position or a more touching issue for the human race than to stand as prize in the combat between Error and Truth ?

ROMAN LAW.

We have seen what roots the old religion of Rome had struck out, how their dislodgment was the work of centuries, and how the highest degree of wisdom, of courage, and of tact was necessary to stifle error without doing violence to human nature, to destroy Paganism without breaking the innocent symbols of the commerce between heaven and earth. But its religious belief did not make up the essence of the Roman civilization; its primitive dogma had come from the Etruscans—Greece had brought to it its fables—the conquered East had yielded her mysteries; but that which was the exclusive property of Rome was her genius for action, her destiny was to realize on earth the idea of justice and found the empire of Law.

A time arrived when Rome no longer remembered the art of conquest, but she was never to forget the secrets of government. The moment even of her deepest decline, when the barbarians revenged themselves upon her in every place, ordered her proceedings, and debated with her the figure of her ransom—when they seemed to have entirely fettered her action—was the period in which all her power was reflected and gathered up into the codes of that legislation which was sooner or later to achieve the conquest of the barbarians, to retain the world under her tutelage after the fall of her empire, and compel the descendants of the Visigoths, Burgundians, and Franks to seat themselves in the schools, and grow pale over the test of the Roman law. We must study now this great victory of thought over strength, and find the hidden force which bore up the Roman constitution at the beginning of the fifth century, and what were to be its respective losses or gains under the mighty blows which demolished the empire of the West.

In the first place stood the mass of jurisprudence of the classic epoch, comprising the works of the entire succession of jurisconsults from Augustus to the reigns of the Antonines. In order that no doubt might arise as to the binding force of these decisions, a well-known constitution, issued under Theodosius II. and Valentinian III., in **a.d**. 426, laid down that in future the writings of Papinian, Paulus, Gaius, Ulpian, and Modestinus should alone have force of law; that in case of difference of opinion the view supported by the majority should prevail, or, in the case of equality, the position taken by Papinian. It might seem a rash measure to canonize, as it were, opinions, controversy, consultations, often contradictory and full rather of subtlety than genius, but there may be seen in it that great principle of Tradition providentially preserved at Rome, and it is a happiness for posterity that those maxims which the disasters of the Empire might well have crumbled into dust were thus preserved, and invested with the character of inviolable law.

On the other hand stood the ever-increasing collection of the constitutions of princes, and especially of Christian princes. In 429, Theodosius the Younger and Valentinian III., to remedy the confusion which had sprung up among them, appointed a commission of nine jurisconsults, or men of official rank, to make a regular compilation, in sixteen hooks, under their respective titles, of those legislative enactments which bore on public or civil life, and to leave the primitive text, as far as necessary correction and clearness would allow, free from contradictory comments. Thus the whole series of legislation of the Christian emperors was preserved to us, and respect was shown, notwithstanding the thoroughness of the reaction which had followed them, even to the works of Julian.

Accordingly the Roman society possessed, in 430, two systems of law, and the barbarians found face to face, on the one hand ancient Paganism tempered by the philosophy of the jurisconsults themselves, acting, as we shall see, under Christian influences, and on the other Christianity tempered by the timidity of the emperors, who only embraced reforms already rough-hewn by their philosophic lawyers, and measured out carefully the blows they were bound to strike at the old institutions: here pagan law just gilded by the rising of Christianity —there the beginning of Christian jurisprudence still entangled in the last shades of the darkness from which the world was issuing.

We must examine these two principles in order, and the result which they had brought about. We see, on opening the text-books of the classic jurisprudence of the vaunted epoch of the Automnes, that all the lawyers whose writings Valentinian had codified, recognized still as a thing of the remote past but as supreme and permanent, the law of the Twelve Tables. They cite, comment on, and often evade it, but still did it homage in refusing to ignore, contravene, or abjure the edicts graven on its bronze by the iron hand of the decemvirs: it was still thus a master from whose scourge they sought in vain to escape. Let us sketch in a few words, not the precepts but the tendency of that ancient pagan and theocratic law-system whose authority, secular in its essence, the jurisconsults did not as yet dare contemn. It was a half-sealed book, a collection of traditions, sacramental formulas, and sacred rites, enveloping the law under the same veils as a religion—a mass of mysteries whose secret the patricians alone possessed, who as descendants of the gods could alone know and enounce law (*jus; fas*, what is permitted; *fatum*, the right, the Divine will). Law, in its primitive aspect, was the true and only recognized religion of Rome. Its first act was to deify Rome herself, who became not only the shrine and dwelling-place of an unknown genius to whom altars were raised, and whose name was known only to the initiated, but herself the mighty goddess who had altars not only in her peculiar territory, but amongst her conquered nations, and even in Asia, on the shores of the Troad. As divine, her will was justice; the law decided through her curies was legitimate if ratified by consent of the gods in the taking of the auspices, and which assumed a commerce between earth and heaven.

To give an act life and a divine character, its accomplishment must be surrounded by rites and ceremonies. God Himself intervened in the judgments and under the strokes of the magistrate to give peace to His earth; execution was an act of sacrifice; the tribunal, as a sacred place, was to be turned to the East, to be closed when the sun, type of the ray of intellect by which judgment is enlightened, had set on the earth. This powerful theocratic imprint was everywhere to be seen, and underlay all the civilization of Paganism. As Rome was supreme in her sphere, so was every father a god in his own family, a genius sent for a time hero below. His will had all the features of law and resistless destiny, admitting no limit, stretching to the right of life and death over his dependants,—over his wife, whom he could judge; his son, whom he could expose; his slave, whom he could put to death.

Authority, the presence of irresistible will in all human actions, marked Roman law, gave to it mystery, and also provoked the greatest awakening of liberty which had yet been seen. Rome's very function, in thus overstraining her principle of authority, was to give a greater volume to the outburst of freedom, and the most remarkable sight her history offers to us is that of the rigour of the private prison, the sale of the debtor cut piecemeal, Virginia's blood spirting over the decemvirs, acting as God's incentive to that very people to show us as an example their eight-century-long delivery.

This was first seen when the plebs, straining to enter upon the sacred enclosure, long defended by the patrician order, tore from their grasp in succession the *connubium*, the magistrate's offices, the auspices; lastly, the very secrets of the Law, and when the freed-man Flavius stole from Appius the Actions of Law, the formulas of which that patrician had drawn up.

The movement, begun under the Republic, lived on under the Empire, which did not close, as has been erroneously supposed, the history of liberty; but the game changed, and whilst under the Republic we see the patrician city stormed and carried by the plebs, the Empire shows us every province, the whole West, besieging the imperial city to gain a place at the sanctuary of law and public justice. The emperor, often himself a foreigner, like Galba or Trajan, sprung from Spain, acted as their representative, as invested with proconsular rank, and so becoming familiar with the provinces whose natural protector he was. Caracalla, after a long period of resistance and partial concession, threw down every barrier, and in proclaiming Rome the common capital, with as many citizens as she had subjects, impelled the Empire to its definitive destiny.

Such was the history of the enfranchisement of the plebs and of the Western provinces, and as races and men were pressing with such energy into the precinct so obstinately guarded, Justice also began to find her place there through the efforts of the praetor.

Every year that magistrate, on entering office, proclaimed by edict the principles on which he would administer justice. He was used to interpret the iron law of the Twelve Tables with equity and clemency, to supply its *lacuna*, to throw light on its obscurity, and softness over its rigour; and in this commenced that struggle entered on by the magistrate against a text he was obliged to apply, regretting its harshness, yet submitting to its authority while blunting its sharp edge. The praetor and jurisconsults, who also had the right, of extenuating law principles, then created the Useful Actions, in order to supply what was clearly wanting in the primitive system; and the emperors, opening their minds to the light, called to their aid such men as Gaius, Ulpian, and Paulus, who were influenced by the Stoic philosophy, and supported it by their authority, not in Rome alone but throughout the Empire. The effort of human reason developed under their sanction a new law-system, in which the law of the *gens* stood opposed to the civil law; to the civil family, composed only of *agnats*, or relations on the male side, the natural family *(cognatio)*, comprising those related through females only; to the property of the *Quirites*, the property by natural right, called *in bonis,;* to succession to legitimate descendants only as established by the Twelve Tables, the right of succession in all alike to whose being nature had given the same author.

This was the work of many centuries, at last effected by the conscience-cry of the plebs and the help of philosophy in the shape of the Stoic lawyers. It was one of the greatest spectacles reason could offer, not only as showing, as in the jurisprudence of the Antonines, a triumph of good sense, of lucidity of thought, a perfect purity of form, an edifice giving with unexpected felicity space and clearness of arrangement to the former chaos of public and domestic relations, but as a first-fruit of satisfaction to humanity, as tempering woman's lot by dower; paternal authority, by suppressing its right of life and death; the condition of slaves, by declaring, through Antoninus Pius, to whoever could escape from his master's rod and embrace the prince's statue, the protection of a magistrate, who must descend from the tribunal, cover him with a fold of his robe, and compel his owner to transfer him to another more humane than himself.

While recognizing the services of human reason and the merits of this ancient jurisprudence, we see beneath the surface what was wanting to this first effort of man's intelligence, the vices still inevitably lurking in it, which gave it up to the time of which we treat that pagan character so difficult to eradicate. Fiction appears everywhere; a superstitious respect for a past openly belauded, but secretly disdained. The entire labour of the praetor was lavished on a succession of subterfuges by which to evade a law he dared not overturn, to escape from their inflexible Twelve Tables, not one of whose long-traced lines he dared efface. If, for instance, they only granted succession to relations on the male side, to grant it to those of defunct female descent a fiction was necessary by supposing in the formula of deliverance the new possessor to be the heir. As the old law willed that certain chattels, called *mancipia*, could only pass by *mancipation*, or by *usucaption*, had an article of that class been delivered to a claimant by simple *tradition*, and been lost before possession had been acquired by *usucaption*, property in it, according to strict law, was gone, yet the praetor allowed a *revendication*, by supposing a previous *usucaption* after the forms of the publician action. Roman law, again, taking no cognizance of foreigners, afforded them no action to enforce respect of their rights. The *actio furti* would not, for instance, lie, as, according to strict civil law, it was not open to a foreigner; but the praetor would grant it by the fiction of supposing him a Roman citizen.

Such things were calculated sooner or later to bring into contempt so essentially simple a system of law. This faithless superstition and dishonest interpretation represents what was passing in Paganism at large— maintenance of form and absence of faith. The old law stood on the same footing as the mythology. It was a mere fable *(carmen serium)* ; serious in the sense of having much which was evil on its pages, and also a mere song, in that its inspiration had ceased. Men listened to its frequent repetition, and then passed on to other and graver occupations. Not an education of some years alone, but that of an entire life, was necessary to find the way through its mazes, which again began to contain a mystery in which very few were adepts; only it was no longer the patricians who held the deposit, but the school, the family of jurisconsults, the few devoted by the state to the study of law, and who alone, in diving into its recesses, could exercise that species of priestly office which Ulpian defined, *Jus est ars boni et æqui cujus merito quis nos sacerdotes appellet** Ammianus Marcellinus, living at the close of the fourth century, leaves us the following picture of the lawyers of his day:—" You would think they professed the drawing of horoscopes or unfolding the Sibylline oracles, to see the deep gravity of their faces, in loudly boasting of a science wherein one can merely grope." So the chief vice of Paganism had not vanished; still there appeared the adepts, few in number and without the vulgar herd; philosophy had succeeded the old religions, detesting, like them, the common people—that is to say, the multitude, humanity itself. Its second vice was the maintenance of the absolute sovereignty of the state over not property only, but life, souls, and consciences, carrying out the old principle according to which Rome was divine and so was her will; and to its legitimate laws human will could find no place of resistance, as no one could he right in contradicting the gods. But a considerable change had still come about, for the name of the genius hitherto dwelling in mystery on the Capitol was at last revealed. It was sometimes named Tiberius, or Nero, or Heliogabalus, and its works were known as well. The Empire became an idolatry, of which the Emperor was priest and god. Altars were raised to him in his lifetime; his images were sent in all directions, to be greeted with light and perfume, and thousands of Christians died rather than cast on the fire at their feet some grains of frankincense. He was a true god, in fact, while living as after death, ordaining this, willing the contrary on the morrow, exercising a tyranny the more intolerable from its being exercised in a moral sphere, and suffering no other will; declaring to the Christians by the organ of the jurisconsults that their existence could not be permitted, "*non licet esse vos;*" crushing the state-right itself in placing the prince above the law, *princeps legibus solid us;* to which privilege it was determined that the sovereign, acceding to her the half of his rights, could also raise his Empress. The will of one thus placed above all law naturally became imperious and irresistible, and the conclusion of the jurisconsults, *quod principi piacuit legis habet vigorem utpote cum lege régia populus ci et in cum omne suum impérium et potestatem conferet* led to that formula so insulting to humanity wherewith princes so often have terminated their acts, " for such is our good pleasure." Not only did the prince's pleasure become the world's law, but he owned beside the pontifical office, the absolute power of making and unmaking legislation, and nearly the whole Roman territory. The soil of the provinces had been divided into two great parts: the tributary, under the Emperor, and the stipendiary, depending on the Roman people. In course of time the former succeeded to the latter, and thus the whole property in the provinces devolved on the sovereign so thoroughly that no private person was considered an actual proprietor, but only a stipendiary maintained and guaranteed till further notice in its use by the Imperial will. Hence no subject could complain when the most sacred treasury *sacratissimum ærarium* claimed some portion of his goods, or when taxes, indictions, or superindictions were imposed, or the land itself distrained, as the prince only took his own. On this principle stood the fiscal system of Rome, full of exactions, which reduced the groaning provinces to such a pitch of distress that the curia responsible for the levy of the impost was gradually deserted by the decurions, whose place was filled by men of evil life and broken fortunes, by concubinous priests and their bastard offspring, since the honour had come to be looked on rather as a disgrace. The provincials, tortured, forced to sell wife and child to satisfy these requirements, began to abandon their lands, and to call upon the barbarians in aid, assured of finding in them less exacting masters, and preferring to render them one or two thirds of the soil than be subject to a system which carried off the total of their revenues. All the confusion at the beginning of the Lower Empire, the responsibility of which has been fixed upon the Christian emperors, flowed naturally from principles long before established. When Aurelian took to himself the diadem of Persia and the pomps of the East, th η Diocletian established that hierarchy of officials which was to crush the Empire with its weight, and the government in the days of its strength sowed the seeds of its ruin.

A third radical vice in Paganism, an unmistakable sign of its last catastrophe, was that terrible inequality which no effort of reason could justify. At the root of its legislation, written though it were by the immortal pen of a Gaius or an Ulpian, lay that heathen emanation principle which supposed that some men sprang from the head, others from the belly or feet of the all-pervading deity. This kept-women in perpetual tutelage, not in the legitimate guardianship of her agnate alone, but in a dative tutelage restraining her capacity in the most trifling actions of civil life. It subjected the child to not only the paternal right of life and death, but to that of sale. He was open to exposal on his birth, condemned to a continual minority, whatever his age or dignity might be, deprived of every kind of property, up to the time of Constantine, except the "peculium castrense," or military pay. It kept up the servile system, the well-known horrors of which existed not only in the heroic and mythical ages, but throughout those centuries of light and philosophical wisdom that were for so many a time of freedom. The opinions of Greek philosophers on the subject were not doubtful. Plato did not admit slavery into the Pie-public, but dared not condemn it in his native city; and Aristotle gave human nature itself for its cause, saying that some were made for rule and others for obedience. Cicero held the same view. *Cum autem hi famulantur qui sibi moderari nequeant nulla injuria est* "There is no injustice in making slaves of those who know not self-government." In his admirable treatise *De Officiis,* the masterpiece of ancient morality, he relates, without commentary, certain cases of conscience proposed by a philosopher named Hecaton. Is a master in a famine time bound to feed his slaves? Economy says No; humanity Yes. Hecaton decides against it. Suppose one's self adrift in a small boat with a bad slave and a good horse on board; a storm comes on, which of the two should be thrown overboard? Hecaton and Cicero will not pronounce upon it. Such was the philosophy of the best epoch of Rome, which time did not do much to modify. To come down to Libanius: in his discourse on slavery he takes care not to repeat Christian complaints about it, nor to let slip any of the old pagan traditions on the subject. Slavery is an evil common to all mortals; all men serve either their passions or their business or their duty— the peasant is the slave of wind and rain, the professor of his audience. Slaves in name are least slaves in reality, but happiest of all in knowing nothing of hunger, that pitiless master; happy in their state of careless lethargy, leaving their master the care of finding them food; and it is thus that passion and selfishness have argued in every age as to slaves of every colour.

The opinion of the philosophers became the doctrine of the jurisconsults, whose duty it was to inspire theory and reduce it to practice. The ancient law had a punishment of death for the slaughterer of a steer; but when Q. Flaminius, the senator, to amuse an abandoned youth, who was his companion, and was regretting at never having seen any one put to death, cut the head off one of his slaves, it was silent, having no penalty for that kind of fault. They had instituted a fine for the murder of a slave,* but hastened to remedy their weakness by taking back from liberty what they had granted to slavery; and by the laws *Ælia Sentia, Junia Norbana,* and *Fusia Caninia,* they calmed the terrors of the serious, who feared revolution on seeing at some funeral games a few freedmen, clad in their caps of liberty, taking their place among citizens, by restraining the frequency of enfranchisement, and closing the city of Rome to the freed. Different orders were distinguished in the Servile ranks, such as *deditii,* who could never become citizens, and the *Latini Juniani,* who could only become citizens in certain cases. The senatus - consult of Silanian, drawn up under Claudius, had ordained torture to all his slaves upon the violent death of any man; and Tacitus paints the terrified stupor of the city when it was one day announced that a senator had died by violence, and that his four hundred slaves were to be put to the torture. Hanging a slave was forbidden, but he might die under the torment, and then his price must be paid to the master. Nourishment was clue to him, and Cato tells us how a prudent head of the family should arrange the matter. " Pour two amphorae of sweet wine into a cask; add two of very sharp vinegar, and as much boiled wine, to the dilution of two-thirds, with fifty amphorae of fresh water. Stir up the whole with a stick for five consecutive days, and then pour in sixty-four measures of sea-water."* Paganism appears clearly here, and the hitter beverage that Cato used to give his slaves reminds us of a certain sponge of vinegar and gall which another Roman, a soldier, was to offer on the lance's point to that other slave who was dying on a cross for the redemption of slaves.

As to their housing, Columella prescribed " *ergastula subterranca,* " in which openings were to be contrived out of reach of the hand, either for the purpose of preventing escape, or of cutting off the sight of the world, which was denied them. Those employed at the mill carried a large wheel round their necks to prevent their raising to the mouth a handful of the flour that they spent the day in grinding. This deprives the Chinese of the honour of having invented their peculiar mode of torture, and it was the mildest method of treatment, as the law of Antonine had not taken away the right of making eunuchs of slaves, and they were to be counted, by troops, *greges pueroram,* as well as crowds of gladiator-slaves who assembled in the lanista, and took the terrible oath to let themselves be burnt, fettered, scourged, and slaughtered, *uri, vinciri, verberari, ferroque necari,* if not men at least merchandise, subject-matter for contracts of sale and purchase, and therefore obliging, in some manner, the attention of the jurisconsults. Gains, in examining the difficulties which might arise in certain cases, in declaring a contract to be one of sale, or merely of hiring, proposed the following question:—" If I tender you a number of gladiators at the rate of twenty denarii ahead for those who survive, as wages for their toils, and a thousand ahead for the dead and wounded, is there a sale or a letting ? The prevailing opinion is that, as to the survivors, it is a hiring; as to dead or wounded a sale, the event deciding it, as if each slave was conditionally an object either of sale or hire, for there is no doubt that either contract may be subject to conditions."* It is a question which is the most wonderful, the calm of the lawyer, or the horror of the prevailing manners. And those manners did not soften; we find Trojan, on his return from Dacia, putting to death ten thousand gladiators. Fear was expressed lest oxen should fail, but no one seemed to fear a scarcity of gladiators. The Roman law of the classic period, as modified by the legislation of the Automnes, was certainly like the Coliseum, a splendid monument, wherein men were thrown to lions ! At the beginning of the fifth century, all this jurisprudence still had force, and had just been invigorated by the law of *Citations,* under Valentinian III., but happily for a Christian period, a rival system was rising in the code inaugurated by Theodosius.

Christianity had early penetrated the Empire, coming as a doctrine that hated fiction, unable by reason of its liberty to suffer enslavement of conscience, or by its charity all those social inequalities which were an outrage to nature. Yet it did not aspire to change violently the world's aspect, but rather to win its point slowly and with patience, and like the Saviour to destroy slavery in becoming itself a slave, *formam servi accipiens*. While Plato daily thanked the gods that he had been born male rather than female, free and not a slave, a Greek instead of a barbarian, it proclaimed by St. Paul that there was no longer male nor female, free nor slave, Greek nor barbarian, but one body in Christ Jesus, a saying strong enough to effect as ages passed the great changes which God had determined. It could not tolerate imperial pretensions over the conscience of mankind, and whilst praying for its persecutors proclaimed that God rather than man was to be obeyed. Finally it repulsed all the pagan fictions, but yet in its contempt for a law which was reserved for a little band of experts, and hidden perforce from the multitude, it did not profess to despise the Roman law-system. As was declared in the Apostolic Constitutions, " God did not will that His justice should be shown forth only by us, but let it shine in the Roman laws; " and St. Augustine said, " *Leges Romanorum divinitus per ora principum emanarunt.* " It received these laws with admiration, recognizing in them the light which lightens every man coming into the world that he might know and adore his God, and was forced to toil with patience to reform in accordance with its principles the legislation whose vices we have examined. Its presence was early suspected and soon perceived, but this is not the place for showing how the new society toiled in its catacombs, hidden deep under another hostile society whose reform it had entered upon; how in every rank of public and domestic life, in the senate and the foulest *ergastula*, it knew how to mould disciples and to enlighten and modify the manners of the time. It has been pointed out how St. Paul, by his speech on Areopagus, his dispute with Stoics and Epicureans, his apology at Corinth before the Roman magistrate, Annaeus Gallio, must have roused the opinions of his contemporaries and of those Greeks and philosophers so greedy of novelty; in particular, Gallio must have informed his beloved brother Seneca, who dedicated to him his treatises *De Ira* and *De Vitâ Beatâ*, of the fame and doctrines of that Graecized Jew who went to make proselytes at Rome in the very palace of Nero. Seneca's own doctrines bear witness to the necessary contact between Pagan and Christian philosophy. His stoicism put in the place of the ancient *fatum*, the third arbiter of our destinies, a Providence, a Divine Father, to honour and obey; it gave him faith in the soul's immortality, and the conflict here below between spirit and flesh, an enemy to be conquered only by Divine help, namely grace, and filled him with a singular pity for all human sorrow, and especially for his enslaved fellow-creature. It is pleasant to believe that this Stoic bore the impress of a Christian philosopher, who was at Rome in the time of Seneca, and was destined to die there more gloriously than himself.

It seems inevitable that the Christians, daily increasing in numbers, filling the forum, the senate, and the army, with the apologies of Quadratus, Bishop of Athens of Athenagorus, St. Justin, Tertullian, and the senator Apollonius, circulating through every rank of society, should influence the Stoic philosophy and the jurisconsults through it. Their admission to the councils of Alexander Severus, who adored amongst his lares the image of Christ, and inscribed in golden letters on his palace walls the maxims of Christianity, points to the growing force of the new religion. The plagiarism of the jurisconsults from its sources, though denied on account of their inveterate hostility, was but the last resource of a baffled enemy, trying to disarm truth by borrowing its principles, "which were attracting every heart. Julian meant this in advising the pagans about him to imitate the Christian priests and open hospitals; and the jurisconsults laboured to disarm the Gospel by infusing it into Roman law, that there might remain no excuse for reforming a society open to legitimate progress, or to destroy a religion so capable of wholesome reform.

When Christianity ascended the throne with Constantine, far from exacting too much and assuming empire as a conqueror, it continued its course with the same calmness. Constantine acted with caution, retaining the title of Supreme Pontiff, and still issuing edicts as to the manner of consulting the auspices. The tactics of his successors were similar: one advanced, another drew back, but all hesitated, and the Theodosian Code still preserved slavery, divorce, concubinage, inequality between man and wife, and father and son, though three great novelties found place in it. In the first place an effort was made to give to law a character of publicity and sincerity. Under Constantine the sacramental formulas relating to wills, stipulations, and other acts of civil life, the sacramental syllables, called by the Christian emperors *aucupatio syllabarum,* as well as the whole system of juridical subtleties, fell to the ground; and by determining the names of the jurists whose decisions should have force, and uniting in one code, as was the case under Theodosius and Valentinian, the scattered edicts of the Christian princes, a popular and accessible form was given to the law. Secondly, the temporal and spiritual orders were separated, and in this respect advance was less easy, for, as Constantine had retained the title of pontiff, his successors were willing to believe that the religion of the Empire alone had changed, and not their old supremacy over the conscience. The Church had to labour perseveringly in preventing their usurpation of the right of convoking and presiding in her councils, saying in the words of Lucifer of Cagliari, ' ' What ! are we to respect your diadems, bracelets, and earrings, and despise the Creator ? " The declaration wrung from Theodosius and Valentinian, " It is worthy of a prince's majesty to pronounce himself bound by the laws," ended the struggle by the victory of the Church, and then the monarch became subject to law, and the temporal power took up the less splendid but firmer position assigned it in the Gospel: " Let him who would be first be the servant of all." In the last place, the hands of the emperors touched with healing the three great wounds humanity bore in the injury clone to women, children, and slaves. Constantine gave mothers a larger share in succession to their children, forbade exposing infants, and punished the child murderer in the same measure as the parricide. He abolished crucifixion as a punishment for slaves, issued an edict against the gladiatorial combats, "not willing," as he said, "such bloody sights in the midst of the Peace of the Empire," and condemned to death the master who had killed a slave. " Let masters use their right with clemency, and let that man be held a murderer who shall have slain his slave voluntarily by blows of rods or of stones, or by mortally wounding him with a dart, who shall have hung him by a halter, or by cruel order had him thrown into an abyss, or made him drink poison, or caused savage beasts to tear his body, or branded his flesh with burning coals, or in frightful torment caused life to flee from his bloody and foam-flecked limbs with a fierceness worthy only of barbarians." This eloquent law, dated **a.d**. 319, well expresses the Christian indignation at the horrors of slavery, and shows the Church, just clothed with the purple, hastening to make a law in favour of her enslaved children.

In this manner did the Theodosian Code remedy the triple outrage offered by the old system to liberty, truth, and humanity, in slavery and domestic inequality. It was no wonder that the reading, by the Prefect of Rome and the consuls, of the edict inaugurating the Theodosian Code throughout the Empire was received by the senate with magnificent applause. The last minutes of its sittings contained this ratification, and its acclamations must have penetrated to the camp of the barbarians, already established in **a.d.** 438, on Roman territory. At the very moment when the Vandals were masters of Africa, the Burgundians and Visigoths of Gaul and Spain, and Attila was advancing at the head of his Huns, by a sublime coincidence the legislation was proclaimed which was destined to master the future. Its fame was to reach those barbarians, whose kings would seek to know the great idea of Roman law which was never to abandon them. The edict of Theodosius, in the year 500, proclaimed the Theodosian Code the law of the Ostrogoths; Alaric gave his subjects, a few years later, the " Breviarium Alaricanum," extracted from the same code; and in 534 the " Papiani Responsa," in great measure collected from it again, appeared for the use of the Roman subjects of the Burgundians. Nor was its destiny to end there; it was taught throughout Gaul, particularly in the schools of Clermont, during the sixth and seventh centuries. Carried into England to the school of York, into Germany in the peaceful train of conquering Boniface, it was to serve as basis to the capitularies of Frankish kings, and thus penetrating into all the barbarian legislation, to give it temper, enlightenment, and system.

It is true that the barbarian chiefs were no less taken by its faults than by its merits, and did not shrink from assuming the heirship of the Roman emperors with regard to their subjects' goods. In this spirit Frederick Barbarossa caused his lawyers to decide, at Roncaglia, that as Trajan's heir he was absolute master of his subjects' property; the same doctrine was adopted by Louis XIV. in speaking of his royal goods, " of which part are comprised in our demesne, the rest left by our good pleasure in the hands of our subjects;" and such pagan traditions have been handed down to become, under other forms, the gravest danger of the present day.

The last traditions of divorce in the family were to disappear in the great struggle of the Papacy against Philip Augustus and Henry IY. Slaves gradually were to become serfs, and serfs freemen. Lastly, the great principle of the separation of the spiritual and temporal orders was to gain its victory at the moment when Gregory VII. gave out his dying cry, " I fought for justice, and therefore am dying in exile." He died, but the principle which he supported so vigorously gained a stronger life, for the ideas which save the human race are those which suffer all that is mortal in them to perish.

Roman law was to rule the world on condition of the fall of the Roman Empire; nothing less was required to dissipate the mist of legal fiction and the remnant of that deep discord which was rooted in the old system. The swords of Attila and Odoacer were to banish the lingering phantom of the imperial throne, and to give breathing space to the world, to revive the soul of the old law on that principle of natural equity which began its struggle in the blood of Virginia and on the Sacred Hill, continued it by tribune's word and praetor's edict, found a new power in the Stoic philosophy, and its ultimate triumph in Christianity. When stripped of its trappings of gold and purple, of imperial pomp and human circumstance, it issued forth lord of the world at the moment of its apparent dissolution.

PAGAN LITERATURE.—I. POETRY.

The deeper we penetrate Roman society of the fifth century the more obvious appears its necessary, but not total dissolution. In religion and law we have already seen the mixture of perishable elements and the immortal principles which were to survive gaining, rather than losing, from the destruction of the former. Literature would seem to afford a different spectacle; that if the idea of holiness was veiled from antiquity by carnal and bloody thoughts, that of justice troubled by the arrogance of the strong and their oppression of the weak, it at least had nothing to correct, nothing to lose, without irreparable loss for the future, and that in respect to art, those men of the North, Celts, Germans, Sclaves, just coming from their forests, could do nothing better than learn at the feet of Latin masters their eloquence and poetry. But it was not so; the fifth century preserved the traditions of art, but overlaid by all the defects and vices of the Decline, and we shall see *what* forces had to be overcome in order to set her free.

The Latin decline in literature began with the reign of Augustus, simultaneously with the end of liberty. The historical commonplace, that inspiration can only flourish with freedom, seems, indeed, contestable, and expressly belied by facts, as in the case of this very age of Augustus, that of the Medicis, and of Louis XIV., and every other in which a huge despotism, covered with a shadow, deadly to liberty, beneficial to genius, the whole aspect of things. But the defenders of this position forget that the great princes who have given name to these golden ages of letters have not opened, but closed them, and, therefore, left, as it were, their inscription on their sepulchres. Augustus began by selling to Antony the head of Cicero;

and so calming, as, according to his contemporaries, he calmed everything —even eloquence—he rather extinguished it, and though surrounded forthwith by poets, they had received their training in the midst of the civil war, within hearing of Philippi and Actium. Later, the Medicis embraced Italian literature, still quivering with Guelph or Ghibeline passion and the breath of Dante, to leave it to slumber for three centuries at the feet of women. Louis XIV. was heir to a century still seething with the tempest of the League and the generous errors of the Fronde, but entered upon another destined to waste itself in the antechambers of courtesans and courtiers; so that all these Maecenas patrons of literature's golden age did but raise a common though splendid sepulchre for both liberty and genius.

Advancing into the ages of the Empire, servitude becomes heavier, and its shadows more obscure. Yet the reigns of Christian emperors, often accused of hastening the Decline, in giving some liberty to men's minds, restored a particle of inspiration to literature. Symmachus, an unsuspected witness, tells us that Valentinian, after Julian's philosophic reign, restored public judicial debates, and as a pagan author, praises him for putting an end to the silence. If eloquence could revive at all, it would have been at these Roman tribunals, haunted by such great memories, still instinct with the genius of Cicero: but it was not destined to gain recognition beyond their precincts.

Poetry, favoured by Constantine's liberality, regained an inspiration to which she had been a stranger nearly three hundred years. The fifth century offering to our view at first sight only palace intrigues, and the quarrels of eunuchs, was of all centuries the most capable of inspiring a great epic poem. Rome had always loved the heroic songs which brought back to life the glory of her great men and military achievement; but she required a form of poetry known to, but not preferred by, Greece—the historic form, rather than the mythical epopee, and from the "Annals" of Ennius to the "Pharsalia " of Lucan and the " Punic War " of Silius Italicus claimed as especially her own the poets who followed the course of her history, and expressed it in language worthy of its glory. The scene was now enlarged, the struggle grown more terrible. The barbarians were at her gates. Though always conquered and repulsed by the prowess of Constantine, the sense of Julian, the genius and firmness of Theodosius, no one could tell which way the balance held by Fate would incline. And another mightier and more lasting conflict was proceeding; and as the poet showed us from Trojan ramparts the phalanxes of heaven joined in battle far above, so we see far over these earthly contests the great duel between Paganism and Christianity being fought out; no one unenlightened by Christian principle being on the morrow of Julian's death able to predict the issue. Here, as in the "Iliad," a world-struggle was in progress, not between East and West alone, but between two halves of the human race, and it was again as if the immortals had descended from the clouds to fight under the light of day in the thickest of the battle. But the poet was wanting to describe it, or rather he was there, but mistook its meaning.

The poet of the fifth century was Clandian, a native of the learned city of Alexandria, and of that Egypt under whose vaunted sky the labourer, served by the waters of Nile, need never call the clouds to his help. He sang passionately of his city, wherein the whole learning of ancient time was stored—parent of Callimachus and Apollonius, at whose schools Virgil and Horace had not disdained to study, and the poet himself had been formed and trained. In 395 he appeared in still pagan Rome amidst universal homage from the partisans of the old cult, who were overjoyed at hearing the brilliant youth belaud their gods at the moment when their fall had been proclaimed. Public admiration bore him to the highest honours, and leave was obtained from Christian emperors to erect him a statue in Trajan's forum beside the great poets of antiquity, bearing on the base an inscription ascribing to him Virgil's intelligence and Homer's muse.

In obtaining such favours for him a more powerful protector was joined with the senate in the person of Stilicho, to whose suite the poet was attached. He sang of his victories, combats, repose, pleasures, vices, and crimes, and accompanied the tutor of Honorius, the conqueror of the Goths, to the end of his career, and when he perished at the assassin's hand was sprinkled with his blood. Clandian thereupon, in disgrace and persecuted, addressed a poem to Adrian, the praetorian prefect, to implore him to show pity, to stay his hand, and suffer him to breathe freely in retirement, and, with the deplorable license of flattery, comparing the prefect to Achilles, reminded him that he did not show fury over the remains of Hector.

This man's genius lay precisely in his errors. Born in a Christian age, he lived by power of an intense imagination, surrounded by the associations of pagan antiquity, and like the gods who walk the earth in mist, so he could only speak in an atmosphere of fable which hid the truth. At this epoch temples were everywhere being closed, except at Rome, where, however, the Galilaean Fisherman had conquered Jupiter Olympus; yet he began a Gigantomachia, to celebrate Jove's victory over the giants. As the time was approaching for the temple of Ceres at Catania to receive the image of the Blessed Virgin on its altar, he was composing a poem in three books on the Rape of Proserpine. The genii of the levelled temples, the inspiration of the Delphic tripod, had passed on to his lips to bring forth no eloquent defence or apology of his menaced gods that would link his fame to that of Symmachus, and confute those of the most glorious confessors, but only to teach us, with great noise and parade, how the infernal god carried Ceres' lovely daughter from the meadows of Enna.

But it was not mere fancy; in Claudian's errors and forgetfulness there was plenty of political significance. The pagan society that had received the new comer with transport and loaded him with favours, in making him the poet of its predilection, and which consisted chiefly of the senatorial families, had embraced the policy, according to the speech of Sallust the rhetorician to Julian, of treating Christianity as a passing whim of some infatuated minds, which would soon fade and leave them to return to the religion of their ancestors. Pagans, formerly so disturbed at these Christians, whom they had treated to menace, to the arenas, executioners, or lions, whom they had accused of treason and a desire to undermine the Empire, contented themselves now with the calmer method of ignoring them as of little account at present, and to be non-existent to posterity. Clandian passed without recognition amidst the Christian glories of the century, in ignorance of St. Augustine and St. Ambrose, who did him on the contrary the honour of quoting from his writings, never attacking Christianity directly but once in his private life, when he hurled the following epigram at Jacobus, a military prefect, for the great crime of disapproving his poetry:

Per cineres Pauli, per cani limina Terri,

Ne laceres versus, dux Jacobe, meos.

Sic tua pro clypeo sustentet pectora Thomas,

Et comes ad bellum Bartholomaens eat.

Sic ope sanctorum, non barbarus irruat Alpes;

Sic tibi det vires sancta Susanna tuas.

So the use of sarcasm against Christianity is not modern, and in writing a history of Voltairianism we have to go hack long before Voltaire.

But the Roman aristocracy rarely allowed its poet such compromising liberties, for it had other services to extract from him. Clandian had been made the poet laureate of its solemnities, of its interests, and of its passions. He was its spokesman; not, indeed, in prose, which might have incurred blame through excess, but in the language of the gods, which could be accused of no liberty, and in which he might recall, from time to time, expressions of Virgil or of Homer. He was spokesman in those great events which were stirring every mind, the war against Gildo or Alaric, the fall of Rufinus or Eutropius; and then it was that he appeared at Rome, Milan, or Ravenna before Honorius, Stilicho, and the high dignitaries of the Empire, to speak in the name of the great senatorial assembly and the aristocracy of Rome; to treat these Christian potentates as he would have treated Augustus and his court; to envelop them in a cloud of words breathing, as it were, I idolatrous incense and the perfume of sacrifice; and entangle them in a sort of complicity with the Paganism which they were not strong enough to disperse. Had he to praise Theodosius, he represented him, after giving his last advice to Stilicho, as taking flight for heaven, like Romulus of old, traversing the milky way, cleaving to right and left the shadows which pressed respectingly on his course, leaving far behind him Apollo, Mercury, and Jupiter, and taking his place on the highest summit of the empyrean, whilst his star rose in the east, to take another loving glance at his son Arcadius, and set regretfully on the dominions of Honorius, in the Western Empire. Thus did the poet of this century sing of the apotheosis of the greatest defenders and crowned servants of Christianity. Still bolder and freer was his tone in addressing the young Honorius, not hesitating on the occasion of his marriage to Mary to picture Love and Cupid coming to pierce the heart of the prince with their darts, and departing to boast of his exploits to Venus in her Cyprian palace, of which he gave a sounding description. The goddess, Rome by a triton, crossed the seas, arrived at Ravenna, and entering the palace of the espoused, found them reading the ancient poets. The odes of Sappho (the reading of which pagans forbade to their children) was what Clandian placed in the hands of the young bride of Honorius.

But there was a greater solemnity for him. In the year 404, when Honorius had reigned nine years, preferring the Christian city of Ravenna to Rome, which was still bound to the false gods, and having issued three edicts against Paganism, he decided, after long hesitation, to go to Rome, to celebrate his sixth consulate. He took possession of the old palace of Augustus, on the Palatine, and gathered around him that divided Senate, the majority of which was still deploring the overthrow of the altar of Victory. In that great assembly, wherein the Christians preponderated by influence, if not by number, Clandian came forward charged to make known the wishes of the Senate and people, and from a parchment on which his verses were written in letters of gold related a dream:—"Balmy sleep gives back to our calmed hearts all the thoughts that during the day have troubled our souls. The hunter dreams of the woods, the judge of his tribunal, and the skilful rider thinks in sleep to pass a fancied goal. Me, also, does the worship of the muses pursue in the silence of night, and brings me back to an accustomed task. I dreamt that in the midst of heaven's starry vault I was bringing my songs to the feet of mighty Jove, and, as sleep has its sweet illusions, thought I saw the hallowed choir of the gods applauding my words. I sang of the vanquished giants, Enceladus and Typhoeus, and of the joy with which heaven received Jupiter, all radiant with triumph. But no vain image deceived me. No ivory gate sent me forth a deceitful vision. Here is the prince, the world's master, high as Olympus. There in truth that assembly which I saw, an assembly of gods. Sleep could show me nothing more excellent, and the Court has rivalled heaven." Nothing at once more polished or more pagan could be said. After this brilliant exordium he continued. First he vowed a temple to Fortune (Fortuna redux), since Rome and the consulate had recovered their majesty. When Apollo abandoned for a moment his splendid home at Delphi the laurel became but a common shrub, the oracles were dumb; but as the god's return gave voice to caves and forests, so did Mount Palatine revive at the presence of the new deity and remembered the Cœsars who for so many ages had dwelt therein. " Truly no other home suits as well the masters of the world, no other mount exalt so highly the imperial power or more dominion to the supreme law, turning as it does over the forum and the vanquished rostra. Behold the sacred palace everywhere environed by temples. How the gods guard it round! Before me I behold Jove's sanctuary, the mighty steeps of the Tarpeian rock, sculptured porticoes, statues that rise toward heaven, holy buildings whose crowded roofs darken the sky. I perceive the columns studded with many a ship-beak in iron and numberless arches charged with spoils. Respected Prince, dost thou not recognize thy household gods? "

There was more than imagination or empty pomp in such verses. They read a bold lesson to the prince who had deserted Rome to hide himself in Ravenna, and it was not without temerity that Clandian called him back to his pagan penates, to Mount Palatine as a place still defended by the divine sentinels which are standing around.

But a fine sentiment of Roman patriotism pushed to a singular degree in a native of Alexandria explains and gives a reason for the poet's unusual audacity. It was a proof of the deep feeling of unity with which Rome had infected all the nations under her sway. Clandian had digested the whole of Roman antiquity, and was penetrated with the spirit of Latin heroism. He filled his verse with the names of the Fabricii, Decii, and Scipios; not as mere verbiage to stock the edifice of an empty poetry, but as living thoughts restoring, if but for a moment, the faded past. Not Jupiter, in whom he only half believed, nor Ceres, nor Proserpine, but Rome was the true divinity of Claudian; Rome as she was pictured on her monuments and seen in the public places or in the temples which even in Asian cities had been dedicated to her name. "Rushing forth on a chariot, followed in breathless course by her two outriders, Terror and Impetuosity, with helmeted head and bare shoulder, in her hand the sword of victory, turned now against Parthian, now against German." Such was the deity of his dreams, and in admiration of her stern beauty he was never weary.

At other times, quitting his rich and florid mythology, he seized the very idea of Rome in her career of conquest and legislation, expressing it with an accuracy worthy of a historian or a lawyer. " She is the mother of arms and of law; she has stretched her empire over the world, and given to law her earliest cradle; she alone received the vanquished to her bosom, and gave her name as consolation to the human race, treating it not as its queen, but its mother. She made citizens of those she had conquered, and bound earth's extremities by a chain of love. By her peaceful genius, we find all of us our country under foreign sides, and change our dwelling with impunity. Through her it is but play to visit the frozen shores of Thule and penetrate regions whose very name caused our fathers horror. Through her we drink at will of the Rhine or Orontes; through her we are but one people, and her empire will know no end. The Sibyl has given her promise, Jupiter thunders but for her, and Pallas covers her with her whole aegis."

I have treated of Clandian in detail, as being the next in the rank of poets to Lucan, and do not shrink from putting him above Statius and all subsequent poets, on account of a singular brilliancy of imagery, an astonishing richness of metaphor, and a warmth of tone which often called forth the true light of poetic diction. But I cannot veil his faults, in devoting such great qualities to the service of a religion which no longer inspired any mind; for Paganism had its time of inspiration in days when it was sustained by a kind of faith, as when Homer pictured a Jupiter the movement of whose eyebrow made the world tremble, with such deep religious truth that the poet himself seemed awed by the mighty image he had just evoked. Virgil, too, in less degree, lighted upon some measure of the same inspiration, when he called us to assist at the foundation of the Roman Destiny, at that assembly of gods wherein it was decided that the stones of the Capitol should never be displaced. But Clandian scarcely believed in these gods; he used them as so many actors to pour forth school harangues, and only brought forward Jupiter, Juno, and Pluto to treat of some commonplace about glory or pardon, farewell or despair. It was worse when he disposed them as so many slaves in the train of his protectors; made them march behind the chariot of Stilicho, or hurled them in pursuit of such of his enemies as Rufinus; and in this all the badness and senility of that pagan society, whose disorders we have glanced at, was at once betrayed. Like his friends, the Roman senators, he offered vows in secret for the triumph of Arbogastes or Eugenius, whom he disowned on their fall—finding, when one had died on the battle-field, and the other had, like Brutus at Philippi, fallen on his own sword, nothing but poetic insults for their memory. "When Rufinus, again surrounded by his enemies, was torn in pieces, his head carried one way, his arms another, and the fragments of his body a third, Clandian showed a savage joy, and could not gloat sufficiently over the blood which he saw flow with the same pleasure as Diana felt when her dogs tore Actaeon limb from limb, and exclaimed, "Happy was the hand which first was plunged into such blood as that."

Mankind could scarcely inspire the poets of this time more than the gods. The familiarity of Augustus, the elegant and prudent commerce he sustained with his poets, was efficient to encourage the muses of Virgil and Horace; he wished for flattery, but the more delicate it was, the more did it please him. Far different was the courtiership of the Lower Empire to which our poet cringed. Stilicho was a Vandal, and Eutropius an eunuch, but Clandian was their hired servant, owing them verses in return for every benefit they conferred. All antiquity then was sacrificed to Stilicho; he was compared to the Scipios, who had patronized poetry, but he was raised to a higher place. Serena, his wife, was invited to give her auspices to the poet's marriage, and in an invitatory epistle in verse, by which he announced it to the great princess, he reminded her that Juno assisted at those of Orpheus, and hints that the queen of earth will not suffer herself to be excelled in generosity by the queen of heaven.* In such phrases he addressed a Christian guilty of the unpardonable crimes in his pagan eyes of burning the Sibylline books, and of snatching from the goddess in the temple of Ceres her necklace, whilst repulsing with a kick the ancient vestal who reproached her with the sacrilege.

Thus all the poet's Paganism was incapable of extracting from him a word of ill-will towards the enemies of his religion, and he includes them all in a generous forgiveness. This leaning towards panegyric was a sign of a degradation of morality; not only did it take from the poet all moral dignity, but was inimical to the spirit of poetry. The panegyrist, in fact, cannot take the truly great and heroic as the object of his verse. He must praise and immortalize everything—take his hero at his birth, and follow him through his childish games; and when Honorius could not lead his armies in person, find a reason for his inaction in declaring the boy of nine to be busied in philosophic study at the moment when he was sought for that he might he made Augustus. Such is the law of panegyric.

The publicity with which these compositions were declaimed, and the custom of public readings of them, brought the poets of the Decline to the oblivion which was their destiny. It has been ingeniously shown how this custom, unknown to the time of Virgil—the self-conceited habit introduced by Pollio, and encouraged later by Nero, of bringing a multitude together at the recital of a poem—contributed profoundly to stifle genius by degrading it to a mere literary game and pastime for men of culture. When a whole people is addressed, there must be some common thoughts, which must be eloquent to gain hearers—simple to gain appreciation. But when only a cloyed and captious handful of so-called fine spirits, who boast of never admiring, because that faculty seems redolent of simplicity, is in question, then, instead of mere emotion, there must be astonishment. It is the principle of periods of decline to strain every nerve to astound by the deep science of the matter and the excessive refinement of the form. As to the former, it is at such times that we meet with those myth-loving poets, astronomers, geographers, naturalists, who will put into their Latin verse everything—whether the phenomena of Aratus, the astronomy of Ptolemy, or descriptions of the earth by some other ancient—except poetry itself. As to the latter, everything is sacrificed to minute detail—to culture, refinement—to the budding of a happy phrase, hid in some word as in a germ, which is developed, enlarged, watered, cherished, till at last it displays its whole foliage to some delighted assembly.

This was the method of Clandian, whereby he struggled to show himself the most learned man of antiquity. His whole art lay in detaching phrases, in rounding periods, refining and polishing the points which were to hold the memory and be learnt by rote, for whereas few knew separate scraps of the " Æneid" or " Iliad," of which the whole or none must be known, no one who had ever heard it forgot the opening of Claudian's poem against Rufinus:—

Saepe mihi dubiam traxit sententia mentem,

 Curarent superi terras, an nullus inesset

Rector, et incerto tiuerent mortalia casu.

I pass over the stirring lines which follow, in which he developes at length the Stoic thesis, and which ended in these verses, to which he was bound to come at any price:—

Abstulit hunc primum Rufini poena tumultum, Absolvitque dens.

One of the chief secrets of the literature of the Decline was this cutting the line and arresting the sentence after the first hemistich, instead of finishing together the poetic period and the idea; another process to excite surprise was hit upon, the finishing the idea before the line, which was thought an achievement. Herein lay all Claudian's defects. He was great in promises, as in beginning his invective against Rufinus by invoking heaven and earth. His works were full of that flourish, that passion for erudition and exaggeration of form, as well as the hidden unbelief suddenly revealed in his pretension of judging and absolving the gods, of whose justice he was not sure. The faults of Clandian himself, and of the Decline, lay in that master-vice of scepticism which had strangled faith, and with it inspiration. We might still after Clandian treat of poets animated by the breath of heathenism, were it good to lengthen the history of a death-struggle.

Some fire still burned in the breast of Rutilius Numantianus, who also honoured in Rome the mistress of law and arms, the uniter of the world into a single faith. Many a feature might be added to our sketch of pagan society from the bold heathenism of this poet's writings. Clandian had scarcely ventured on one stealthy epigram against Jacobus, but Rutilius, on his return voyage from Rome to Marseilles, having passed the island of Capraria, which he found tenanted by monks, shows us what he thought of these men of black robe and stern countenance, whom he qualified as hating the light:—"Called from a Greek word monks, as wishing to live without witnesses; flying the gifts of fortune to avoid the blows, making themselves wretched that they may not know misery. What can that fury of the troubled brain be which carries so far the terror of evil as not to undergo what is good?" These words of Rutilius were to be repeated later by the Provençal poets, by the calumnious minstrels of the *langue d'oil* in their perpetual strife with the clergy, and so to be handed from age to age, to our fathers, to ourselves, who, perhaps, may think them new.

It would be more interesting to follow this pagan poetry at the moment in which it fell in some manner under Christian influence, in the writings of Ausonius in the fourth and Sidonius Apollinaris in the fifth century. The latter followed his master Clandian; like him framing epithalamia, panegyrics, and sonnets on pagan models, evoking with his pen Thetis and Peleus, Venus and Cupid, and composing pieces to be learnt by heart. In one of these he shows Rome appearing helmetless, dragging painfully her lance and buckler in the assembly of the gods, and complaining that she, the former mistress of the world, should now be under the domination of the Caesars, but at least, she exclaimed, if I must serve, let heaven send me a Trajan! Jupiter accordingly sent her Avitus, who reigned but one year, and amid thorough disorder, but he was the father-in-law of Sidonius. The poet excused the imperfection of his verse by the presence of the barbarians—those men of six feet high, with hair greased with rancid butter, who surrounded him importunately, stunned him with rude songs wild as their own forests, and took from him the liberty of mind necessary to inspiration. Fortunatus was not so sensitive, but though he lived at the court of these terrible patrons, he had not forgotten his Clandian. In leaving Italy he had brought carefully under his mantle the roll of his master's poetry, had studied and assimilated it, and when the great event of a marriage between Sigebert and the beautiful Brunehaut came to pass, was happy in finding an occasion for his recollections, in bringing Cupid from Cyprus to the wedding, to affiance these barbarians, in making Love sing the praise of the prince and Venus of the princess, another Venus, fairer than the Nereids, to whom the river gods were happy to offer their nymphs.

Ipsa sua subdunt tibi flununa nymphas.

Venus and Amor little knew that the lovely Spaniard, the young princess of the barbarians, the world's delight, would one day be dragged by the hair at the tail of a wild charger, amidst the yells of a barbarian army. As the pagan divinities and Jupiter himself had lost their power of foretelling such a future, so also had the epopee left these undiscerning deities for the camp of the once despised barbarian; and was to be found then, as ever, to her shame, on the side of the victors. As with Greek against Trojan, as with the Roman against the world, so now with the barbarian against Rome. It lurked in those songs of the people which told of the beautiful Sigurd, conqueror of the dragon, and grouped around his myth the heroes of the invasion; in those which pictured Attila, the world's subduer, dying of hunger, a despairing captive in the depths of a cavern, gold-surrounded but shut in by iron doors, while his enemy bade him " Surfeit thyself with gold—take thy fill of money." It was with Theodoric hunting wild beasts in the forest, and then having become Christian in his old age, appearing on earth from time to time, in the belief of the Swabian peasantry, to announce to men the disasters of the Empire. Such was the destiny of the poetry which Rome had thought all her own.

The theatre had not fallen before the vices of the degenerate Romans of the Decline, or the scandal of the gladiatorial and mimetic shows, or before the rivalry from the readings, or an exhausted treasury. It had not succumbed to the decrees of Christian emperors, for though they had at first expressly suspended theatrical representations, a law of Arcadius in 399, levelled against certain impurities therein, disclaimed any intention of suppressing them, lest the people should be dispirited. It remained, and Clandian reckoned among the inaugurators of the consulate of Mallius, actors of the sock and of the buskin, devoted respectively to tragedy and comedy: thus at the end of the fourth century we find two contemporary comedies: one the " Game of the Seven Sages," from the pen of Ausonius, a subject dear to the Middle Age, and often repeated, consisted of monologue in which each of the seven successively enunciated his wise maxims with all fit dramatic surroundings; the other, " Querolus," was also a work of the fourth century, and has been brought forward in the skilful comments of M. Magnin as a strong proof of the continuity of theatrical tradition.

The prologue commences by asking silence and a hearing from the audience for a barbarian who wished to revive the learned games of Greece and Latin antiquity, for he followed the steps of Plautus in imitating the " Aulularius." The first who entered on the scene was an entirely pagan personage in the shape of the family Lar, and he appeared, as will be seen, before a society in full decay. The plot was as follows:—An old miser named Euclion, having hidden his money in an urn, filled it for better concealment with ashes, and inscribed upon it that it contained the remains of his father; he then departed with light heart on a long journey. On the way he died, having made one of his parasites co-heir with his son, and charged him to tell the latter that all the gold the old man had amassed was to be found in a certain urn. The parasite arrived and, fully resolved to reap the sole profit of the legacy, passed himself off as a magician, and was introduced by Querolus, the miser's son, into his house. There he was left alone, and having ransacked the premises and found only one urn, the inscription of which told him that it held ashes, in a rage threw it out of window: it broke at the feet of Querolus, and thus betrayed the secret. The parasite was imprudent enough to claim his share, and brought forward the will, but Querolus replied, "Either you knew what the urn held, in which case I shall treat you as a thief, or you did not, in which case I shall have you punished as a violator of tombs." And so the comedy ended. But it affords another page to add to those already cited, and complete what our classic education often slurs over—the reverse side of that splendid Roman antiquity; for not only does Querolus lash with his satire everything public, official, and solemn in the old society, and expose the perfidy and cupidity of the pagan priests by showing, for instance, how they denounced all the offerings and other impostures which were essential to the system of worship ; not only does he ridicule the whole crew of divines, augurs, and astrologers who fattened on public credulity, but he shows us the honest man of Paganism one to be honoured by mortals and protected by the gods.

The Lar set forth the plot in these terms:—" I am," he said, "the guardian and inhabitant of this my assigned house; I temper Fate's decrees for it; if any good luck is promised I press it on, if bad, I soften the blow. I rule the affairs of this Querolus, who is neither agreeable nor the reverse. At present he is in want of nothing; soon we shall make him very rich, and he will deserve it, for if you think that we don't treat worthy people according to their worth you are mistaken."

Knowing Querolus' bad temper, he promises himself a laugh at his expense. Soon Querolus enters, and asks why the bad are always happy and the good unfortunate, and the Lar tells them he will explain it. Querolus declares that he does not count himself among the unhappy, whereupon he puts this question to him,—

The Lar. " Have you never stolen, Querolus ?"

Querolus. " Never since I have lost the habit of doing so. When I was young I admit that I did play some young man's tricks."

Lar. "Why then give up such a landable crime? and what shall we say as to lying ?"

Querolus. " Well, who does tell the truth ? That little sin belongs to everyone. Pass on to the next thing."

Lar. "Certainly, as there is no harm in lying; but how about adultery?"

Querolus. "Oh; but that's no crime."

Lar. " When did they begin to permit it, then ? Tell me how often you have sworn, and be quick about it."

Querolus. "All in good time. That's a thing I've never been guilty of."

Lar. "I allow for a thousand perjuries. Tell me the rest, or at least how often you have sworn love to people you hated."

Querolus. " What a wretch I am to have such a

pitiless judge. I confess I have often sworn and given my word without giving my faith."

The Lar, content with this confession, tries to reassure Querolus by proving once more that the gods overlook the peccadilloes of good fellows. And this, be it remarked, shows us the more innocent side of that society, so we can judge of the dangers which must have surrounded it. The Lar, wishing to reward Querolus for his candour, promises to grant his wishes but to warn him of their peril. His wish was the glory of battle but not the blows. He longed for Titus's cash-box but not for his gout. He wanted to be a decemvir, but not to pay the fee for the honour; to be lastly a simple citizen, but powerful enough to rob his neighbours without any one gainsaying it. To which the Lar answers, "It is not influence, but sheer robbery, that you are hankering for."

Such was the visible and glaring disorder ranged at the gates of that wealthy and learned society. But we must examine what lay beneath and within it amongst the redoubtable and implacable slave-caste. One of them named Pantomalus appears in " Querolus," and shows us of what sort they were, and in what their wishes and thoughts consisted in the fifth century. " It is acknowledged," he says, " the slave-masters are bad, but I have found none worse than mine; not that he is actually cruel, but so exacting and cross. If there's any theft in the establishment he flies out as if it was a crime. If one happens to throw a table, chair, or bed on the fire, see how he scolds; he calls it hastiness. He keeps the accounts from end to end with his own hands, and if anything is wrong pretends that we must make it up. How unjust masters are ! They find us taking our nap in the daytime, the secret of which is that we are up all night. I don't know what nature has made better than the night. It is our day. Then we go to the baths with the pretty female slaves. That is freedom in life. We shut our masters up at home, and are sure of their being out of the way. We have no jealousies; there is but one family among slaves; for us it is one long festival, wedding games and bacchanals, and therefore few of us want to be freed. What freedman could stand such expense or be sure of such impunity? "

We see then that family life at this time was menaced as well as property; deep-seated perils were shaking that world with its thin crust of marble and gold; domestic danger was besieging those haughty patricians who owned the world, in the very days which they passed on the benches of the Circus applauding the course of the chariot.

One of two things—either the poet wished to crush the slave with his own vices, and answer the complaint of Christianity by showing him to be unworthy of enfranchisement, which would be an eternal proof of the pitiless cruelty of Paganism towards the portion of mankind which it held in fetters, or to show the peril society was running, in which case we must admire the boldness of the Fathers in reading, whilst tolerating slavery, such severe lessons on the equality of all men before God; and even now may ask ourselves whether the fears of those are well-founded who wish to relegate to times of security such dangerous truths, as if the truths of the Gospel were not made for a period in which suffering and sacrifice alike are frequent.

The dramatic shows lasted through the following centuries. In 510 Theodoric rebuilt the theatre of Marcellus at Rome, and the Senate undertook the expense of providing actors. In Gaul Chilperic repaired the stage at Soissons, and Terence was acted there in the seventh and eighth centuries. Of this we have proof in a fragment which has been preserved to us. It opens with a prologue, in which Jerome, the manager of the theatre, announces to the audience the performance of a comedy by Terence. A buffoon *(delusor)* then appears, who expresses disgust at the idea, and wishes them to pack off such a broken-down poet. Terence thereupon enters in person, and encounters the young man who had insulted him, whereupon there is a dialogue and the commencement of a new and barbarous comedy. The clown replies to Terence, " I am worth more than you. You are old, I am young. You are only a dry old stick; I am a green tree." The latter asks where his fruit is, and the two begin to use strong language, then threats, and the pageant breaks off just as they are coming to blows.

A council held at Rome in 680 forbade bishops to attend at the shows of mimes, and a letter of Alcuin a little later exhorts certain abbots, priests like himself, to abstain from theatrical amusements. In the eleventh century, at the marriage of Beatrix, mother of the Countess Matilda, mimes were still playing after the old method. Later Vitalis of Blois composed two comedies; one called "Geta," the other "Amphitryon." Thus "Amphitryon" was played for the men of the twelfth century, as Molière was to bring it again under the eyes of the staid and learned court of Louis XIV. So hard was it to subdue that lusty spirit of antiquity, which was to reappear in every age, not only in the centuries of the Revival, but in those of purer and severer character, which seemed farthest removed from the taste of the ancients.

In fact, mythology was not, as has been supposed, a posthumous resurrection, a wonder of the Revival, an effort to bring back a departed element into literature. Tasso, Camoens, and Milton are not open to the accusation of having revived the pagan muses; it was rather Paganism perpetuating itself in literature, as in religion by superstition, in law by the oppression of the weak, by slavery, and by divorce; and as astrologers continued the science, so did mythologists continue the literature, of heathendom.

Mythology had entered deep into the manners of antiquity. Rome, disputed for by Belisarius and Totila, still kept the vessel in which Caesar was fabled to have touched the shores of Italy. The teeth of the Erymanthian Boar were still shown at Beneventum, and upon the ornaments Rome by the Emperor at Rome on days of feasting were embroidered the Labyrinth and the Minotaur, to signify that his thoughts should be impenetrable to his subjects. In the mosaics which beautify the churches of Ravenna and Venice a number of subjects borrowed from the old fables arc to be found. Thus, in the baptism of Christ, the Jordan is depicted as an old man, nude, crowned with rushes, pouring from an urn the waters of the river. The earth was represented as a female, sometimes nude, sometimes covered with flowers; the sea under the features of a man vomiting forth water. The Caroline books alluded to these abuses, and condemned them in vain, so that under Charles the Great artists employed all their time in painting Actaeon, Atys, and Bellerophon, until mythology triumphed everywhere. Later, in describing the palaces of the time and their mosaics, they inform us that the principal group represented Amor discharging his arrows, and around him were the beautiful women of old whom he had struck. At Florence, during festivals, bands of youths paraded the city, the handsomest at their head, who was called Love. At marriages during the Middle Age it was customary to play little pastoral dramas, in which Cupid appeared levelling his shafts at the ladies present. The first Spanish dramatic poem by Rodrigo de Cota (1470) was a simple dialogue between an old man and Love. It cannot be supposed that, since mythology still held the manners and the arts, that it would relax its hold on poetry, and we find the barbarians composing works of entirely pagan character, and revelling, in the seventh and eighth centuries, in all the impurity of Catullus. The fables of Ovid were translated in verse, and I have seen at St. Gall a complaint of Œdipus, rhymed like the chants of the Church, and so noted that the music was joined to the text, which proves it to have been the work of a man who laboured for the public. Mythology even returned in the works which came from the pen of men of heroic courage and virtue, as St. Columba and St. Boniface. The mythology of Dante's Hell has been condemned as a pedantic contrivance to bring science into his art, fit only to astonish the mind; but he did but follow in this the inspiration, tastes, and prejudices of the men of his time, and, far from being pedantic, he obeyed the feelings of a people which still believed in such things as the hidden virtue of the statue of Mars, the geese of the Capitol, and the *ancilia*. The ancient deities had but changed their form and become daemons or fallen angels; in this sense the poet used them, according to his belief in them; and it is not till we come to his Purgatory and Paradise that we feel that poetry was entering its true destiny.

We must traverse the Middle Age, the Revival, the quarrels of the Jansenists and Molinists, of ancients and moderns, to find the end of mythology; and can we say even now that we have found it? All this time had to elapse that, in religion, faith might rise in triumph above the creed, in law the spirit of equity might conquer the arbitrary and changeful letter, that in literature thought might become mistress of form and independent of tradition.

The literature of the fifth century then preserved the tradition of its art, as treasure in a vase which must ultimately be broken; but we must confess that the receptacle was sculptured with art, and its fair exterior was calculated to excite the desire of many. When it had been shattered, and its contents were in dispute, the majority thought themselves rich in having picked up a morsel of the painted clay, but few were found to grasp the treasure which had been hidden within.

THE LITERARY TRADITION.

We have seen what poetic inspiration could effect in the fifth century, how the majesty of the epopee was sustained as by a last effort in the poems of Clandian, how the drama remained popular, and how the comedy of Plautus lived again in the merry scenes of" Querolus." The tales which had charmed the polished imagination of antiquity did not weary the barbarian world, and the fables which had been expelled from their religious shrines long took refuge in the manners, arts, and poetry of the Christianized nations. But the old inspiration was burning itself out day by day. The ancient poetry had been essentially religious in origin and principle, the only form of preaching known to Paganism; it was the accompaniment of the mysteries, and the histories, destined afterwards to be gathered up into the epic celebrations of god-born heroes, were originally a part of divine worship. Hymns to the immortals had been the earliest form of poetry. The theatre had only opened for tragedy on the feasts of Bacchus, and as a form of public worship. The destiny of poetry was lowered when it went forth from the temples to be given to the people in the works of Homer and Hesiod, to enter with Virgil into familiar intercourse with Augustus, to sit as a courtier at the feet of

Nero, and lastly, to justify all misgivings on its behalf, in stooping under Clandian to the domestic life of Stilicho and the other minions of Honorius. Inspiration it had no longer, but tradition still lived tenaciously in the ancient literature; its genius had departed, but its methods survived. Genius is but a lightning-flash, playing on the human mind, but in such vivid beauty that man would fain fix it there forever; science grasps by one intense effort the passing words, holds them in meditation, and thence unfolds the ideal of an eternal beauty. Thus the tradition of the beautiful is preserved through those masterpieces of genius which became the property and educating principle of the human mind. No century can be so unhappy as not to find pleasure and consolation even in its most barren period from some productions of literature's golden age. We must sum up the services and show the conservative spirit and method of tradition, and now, especially, observe the labours whereby it was perpetuated in antiquity, and by dint of which it passed into the bosom of the Church.

The traditions of literature lived through the old times, as indeed ever, principally in schools and by teaching. What was the Roman method of teaching. Was it—and this, like all great questions, is a perpetual one—carried on under a principle of authority or one of liberty?

In the earliest period of Roman history teaching seems to have been free, or rather it fell under that omnipotent domestic authority which hitherto the legislature had not dared to touch. The father at his family hearth amidst his household gods was a type of Jupiter, and his rule at home symbolized, and was the secret in Roman eyes, of that universal empire destined to be

Rome by them abroad to the world's extremity. The law did not trouble itself to know what masters he seated at his side, or to what schools his sons were sent; and when Crates of Mallos opened the first school of grammar and Carneades of rhetoric, fathers purchased in open market the expensive services of some of these philosophers at the cost of about four hundred thousand sesterces a year. But teaching spread so rapidly that in Caesar's time no less than twenty public schools were to be counted, and the number of rhetoricians, the dangerous facility of their art, undertaking as it did to prove the *pro* and *con.*, the true and the false, began to startle the old Roman gravity and provoked from the censors, Cnaeus Domitius and Licinius Crassus the following decree: "We have learnt that certain teachers, calling themselves Latin rhetoricians, have introduced a new kind of discipline. Our ancestors have laid down what it pleased them that their children should learn and what schools they should frequent. These innovations, as contrary to the customs of our fathers, displease us and do not appear to us proper. Therefore we have thought it necessary to make known to those who keep and those who frequent these schools that they are displeasing to us."

In this decree appears the severe censorship of old Rome, but it was powerless, for the schools of the rhetoricians were soon reopened on every side. Later Roman policy perceived that private tuition could not be stifled, but might be directed, usefully aided, and enlightened by the foundation of a public instruction. Caesar was the first to grant it privileges, and whilst honouring to keep it within bounds. Vespasian fixed the salaries of the public professors at a hundred thousand sesterces, and the imperial schools of the Capitol, destined to be the haunt of the youth of the whole world, were founded. Adrian built the Athenaeum, and granted honourable privileges to public instruction, and Alexander Severus founded burses *(stipendia)* for poor scholars of good family. Thus the imperial system of teaching was constituted, its professoriate became a magistracy, a literary tradition was infused into many of the public institutions of Rome, and liberty flourished under its shade; for at this epoch we find from the letters of the younger Pliny families associated in one city, under the auspices of a man of influence, to found there the first literary resort open to the children of the town. One day at Comum the young son of one of the inhabitants came with his father to visit *Pliny* in his library. " Do you study? " asked

Pliny. "Yes," was the youth's answer. "Where ?" "At Milan. " "Why not here ? ' ' (The father) " There are no masters." " And why ? is it not your interest, as fathers of families, to keep your children near you. What can be more consoling, more cheap, and more satisfactory as regards their morals ? Is it so difficult to get funds to engage masters ? I, though childless, am ready, for love to this city, which I look on as daughter or a mother, to undertake a third of the sum required. I would promise the whole did I not think it would be dangerous, as it is in many places where professors are paid from public funds. Those who are careless of the money of others keep good watch over their own, and will always take care that what they spend shall not fall into unworthy hands. Let your children, educated on their own native soil, learn early to love it, and may you be able to attract professors of such mark that one day the neighbouring cities may send their children to your schools." Nothing can be more modern in spirit, more judicious and benevolent than this, worthy in fact of times much nearer our own; but still antiquity opened no slave-schools—no such idea of literary benefits for high and low ever entered its philosophy.

To come to the Christian emperors. Constantine, instead of extinguishing the old lights, became their protector, and as a benefactor to public tuition wrote to the poet Optatianus, "I wish my century to afford an easy access to eloquence, and render a friendly testimony to serious studies." Three of his laws, dated ann. 321, 326, 336, re-enacted the old imperial constitutions, and granted to public professors of medicine, grammar, and literature in general, exemption from municipal taxes, military service, and every call on property and residence which the imperial tax-system required; extending the same privileges to their wives and children, that many might be called to liberal studies, " *quo facilius liberalibus studiis multos instituant.*" The law also guaranteed them against personal injury, punishing by a fine of a hundred thousand pieces of gold anyone who publicly insulted them, or if a slave was the offender, by beating with rods before the person aggrieved, that the latter might enjoy the sight of the penalty. A decree of Gratian and Valentinian in **a.d**. 76 took the more solid measure of fixing the salary of all professors throughout Gaul, desiring that in each metropolis a yearly stipend of twenty-eight annones, or twenty-four times the military allowance, should be given to the rhetoricians, and twelve to the Greek and Latin grammarians. At Trèves rhetoricians received thirty annones, Latin grammarians twenty, and Greek grammarians, if found able, twelve only. In the West Greek teaching was sacrificed to the Latin, but the contrary was the case in the East.

Thus were established the privileges, payment, and right of public instruction. But it was more important to think of the pupils than the masters, and the police of the schools were settled by an enactment of Valentinian dated 370. " Those who come to Rome to study must be furnished with a certificate of consent from the magistrates of their province. They must announce their intended subject of study on arrival, and make known their lodging to the office of the Censorship, the functionaries of which must strictly admonish them to worthy behaviour, to fear a bad name, and avoid those associations which are the first step towards crime; *consociationes quas proximas esse putamus criminibus*. They must warn them against too great a passion for public spectacles, and against disorderly banquets. They shall have power to punish the disobedient by scourging, to send them back from Rome to their province. All who do not fall under censure may pursue their studies till twenty years old, then the magistracy must insist on their departure and provide for it in spite of them. A report must be sent from the offices at Rome every month to the provincial magistrates, and a yearly memorandum to the emperor, of those who are most worthy of employment."

As the tree grew and its foliage became thicker there was less room for the sun to reach it, and so private tuition gradually lost its freedom. A law of Julian, in 362, considering that masters ought to excel in morality and in eloquence, ordained that postulants for the honours of teaching must submit to be examined by a municipal commission chosen from the *curia*, whose judgment was then to be ratified by the prince. This was aimed at the Christians, to exclude from the chairs those whom he hated as Galileans, but the decree was to recoil one day on its authors. In 425, a decree of Theodosius the Younger and Valentinian III. gave permission to private professors to teach in families, but forbade their keeping public schools, to debar them from that road to fortune and even dignities, and at the same time interdicted public professors from domestic tuition on pain of losing their privileges.

We have to consider, then, three periods in Roman instruction. At first an absolute liberty for private tuition, but no official teaching; secondly, private teaching still existing, but the public system all-powerful; and during the golden age of the Empire, its longest and brightest period, an official instruction honoured and sustained by state aid, side by side with a general liberty which enabled every capable man to give proof of his learning by undertaking the education of his young fellow-citizens. But neither the measures of Julian nor those of Theodosius the Younger receivedtheir full accomplishment, for on every side private schools were opened which caused alarm and disquietude to the legislators. The year 425 approached too nearly those formidable invasions which had already carried off Spain, and were destined to sever Gaul and all the provinces in turn from the power of the Roman Caesars. The laws never were in full vigour, and as, under the continual menace of invasion and before the tide of barbarism, the impoverished cities were little able to provide the large charge imposed by Antoninus and renewed by Gratian, public teaching had to disappear in favour of the private schools. Toulouse, at the end of the sixth century, possessed barely thirty grammarians, left at perfect liberty to assemble in deliberation amongst themselves, but hardly calculated to excite the jealousy of the Merovingian executive, since the object of their gatherings was only to know whether the adjective must always agree with its substantive, or if the verb had always a frequentative form, making *lego, legito,* as legitimate as *moneo, monito.*

Instruction thus constituted had a power of extension to the very ends of the Empire. We have marked its establishment at Trèves, and at Xanten on the Rhine an altar has been found attesting the restoration of a school in that northern region by Marcus Aurelius and Lucius Verus. At Autun, Clermont, Bordeaux, Poitiers, Auch, Toulouse, and Narbonne flourished numberless schools, whose professors and grammarians, Greek and Latin, Ausonius landed to the sides, and even Homer found in one of them a new Aristarchus to throw light on the obscure and doubtful passages. Britain offered the same spectacle, since the conquering Agricola introduced eloquence and Roman manners hand in hand, in the belief that, by throwing the toga over its haughty islanders, he would enervate their courage and disarm their opposition.

When Britain ceased to form part of the Empire, Roman culture survived in such a manner that the traditions of the "Æneid" were confounded with the fabulous tales of Cambria. The same songs celebrated the fame of Merlin, the enchanter, and of Brutus, the founder of the British realm, or vaunted the greatness of the old Latin city of Caerleon, with its baths and palaces, its schools and its forty philosophers.

The same movement of intellect was seen in Spain. In the days of the republic Sertorius had founded a school of the liberal arts at Huesca, and later a legion of brilliant minds, such as Quintilian, Seneca, and Lucan came out of that province to Rome. So many poets and actors, indeed, did it produce in the time of Theodosius, that, unable to gain a livelihood in their own country, they passed the Pyrenees to seek their fortunes beyond.

Moreover, when all intercourse seemed suspended between the central seat of empire and the provinces, the learned tradition survived through the most uncongenial time, and lightened the obscurity of the darkest age. The imperial schools subsisted to the end of the seventh century, not only in Gaul but in Italy, Spain, and on every point of the old Roman world. In Italy, till the eleventh century, lay teachers pursued their course side by side with the ecclesiastical schools, as if to unite the end of the old imperial system to the origin of that of the universities, and especially the university of Bologna, which, in spite of difference from one another, and from the old schools of the Empire, perpetuated the public method of antiquity through a privileged professoriate and an universally accessible system of instruction.

As Alexander Severus had founded burses for poor scholars, so numberless colleges were opened during the Middle Age for students, who sat on straw at the feet of their masters to receive their tuition. On one side, the spirit of the universities was derived from antiquity, while the new principle brought forth in the schools and the laws of the emperors was entirely modern and moulded by Christianity—then a power in the world, and straining to penetrate its institutions. Antiquity loved science, but as a miser loves his gold; it loved it more than humanity, and feared by spreading to dishonour it. Christianity loved science also but as it said, *Venite ad me omnes;* and it loved mankind more. It honoured public eloquence, and encouraged it by the canons of its councils, as the favoured weapon which had brought the world under its dominion, and it distributed the gift with profusion. Therefore, from the time of Charles the Great, every province opened schools for the children of its peasants and serfs, and the bishop kept a higher school, supported by the alms of the rich proprietors of his Church, the benches of which were open to all. Around sprang up in numbers colleges and hospices for needy students and pilgrims from afar. Pious legacies for these purposes were encouraged, and we have ten or twelve enactments of St. Louis relating to the foundation of scholarships and colleges. Christendom's greatest minds, like Albert the Great and St. Bonaventura, did not think their vigils wasted in multiplying abstracts of Holy Scripture for poor students, *biblia pauperum,* and feared not, in opening the gates of knowledge to their widest, to encourage by too liberal a training vocations that would be useless or dangerous to society. Christianity had no such scruple. It made science shine as its God makes the sun to beam upon the good and the evil, leaving all responsibility to those who abused the light, but not dreaming of extinguishing it.

What, then, was the nature of the teaching afforded by those schools whose origin, number, and duration have just been considered? In the fifth century its spirit was still profoundly pagan, and proof of this is given in writings of Macrobius, the learned author of a " Commentary on Scipio's Dream." He compiled, also, under the title of " Saturnales," a sort of encyclopaedia of the old learning of antiquity, as it had been handed down in literary tradition, and, to give to so dry a study the advantage of the dialogues introduced by Cicero into Latin literature, supposed a group of men of birth and letters, such as Symmachus, Flavianus, Caecina Albinus, Avienus, Eusebius the rhetorician, and Servius the grammarian, to have assembled during the Saturnalia at the house of Praetextatus, to pass the time in social festival and philosophical discussion. The mornings were devoted to serious pursuits, and in the evening a more playful mood and mirthful sallies enlivened the board. This assembly of sages, enjoying the repose so rare in the Rome of Theodosius, agitated, as it was, by incessant business and political anxieties, sought their natural recreation in the sciences, whose elements they had acquired in their youth, and show us, by the tenor of their conversation, what constituted the education of the man of culture at the end of the fourth century. The discussion was opened upon the origin of the feast of the Saturnalia, which Praetextatus, as being the best versed in matters religious, was asked to expound. He did not " seek for its cause in the hidden nature of any deity, but drew his explanation from some fabulous stories or the philosopher's comments upon the same for the secret causes which spring from the pure source of truth cannot be revealed even through the mysteries, and even he who can raise his spirit to their contemplation must keep the result in the depths of his intelligence "—and herein again appeared the old jealousy of heathenism, and its determination of having two theologies, as it had two kinds of science and politics—one theology for the learned patrician, another for the ignorant plebeian. Prretextatus only gave out half his idea, for fear of betraying the secret of the mysteries, but he went very far in his avowal by urging, in conclusion, that the gods of different name really made up but one deity, the Sun, to whom, by physical and allegorical interpretation, must be referred all that was said of those gods who, of old, had crowded the heights of Olympus and Parnassus. In this attempt to serve Paganism he destroyed it, and forgot, in giving his gods a refuge in the Sun, that Christians saw, in his deified luminary, the first of the servants of the Almighty. Prœtextatus would have been surprised could he have met at his table another writer of the time, who, in an admirable and too little known essay, gave speech to the constellation which the ancients adored, making it reprove with energy the worship whereby it was insulted by setting up it, the eternal slave of God, as His rival and enemy. So deeply was the theology of Prœtextatus, the essence of this teaching, tainted by a Paganism not yet transformed and purified by the wisdom of Alexandria.

In his discourse he had named Virgil, and Evangelius the rhetorician present to act as critic and general opposer, seized the occasion of saying that many intentions had been assigned to the poet which he had never entertained. Symmachus replied by an eulogy upon Virgil; and Praetextatus himself undertook his defence, regarding him as of all the ancients the most versed in priestly law and the lore of religious antiquities, showing how Virgil had distinguished the parts of the sacred rites, had never confounded different kinds of gods and victims, and had known the worship proper to deities at home and from abroad. Flavianus claimed further for him an intimate acquaintance with the science and rules of auspices and omens, and then the whole literary clique pointed out how he had scattered philosophic theories throughout his poems, the knowledge of astronomy displayed in them, what he borrowed from the Greeks, stealing the gold from Homer himself with consummate art, sometimes showing and at others hiding it, and how he had profited by the treasures of Ennius. Lastly, they placed him above Cicero, as having known all the depths of pathos and exhausted the resources of eloquence, and being equally great as an orator and as a poet. In such grave debates the mornings of these days were passed, and in the evenings another portion of the teaching given by grammarians and rhetoricians was reproduced. Proof of this lies in the jokes and wagers the feasters proposed to each other, as indicated by Seneca the rhetorician. In the schools of his time, wherein discussions on agrarian law or imperial interest were no longer permitted, we find, among questions thought fit to exercise the eloquence of the Roman youth, and to occupy the leisure of the idle patricians, such an one as this—"Which is the first, the egg or the chicken ?" Was the world the creation of chance or of some supreme wisdom? If of the latter, it needed a good beginning, and would a logical nature commence with that of the hen or of the egg? We may leave the question where it was left in the dialogue of the "Saturnales," for it is enough to give an idea of the futility of that teaching, so grave and learned in pretension, which claimed to be a summary of the relics of antiquity. Yet Macrobius lived to posterity, and was to bo found in a work by Alard of Cambray, entitled "Extracts of Philosophy and Morality," named after Solomon, Cicero, and Virgil, and was popular enough to be quoted by a poet, not in Latin only, but in the vulgar tongue.

If such was the spirit of Roman instruction, what were the sciences expounded in detail by the voice of its masters? It comprised three subjects, grammar, eloquence, and law; grammar and rhetoric were taught in all the cities of Gaul, as at Rome. Law had special chairs, though there was no official instruction on it in the provinces generally. Under Justinian, its schools were placed at Rome, Constantinople, and Berytus. As the science of law was to be studied at Rome, so had the other indispensable accessories to a thorough literary education been professed there, since Cicero, like Plato, demanded that orators should he made out of musicians and geometers, thinking that without such experiences eloquence would consist merely of empty declamation, sallies of humour, sonorous tirades, instead of entering the depths of its subject through a well-grounded system of teaching; and so geometry, dialectics, astronomy, and music formed part of the galaxy of science taught to the youth of Rome.

Grammar, which formed a summary of the whole, was not confined to the elementary art of speaking and thinking correctly. Suetonius and its other professors expressly declared that, far from narrowing its sphere to the study of language, it comprised a criticism of all the great works of antiquity, and a reading and interpretation of its poets, its function being not merely to read, but to analyze and compare. It had two parts, philology and criticism. In France, it extended into the domain of rhetoric, comprising the humanities, and a critical reading of all the great orators and poets of antiquity.

With the ancients, philology was no such rudimentary science as might be supposed in hearing Varro and the old jurisconsults derive *lucus* from *non lucendo*, and *testamentum* from *testatio mentis*. We have no idea, while smiling at this, of the learning and labour necessary for the unravelling of the chaos of the old languages. One section derived the diverse and confused elements of which Latin was formed from the old national idiom, whilst the other found them in the Greek, and hence arose for many centuries the disputes of the rival schools of *Romanists* and *Hellenists*. Another problem worked out with different results, was to find which was the oldest and most masterful principle in the universe—authority or liberty, the finite or the infinite. Those who believed in the principle of mobility referred everything to usage gradually corrupting words, to irregularity and anomaly, while the believers in the infinite, immovable, and eternal principle proposed to subject everything to a fixed law, which subjugated custom to reason, and ruled through analogy; and thus arose two other sects, the anomalists and analogists. Thus every controversy was carried into the sphere of grammar, in which all the treasures of antiquity were reunited. In the laborious agony of the Latin language, the origin of institutions whose traces had long been lost were to be found, and through the dry and ungrateful study of etymology the secrets of those which had remained a sealed book in the hands of the jurisconsults were again laid bare. In the matter of criticism, we see grammarians early taking in hand the works of the old poets, as

Naevius, Ennius, and Pacuvius, which, before Lucretius and Virgil appeared to efface all other models, had been commented on and criticised in a thousand ways. The figure of Virgil, long surrounded by clouds, stood out in such radiant beauty that posterity took it for that of a god, as which the poet was honoured in the *lararium* of Alexander Severus; his name was placed on the calendar, and his birthday, the eve of the ides of October, marked and honoured like that of the emperor; while the Mantuan women told of his mother's marvellous dream, of the budding laurel, and would, when near childbirth, bear votive offerings to their poet's oratory. His fame grew from day to day, and upon it the Roman scholiasts concentrated all their labour. Donatus, Servius, Charisius, Diomed, and many others might be instanced, but Servius especially, preserved through the Middle Age to our own day, saw in Virgil not merely a poet, but an orator, philosopher, and theologian, finding so rich and various a store of teaching in the sixth book of his " Æneid," that he did not wonder that whole treatises had been composed in comment upon it.

But the ancient teaching, and especially the labours of the grammarians, were concentrated to a special aim, of which their prodigious activity, never greater at Rome than in this century, was the proof. It seemed that they were struggling to save, verse by verse, fragment by fragment, the remnants of that splendid language, to rescue portions of so many authors destined to perish, save in the morsels which the grammarians had preserved. Donatus and Priscian were the two most eminent of the time; the latter was so honoured in the East that Theodosius the Younger copied, with his own hand, the eighteen books of his " Grammatical Institutions." The former had St. Jerome for a disciple, and was so perseveringly commented upon in every generation, that his name became a synonym for grammar itself. His work lived as the ground-plan and type of all modern grammars, and by its clearness and brevity held the Middle Age, though it was as the bed of Procrustes for the different idioms which adopted it, too short for some, too long for others. Thus the " Donatus Provinciális," omitting the article which existed in Provencal, said that there were but eight parts of speech, and in the French adaptation, there being no declensions in that language, it was somewhat hard for the author to find place for all the nouns in his scheme.

But all the labours spent on grammar and criticism were summarized, in these essential points, under a taking form, in the work of Martianus Capella, written at Rome about 470, and under this guise the treasures of antiquity were to traverse with some safety the stormy period in which what was less valuable was destined to perish. The author was an old African rhetorician, plunged in all the contention of the Bar, and who, in his own words, had not found wealth in pleading before the proconsul. He composed, for the instruction of youth, a book entitled " De Nuptis Mercurii et Philologiae," of the nuptials of Mercury, the god of eloquence, with Philologia, the goddess of speech, a vicious title, as all are that require an explanation. The two first books related, in prose mingled with verse of frequent elegance, how Mercury, seeing that the gods had yielded all things to the laws of love, determined to act in like manner. He went to consult Apollo, who points out to him in oracle a virgin for a wife, who read the stars by her glance, and in spite of his lightnings revealed the secrets of Jupiter. The latter, being warned of it, called a meeting of the gods, to announce that a mortal was to be called to take a place in their midst, and demand a decree to naturalize in heaven the virgin of earth. But Philologia, from the depths of her retreat, lost nothing of what passed; and, knowing some noble alliance was in store for her, combined, by Pythagorean processes and calculation, the numerical value of the letters of her name with those of Mercury, and finding a perfect harmony between them, decided on submitting to fate. Her mother, Phronesis, and her handmaids, Periagia and Epimelia, hastened to complete her attire. Scarcely had they finished, when the Muses appeared to sing at her door, and Athanasia hurried in to wish her joy; but, as before becoming immortal all that was perishable must be put off, the goddess of immortality placed her hand on the breast of the virgin, who instantly vomited a frightful quantity of books, parchments, letters, hieroglyphics, figures of geometry, and even notes of music; no one being able to tell, as the poet says, what a chaos escaped from the half-opened lips of Philologia: and then, nothing hindering her upward flight, she was assumed into heaven. Her dowry was fixed, and Apollo appeared with the seven virgins assigned by Mercury as her companions—Grammar, Rhetoric, Dialectic, Arithmetic, Geometry, Astronomy, and Music—being the seven liberal arts of antiquity, which allegorical personages, each with its accompanying attributes, briefly summed up, now in verse, now in prose, the group of sciences committed to the share of each. Geometry was not understood in the modem sense, but embraced geography; music was not confined to music proper, but it united the art of melody with that of composition, the secrets of harmony and the rules of versification.

Such was this encyclopaedia of antiquity, which sought to reduce all sciences to the arbitrary number of seven: the old world had not dreamed of straitening its wealth to so narrow a compass, that task was left to a deeply imperilled society, which, like a traveller, clutched its treasure lest any should be lost by the way. The mythological machinery in which science was enveloped saved it by making it popular; for we know the barbarian passion for the mythical, and how readily their conquering hordes would open their ears to the new fables related to them by the Romans, to the graceful myths of the grammarians and men of letters. The nuptials of Mercury and Philologia were to be the delight of Gauls and Germans, who would desire them to be embroidered on the tapestry of their churches and the saddles of their horses, so easily would they have been gained over to the worship of false gods, had not Providence impelled them to other temples and far different priests. The legendary scenery in which Martianus had concealed the graceless subject of his poem was especially calculated to charm them; and he once also formed a natural mnemonic, whereby the meaning he had wished to convey was deeply imprinted on their minds. His book became the text and groundwork of elementary education during the sixth and seventh centuries, was translated into German in the eleventh; and in the ninth, thirteenth, and fourteenth, was commented upon by Scotus Erigena, Remy of Auxerre, and Alexander Nicasius. It gave, in one word, law to the whole Christian education of the Middle Age, and fenced whole generations of intellects around with the limits of the *trivium* and *quadricium*, until the Revival came to burst these barriers and give a larger sphere to genius, which languished in such confinement and aspired to the infinite. In going over the catalogues of the monastic libraries of the time, and especially those of Bobbio; of York, in the time of Alcuin; and of St. Gall, at the same period, we find therein, next to the chief Latin poets— Virgil, Horace, and Lucan—grammarians and commentators, the last writers of antiquity, perhaps, whom we should count worthy of the preservation, which, however, our ancestors did right in affording them.

It was only on the condition of bringing the heavy hammer of the old grammarians to bear on their iron nature that Vandals, Suevi, Alani, and Sarmates could digest their knowledge, and become capable of studying a language so little made at first sight for their ears or their spirit. It was only by constant repetition that their lesson was retained. Without the labours of those commentators who guarded Virgil's works down to their last verse, syllable, and *lacuna*, poetasters would have arisen, undertaking to finish his incomplete rhythms. It needed the Argus-like jealousy of these watchful guardians to prevent the profane from actually laying hands upon them, and so justifying the suspicion of Père Hardouin and his successors.

Their labours, so repulsive at first sight, were destined to mould both our ancestors and ourselves. Impelled to the lowest depth, it was to become the effort whereby genius was to rise again under that admirable law of the Almighty which makes it the prize of labour.

Long ages indeed, and many a generation, passed away in their course before the spark was struck out, to fall at once into eclipse, till other generations came to dash in their turn against the cruel rock of labour, and to end by finding another stone from whence the fire of ignition must spring. The schools of the Middle Age were for a time buried as in the earth out of sight, but the day came when a blaze of light arose from beneath their blows, where Dante and Petrarch, the precursors

and prophets of the Revival, hurried to kindle their torches. It must now be seen how this century, so pagan in its memories, so filled with traditions of mythology, became Christian, and after what repeated efforts its heathenism was transformed and thrown into the great movement which bore away the age in its current.

HOW LITERATURE BECAME CHRISTIAN.

Whilst poetical inspiration was dying out, the tradition of literature was gaining a lasting power, under the shelter of the schools which the imperial policy had endowed and multiplied, by making a magistracy of their professors, and organizing science as an institution. The Roman law, in respecting the liberty of instruction, gave to it an authority that the culture of minds might not be left to chance. It sustained the right of a father to send his son to the schools of the mercenary grammarians, evidenced by their purple hangings, or to buy a professor of rhetoric in the slave-market; and at the same time founded a public system as a model and rule for the others, thereby preserving from destruction the wealth of human intelligence, and handing it down under a severe and scrupulous control. We have seen with what ardour that tradition was taken up and cultivated in the fifth century by a whole people of grammarians, rhetoricians, and scholiasts, who extracted from the ancient text-books the rules of language and the principles of every branch of science, until the whole cycle of human knowledge was enclosed in the encyclopaedia finished at Rome in **470** by Martianus Capella. Whilst the Empire was tottering, its literature must be saved at any cost, and though Clandian, Rutilius, Sidonius Apollinaris, and the rest of the poets, in deed or in name, would have wondered had they been told that posterity would prefer to them such obscure bookworms and word-splitters as Donatus, Servius, and Macrobius, yet posterity was wise; for in the works of the latter they found the ancient language, the essence of the knowledge, ideas, and experience of the old world, and the text of the classics, preserved with scrupulous accuracy, transmitted with a care that had not let a page perish; and, lastly and especially, an example of labour of thorny and disinterested study on the part of men who could not foresee their recompense. This was the most precious fruit gathered from it by a barbarian age. Horace speaks of the lyre of Orpheus civilizing the nations, but his imagination led him astray. Doubtless the Muses have their share in the march of civilization, and the nations have ever loved to see poets in their van, especially in ages of difficulty; but whereas these guides have often failed, toil has never been lacking to a people struggling for improvement. The period we are traversing is eminently one of labour, and will teach us the difficulty and merit of the task of binding to the study of mouldy texts on the benches of the crowded school the descendants of the barbarians whose fathers had found their home in the German forests; men who had to be civilized by a process full of anxious labour, of which the light of genius was to be the result and the recompense. The traditions of ancient literature, in order to reach the Middle Age, must pass through the ordeal of Christianity; the School must desire to enter the Church, the Church to receive the School. It was no easy question to solve, but a problem which was to be for long ages the torment of the human mind, as to which the treaty concluded seemed never to be definitive, so often has it been reopened and recontested, even to our own day; it was the immortal problem of the connection between science and faith, the alliance of the Gospel with profane literature, the agreement of religion with philosophy— questions which are proposed anew every day to ourselves, and were the special difficulties of the times of which we are treating.

Moreover, they were rendered especially obscure and dangerous in the fifth century by the profoundly pagan character of the schools. We know all that the Alexandrian Syncretists attempted in order to reunite religion and literature, how under the influence of its doctrines poetry became a means of popularizing the worship of the false gods, eloquence a propagandism, and philosophy a theology; that whilst Clandian reproduced in verse the history of the Rape of Proserpine, and brought the deities of Paganism into the councils of Christian princes, Acacius, the rhetorician, was triumphantly telling Libanius by letter that he had preached in the temple of Æsculapius, and in making the innovation of praising the gods in a prose discourse, pronounced before pagans, had not forgotten to insult the Christians, the very neighbourhood of whom was an outrage to the immortals. Jamblichus, Maximus of Ephesus, and all the later disciples of Plotinus, who had embraced or adopted these doctrines, and plunged in all the errors of theology, spent their time in invoking gods and demons. The last bulwark of Paganism, both in West and East, was among these poets and philosophers, and Libanius, congratulating himself on the fact, tells us that the Greek Septints still had many allies at Rome, Ausonius also bears witness to this fact, and among the public professors of Bordeaux specifies one named Phrebitius, priest of Balenus, who vaunted his descent from the caste of Druids. So essentially pagan was the school, that it was a question to what point a Christian might continue to teach literature, and Tertullian did not scruple to maintain the negative; " for," he said, " they must of necessity teach the names of the gods, their genealogies and the attributes given them by mythology, and observe the pagan festivals and their solemnities, on which their emoluments depend. The first fee paid by the pupil is conserved to the honour and name of Minerva; presents are given in the name of Janus; if the aediles sacrifice, it is called a ferial day;" and concludes by defying any teacher of letters to disengage himself from these bonds of idolatry. But a stronger tie was found in the charm of these discredited fables, which had raised the shoulders of Cicero and embarrassed Varro.

In the presence of Christianity they seemed to revive; before its severe doctrine, so filled with austerity and mortification, their carnal and seductive spirit rose again, to throw its power on the side of graces, muses, and pleasure. Literature had to be shorn of their fascination before it could become Christian—to resist such tendencies before it could enter the pale of the new truth, which commanded an abandonment even of the charms and illusions of the mind. It was not to be wondered at, that many apostasies came to pass at this time among men of learning; and it was the influence of the Muses, or of Homer himself, which was guilty of that of Julian. When he assumed the purple, it was no marvel that men of letters in crowds rushed into the temples in his train. The terrible edicts put forth by Theodosius against apostasy make us feel how deeply the evil had corroded Christendom. Licentius, pupil of St. Augustine, a youth in whom he had placed all his sympathy, who had passed many months with him in the elevated and familiar intercourse of Cassiciacum, was pursued and tormented, though a Christian, by the daemon of poetry, and escaped to compose a piece upon Pyramus and Thisbe. It was touching in the extreme to see the efforts of the saint on his behalf. At first he bantered Licentius, and tried to draw him from the influence of his Muse; then, thinking advice the wiser course, begged him to continue and complete his fable, but, when he had represented the two kings dying at each other's feet, to give way to his rapture, and extol the conquering love which leads souls to the light, which gives them life, and never suffers it to die. Advice like this seems instinct with supreme wisdom, but it was dangerous. St. Augustine returned into Africa; Licentius was attracted by the honours and pleasures of Rome; he found jovial mirth there, and was soon surrounded by all the pagan aristocracy. He dreamt one night that the gods appeared to him, and promised, if he returned to their allegiance, that he should become consul and sovereign pontiff; and under the joint effects of the dream, the festivals, and poetry, he embraced Paganism.

Such was the irresolution of the souls of the poets, philosophers, and men of letters, whose eternal curse was a kind of incorrigible weakness, a softness of heart open to seduction, an activity of mind which perceives at a glance strong points and weak, and at the same time is incapable of decision and of choice, through excess of knowledge; for fine intellects are often served by feeble wills, and we may find in all ages the irresolute souls who have not the courage of faith.

To meet this, St. Paulinus wrote to Jovius, to engage him on the side of Christianity, and to conquer his doubts. " You breathe the perfume of all the poets, carry in your breast the streams of eloquence which have flowed from the orators, bathe in the fountains of philosophy, and taste the honey of Attic literature. Where is your business, when you read and read again Demosthenes or Cicero, Xenophon, Plato, Cato, or Varro, and all the rest whose names I hardly know, but whose works you know by heart. You are always able to give yourself up to such as these; but when the knowledge of Christ, which is the wisdom of God, is in question, then you are a slave to business. You can find time to be a philosopher, but not to be a Christian. Rather change your thoughts, carry your eloquence into another sphere; you need not abandon your philosophy, if you will but hallow it by faith, and employ it wisely by uniting it to religion. Become the philosopher and poet of the Almighty, no longer eager to find, but to imitate Him. Show your knowledge in your life rather than in your words, and produce great actions rather than wise discourses." Such firm and manly language was necessary for that effeminate generation of men of talent and sense, but whose minds were crippled by weakness, and had to be dragged, as it were, under the yoke of the holy and fertile austerities of the Faith.

But these efforts were blessed, and a certain number of hardier souls had early the courage to bury themselves in the mysteries, which gave a recompense to their boldness. Quadratus, Athenagoras, St. Justin, pupils of the most brilliant schools of Greek philosophy, were among the first of these; and the rhetoricians, Tertullian, Arnobius, and Lactatius, followed them. They began, on entering the Church, by shutting their schools, and abjuring a vocation of which they were ashamed, as irreconcilable with the literature of Christianity; but soon the further sacrifice was demanded of them, of remaining in their places, to preserve science amidst all its dangers, in spite of the requirements and newly-arisen difficulties of their faith. St. Basil, accordingly, in the fourth century, found a Christian master in the person of Preheresius. The two men named Apollinaris, one a poet, the other a rhetorician, reproduced the form of the epic in a versified New Testament, and the Platonic dialogue, by adapting it to that method, that the precious treasure of the literary tradition might be preserved; and Julian showed his fear of these Christian masters in that masterpiece of hypocrisy in which he enacted: "As we are now, thanks to the gods, enjoying liberty, I hold it absurd to lead men to teach the works of poets whom they condemn; for do not Homer, Hesiod, Demosthenes, and Virgil, recognize the gods as authors of their knowledge ? Were not many of their works consecrated to Mercury and the Muses ? If these masters think them to have been in error, let them confine themselves to interpreting Luke and Matthew in the churches of the Galilseans." This persecution, held by Christianity to be the most hateful to which it was ever exposed, attests in the loud protests raised against it on every side to the number of the Christian masters, some of whom closed their schools, while others maintained them, and sought to elude the rigour of the new enactment.

But the time came when such a resistance was useless, when

everything yielded to the subduing power of the Church, and the last rhetoricians were obliged to give up the contest. Witness the history of Victorinus: "He was an African, who had for long been a teacher of rhetoric at Rome, had seen the noblest senators among his pupils, and had received as reward of merit a statue in the Forum of Trajan. He had remained an idolater till his old age, but was at last converted. Having read Holy Scripture, and carefully examined all the Christian books, he said in secret one day to a Christian friend of his, named Simplician, ' Know that I am a Christian.' 'I cannot believe it,' was the answer, 'till I see you at church.' Victorinus said, scornfully, ' Do **walls** make one a Christian ? ' They held similar conversations from time to time, as Victorinus feared giving offence to certain influential friends of his among the idolaters. At length, strengthened by reading, he began to fear lest Jesus Christ should deny him before the holy angels if he dared not confess Him before men; so he sought Simplician at a time when he least expected him, and said, 'Let us go to church, for I wish to become a Christian.' Simplician, in a transport of joy, brought him there; he was admitted as catechumen, and shortly after, to the great surprise of Rome, and disgust of the pagans, gave in his name for baptism. When the time for his profession, made at Rome from an elevated place, so as to be in sight of all the faithful, approached, the priests offered to receive it privately, as was the case

with some whom shame otherwise might overcome; but he preferred pronouncing it in public. When he rose to recite the Creed, as everyone knew him, a general murmur went round, every one saying, in accents of joy to his neighbour, Victorinus ! Victorinus ! Then as the desire of hearing it from his lips caused an intense silence, he pronounced the symbol in a firm tone, each of the congregation following him from the heart with joy and love."

Thus the School entered the Church, but did the Church receive it with open doors, or did a new difficulty arise to prevent literature from reconciling itself to a system so foreign to its spirit? It would seem, at first sight, that Christianity ought not to give help to the alliance of learning and faith, for the latter presents itself as a dominant principle, ready to crush human science. Such is the language of St. Paul, glorying in the fact of Christianity being reputed as folly by the Greeks, delighting that in its turn it had confounded the haughty wisdom of antiquity; happy in its having few sages of its own, but rather choosing the ignorant and the insignificant to confute by their aid the learned and the influential. The apostle rightly charges them to join the battle, with no speeches learned in the schools of eloquence and philosophy, but tells them, with Cicero, that though philosophy is the ornament of human minds, no rule of life must be sought for in it, but rather on the stronger and surer ground of ancient custom, *mos majorum;* for every error has in its turn been brought forth by philosophy. We think the Apostle right at the sight of philosophy bringing Gnosticism into Christianity, reducing it to a mere mythology, in opposing to each other two eternal worlds of matter and spirit, renewing all the errors of Pantheism and Oriental Dualism. Philosophy held a fragment, but not the whole of Truth. Christianity also taught that the Word was the Light which lightened every man who came into the world, and that the reason which had so divine an origin could not be trampled underfoot. So St. Paul did not fail to add that the philosophy of old had known God, that His works, manifested to man, had sufficed to show him his Creator, and that the crime of its experts had consisted not in ignoring, but in hiding the truth, in keeping it from sight, lest they should suffer the fate of Anaxagoras and Socrates; of having abandoned by their cowardly retreat the truth they were bound to serve. Hence flowed the two principles maintained by St. Paul, and by Christianity after him, the insufficiency of reason and its power, the danger and the usefulness of literature—principles which were one in essence, but which had separated and formed the guiding influences of two different schools.

However, the agreement wished for by the Apostle seemed to have been understood. The East, enlightened by the luminaries of Alexandria, Greece enchanted by the eloquence with which Athens was still resounding, those speculative races occupied with the beautiful and the true, could not suffer the heritage of so many masterpieces, and of the instruction which they had received from their ancestors, to be snatched from them. Early were combined efforts made to bring together in a lasting peace the two rivals, faith and knowledge; and this was the motive for the foundation of the catechetical school of Alexandria, which could trace its origin almost to apostolic times, of which one of the first known masters was St. Pantaenus, in the second century. At the same time great schools of theology rose at Antioch, Caesarea, Nisibis, and Edessa, the work of which was to throw on the darkness of ancient philosophy the rays of Christianity, and reciprocally to illustrate the mysteries of the faith by all the legitimate light of human reason. Of this great scheme, St. Clement of Alexandria gives us an example in his three works, "An Exhortation to the Greeks," " The Pedagogue," and " The Stromata." It is impossible here to examine these admirable treatises in detail, or do more than sketch their principal thoughts. The saint wished that philosophy and profane science should become like Hagar to Sara, a handmaid to the Faith, but that the servant should be treated as a sister, and thus expresses it:—" No, philosophy does no harm to the Christian life; those have slandered it who represented it a treacherous and immoral attendant, for it is a light, an image of the Truth, a gift from God to the Greeks, which, far from seducing us from the Faith by an empty fame, gives it another bulwark, and becomes its sister science, affording it a further demonstration. For it was the schoolmaster of the Greeks, as the Law was of the Hebrews, both being means to bring them unto Christ."

The method of St. Clement was also that of Origen, whose efforts tended to compare and balance the philosophical doctrines of his time, to bring out, not their contradictions, but their harmony, as fundamental verities on which the edifice of the faith might rest. And so also taught Gregory of Synesius, Nemesius, and all those Orientals who were still held spell-bound by the Platonic doctrine.

But it is in the works of St. Basil in particular, the friend of St. Gregory of Nazianzum, the rival of Julian, the pupil of the school of Athens, when it was just newly lighted by Christianity, that the true and wholesome doctrines on the share of the Church in the profane legacy of antiquity were to be found; he improvised, and afterwards committed to writing, for the benefit of the schools, that homily on the right use of the pagan authors, which, beginning by establishing the necessity of subordinating everything to a future life, recognizes promptly that the future itself can gain lustre from the literature which adorns the present; for, as he says in his beautiful language, which in its comparisons well recalls that of Plato: "As dyers dispose by certain preparations the tissue which is destined for the dye, and then steep it in the purple, so, in order that the idea of good may be traced ineffaceably in our souls, we shall first initiate them in the outer knowledge, and then will listen to the hallowed teaching of the mysteries; and as the real property of trees is to bear fruit in their season, and yet they clothe themselves with flowers and green branches, so the holy truth is the fruit of the soul, and yet there is some grace in clothing it with a different wisdom, like the foliage which covers the fruit, and lends it the charm of its verdure." He then applies these maxims in considering how much of the old learning could be received, and how much must be cast away, as with the poets the pictures of vice and of the nature of the false gods, the voluptuous sentiments which too often formed the essence of the work, the fierce Paganism which knew neither sister nor mother, nor any loving influence; at the same time separating and prizing whatever might tend to virtue in them. Homer was, according to him, to he looked upon less as the narrator of the fabulous loves of the gods, than as the learned oracle who covered in allegoric form the wisest doctrines of antiquity, and showed, under Ulysses, the symbol of worth; for what could be grander than the idea of that man arriving naked on the Phaesacian shore, but enveloped as in a cloak by his courage, virtue, and wisdom, so that the young princess, daughter of Alcinous, could not look upon him without respect; then appearing in their popular assembly to confound it by his heroic aspect, all battered, as it was, by battle and shipwreck, so that no Phaesacian among them all but longed to be Ulysses, even in his piteous plight ? Thus it pleased the Christian bishop to dive into the most mysterious depths of Homer's thought, to show the sweetness which it contained, and to run through the other poets of old time—Hesiod, Theognis, Euripides, Plato— to repeat whatever he found therein that could elevate the human mind. He had no wish to deny the good in pagan virtues, for he did not fear them, and cited boldly and joyfully the examples of such as Aristides and Themistocles, for he knew well that Christianity need not fear the comparison.

In this way the Greek Church accepted in part the literature of old, as both a preparation for Christianity, and as its proof ; as a preparation, because philosophy had acted as schoolmaster to the heathen world, and it was fit, according to St. Basil, to steep in the science of antiquity the young souls that aspired to become Christian, that they might then be imbued with the principle of the Faith, as a means of proof, because Faith, its mistress, would act herself upon the intellect which sought the light that it had perceived afar off in the bosom of the Almighty. And the schools and their science came forward to lend their aid to religion, and surround with a new and ever-enlarging light the elements of Christianity. And so the alliance was completed. It has been thought that Clement of Alexandria did but enslave philosophy, and that the chart of the human mind remained torn until the day when Luther brought it anew out of the convents of Germany—a strange error, for at the very hour when Faith seemed to bind philosophy in her fetters, she is seen, if closely watched, to deliver it from the tyranny of the schools, and their masters from that word *αυτός εφη, ipse dixit,* the last argument of antiquity, which had been repeated from one generation to another without any making the necessary effort to break its yoke. The eclectism which Alexandria named, but never grasped, is found in the writings of the Fathers. Truth must be sought not in one school, but in all; Aristotle and Plato must be weighed in an even balance. The eye must be turned from the fascinating page of error; and the mind, absolute master of what lies within human scope, acknowledge an authority in things divine.

And whilst faith freed the human mind from its old tyrants, it snapped also the old bonds of everlasting doubt, which lay at the bottom of those schools that were forever beginning anew their search after God and the soul, which they never found. It was the glory of Christianity to have bidden the quest to cease; it gave itself to the world, rather than the world to it, and, forbidding the light to be longer withheld, said to it, " Christ is here, go no further in pursuit of Him." By taking from man uncertainty, the Church gave him liberty, and broke the chain which was hindering him from carrying his investigations with ambitious ardour to the extreme limits of the finite and the infinite.

But side by side with this school, which was to last fourteen centuries, another, less in number and in influence, but of equal vitality, was forming itself. Struck with the danger, it found it easier to fell literature than to prune it; finding philosophy dangerous, and rightly in the hands of the Gnostics, the Epicureans, and the Stoics, it declared it impotent, and sought to bring man to faith through despair of reason. It resolved to disgust men with it by proving it incapable of anything, and by bringing forward as a proof of this its perpetual contradictions. This work was undertaken by the whole line of apologists, beginning among the Greeks with Hermias, but was taken up especially among the Latins, whose spirit had always been practical rather than speculative, to whom literature had always been somewhat an exotic, and whom Cicero had found so wedded to the business of life, that he had been forced to apologize for his philosophical labours, and to evince, or at least to feign, a profound contempt for Greek subtlety. In the train of Hermias, who undertook to prove the contradictions of the various schools of philosophy, followed Tertullian, Arnobius, and Lactantius, eager to repel all possibility of accord between religion and letters, and disclaim the services of Dialectic itself. Tertullian contemptuously pitied Aristotle as architect of the art of construction and destruction, of that logic of thorny argument which was a mere nest of eternal controversy, and source of division among men; which returned upon every question ceaselessly as if discontented at having settled it. He was indignant at the efforts of some of his contemporaries to bring about an union between philosophy and the Faith. " What is there in common," he exclaimed, "between Athens and Jerusalem; between the Academy and the Church; between Heretics and Christians ? Our doctrine comes from the Porch, but the Porch of Solomon, and teaches us to seek God with a simple heart. Let those who wish to give us a Stoic, or Platonic, or logical Christianity come to terms with it, for we have no want of science with Christ, nor of study with the Gospel, and when we believe we search no more."

This proud, self-confident language points to the fall into error, its fitting punishment, which we soon perceive in its authors. Lactantius reproduced the same views up to a certain point, when he finally modified them in assigning to philosophy a subordinate place in his scheme. It was not only a small number of Christian orators of the third, fourth, or fifth century who spoke thus; they had disciples and imitators in all subsequent ages; in the Middle Age, among the schools of Mysticism, some of which were destined to go to the last extremity of opposition to human reason; in the seventeenth century, in the person of Huet, who devoted his labours to the establishment of a kind of universal scepticism; and in the person of the great Pascal himself. The school has even its disciples among ourselves. It has never closed its doors, its adopted thesis has never lacked supporters, for some have ever been found ready to throw the gauntlet down to reason, and to attempt, by the production of an artificial Pyrrhonism—a system of organized doubt—to overturn the labours of the human mind, and to give faith a freer and wider sphere.

Against these men are ranged the general tradition of the Church, the great and glorious names of Christendom, and especially their own errors. Their excesses were not without peril in the midst of that doctrine which abhorred extremes, and was ever characterized by wisdom and moderation. The eagerness to burn what had been once adored, without distinguishing the precious metal 'from the idol—perhaps an excusable exaggeration in newly-made Christians—became more perilous in the reasonings and dogmatizings of these doctors, as showing a want of faith, or at least a faith which trembled before reason and the ancient literature, as if the Church had anything to dread in philosophy, or her faith was destined to pale like a torch of night before the light of day.

And this weakness betrayed itself by remarkable lapses. Tertullian gave up science forever to follow in the train of the heretic Montanus and the two women who believed in him. The Mystics of the Middle Age were travellers on the road which led to the heretical excesses of the fifteenth century, and Pascal himself followed one of the tracks of error. We must remember that, however stubborn their doctrine might be, it never had the character of authority or general prevalence, and its most illustrious follower of our day has finally abjured it, and redeemed the rashness of trampling reason under foot by his pregnant saying, that "Plato wrote a human preface to the Gospel."

But the union of science and the faith, of religion and literature, was no easy question, presented as it was in the fifth century with a host of partisans on either side, with the East in its favour and the West in opposition; and its solution was entirely doubtful until the West decided it in the person of her two great doctors, St. Jerome and St. Augustine. Up to this time, whilst the masters of the West had abjured their literary heritage, those of the Greek Church had inclined to avail themselves of their right. The hesitation of St. Jerome was natural before the formidable duty of deciding under the eyes of the whole Church, bent upon the question in anxious attention. Moreover, he was imbued with his readings of grammarians, rhetoricians, and philosophers, though burning with faith. Plato had been his meditation, the declamation of oratorical controversies after the school-methods his exercise. When the Spirit of God came upon him he fled into the desert, but having carried his library with him, he read Cicero as he fasted, and devoured Plautus whilst he bewailed his sins. He came to himself and took up the sacred writings, to be disgusted at their unpolished style. Towards the middle of one Lent he fell dangerously ill, and was transported in a dream to the foot of the throne of Jesus Christ. "

Who art thou ?" asked the Saviour. "I am a Christian," answered St. Jerome. " No," replied Christ, " you are not. Christian, but Ciceronian." Confounded by the reproach, the Saint promised, with many tears, to abandon forever his profane studies.

It was a grave engagement, and he seemed to contract it anew in a letter written soon afterwards to Eustochius. About the same time he sent to Pope Damasus an elaborate commentary on the parable of the prodigal son, in which he denounced the priests and bishops who knew Virgil by heart, who used to recite bucolic poems and love-songs, and occupied their leisure in declaiming entire tragedies. " For all," said he, " these muses of poets, this eloquence of orators, wisdom of philosophers, are but daemons' delights; truth doubtless may be found in them, but it must be sought with prudence, that the faithful may not be scandalized." These harsh maxims, however, were written in the years 383, 384, in the first fervour of conversion; the Saint was accusing himself, his hard blows were brought from the depths of his remorse to punish his own faults, but wisdom and good counsel came to him from the solitude of his desert retreat, to change his tone. He continued his writing, Virgil still filled the fourth part of his correspondence, Plato and all the ancients threw over it their eloquence in turn, for his fine intellect could not separate itself from the influence of the old literature, which overflowed his mind and escaped inevitably into his writings. Some were scandalized at this, and Magnus, a rhetorician of Rome, who was somewhat jealous of Jerome, reproached him with having filled his works with pagan memories, of having profanely stained the whiteness of the Church's robe, and of being unable to write a page or a letter to a woman without allusion to those whom he called our Cicero, our Horace, and our Virgil. But St. Jerome retorted, " that his critic could never have applied such a reproach to him had he known the sacredness of antiquity.

St. Paul, pleading the cause of Christ before the Areopagus, had not scrupled to use the inscription on a pagan altar in defence of the faith, and to invoke as a witness the poet Aratus. The austerity of his doctrine did not hinder the Apostle from citing Epimenides in his Epistle to Titus, and a verse from Menander in another place. It was because he had read in Deuteronomy the Lord's permission to the Israelites to purify their captives, and then take them to wife. What wonder, then, that I, struck by the science of the age in the beauty of its features, and the grace of its discourses, should wish to transform it from the slave it is now into an Israelite."

And St. Jerome was so regardless of his dream, and the promise given never again to open profane books, that he made his monks copy the " Dialogues of Cicero," and carried a copy of Plato with him on a journey to Jerusalem, so as to lose no time on the road. He taught grammar at Bethlehem, and expounded Virgil, the lyric and comic poets, and historians to children confided to him for training in the fear of God, and did not hesitate to plead that it had been but a dream, to the accusations of Rufinus. "Rufinus," he said, "has accused me of the promise I made in a dream, and has brought proofs of my perjury from my writings. But who can forget the days of his infancy ? My head is bald twice over, and yet in sleep I think I see myself young again, with long hair and well-draped toga, declaiming before the rhetorician. Must I drink the water of Lethe? I should give this answer, if there was any question of an engagement undertaken in the fulness of my wakeful senses. But I send him who reproaches me with a dream to those prophets who teach that dreams are vain and deserve no faith." It is a grave and remarkable fact that St. Jerome wrote this between **a.d.** 397 and **a.d.** 402, when old and full of experience of life; when he had played his part and taken his side advisedly in the great questions in debate around him; when he had gained a greater wisdom, and freed from the excesses of his youth had learnt in the moral order to pardon much to human wills, and to be tolerant of the intellect of mankind.

What was the doctrine of St. Augustine on the subject, the result of the mental labour of which that great soul gave us the sight, and by which, in greater measure than St. Jerome, he was to decide the vexed question of the whole of Christian antiquity '? We need not speak of his early passion for ancient literature, the tears which Dido's fate caused him, or the ardour with which he devoured the " Hortensius " of Cicero, and later, the works of the Neoplatonists, but stop at the period when, upon his conversion, he abjured all his errors, and follow him into his retreat at Cassiciacum, where he passed many months of peace with his friends Trygetius and Licentius, devoting the mornings to discussion of grave questions of philosophy, commenting on Cicero, and reading every day the half of one of Virgil's cantos. He was in no haste to abjure all that he had once admired, and ignored the declamations of Tertullian, Arnobius, Lactantius, and all those other men whom the Church has never counted in the number of her saints. In the " Confessions," that deep outpouring of a devout soul, he recalls the time when the Neo-platonic books first fell into his hands: " Thou didst send me, Lord, several works of the Platonists, translated into Greek and Latin, and in them I read, though in other terms, that in the beginning was the Word, and the Word was in God, and the Word was God, and that It was the true light which enlightened every man that came into this world. But that He came to His own, and that they received Him not, and that to those who did receive Him He gave power to be made children of God, that the Word was made Flesh, and dwelt among us, I read not in those books;. . . that He existed before time, beyond time, in an immutable eternity, that to be happy, souls must partake of His fulness, I found indeed in the writings of those Platonists; but I did not find that He died in time for the wicked. Thou hast hidden these things from the wise, my God, and hast revealed them to babes, that all who suffer and are heavy laden may come to Him for comfort."

This was the measure and the secret of the question which for so many centuries has tormented the world. Philosophy was not without power to lead men to the feet of God, but Beason could not bring the human mind to comprehend the God-man, or the charity and mystery of His infinite love. St. Augustine was continually repeating this in the Church at his first conversion, when writing his "Confessions," and when he had become the great doctor of the Western Church.

He spoke with respect of the Platonists on every page of his " City of God," and finished it with this fine saying : " I could have pardoned the pagans if, instead of raising a temple to Cybele, they had reared a shrine to Plato wherein his hooks should he read."

The door, thus opened to Philosophy, could not he closed to the rest of human learning; and thus, iu his work " On Order," in tracing the plan of Christian education, St. Augustine followed the changeless law of God, written by Him on the hearts of the wise, and divided it into two parts, discipline of life, and discipline of knowledge; the first proceeding from a principle of authority, the second from that of reason.

"Reason is an effort of the soul, capable of bringing man to a knowledge of himself, and even of God, were he not arrested by the preoccupation of the senses. It seeks intercourse with men in whom reciprocally it resides, from whence springs Literature, and *Grammar,* which embraces whatever the former hands down through the memory of man, and is in consequence history. Reason then bending to its work, and taking account of the definitions, rules, and divisions produced, forms *Dialectic* ; and to it, as it is not in itself sufficient for persuasion, adds *Rhetoric.* Having compassed man, it goes in search of God, or of steps by which to reach Him; and thence comes the idea of Beauty, which, grasped by hearing, sound, rhythm, and number, forms *Music,* and by sight, symbol, dimensions, and numbers becomes, again, *Geometry* and *Astronomy.* But what is seen by the eye is incomparable to the harmony discovered to the Soul. In this course of study everything is reduced to number, of which the shadow rather than the reality is perceived; and thereupon Reason takes courage, and begins to suspect that a number must exist of capacity to measure all the rest. From its efforts in this direction Philosophy is born, and with it the two questions of the Soul and God, our nature and our origin, one rendering us worthy of happiness, the other giving bliss itself." Such was his order of study, a system of wisdom by which the soul was to be rendered worthy of knowing the sovereign order of things, of distinguishing the two worlds, and rising in thought to the Father of the Universe.

Moreover, it is remarkable that this scheme was nearly the same as that of the ancients, but renewed and regenerated by the loftier spirit of Christianity. It contained their entire encyclopaedia of the seven arts, modified by the conjunction of arithmetic with geometry, and giving to philosophy, which in the system of Martianus Capella had been confounded with dialectic, a distinct place. But it was far grander in conception, regarding the sciences, as it did, as so many steps fitted to lead mankind from the earth it dwelt on to the presence of its Supreme Governor. St. Augustine did not shrink from the objections hurled at his method, that it degraded the sacred science which man could gather from faith alone, and replied, with conscious superiority, that God could have used the ministry of angels, but He willed to. honour humanity in giving forth His oracles in a human temple, and charity itself would perish if man had nothing to learn from man, if one soul could not pour its overflowings into others.

" If those, then, who are called philosophers, and especially Platonists, hold doctrines which are true and in agreement with the faith, not only must not their tenets be held in suspicion, but must be reclaimed from their wrongful possessors. For as the Ægyptians had not only idols which the people of Israel were bound to fly from and loathe, but vases and ornaments of gold and silver and garments "which they carried with them in their flight, so the Gentile science is not entirely composed of superstitious fictions which the Christian must abhor, but contains liberal arts, serviceable to the truth, wise moral precepts not created by them, but drawn like so much gold and silver from the mines of Providence, which are dispersed over the world; and these the Christian may carry away when he has purged them from their surrounding dross."

Thus the question was solved, and the dispute closed for many centuries. On the word of St. Augustine, and upon the same motives, following ages accepted their inheritance from antiquity; but the Church held it as a wise trustee receives the property of minors, with a privilege of inventory. The same reason determined Cassiodorus, Bede, Alcuin, who all, by a phenomenon of the intellect which it is well to mark, actuated rather by comparisons than by reasons, by images rather than great motives, repeated the metaphor that Christendom was bound to act like the children of Israel on coming out of Egypt, and to carry off the gold and silver vessels of their enemies. With this saying the science, art, and tradition of antiquity passed into the Middle Age, the great problem was solved, and the literary and intellectual knot was formed which bound the two periods into one.

It remains to show how Virgil, deified by pagan science, raised to the rank of Pontiff, Flamen, and inheritor of the priestly tradition, became also the representative of the religion of the future, the barbarous ages having, in order to save him, thrown over his body the end of the prophet's robe. Thanks to his " Fourth Eclogue," the Christian world regarded him as a foreteller of the new religion; and this interpretation, first given by Eusebius in the fourth century, continued through the mediaeval time, placed him among the prophets, and afforded to his works an increase of respect. A tradition relates how St. Paul, the fierce contemner of the profane sciences, on his arrival at Naples, went to visit the tomb of Virgil, and having opened the "Eclogues," and read the Fourth, burst into tears; and the memory of this was preserved in a sequence chanted long in the Cathedral of Mantua, which recalled the legend in the following graceful lines:—

Ad Maronis mausoleum

Ductus, fudit super cum

Piae rorem lacrymae:

Quern te, inquit, reddedissem,

Si te vivum invenissim,

Poetarum maxime.

Popular tradition was also desirous of adding to this more ancient legend, and for long the shepherd who guided travellers to the poet's tomb used to show a little chapel near to it in which he said Virgil heard mass.

Thus the pagan civilization did not perish entirely, or deserve to do so. One portion of it was preserved by the Church, another remained in spite of her. So great was the necessity for the culture which we have seen, although stricken by a mortal malady, continued for the education of races yet to come. We might easily believe in the fitness of its dissolution, in order that Christianity alone might hold the ground. But no. Christianity itself gathered up all that was lofty, equitable, generous, and beneficent in the old order, and at the same time, and in spite of her efforts, mythology was perpetuated in literature, though proscribed by the Church; in religion itself a superstitious element appeared, and gave the hand to the defunct Paganism of old, and in the order of law there remained an odious system of taxation, which kept alive political oppression, divorce which brought domestic tyranny in its train, and the confusion between the power of the priesthood and of the Empire which went far towards engendering the bloody struggles of the Middle Age.

The Church, then, preserved the ancient literature, which also in spite of her kept alive, amidst a mythological Pantheism all the voluptuous and carnal feelings which were to reappear in full fury in moments of disorder and intellectual anarchy. Antiquity gave, in a word, its vices as well as its enlightenment to the dark ages, and, when tempted to accuse our ancestors and reproach them with their barbarism, we may well recognize in them the heirs of the refinements of the Decline; for there is a singular analogy between the vices of an used-up society and those of a savage state, and a moment comes in which the impotence of the aged is brought near to the weakness of babes, and we know not whether we are treating of a people which is perishing, or of one rising into life.

It has been wished to separate arbitrarily antiquity from modern times, by assuming a kind of abyss at the year 476, and saying, Here is modern history to the right, to the left antiquity, and the two have nothing in common; but God, who is stronger than the chroniclers, suffers no such break, for He sets order and unity everywhere, in time as in space, and makes even the disordered passions of man the bond-slaves of His design. The times which we divide so arbitrarily are bound by two ties, the golden chain of weal, wrought by God Himself, and the iron chain of evil, which He tolerates; and history has no other end but to weld together all these links, and thus establish that dogma of continuity, so fundamental in Christianity, to which human society is aspiring. This task is assigned to us, for we are not as independent as we would think, but are bound to our forefathers by our responsibility for their sins, no less than by our gratitude for their benefits.

*

THEOLOGY.

In the pagan civilization of the fifth century we have seen the works whereupon antiquity had expended her light and her strength. The human mind could go no farther than that mighty labour of the Alexandrian philosophy towards attaining to truth, or than the admirable perseverance of the Roman Law in establishing the reign of justice. We have not hidden the grandeur and merit of these efforts, and as mere admiration profits but little, have followed their effects down into Christian ages, and have seen the institutions, knowledge, literature, and even the industry of the old world entering, so to speak, into the construction of modern society to be the teaching principle for those barbarians who had encamped on its ruins. There is assuredly no spectacle in which the power of human reason breaks forth more, and none in which it more plainly manifests its insufficiency. For all that pagan civilization, to the preservation of which Greek genius and Roman common sense had been alike devoted, perished without hope; and while the statues of Aristotle and Plato before the schools did not hinder their successors from giving themselves up to all the aberrations of theurgy and superstition, the wisdom of Paulus, Gaius, Ulpian, or Papinian had not closed the doors of the Empire against the vices of the Decline. In that learned and polished society we have seen fetichism reduced to a dogma, philosophers believing in a constant presence of the deities in their idols, religious prostitution, and human sacrifice; in the political order, gladiators, eunuchs crowding the imperial seraglios, and slavery, profound excesses which Christianity was bound to dissipate; literature itself degraded, reduced to be a domestic pleasure for some few favourites, or at the service of a corrupted aristocracy. Moreover, Alaric was at the gates of

Rome, afar off too was heard the tramp of the horses of the Vandals, Huns, and Alani, who were rising in masses round their chief, and were about to bring Attila to the foot of the Alps.

So it would have perished, had it not been for the new principle of Faith which came to penetrate and regenerate it. Reason is powerful, no doubt, and is always present in man, for there has never been an age so unfortunate as not to give some sign of its presence and influence; but it is bound within us—held in inactive captivity till awoke by the Word from without, which calls it from its repose; then it becomes conscious of and holds intercourse with itself; and that it may fully realize its own existence and its faculties, using the same language which has come to its ear from without, becomes self-regarding, and names itself in saying, "I think, therefore I exist."

Therefore, as the Word which provokes the reason comes from something external to the reason, it comes as an authority and impulse, an invading force from without, and as a forerunner of some other reasonable existence, which draws it to itself by an irresistible influence. The soul, when addressed, is bound to respond, and as the first effort of persuasion is to provoke the adhesion of our intellects, to draw them into the path of that other intelligence which approaches them, so is that adhesion to the spoken word, called in the order of nature human faith, to which divine and supernatural faith are correspondent in the order of theology.

Thus Reason and Faith are two primitive principles, distinct from but not hostile to one another, for neither can dispense with the other, reason being aroused only by the persuasion which provokes its energy, and faith only yielding itself when the object proposed is reasonable. These principles were brought into the world by Christianity, which gave to reason a perpetual honour and sanctification in recognizing in it the Word which enlightened every man that came into the world, and having thus surrounded it with a divine glory, and acknowledged in it a ray from the Almighty Himself, could never again trample it under foot. But it established also the necessity of an exterior word to provoke responsive action, which was expressed in a series of revelations, the first of which was to be traced to the world's commencement, and having given mankind its elementary education, was renewed through Moses, and, lastly, sanctified, extended, and fixed forever in the Gospel dispensation. And so Christianity realized, in a diviner form, and proclaimed, with a deeper truth, what had been always a necessity to society, and had ever existed in the depths of human nature—the perpetual agreement of reason and faith—and raised, at the same time, reason and nature above themselves.

And in the Christian view, this external and open word of revelation, which had kept the light of the ages alive from their commencement, had uttered two varieties of truth—the first of an order to which reason, unaided, could never attain, for religious truth is the expression of the relation between the finite and the infinite, and one of its elements, the infinite, being beyond the power and scope of human thought, it results that a portion of it is by nature inaccessible, to expound which a revelation, withdrawn from all supplement and development by the human intellect, was an imperative necessity; the second variety embraced those natural truths to which the reason of man could attain, and which Christianity attested to have been actually compassed by science, avowing, with St. Paul, that the ancients had known God, but had lacked courage to glorify Him as God; truths grasped only by a few, and still mingled with obscurities, doubts, and errors, which had cost the human race more than three thousand years of painful wandering before the genius of Plato and

Aristotle laboriously produced them, still enveloped in error and false principles, but which revelation established by a short, sure, and supremely popular method, making them no longer the monopoly of a minority, but the possession of each and of all.

Never had a stronger appeal been made to the inner power of the human soul than that addressed to it from the height of Calvary, and when that word which called for faith from the human race, *consummatum est,* went forth from the lips of Him who had come to bring it life and deliverance, the unexampled prodigy was manifested of a power of faith which no one could have pictured excited in that decaying world in which all good feeling seemed corrupted, if not extinct. A German theologian, in criticising the text of the Gospel, has declared that the marvel of it broke upon him in a vivid manner on reading the passage which relates how Christ, walking by the Lake of Genneseret and meeting some fishermen, said to them, "Follow me," and that had he been in their place he would never have done so; that he cannot comprehend the inconsequence and logical deficiency of those boatmen who abandoned their nets and fishing-boat to follow the first passer-by who promised them life eternal. That was, indeed, the prodigy, and it appears less in those two or three Galilaeans than in the numberless multitudes of the Greek, Roman, and Asiatic world who tore themselves, not from their boats and the daily labour and sweat of their brow, but from the pleasure and luxury of an existence of delight, which the ancient world understood very differently from ourselves, to throw themselves into the difficulty, privation, and sacrifice of a Christian life—a life far harder than death itself; for, though the faith of the martyrs may move us, that of those who lived in the midst of a world which no longer knew them, devoted to the hatred and execration of the whole human race, must touch us more. But that their number grew, and their energy lasted, and that the early ages passed entirely under the dominion of their faith, is attested by the writings and letters of the chief pastors of the Christian commonwealth, as St. Ignatius, St. Clement, and St. Polycarp.

But faith could not dispense with reason, for the Apostle himself had said, " Let your submission be complete, but rational." *Rationabile sit obsequium vestrum.* The moment came when it was necessary that the revealed dogmas and heaven-born principles must be arranged and defended as with a bulwark by all the lights of knowledge. The provocation came from without, and the attacks of pagan philosophy compelled the early Christians to defend themselves, to prove their doctrines by an appeal to history, philosophy, and eloquence; and this gave rise to the works of Justin, Athenagoras, Tertullian, and the many other apologists. But although those early labours imposed by polemical necessity were little, yet the combat with external enemies was to bring out the necessity of rendering an account to the disciples of the school they were forming of the dogmas they wished to defend, and so gave rise to the catechetical school of Alexandria, whose illustrious children, Pantaenus, Clement, Origen, were to be seen devoting their lives to the exposition of the Scriptures and of dogma. We have scarcely arrived at the third century, and yet Origen had not bound himself merely to the task of collating and comparing different texts, of publishing editions in some measure polyglot, in which the translations of many Jewish authors were confronted with the primitive text, but, grasping these eternal sources of verity, had developed them and drawn thence theology, not only in its first elements, but in its complete form, as we find expressed in his eulogy by St. Gregory Thaumaturgus, resulting in the unison and powerful harmony of that novel science which was moulding itself into what was to be theology.

In the first place, he taught them logic in accustoming their minds not to receive nor to reject proofs at hazard, but to examine them carefully without stopping at their surface-appearance, nor at sayings whose lustre dazzled or whose simplicity disgusted, and not to reject what at first may seem a paradox but afterwards is shown to be most true, but in a word to weigh everything healthily and without prejudice. He also applied their minds to physics,—that is, to the consideration of the power and infinite wisdom of the world's Author which are so fitted to humble us. He also taught them the mathematical sciences, especially geometry and astronomy, and lastly morality, which he did not confine to empty discourses, to definitions and barren divisions, but taught practically, making them mark in themselves the motions of passion, that the soul, seeing itself as in a mirror, might tear up its vices by the roots, and strengthen the reason which produced the virtues. To discourse he joined example, being himself a model of every virtue. And last of all he brought them to the study of theology, saying that the most necessary knowledge was that of the First Cause. He made them read whatever the ancients, whether poets or philosophers, Greeks or barbarians, had written on the subject, except when they expressly taught atheism. He made them read it all, that, knowing the strong and the weak in each opinion, he might guarantee them against prejudices. But he was their guide in the study, leading them as it were by the hand, that they might not stumble; showing them what every sect had which was useful, for he knew them all perfectly. He exhorted them not to cling to any philosophy, whatever the reputation, but to God and His prophets. And then he explained to them the Sacred Scriptures, of which he was the most learned interpreter; and in this exposition he gave them an idea of the order and gist of the whole Christian doctrine, and so raised their souls to the understanding of revealed truth."

Thus theology was already in existence, and the time which elapsed from the fourth to the end of the fifth century was its golden age. It was then that these great men appeared who were the glory and admiration of the East—St. Athanasius, St. Basil, St. Gregory Nazianzen, and St. John Chrysostom, not to be treated of here, as we have separated Oriental civilization from our task, though their writings, translated into Latin and inherited by the monasteries of the Middle Age, form part of the education of our times.

In the West these men continued the development of the new science. St. Jerome, who attached himself to fixing the sense of the sacred text by Latin translations of the Bible, and so commenced true exegesis; St. Ambrose, who founded moral theology; and St. Augustine, who undertook dogmatic theology. Time would fail to give the history of these great men in a work confined to that of ideas. We must rather see, within our narrow limits of the theological history of the fifth century, at the price of what struggles and by what genius Christianity succeeded in keeping its ground in spite of the heresies which threatened it, on the one hand, with sinking into a mere mythology (a new form of Paganism), on the other, with the danger of becoming pure rationalism, but one more philosophic system to add to history. The weighty subject for our present attention is to find how amid perils so various Christianity was enabled to remain as it was, a verity revealed but reasonable, full of mystery in that it touched the infinite, but at the same time intelligible to the human mind.

Paganism had hurled two menaces against the nascent faith, persecution and the Alexandrian schools. These two dangers, which first engage the Christian historian's attention, were, however, insignificant. The former multiplied believers, and the apologies of the latter failed to replenish the deserted fold of heathenism. But at the moment in which the old religion, conquered in every field, powerless to defend itself, seemed in its agony, it was on the point of revival, or at least of dragging its opponents after it, by conforming to Christianity. However exorbitant such an expression may seem, it is no vain utterance of words, but an historical reality. For the epoch in which our work is placed was that of a general syncretism, in which every doctrine, every error, and some few truths were struggling to bind themselves into a single and comprehensive system. So true is this that the Roman world, so long enclosed in its pride, which had cast such scorn on its vanquished peoples, had gone to seek on its knees, one after another, all the gods of the Orient to enshrine them in its temples. We have seen Cybele arriving from Phrygia, Osiris and Serapis from Egypt, Mithra from Persia; and when Heliogabalus, that madman whose frenzy proceeded from a deeper source than has been supposed, who was possessed by idolatry as by a daemon, that young priest of the Syrian god Heliogabalus, or the Sun, was transplanted suddenly to the throne of the Caesars, and wished to celebrate his own bridal with the Roman Empire, he ordered three beds to be prepared in the Temple of Minerva, and the image of the Sun, the divinity of Asia, that of Astarte, the African Venus, and of Pallas, the deity of Europe and of the "West, to be laid upon them together. In the marriage which he desired to solemnize between the gods of the three quarters of the world, Heliogabalus did but express, with singular force, the spirit which was tormenting his age—the necessity for Paganism to gather up all its forces to resist an enemy which it had tried in vain to stifle by punishment, and must now attempt to conquer by a novel method. And if this tendency was thus manifest at Rome, what must it have been at Alexandria?—that city, along whose streets, of two leagues in length, amidst colonnades of rich workmanship raised by the Ptolemies, thronged Romans, Greeks, Ægyptians, and all the navigators who came from the East, traversed the Red Sea, and descended the Nile to this emporium of the world. Here reigned all the doctrines of Greek philosophy, regenerated by the sages of the Museum, by Callimachus, Lycophron, and the rest who had sought out the origin of those fables which men had but weakened by adornment. Those memories of Chaldaea and of Persia, those traditions of Zoroaster and the naturally nearer traditions of ancient Egypt, that multitude of philosophies and apocryphal predictions which filled the first ages of the Alexandrine science, witnessed to the effort made to lay hold again on the ancient sacerdotal traditions, in order to revive that hieratic science which was half extinct.

Whilst all these doctrines were approaching each other, a great movement Avas at work behind them, which perhaps explains this sort of revival in the first Christian ages; for the time had arrived for a new form of heathenism to seize upon Eastern Asia. The sect of Bhuddha, born about five centuries and a half before our era, for long firmly enclosed within the limits of Hindostan, and in the bands of a philosophic school, had taken flight with its brilliant mythology, at once popular and learned, and capable of fascinating and subduing the minds and imaginations of entire nations. Having burst over the borders of the country to which it had once been confined, Bhuddhism at the year 61 **b.c.** made a new appearance on the scene, and invaded all Northern Asia, so as to extend from the sea of Japan to the coasts of the Caspian, filling all the intervening countries and rekindling the religious zeal of their countless populations. This great movement evidently could not but influence the pagan development of the West, and was destined to stir nations who remained at a certain point strangers to it. As it was in the East and among the Tartar tribes that the agitation began which, spreading from man to man, was to end in throwing the Huns, Alani, and Goths upon the Bhine banks, and even beyond the Pyrenees, so an Orientalized Paganism put forth its last effort to penetrate the faith of Christendom.

It effected its entrance through the Gnostic sects. The Gnosis was the designation of a higher science or initiation reserved for a handful of chosen spirits. It was one of the chief characteristics of Paganism to divide the human race, to refuse recognition to its primitive equality, to make certain classes to spring from the head of the Deity, others from the stomach, legs, or feet, and to measure out enlightenment, like justice, with a grudging, unequal, and jealous hand. The Gnosis possessed the other pagan principle of confounding creation with the creature, and by whatever means it tried to explain the commencement of things ultimately to unite them in one substance. It represented God as a *pleroma*, a plenitude of existence which overflowed, a vessel surcharged, which let its superabundance drip over in a multitude of emanations, firstly in the form of *Mons*, semi-divine essences which descended in steps of successive existences to the lowest ranks of creation. These divine outpourings, which had as it were a perpetual migration to accomplish, had names, were divided into gods and goddesses, and became in consequence mythological personifications; so that the Gnosis tells at length of the adventures of *Sophia*, the divine wisdom, one of the first emanations of God, which, wandering on the brink of chaos, fell into the abyss, and could only escape by the intervention of Christ. She then was to be manifested in a female devotee, who was shown as the destined propagator of the Gnostic doctrine; and accordingly Simon Magus led about with him a woman called Helen, as the incarnate soul of the world. The pagan influence breaks out again in these poetical adventures lent to the divine emanations, but especially in the eternity of matter, a principle common to every scheme of Gnostic doctrine, which thus seated a resisting power by the side of the Divine Power, an evil face to face with a good principle, assigned two causes instead of one, and sowed the seeds of dualism by its own pantheism. Such is an abridgment of the doctrine of Valentinus, one of the first Gnostics, as developed by

Basilides and corrected by Carpocrates and Marcion. Its sects multiplied and brought about their division, and thence their ruin.

Like all false doctrines, it perished by that propagation which is the salvation of truth, but by which errors disappear in their variations.

At the end of three centuries, when the sects who sought to bring Paganism into Christianity seemed near their end, their errors were reunited and strengthened in the new doctrine of the Manichaeans. Manes was a Persian by origin, and two distinct but reconcilable traditions as to his life, and the circumstances under which his system was founded, have come down to us. One relates that he was born in Persia, and in the course of long travels in Hindostan, Turkistan, and China, encountered Buddhism in its rise, or at least in the ardour of its first propagandism. The other tells how the true author of the system was not Manes, but a certain Scythianus, who had a disciple named Terebinthus, or Buddha, the latter having a slave called Manes, who received from the widow of Buddha his liberty, and doubtless his doctrine also. Both accounts agree in assigning to Manes a birthplace in Persia, a long period of travel, and the work of uniting the belief of his own country with the Oriental dualism, and the other dogmas which the disciples of Buddha had circulated through the East.

It is not astonishing, then, that this heresy, presenting as it did some features of the Oriental mythology, was not wanting in a certain grandeur. It admitted two Principles—the one, God, or Spirit; the other, Satan, or Matter; the former dwelling with His Æons, or primitive emanations, in the immeasurable world of light; the latter in the sphere of darkness, equally eternal, but limited by the realms of light, over which it cast its shadow, as a cone of obscurity veils in part the face of a star. The powers of darkness, beholding the splendour of the Deity, undertook the conquest of those fields of light of whose beauty they were enamoured. Thereupon God, the author of Good, sent forth as a guardian of the frontiers of His kingdom a new emanation, the Soul of the World. Planted between the limits of the light and the darkness, it fell to pieces before the inevitable assault of the powers of the latter.t Then God sent His Spirit in aid of the World-Soul given over to the fury of the shadowy forces. It came and took from its shattered fragments each of the members of primitive man, and therewith made the world. It chose the brightest and most spiritual constituent to create therefrom the sun, the moon, and the stars; from its aerial but more material parts it made the atmosphere and the purer existences; from its entirely material elements the animal and sensible portions of this world. But the latter was under the empire of those dark powers to whom Matter appertained, and so the World-Soul, dispersed everywhere, existing in every atom of the visible world, was held in a sort of captivity. The divine essence spread through it had to struggle against its shackles with a long effort for deliverance, and this, alike of heavenly origin, and a suffering prisoner, was no other than *Jesus patibilis,* whose conflicts formed the true and only Passion endured by the Word which went forth from God.

Moreover, the soul of the primitive man, which resided in the sun and moon which it had helped to create, had become a power which had taken the name of Christ, who, according to the Manichaeans, dwelt in the heavens—now in the sun, now in the moon—but seeking from the former to attract to Himself the spiritual particles which were wandering through matter. He had become incarnate in a human body, but which was unreal, and had vanished at the moment in which the Jews stretched it on the Cross. Thus, therefore, He had not come into the world to shed the blood which He did not possess, but to infuse into it a truth which would raise the divinely emanated souls of men to the light, and bring them to Him. There were three categories of souls. The *pneumatic*, or most perfect souls were able to discard the flesh and purify themselves in the Sun. The *psychical* souls were passionate and weak, but not evil; their struggle, though real, could not affect their triumph, and they were forced to pass through another existence in another body. The *hylic* souls were entirely material, daemon-possessed, and reprobate, without any hope of future immortality. Those who between these two extremes were struggling to return to God had to traverse, according to the dogma of Metempsychosis, a fresh series of existences in other men, or beasts, and even plants, before their return to Him. Such, according to the Manichaean conception, was the law of the Universe; its end being to reunite all the dispersed particles of the divine power, and bring them back to their source; for the soul that, triumphing over every obstacle, arrived at the close of life, was at once transported to the presence of the Supreme Power in the realms of light.

The Manichaeans reduced their moral system to the three seals of the lips, the hands, and the breast. The object of the seal of the lips was to close them against blasphemy, and particularly all animal food, the use of which was forbidden as a Satanic corruption, tending naturally to weigh clown the divine particles within, and bind them to earth. The seal of the hands forbade on the same motive the slaughter of animals, or the gathering of plants, which were purer still, as being so many vents whereby the perfumes and exhalations of earth rose to heaven, to restore in their light mists the portions of divinity which longed to remount to their source. The seal of the breast was to close the heart to all passion, for Manes forbade marriage and the procreation of children, as tending by the increase of the human race, in long series of generations, to lengthen the divine captivity and send new souls to languish and groan upon earth, and so commit the greatest crime against the Soul of God whose deliverance mankind was bound to further.

Such were the fundamental principles of the system, and in them its utter immorality is manifest. These distinctions of souls into three classes, the division of mankind into two parts, the *elect* and the *hearers*, the denial of any enlightenment to non-Manichaeans, made the system an outrage to the human conscience. Thus, giving alms to any one external to the sect was forbidden, as affording him a means of insinuating as nourishment to his impure and material body substances which, if placed on Manichaean lips, would be cleansed and raised towards God; t and the contempt thrown over the whole of nature degraded the Divine workmanship, and resulted inevitably in an interdiction of all property as one more bond to fix man to the corrupted earth, whose curse extended to those also who tilled it with harrow and plough, whose plants were full of hallowed life, and those who reaped them guilty of a crime. It tended to the destruction of the family, for marriage was under a ban, and the giving of children to the state and fresh shoots to the Manichaean Church accounted the greatest of sins, and its doctrine, owing to human nature's inextinguishable passions, had for a result, by inevitable though unavowed consequence, the ruin of man himself. To this pointed those maxims, inexpressibly true, which established distinctions between the requirements of nature and the prohibitions of law, the forbidden and the tolerated among the pleasures of sense, and which inaugurated a state of manners to the real and frightful corruption of which contemporary evidence bears witness. We have thus sufficiently shown the profoundly pagan character of the Manichaean errors; but on closer consideration of its origin, of the country and personal adventures of its chief apostle, we can easily recognize in it traces of the Persian dualism, the opposition of Ormuzd and Ahriman, and the eternal struggle on their respective frontiers of the realms of light and of darkness. This was the essence of the religion of Zoroaster, but in the battle between these principles there was a third, of mediating character, called Mithra, the worship of whom had attained such singular popularity on its importation into the Western Empire that Commodus even dared to immolate a man, and Julian at Constantinople established games in his honour, while

numberless monuments bear witness to the worship of him at Milan, in the Tyrol, throughout the two provinces of Gaul, and in the remotest parts of Germany. But Manichaeism had an element ignored by the system of Zoroaster, which in approaching nearer the infancy of the world had never hurled an absolute curse at the flesh, nor believed in the entire degradation of created matter, nor the captivity of the divine essence, nor dreamt of prohibiting marriage and procreation of children—doctrines which sprang from that worship of Buddha, the energetic and passionate propagandism of which we have observed in the early centuries of the Christian era. But it is difficult to decide whether Manes drew his system originally from these Buddhist sources, or found the teaching which he handed down to his disciples held by former Gnostic sects, themselves impregnated with the Oriental doctrine. Yet, however this may be, it was instinct with Paganism, and from that one cause, perhaps, the Manichaean belief exercised so incredible an influence over the minds which had seemed entirely severed from the errors of the pagan world.

At the end of the fourth century, under Theodosius, when Christianity had enjoyed a century of sway over the mind of man and the provinces of the Empire, Manichaeism became bolder than ever, and the idolatry of old seemed to have found its avenger. Its tenets spread with marvellous rapidity in both East and West, and made a conquest of St. Augustine himself, who for nine years was one of the hearers of Manes, and struggled vainly against the problem of the origin of evil, which he used to turn in every sense on his tear-bedewed couch, to return always to the same question, "How was evil created." Finding no solution in the early notions of Christianity which he had received from his mother, he suffered his mind to be drawn towards the fables of Manichaeism, and hung upon the lips of the eloquent preachers who told of the strife of the two principles, of the agony of *Jesus patibilis*, the sufferings of all creation, even, as he says, to the tear shed by the fig when dissevered from the branch to which it had clung.

Such were the errors to which this great intellect had fallen a prey, until the wiser philosophy of the Platonists and the eloquence of Ambrose snatched it from these delusive fables, and made it their most formidable opponent by assigning him the mission of refuting and destroying them, by rehabilitating in the face of the heathen world a philosophical, holy, and reasonable view of the origin of evil. In default of an analysis of his works on the subject, the following passage from his book, "De Moribus Manichaeorum," will suffice to show their tendency:—

" That which especially merits the name of being is what always remains in its own likeness, is not subject to change or corruption, or to lapse of time, but the same in conduct in the present as in the past. For the word Being carries with it the thought of another permanent and immutable nature. We can name no other such but God Himself, and if you seek a contrary principle to Him, you will not find it, for existence has no contrary but non-existence.

" If you define evil as that which is against nature, you speak truly; but you overturn your heresy, for all that is contrary to nature tends to self-destruction, and to make what is non-existent. What the ancients called nature we name essence and substance, and therefore in the Catholic doctrine God is called the author of every nature and every substance, and by it is understood that He is not the author of evil. For how could the author of being to everything which exists be the cause by which anything already existent should cease to be, lose its essence, and tend towards nothing ? And how can your evil principle, that you pretend to be the supreme ill, be contrary to nature, if you attribute to it a nature and a substance? For if it works against itself it will destroy its own existence, which it must succeed in doing to arrive at the supremacy of evil, but which it cannot do according to you, as you predicate of it not only existence but eternity of existence.

"Evil, then, is not an essence, but a deprivation and a disorder. All that tends to existence tends to order. For to be is to be one, and the nearer anything stands to unity so much the fuller is its participation in existence, it being the work of unity to give concord and arrangement to its constituent part: this order gives existence, disorder takes it away, and everything that has an internal principle of disorder tends to dissolution. But the goodness of God forbids things to arrive at that point; and even to those creatures of His who miss their end He gives such order that they are placed in their most congruous place, so that by regular effort they may again ascend to the rank whence they had fallen. For this cause reasoning souls, in whom freewill is powerful, if they distance themselves from God, are arranged by Him as befits them in the lowest degrees of creation, so that they become miserable by a divine judgment, in accordance with their merits."

These theories, though abstract, afforded a vast comfort to the human mind as it emerged from its Manichaean frenzy, from the pagan fables which were wafting it back to all the spells of Greek mythology, into the light of a purer philosophy and possession of the innate reason. In accepting them, the Christian world divorced forever the tales which too long tyrannized over the intellect, but yet while it escaped the peril of becoming a mythology, it fell under the risk of reducing its system to so rational a form as to sink into mere philosophical speculation.

Among these new forms of heresy two stand out as especially to be noticed. Arianism and Pelagianism, infants of those two philosophical systems of antiquity which had most attraction for Christian minds, were most calculated to strike them by their metaphysical character or pure morality, the doctrine respectively of Plato and of Zeno.

The former gave a lofty notion of the Deity, whom it represented as acting on the world by means of ideas, which Plato abstained from defining, and, in calling them only the principle of all knowledge, avoided explaining their place of residence, whether within or external to the Deity, whether they were reduced to one idea or the many, whether, reunited, they formed the *Λόγος,* or Divine Word, or continued in distinct and personal existence.

On all these points the master kept silence, but as the disciples did not imitate his reserve, these questions have been the continued torment of the schools of Platonism. An Alexandrian Jew named Philo, tortured by the wish of adapting his Mosaic creed to the doctrines of their philosophy, undertook to establish God's creation of the universe by the aid of a perfect idea or archetype, wherein was reflected the creative law, which was personified in the wisdom of Solomon and the Word of the sacred writings. God, not being able to act directly on matter, as too evil and weak for His action, had created the Word before the world to serve as intermediary between the Divine Will and this imperfect and corrupt universe. Therefore the Word was inferior to God, and beneath it were produced a series of emanations to which Philo gave a distinct personality, and named them sometimes ideas, sometimes angels.

His doctrine was destined to inspire that of the Alexandrian commentators Numenius and Plotinus, who evolved a trinity formed of unity (τὸ ἕν), absolute intelligence *(νοῦς)*, and the soul of the world *(ψυχή του παντός),* which, far from inspiring the idea of the Christian Trinity, did not appear in any precise form till Christianity had promulgated its doctrines, and made known the mysteries on which this philosophical triad was designed. But a certain number of minds fell into 'error on comparing the two dogmas, especially those of a philosophical bent, who were fascinated by the old lore and the Platonic doctrines, nourished on Plotinus, and steeped in that Alexandrian speculation which Tertullian had especially defied when he cast his ban upon pagan philosophy and letters; the Judaizers also, who though believing in the Christian scheme, found it heavy for their faith, and therefore sought to rob it of its aureole; and lastly the mighty multitude who had entered the Church in the train of the emperors, and sought to attenuate its mysteries by seeking refuge in the reception of a dogma of higher morality than any antiquity had known, but which would ill support the miraculous element of Christianity. And these three classes of minds became the components of the Arian sect, Arius himself, on his appearance, speaking only as their organ.

Arius rehabilitated Philo in professing that God was too pure to act upon creation, and that the world could not support the divine action, that it was necessary to utter a middle existence, purer than creation, less holy than God Himself, namely, the Word, created and not eternal, enjoying a great but not infinite share of light and wisdom; holy, but not so immutable in sanctity as to preclude the possibility of a fall, submitted in fact by God, who foresaw the triumphant issue, to the supreme probation of an incarnation, and assigned in recompense as the Creator and Saviour of mankind. This Word, united to a human body, became the man Jesus; and thus Christ had no real divinity, and as man had never been in immediate relation with God, the original fall had not the same gravity, nor redemption the same effect; it could not bring man, still too feeble, into communion with the infinite Goodness and Wisdom, and so became a bald teaching by the example of a divinely-inspired man named Jesus, who was a mere prophet or sage, with superior enlightenment to his fellows.

At the same time the doctrine of Zeno made many converts. Its Stoic morality, so nobly stern and mortifying to carnal impulse, had a great fascination for manly and ascetic natures, like those of the men who took refuge from the world in the deserts of the Thebaic that they might bring their body into subjection. It need not astonish us to see St. Nilus putting into the hands of his anchorites the manual of Epictetus, or Evagrius of Pontus falling into heresy through the system of Zeno. It exalted human nature as being that of God Himself, whence it followed that the two laws of nature and of reason sufficed as a rule of life, and that by their aid man could rise to the same or even a higher level than the Deity Himself. "For," said Seneca, " what difference is there between the wise man and Jupiter? the latter can effect no more than him; the only advantage he has over him is that of having been good for a longer time, but virtue itself is not enhanced by a longer duration. The sage despises material advantages as much as Jupiter, and excels him in this respect, that the god abstains from pleasures which he cannot, the sage from those he will not, avail himself of." And so man by his own strength rose superior to his God; and such dreams seduced many a hermit's soul in the contemplative hours of his long vigils; till, carried away by this stoicism, the monk Pelagius arrived at the profession of the doctrine that nature had never suffered original sin, but had remained intact and always able to raise itself to God by its own strength; that grace was useless, and if it existed at all was nothing but the possibility of well-doing, the fact of human liberty, the divine law promulgated in the gospel, a light innate to the intellect and shining there without any impulse or aid to the will from without; prayer had no meaning, and with it vanished the consolation which feeble man found in recourse to the Almighty.

Such were the essential errors of Pelagius, against which St. Augustine declared war as Athanasius had done against the heresy of Arius. The two systems, near in point of time, filled a century and a half with controversy, which roused into activity the whole Christian world, moulded its polemics, and gave inspiration to its genius. *We* need not speak of the councils without number which forced men to occupy themselves with the most difficult problems in the cycle of Christian metaphysics, and roused their minds from their sloth to precipitate them into that pregnant strife which called for crucial proof of their subtlety and skill in handling all the resources of dialectic, nor of the mighty travail of the intellect which was destined to give birth to modern theological science, but need only mark that in repelling the double error, Christianity repudiated as well the idea of being but a system of philosophy, to remain a religion, as it had been first announced. Lactantius summed this up in his memorable sentence, " Christianity can never be a philosophy without religion, nor a religion without philosophy." The faith is dogmatic, and therefore more than an opinion, but a dogma that is entirely reasonable. Had Pelagianism or Arianism triumphed, and the Church creed become a philosophy, the consequences would have been that as Arius suppressed the relation of Christ with God, and Pelagius those of man with Christ, in denying grace, original sin, and redemption, so all the supernatural intercourse between God and man being snapped, all religion would have perished, for religion *(religare)* is but a bond between the two extremes of God and man, the Infinite and the finite; and with the disappearance of the mysteries which enshrined the two principles of faith and love, nothing would have remained but a learned, subtle, but feeble deism, impotent, as the mere scientific opinion ever will be, to fertilize and regenerate humanity in its entirety.

Science has a sufficiently ample and glorious domain, but it is not her mission to be popular and universal, for limitation to a small minority of the race is the condition of her existence. Even to-day, in the full light of civilization and of Christianity, how many metaphysicians in Europe are there who, by the effort of their own unaided thought, can arrive at a precise notion of God and of man's destiny ? And if so, how much the more, when the world had but just emerged from her proof by blood and fire, and was still groaning beneath the sword of the barbarian ? What would then have been the issue had not the principle of Faith been endorsed in the flanks of that new society, and the reconstructing influence been revealed at the period of seemingly utter ruin? More than knowledge was wanting for the training of those bloody and coarse-minded hordes which were vomited from every quarter of the East, and to bring them to that Middle Age whose entire civilization was to be but a development of theology.

The most salient feature of these barbarous centuries of the Middle Age, and that least open to doubt, is their supremely logical character. From that proceeded the intense fascination exercised by syllogistic reasonings upon a period which could never lay down a principle without seeking to deduce its consequences, nor realize a great event without labouring to find its cause. From this sprang all the great efforts and mighty achievements of the mediaeval epoch. Theology was destined to bring about not only the marvellous intellectual development of the thirteenth century, under the grand intellects of St. Thomas Aquinas and St. Bonaventura, but also the

Crusades, the struggle of the priesthood and the Empire, the reign of St. Louis, and the constitutions of the Italian republics. It was to influence all the great political movements of the time, to penetrate the universities, to be found in the painter's studio and in the poet's song, and, further still, to open the fields of ocean, pregnant with stormy peril, to the genius of Christopher Columbus, who, in obedience to his own interpretation of a Scripture text, set foot on his ship to find another road for a new Crusade which might release the Sepulchre of Christ, rendered up, to his despair, to Moslem oppression.

The logical principle of every great achievement of that period was faith, the desire for belief, and the power man finds in himself when he believes; for, as it is only on the condition of faith that mankind can attain to love, the power of theology lies in its being the native principle of both faith and love. For mankind only loves what it takes on trust, not what it can easily compass; the not understanding a thing is the condition of loving it; and whatever is capable of mathematical demonstration gives little warmth to the heart. Who has ever been in love with an axiom, with a truth which leaves no need of further search ? The unknown is the most powerful constituent of love, for nothing fascinates the human mind like mystery, and, on the contrary, we soon weary of what we comprehend. How many illustrious men of letters or of science have finished a long life of toil in weariness at all they knew, and have acted like Newton, who, disgusted with mathematics, forced himself to expound the Apocalypse, attracted by speculations on that which was indemonstrable ? Mystery is the secret of love, and in love there is faith. We need not wonder at the great works of the Middle Age, when we see how it believed, still less when we see how it loved. It was the power which inspired St. Francis of Assisi, and all those generations of devoted men to whom no cost was too dear to bring another soul to the threshold of truth. It was in its faith and its love that the Middle Age found its strength, and therefore our treatise on the theology which produced them has been long. St. Anselm has spoken of Faith seeking understanding, *Fides quærens intellectum*, and in the words of St. Augustine, *Intellectum valde ama*.

CHRISTIAN PHILOSOPHY (ST. AUGUSTINE).

We have seen amidst the ruins of the fourth and fifth centuries theology arising as a new power, unknown to antiquity, but destined to dominate the Middle Age. Antiquity had possessed learned priesthoods, and had made attempts at bringing its religious traditions to order and light, but had no true theology in the sense of a science founded upon a serious alliance of reason and faith, because in Paganism there was no faith and but little reason. These two principles, on the other hand, were of the very essence of Christianity; faith had given it three centuries full of martyrs, and reason, applied to the understanding of dogma, had given it the Fathers. We have also seen what a degree of rectitude, perseverance, and toil was necessary to maintain the dogmatic deposit free from the two perils of a return to heathenism with the Gnostics and Manichees, or of losing itself in philosophy under the guidance of Arius and Pelagius.

And these questions had a right to occupy us in spite of their difficulty, for the fifth century was labouring far less for itself than for the ages to come, thereby manifesting the admirable economy in the laws of Providence, which causes nothing to be lost to the Christian family, but that each generation should show itself bent under the burden and heat of its own day, and weighed down also by that of its successors. Arianism did not perish at Nicasa or at Constantinople. Banished from the Roman Empire, it took refuge with and made rapid progress amongst the barbarians, to return again with the clouds of Goths, Alani, Suevi, and Vandals, which, in the course of another century, were to break over the Empire, and to become dominant in Italy, in Southern Gaul, in Spain, and on the shores of Africa.

The greatest of the Arian princes, Theodoric, seemed as if raised up for the purpose of founding a new empire with an Arian civilization, which, however, was soon destined to fall before the breath of Providence. Behind these Arians were others, the Moslems, possessing a newer edition of the same error—the unity of God, and Christ considered as a prophet, under which novel appearance the heresy was to cover the East, and even the West, till its recoil before the little kingdom of the Franks, founded by bishops and built upon theology, before the theologian monarch who called himself Charles the Great, and before the age which left upon the whole of Christendom so deep an impress.

Neither had Manichieism irretrievably disappeared, though hurled back by the puissant eloquence of St. Augustine to the boundaries of the Eastern Empire and Persia, and into the mountains of Armenia. It was there that Petrus Siculus, a Sicilian bishop, and envoy of the Greek emperors, found in the ninth century a powerful sect, possessed of a perfect hierarchy and organization, and which sought to propagate itself under the name of Bogomites, or as Paulicians in Bulgaria. It was Manichaeism again which reappeared during the eleventh century in France, Italy, and Germany, in the errors of the Cathari, Patarini, and Albigenses, and suddenly enveloping, as in a net, the greater part of Southern Christendom, threatened the Catholic civilization with the gravest perils. At the rumour of these heresies, which alike denied the Christian's God and attacked the principles of property and the family, and consequently the very elements of society, Europe roused herself and chivalry grasped the sword; and though we must ever deplore the excesses and horrors of the Albigensian crusades, yet the smoke of their conflagrations must not conceal the truth, that if the victory won by the sword was tarnished by cruelty, the triumph of thought and reason leaves no room for regret. From that furious struggle proceeded all the great theologians, in whom the age was so wealthy—St. Thomas Aquinas, St. Bonaventura, and Italy's great poet, Dante; and from their theology, which had profoundly agitated the human mind and fertilized its thought, had penetrated during the long gestation of the fourteenth century, in the mid-chaos of its stormy years to the last ranks of Christian civilization, went forth the marvels of the sixteenth century, its grand expansion of human genius, which, in less than a hundred years, discovered printing, sounded with Copernicus the secrets of heaven, and brought to light with Columbus a moiety of the world; all long before the appearance of the man to whom the honour of having aroused the human intellect has been awarded —Luther, the German monk. Theology, then, was the soul of the Middle Age, and in looking upon the working of all the great thoughts which gave birth to the crusades, to chivalry, and the great movements which carried away our forefathers, we must confess that, amidst the general confusion, it was the only influence that made its impulse felt. *Mens agitat molem.*

Theology descends from faith to reason, and philosophy ascends from reason to faith. This return of the soul towards truths which it has perceived from afar under mysterious shadows, only to desire their contemplation anew, and face to face, is an irresistible and imperishable want in human nature. And what religion, true or false, has not given faith a philosophy to confirm it or to contradict ? Those two great verities, God and the immortality of the soul, at once supremely attractive and supremely terrible, have never ceased to pursue humanity, and to strive by one way or another to come under its cognizance. But every time philosophy has pointed out two ways towards grasping the ideas by whose aspect it has been attracted, one way by the laborious reasoning process, which is continually pausing to consider the steps it has made, the methodical reasoning of logic, the science of binding ideas together, as if to mount to the seat of the Deity by piling Ossa upon Pelion; but these mountains are heavy to raise, dialectic is no moderate effort for the human mind, and its ambitious edifice often falls before it has been half constructed. And, therefore, man turns to the other path, and perceiving that now and then unsought truth has beamed in upon him, that inspiration has its instincts and contemplation its lights,' demands wherefore they are not his, and so he seeks another method in the effort of will, in the purification of the heart, in the interior labour of love; in short, he puts his confidence in morality instead of in logic, and thinks that in making himself more worthy of God he may arrive at the contemplation of Him. These two methods, then, the former proceeding from logical reason, the latter from morality and contemplative love, have constituted the two philosophies of dogmatism and mysticism.

It is not our task to remount to the origin of mysticism, nor to point to the highest antiquity of India, to those motionless contemplators who lived whole lives on the point where on their resting-place had first been fixed, forbade themselves any movement, and with eyes strained forward, gave themselves up to the last degree of privation and mortification, in order to conjure their Deity to descend upon them; neither those speculative philosophers who, in expounding the text of the Vedas, drew in imagination from them many systems to elucidate the revelation which they supposed had been confided to their charge. We may leave this too remote antiquity, and pause at the same efforts appearing in Greece, whose mystics, with Pythagoras, made wisdom consist in abstinence and continence, and which, in the persons of Thaïes, the sophists, and half the school of Socrates, contributed to the dogmatic system. We may be content with the results of Greek genius, that finest shoot of the human mind, and ask what conclusion its mightiest intellects, Aristotle and Plato, arrived at on the weightiest problem of the reason, the knowledge of God.

Plato, indeed, pushed the knowledge of God farther than any other sage of antiquity. He conceived of God as the Idea of Good, from whom all beings receive their intelligence, and by whom they exist; his God was good, and by his bounty had produced the world, not out of nothing, but from previously existent matter, which he drew from the chaos in which it was labouring, and which he was ever opposing as the rebellious principle by which his works are modified, corrupted, and spoilt. The God of Plato was a great conception, but he was not a free agent nor a sole existence, but living eternally side by side with undisciplined matter, and, conquered in his efforts by its resistance, was but half master, and though great and good, if not free and sole, was not God.

Aristotle, on the other hand, in the fourteen books of his " Metaphysics," put forth his utmost efforts to surpass Plato, and brought together the mightiest scientific apparatus that human hand has ever moved. Yet the man who knew the history of all animals, who had laid a basis for a republic, studied the laws of the human mind, and classed thought in categories, felt at last the necessity of recapitulating all his toil; he stretched his hands to right and left, and reassembled the knowledge which he had gained in the study of the universe in its totality, and from the most profound notions as to substance and accident, potentiality and action, movement and privation, hewed steps, as it were, on the summit of which, breathless and panting from the immense labour to which he had condemned himself, he believed at last he had reached God. He proclaimed him as a First Motor, necessary and eternal, of a world as eternal as himself, as guiding the universe without volition and without love, submitted with a capacity of directing it to a kind of physical attraction. He was powerful and intelligent, and found his pleasure in self-contemplation; but as he was not good, did not love his works, but only himself, was still more imperfect than the God of Plato.

Such were the results obtained by the human intellect, aided by the light thrown upon it during ages of infinite laboriousness, and by the immense advantages afforded in the congenial and brilliant epochs of Pericles and Alexander. Epicurus and Zeno followed, the former with his system of atoms, the latter making God a corporeal substance—a great animal, as it were; and then Pyrrho, with his universal scepticism, which Cicero struggled against in vain, by surrounding with the brightest lustre those two fundamental verities of all true doctrine—the existence of God and the soul's immortality. In vain, for, tainted himself by scepticism, he ended by finding the former a mere probability, and the latter eminently desirable for men of worth. And this was the issue of philosophy at the dawn of Christianity.

Christianity appeared to refresh the forces of the human mind, in giving it that certitude without which its action is paralyzed; for that which has been hurled as a chief objection against Christian philosophy constituted in fact its strength, its novelty, and its merit. It has been constantly said that the Church only suffers a verification of dogma already pronounced certain, that she fixes the goal, and leaves only the road to it open to search. Yet surely no great minds, no deep thinkers, have entered upon the ways of science but with a firm and settled idea as to their end; the human intellect only resigns itself to the formidable task of philosophic reasoning on condition of seeing their result in the distance. When Descartes went on his pilgrimage to Our Lady of Loretto as a Catholic pilgrim, he had a fixed determination of arriving at the proof of the existence of God and the immortality of the soul. It is in a settled certainty as to its aim that genius finds its power. Kepler's dying speech was that he knew that his calculations were inexact, but that, by God's help, sooner or later, someone would come forward to correct their errors, and prove the truth of the conclusions. This was true genius, science, and philosophy— the light destined to guide the intellect of mankind for the future. Christianity brought certainty to it, and to the gift added the liberty of choosing among the different paths which led there, and freeing human thought from mystic or dogmatic schools, spoke at once to the mind and to the heart, and imposed upon man the duty of arriving, by aid of his faculties and feelings, at a supremely lovable and supremely intelligible notion of God Himself. In this lay the novelty of the Christian eclecticism, and the road was followed by the Fathers of the Church in succession; but as the majority of those great minds, being involved in pressing polemical struggles, had no leisure to summarize and reduce into philosophical form the issues of their thought, that labour was reserved for St. Augustine, as being one out of the three or four great metaphysicians assigned by the Almighty to modern times; it was his task to clear the two roads open to Christian philosophy, and to inaugurate its two methods of mysticism and dogmatism.

No soul had ever been more troubled with an insatiable love for truth which could not be seen—a feeling happily described as a heavenly home-sickness, a deep craving for the eternal fatherland whence man came and whither he is tending. No soul, on the other hand, ever seemed thrown upon this world at a greater distance from its God. He was born on that African coast, already given up to the last state of disorder, which required nothing less than the Vandal torrent to cleanse the impurity in which it was steeped. His father was not Christian, and, greater danger still, designed his son, not only for the study but the profession of the corrupt literature of the Decline; to hire out his eloquence, and teach the art of lying on lucrative terms.

Amidst the traffic in rhetoric of the schools of Madaura and Carthage, the young Augustine began to grow skilled in tricks of speech, in the dangerous art which holds thought cheap and seeks an empty pleasure for the ear. His fellow-pupils, the students of Carthage, had earned, from their wild reputation, the nickname of *ever sores* (ravagers), and, according to the Saint himself, were in the habit of attending the lectures of some favourite master through door or window, breaking everything in their way. We can judge of the peril Augustine encountered among such wild freaks, and his " Confessions" show us, in fact, that he resisted none of the temptations by which early youth is generally assailed. But God had given him a restless heart, which could find no repose but in Him, and the secret disturbance of a soul which aspired to purity revealed itself in the very midst of its pollutions. When a mere child, he used to pray to God that his masters might not flog him, and later, when it seemed as if every remembrance of Him must have been banished in those nights of wild debauchery, the idea was still present, though unrecognized. His strong admiration of the beautiful began to reveal his literary vocation; it drew tears from him on reading of the woes of Dido, and took him as a spectator, not so much to the games of the circus as to the representations of the theatre, and especially to those tragedies which placed beneath his eyes the heroic misery of the great ones of antiquity. It pursued him as an insatiable passion into the pulpit of the rhetorician, and caused him constantly to ask his friends, " *Quid amamus, nisi pulchrum ? Quid est pulchrum ?* " whilst his first literary labour consisted of three volumes on Beauty.

But Goodness attracted him as well as Beauty; friendship, the communion of soul with soul, showed itself with great force in his breast when, on the loss of a beloved fellow-pupil, he bewailed him with an agony which nothing could console. " My eyes looked for him in every place, but no place gave him back to me, and I loathed everything, because nothing could show me him, nor say, ' Behold, he is just coming,' as when he lived and was absent from me. I bore then within me a torn and bleeding heart, which hardly suffered me to bear it, and yet I knew not where to lay it down, for it would not repose in charming thickets, nor in the country with its sports, nor in perfumed chambers, banquets, or voluptuous delights, neither in books nor in poetry."* Such was the affection of St. Augustine; and if he could thus love a friend, what must have been the nature of those other passions of his heart ? for amidst the horror with which the wild disorder of his youth inspired him, mark that he maintains that his soul plunged into unlawful love because it was famishing for some love, and divine nourishment had been withdrawn from it. At nineteen, the " Hortensius " of Cicero fell into his hands, caused him a disgust for fortune, and made him to swear to love nothing thenceforth but the Eternal Wisdom; " for already," he says, " I was aiming to return, O my God, to Thee." But he was but half satisfied with " Hortensius," and troubled at not finding therein the name of Christ—a word which, with its sweet and tender influence, had remained rooted in the depths of his heart.

The Manichaeans spoke of Christ, and that drew his mind towards them, as, tormented by the thought of God, he asked himself ceaselessly, "What is evil? from whom does it proceed ?" A sect which promised an explanation of the problem could not fail to fascinate him. The Manichaeans brought him up to the point of admitting, with them, a corporeal God and a corporeal soul; no notion of things spiritual entered his intellect; be believed that Christ resided between the sun and the moon; that He had taken only a fantastic body; that primitive man had been broken in pieces by the spirit of darkness; that plants exhaled in their perfumes different particles of the soul of the World, and the fig plucked from the tree shed tears of pain. All this St. Augustine believed, rather than nothing, so deeply did his soul crave for sacrifice and for entire self-devotion. But the Manichaeans themselves at last wearied him by the demands they insisted on from his lofty reason, and the works of the Neoplatonists having, at the same time, come in his way, he again found a philosophy which told of God as the Author of good. He gave himself up by preference to their guidance, and under it began to conceive of God otherwise than under corporeal forms, as a hallowed, invisible, impalpable Light; and yet these notions had difficulty in penetrating his still hesitating mind. "And I said, ' Has Truth, then, not existence, seeing it not spread over finite nor over infinite space ? ' and Thou didst cry to me from afar, 'I exist, I am that which is; ' and I understood in my very heart, and I could no longer doubt more of Thy Truth than of my life!"

But at the moment of this revolution in his soul, St. Augustine left Carthage, **a.d**. 383, and set sail for Rome, leaving his mother kneeling on the shore as the scudding ship bore far away that *child of so many tears*. At Rome, the prefect of the city, who had been asked for a professor of rhetoric for Milan, where the court was then residing, summoned the young African, whose fame had reached him, to his presence, heard him, and entrusted him with the appointment. The man who played the part of protector and Maecenas to St. Augustine was, by strange fatality, the pagan Symmachus. Arrived at Milan, St. Augustine saw St. Ambrose, heard him with admiration, and went again to listen to him at the Church. At other times he went to behold him working, reading, compiling manuscripts, writing in his house, which was open to all, and constantly thronged by the curious, though Ambrose never raised his eyes, except on some demand of charity. Augustine saw him in meditation, and went out again in silence. He had his mother also at his side, for she, counting always upon his conversion, had not feared to cross the sea to rejoin him, reassured, too, by the speech of a bishop to her: "It is impossible but that your child of many tears should be restored to you." His friends were with him; his pupils, who had followed him from Africa, unable to detach themselves from their beloved master, and in their midst his soul began to seek for the calmness and repose of a better regulated life. They discussed together the formation of a philosophical community, which had been the dream of so many philosophers, and which Pythagoras had attempted; but their difficulty lay in the admission of women, for Augustine had not resolved on tearing himself from the pleasures of his youth, and his old lusts still kept their grasp on "his garment of flesh." When in this condition, he learnt the story of Victorinus, who had left everything at the summit of his fame, and ripe in age, to follow Christ; and was captivated by that other history of the two imperial officers, who, whilst walking in the suburbs of Trèves, had entered a monastery, and struck with admiration at their life, had decided to abandon everything to live in perfection with its inmates. All these stories troubled the mind of St. Augustine, and drew him on insensibly towards Christianity, which St. Ambrose had lately taught him, and whose marvels excelled so infinitely those related by Plato and his disciples. At the conclusion of the conversation, in the course of which the account of the two officers had been related to him, he felt that decisive blow of which he has left us so vivid a picture. We must give it here, in remembrance of that memorable day at the close of August, 386, in which this great soul was snatched from its errors, and thrown at the feet of the Truth, into the bosom of that doctrine which henceforth he was so gloriously to serve.

"I advanced into the garden, and Alypius followed me step by step. I could not feel alone with myself as long as he was with me, and how could he desert me in the trouble in which he beheld me. We sat down at the farthest spot from the house, and I shuddered in my very soul with ardent indignation at my tardiness in flying to that new life to which I had agreed with God, and into which my whole being cried out to me to enter. . . I flung myself on the ground, why, I know not, under a fig-tree, and gave free course to my tears, which gushed forth in streams, as an offering agreeable to Thee, O my God. And I spoke thousands of things to Thee, not in these words, but in this sense: ' O Lord, how long wilt Thou be angry with me ? Remember no more my old iniquities,' for I felt that they held me still. I let these pitiable words escape me: ' When ? On what day? To-morrow? The day after? Why not yet ? Why is not this very hour the last of my shame ? ' So did I speak to Thee, and wept bitterly in the contrition of my heart, when, behold, I heard proceeding from a house a voice like that of a child, or a young girl, which sang and repeated as a burden, these words, ' Take up, and read ! take up, and read ! '

" Then I returned with hurried steps to the place where Alypius was sitting, for I had left the book of the Apostle there on rising from my seat. I took it, and opened and read silently the first chapter on which my eyes fell: ' Live not in rioting and drunkenness, not in chambering and impurities, not in contention and envy; but put ye on the Lord Jesus Christ, and make not provision for the flesh in its concupiscence's. I would read no farther, nor was there need for it, for instantly, as I grasped the thought, a light of certainty spread over my soul, and the mists of doubt vanished. Then I marked the passage with my finger or some other sign, shut the book, and gave it to Alypius to read."

All the darkness was, indeed, dispelled, and from that day Augustine was in possession of the .God whom he had so long pursued, who had sought him, too, and at last had gained him. So perfect was the communion, so real the contemplation, that in that other famous moment of which he leaves us the history, in his intercourse with his mother, we feel that he reached the farthest point open to mortal man in relation with God.

A short time after this day of his conversion, when Monica was on the point of giving back her soul to God, though the approach of that hour was not yet known, both mother and son were at Ostia, preparing to embark on the vessel which was to bear them back to Africa. As one evening the two were leaning on a window in contemplation of the sky, they fell to talking of the hopes of immortality, and then, said St. Augustine, having traversed the whole order of things visible, and considered every creature which bore witness to God, far above stars and sun they reached the region of the soul, and there found their aspirations were not satisfied, and so they turned to the Eternal and Creative Wisdom; and whilst we spoke thus, continues the Saint, we seemed to touch It; and, in conclusion, he declares that had that moment's contemplation lasted for eternity, it would have sufficed, and far more than sufficed, for his everlasting happiness.

Thus did St. Augustine, by the way of purification, of illumination, of contemplation, reach the true idea of God, and in this sense his " Confessions" become a grand work of mystic philosophy; and that he thus considered them himself is evidenced by the concluding address: " And what man can cause man, what angel his fellow-angel, what angel can cause man to understand these things ? It is Thou "Whom we must ask, O God ! Thou Whom we must seek, at Whom we must knock, and it is then only that we shall find, shall receive, and he opened to. Amen." To him these " Confessions" were nothing else than a mystic method of reaching God, and in them we find every characteristic of mysticism, and especially asceticism, the effort to create a moral and not a logical method of purifying self, and so rendering it worthy of an approach to God, to which end alone the long struggle against passion must ever tend; the careful cleansing of the intellect, in banishing every error which had crept in, whether Pagan, Manichaean, or Neoplatonic; and, lastly, the raptures of a heart henceforth free in its aspirations towards the Eternal One, and able to enter into closest communion with Him. These are the three degrees and phases through which great mystics make every soul pass which is under their guidance—the life of purgation, the life of illumination, the life of union. And, again, it contains another force; the soul, no longer given over to itself, as when a guidance towards reason is in question, for love cannot stand alone, but must have a proper surrounding, its philosophy cannot go alone, but only in company, so Augustine was accompanied by his mother, the guardian angel of his convictions, and one of their living and necessary elements—the soul, as it were, of his loving and inspiring philosophy; it was his mother who guided and stood by him from his dark youth to his brilliant maturity, whilst his friends, such as St. Ambrose, or the Church Universal, greedy of his presence, brought him on to the threshold of truth.

This method, then, condemns mankind to no unnatural isolation, it appeals to nature in its entirety, with all its splendours, errors, and illusions. By the aid of Beauty St. Augustine returned to God; the things of earth, which had charmed and deceived him, held amidst their seductive errors a true reality, making itself felt as alone capable of filling his heart. At last he cleft the veil and found the deep and creative beauty which lay hid under the form of every creature as a ray from the Creator, the symbolism which is another note of mysticism seeking in natural objects the reflection of the Deity and the footprints of the Invisible. Mysticism, with these three characteristics, is the same in every time; and during the Middle Age the mystic philosophy of St. Augustine blossomed into that of Hugh and

Richard of St. Victor, of St. Bonaventura, and the other great masters of the Western Church.

But the fact that this doctrine has its dangers was proved in the case of St. Augustine himself, and was to be shown by many subsequent instances. Like love, it brooks no control, and will be responsible to no one for its raptures and abandonments, and so it lies open to extravagance, to be drawn into paths in which the ties of its wings may break, and its aspirations towards the Sun end in a fall into the abyss. Control is essential to it, and so Christianity did not call for a mystic philosophy to stand alone without guide or rule, but placed at its side a dogmatic system, as the mysticism of St. Augustine was supported by his dogmatism.

In the earlier portion of the intellectual history of this Saint, it was God who was pursuing him pitilessly in the doubt of his mind and the struggle of his heart, as well as through the deep abasement of his carnal nature; and though he could fly from his country and his mother, he could not escape from his God, Who found him at Milan in that garden and under the fig-tree, whither we have followed him; but when He had once possessed him, it was St. Augustine's turn to follow after his God: he found Him, indeed, but never sufficiently—he forever was wishing to enter into deeper enjoyment of His perfection, and his whole philosophical toil lay in the attempt to return by dint of Reason to that Being whom he had already grasped by Love.

At the moment of taking the great resolution of an irrevocable self-devotion to God, he had also determined to quit the school in which he now saw a mere traffic in vanity. From one of his friends, Verecundus, he had sought and found in his beautiful villa of Cassiciacum, at some distance from Milan, the reposeful asylum so necessary after the struggle through which he had passed. Though out of health and with an affected chest, the dauntless activity of his mind forbade repose. Surrounded by his mother, his brother, son, and other relations, as well as the friends who had followed him, his days were passed now in reading a half-canto of the "Æneid," now in commenting on the "Hortensius" of Cicero, to which he used to refer the earliest motions of his heart towards virtue, now in talking philosophy with Trygetius, Alypius, Licentius, and others; obscure enough, indeed, by the side of the illustrious interlocutors in the "Dialogues of Cicero," but touching in their obscurity when viewed in the light of Christian philosophy, which counts none insignificant, the meanest becoming, as St. Augustine says, great when occupied with great things. One day his mother came to take part in these discussions; the Saint took care not to repulse her; and as she wondered at herself, as a woman, being thus admitted to philosophize, her son gloried, and rightly, in the idea. These conversations, preserved by stenography, form the first of St. Augustine's treatises on philosophy, and are found in his books, " Contra Academos," " De Ordine," " De Vitâ Beatâ," to which may be added the "Soliloquies," and the works " De Quantitate Animas," " De Immortalitate Animas," "De Libero Arbitrio;" and though no single volume amongst these furnishes a complete system of his philosophy, which must be sought for throughout the whole of his writings, this is due to the manner of composition assumed by this most laborious of men, whose time was disputed between an infinite variety of occupations; now engrossed in settling law-suits and other difficulties between the worthy people of Hippo, now called upon to direct the Church in her gravest decisions; and amidst such calls he was able from time to time to devote himself to some discussions on philosophy. All that we possess from him has, moreover, been written in haste, collected by reporters, and hardly ever revised by its author. Treatises were commenced by him and never finished, and in others the plan adopted at the outset was changed in the sequel. But yet, beneath apparent disorder, is found the most powerful internal arrangement; and it is not the least satisfaction to the mind which penetrates into the heart of his works, to discover therein the strength and unity of a genius ever master of itself, like the Christian faith which inspired it, marching without the slightest deflection in the straight road which was to lead it to God.

Moreover, he never reached the point of despising philosophy or of sacrificing reason to faith. Far from it; he wrote to Romanian urging him to embrace that system into the bosom of which he had plunged his own mind, and by which he had learnt to condemn Pelagius and throw off the Manichaean errors which had sustained him through his researches, and promising to show him God had, in fact, given him a glimpse of Him, though veiled in lustrous mist. Whilst he pointed to the weakness of the old philosophers, he gave them credit for their glory. He admired the chief of the Academy; to him Plato's approach to God seemed near; but he did not deny the impotence of the essays of the human mind. He declared that a handful of men, at the expense of great genius, leisure, and toil, had grasped the notion of God and of the soul's immortality, but had found truth without love; they had perceived the goal, but had not taken the path which alone led up to it, and so the truth they held was imperfect. " It is one thing to gaze down upon the land of peace, as from the peak of a mountain, whose sides are covered with forests haunted with wild beasts of prey and fugitive slaves, without knowing the road to follow, another to be upon the highway traced out by the Supreme Master." This was the distinction he drew between the philosophy of antiquity and that of Christianity, of which he was one of the most illustrious representatives—the necessary union of reason and faith. God Himself, he said, cannot despise reason, for how can He despise that principle which distinguishes man from His other creatures

? Nor does He desire that we should seek faith that we may cease to reason, but, on the contrary, that the possession of faith should make us reason more—should give it stronger and more ample pinions, for, were we not reasoning creatures, we should not know how to believe. Reason precedes faith, to determine where authority lies; it follows it too, for when the intellect has reached God, it seeks Him still.

St. Augustine was far from wishing to discourage the reason by dwelling on the contradictions of the old schools of philosophy, and rather blamed the new Academy for seeking refuge in a state of doubt between Epicurus and Zeno. He destroyed its specially adopted doctrine of probability, showing the disciples of the school that, in speaking of probability, they held an idea 'of truth, and even supposed the presence of what they denied; and in order to refute doubt, he sought for certitude in thought by the psychological method.

"In truth," he said, "those who doubt cannot doubt that they are alive, that they remember, wish, think; for, if they doubt, it is from a desire for certainty, and so they refuse to consent to anything without proof. You, then, who wish to know yourself, do you know if you exist ? I do know it. Whence? I am ignorant whence. Do you think yourself to be simple or complex ? I know not. Do you know whether you are in movement ? No. Do you know whether you *think* ? I know that I do. Then it is certain that you think."

This is, in fact, the *Cogito ergo Sum,* as expressed in the second hook of the " Soliloquies" of St. Augustine, in a dialogue between his reason and himself, and in which he thus lays down the very foundations of certainty. It was in the deep trouble of his mind, when, as philosopher, he beheld within himself the ruin of every system of philosophy, on the point of giving up reason in despair, he sought the corner-stone whereon to raise the fabric of his knowledge, and found no other but the *Cogito ergo Sum*. The advance of Descartes consisted only in putting the same idea into higher relief, in seizing it to hold it forever, and so never to be drawn into empty speculation again. He was to stop his course at the point marked out by St. Augustine, by whom, indeed, the seal was placed upon the page which would draw succeeding generations to return upon it in meditation, and extract from it so many others equally immortal.

Thus the soul is at least sure of its own thought, doubt, or volition, the witnesses of its own consciousness; it is aware of sensations also, and demands whence they come. The Platonists alleged that the senses were full of error, and compared them to the oar, which appears broken when plunged into water, or to a tower on the sea-coast, which seems falling when observed from the sea; but St. Augustine replied, with all the superiority of philosophic truth, " The senses do not deceive us as it is; they would do so did they make the oar look straight or the tower steadfast; it is you who deceive yourselves, in asking them to give judgments when they can only give impressions." And, taking higher ground, he perceived in the soul and conscience something higher than the inner sense, the most solid of sensations, namely, ideas, universal and evident notions, everything, for instance, which constituted the elements of dialectical science. Thus the same thing cannot he existent and non-existent. He found therein numbers, which were the same in relation to everything, and of which no one could doubt; mathematical verities, and also moral principles, likewise the same to all, which he sometimes called numbers, with the Pythagoreans, more often ideas, after Plato; and this was all discussed by him at a time of absorption in all the duties of a religious life. Thus the philosopher subsisted in the Christian, and the excellent tradition of disdaining nothing of real utility in the results of the old reasoning was perpetuated.

" Ideas are certain principal forms, certain reasons of things fixed and invariable, not formed themselves, and therefore eternal, acting ever after the same method, and contained in the Divine Intelligence: and as they are never born, and can never perish, it is upon them that a very thing which must have a birth and a decay is formed. The reasoning soul alone can perceive them, which it does through the highest part of itself, namely, through the Reason, which is to it as an interior and discerning eye. And again, the soul, to be capable of this vision, must be pure, and its interior eye must be healthy, and like to that which it seeks to contemplate. Who dares say that God created without reason ? For the same reason, the same type could not equally subserve the creation of a man and a horse.

Therefore every particular being had its particular reason. But these reasons can only reside in the thought of the Creator, for He did not regard a model placed exterior to Himself, and so the reason of things produced were of necessity contained in the Divine Intelligence."

Thus the Divine Beason is present to the reason of man through these eternal truths, by this sight of numbers and the essential reasons of all things; and so when speech external to ourselves gives names to these things invisible and absolute truths, it does not itself convey to us the idea of them, but only warns us to consult that internal monitor whom we name the true, the beautiful, and the just, in that language of ours which, though neither of Hebrew, Greek, Latin, nor barbarian tongue, has been understood by all the world from the beginning; an eternal language taught us by a Master who is no other than the Word, the true Christ, present in the depths of human consciousness.

Such was the psychology of St. Augustine, which we now leave aside to examine his treatment of those two propositions as to the spirituality and immortality of the soul which will bridge the space that divides us from the second point in his metaphysical system—the search for God. For he let not the scruple of there being any inconvenience or culpability in making self-knowledge the preliminary step to a knowledge of God arrest his course, but affirmed, on the contrary, that the science of the human soul was a necessary and legitimate introduction to the science of God. It was through his adoption of the psychological method of the ancients that he went far beyond Socrates: while the latter had said "Know thyself," the cry of the former was, *Noverim me, sed noverim te.* But in what manner would he know God ? He wished for an essential knowledge of Him, one deeper than of the truths of mathematics, and shrank from a cold and freezing scientific appreciation of Him, as he promised himself therefrom happiness as well as enlightenment. The way along which he was to seek for God was that passed by David as he uttered the sublime hymn of praise, *Coeli enarrant gloriam Dei;* by Xenophon in the memorable Discussions of Socrates, to develop the old but eternal proof of God's existence, as he says in the passionate language of Christian love:—

" Behold the heaven and the earth; they exist, they cry out that they have been made, for they vary and they change. For that which exists without creation has no particle which has not forever existed; so these exclaim, ' We stand because we have been created; we did not exist before our creation, that we might create ourselves,—and this their voice is their evidence. It is Thou who hast made them, Lord; Thou art beautiful, and so are they; Thou art good, and they are good; Thou art, and they are."

In this lay his whole physical proof of the existence of God; but it was upon the metaphysical proof that he innovated in conveying to it all the power of a genius hitherto unique.

By his study of the soul, St. Augustine recognized immutable principles of Beauty, Goodness, and Truth, to which he was bound to give the adhesion of his mind and heart. But these principles did not merely reveal themselves to him, but gave the impulse towards some unknown existences whose manifestations he already felt. He did not resist it, and thence came the reason for insisting on that idea of beauty which had fascinated him from his infancy, and been the food of frequent meditation—which made him the first among Christians to lay the foundations of an aesthetic philosophy, to write treatises on Beauty, and utter the sentiment, *Omnis pulchritudinis forma unitas est.* This road, then, led him to God through his idea of beauty, but it did not suffice, and unwearied of the chase he sought Him also by the path of goodness.

" You love," said he, " nothing but what is good; you love the earth because it is so goodly, with its lofty mountains, its hills and dales; you love the human face because it is comely in the harmony of form, colour, and feeling; you love the soul of your friend, which is beautiful by the charm of ordered intimacy and faithful love; eloquence, because it teaches sweetly; poetry, which is lovely in the melody of its numbers and the solidity of its thought; in all that you love you find some character of goodness— suppress that which distinguishes all these things, and you will find the good itself. We compare these various goodnesses; and how, if not by a perfect and immutable idea of good, by the communication of which everything is good? If in each of these particular excellences you behold only the supreme excellence, you gain a sight of God."

And so Goodness, by a similar way, leads to the same goal as Beauty. But the perception of the philosopher still distrusted this idea of what was beautiful and good; it feared the empire of mere fame, and dreaded yielding to the raptures of a spell-bound imagination. Severe in its reason, it sought a conviction of its own, and, to escape all possibility of delusion, determined to seek God through the idea of a Truth which was pure, absolute, and mathematical. In his treatise, " De Libero Arbitrio," he therefore recommenced the demonstration of the existence of God, and, that it might be complete, plunged into the very abysses of human nature. Considering man as possessing three qualities of existence, of continuing life, and of intelligence, he devoted his mind to the last, leaving the two former out of the question, and found in it both the external senses and that innermost feeling which is their moderator and judge, and, in a word, Reason. "Reason," he said, "surpasses all the rest; if there exists anything above it, that must be God."

Thus, by a third effort, and, as it were, by a third assault, he made a breach in the metaphysical barrier, and entered on possession of the Divine Idea; but knowing well the danger of confiding the notion of which he now was master to human language, declared, at the moment in which his possession seemed sure, that perhaps it would profit more to know less— *Scitur melius nesciendo*—recognizing the inexactness of all human speech in describing the attributes of the Divinity. Right and left, with the dread of one long entangled in Manichaeism, he beheld the perils of Dualism and Pantheism. He avoided the danger in declaring that evil formed no opposing force to good; that there were not two principles, but that evil does not exist in itself, but only relatively as a deprivation of, an apostasy from, or an inferiority in good; that beings have no existence that is not given them by God; and that, in consequence, there is nothing external to God—thus dispelling at one blow the perils of Dualism. But, then, did he not seem to fall into Pantheism—especially in such strong expressions as that existences have no real existence ? No; there was no fear of his relapsing into his old error, and seeing in all beings an emanation of the

Divinity. He drew himself from the toils by what was then a novelty in philosophy, and severed his mind from Pantheism by the dogma of Creation. The ancients had held with Plato an eternity of matter existing at the side of God, or had thought, with the philosophers of Alexandria, that God had drawn, and was forever drawing, all existences from Himself by a continual emanation. St. Augustine was the first to profess a Creation from nothing; that, external to God, there was nothing from which the world could have been formed, and if it had flowed out from God, would itself have been God.

He thus establishes the doctrine of Creation, and, in answer to the philosophical difficulties of the dogma that creation was in time and God in eternity—why and when had God created—what had been His occupation previous to creation—replied, with calm superiority, that God had created the world in freedom, but not without reason, that He, as the good God, had created it for a good purpose.

" We must not inquire when He created, nor whether, in the creative action, He went forth from His immutability, nor as to what His previous work might be. He willed from eternity, but produced time with the world, because He produced the world in movement, of which time is the measure."

He thus abandons his mind to the highest and boldest considerations, with the' utmost judgment and accuracy, and without the least subtlety. Having established time as being the measure of movement, he thus concludes:—

" Thus all my life is but succession—dissipation. But Thy hand, my Lord, has brought me together in Christ, the Mediator between Thy unity and our multifariousness, so that, rallying my existence, once dissipated by the caprices of my early days, I dwell under the shadow of Thy Oneness, without memory of what is no more, with no anxious aspiration towards that which has to come."

And so his reason brings him back to love, as love had brought him to reason; and as all his mystic philosophy, under the guidance of divine love, tended to a rational and pure notion of God, so all his dogmatism, under the reasoning principle, ended in love to the Almighty. This impossibility of severing these two great forces of the soul is the essential characteristic of Christian philosophy. As antiquity pictures to us the aged Œdipus weighed down under a sense of guilt and by blindness, its punishment, supporting his painful steps by the aid of his two daughters, Antigone and Ismene, so the human mind, like a blind and age-stricken monarch groping from the beginning of time in search of its God, has need, indeed, of its twin-offspring, love and reason, to help it to its goal, the knowledge of the Divinity; and we must shrink from depriving it of either.

But the philosophy which St. Augustine opened, that new dogmatic system which compassed a true notion of God as Creator, as One, and Free, loving and really to be loved, did not stay its progress with its author. Truth, we have said, lay scattered throughout his many writings, and if any reproach is due towards the great genius of Hippo, it lies against the inevitable diffusion of his thought in the midst of innumerable works, interrupted as they were by the duties of a thoroughly occupied life. But these germs were not useless; they bore their fruit, and were carried over the stormy centuries of the Middle Age, and cast upon fertile ground in France, Italy, and Spain, the native lands of great intellects in the future, and where another great metaphysician and profound thinker was to appear in St. Anselm, whose predestined labour was to bind together in one group the proofs of God's existence given by St. Augustine, and present them by a more rigorous method and in an exacter form. St. Thomas Aquinas was also, in his turn, to develop the theories of St. Anselm, so that the seventeenth century, with all its right to be captious in the matter of genius, philosophy, and truth, could find no greater work than that of bringing to its light, in another form, the doctrines of St. Augustine, by the aid of Descartes and Leibnitz, who reproduced his metaphysics with certain corrections and greater accuracy. This was alike the labour of these great minds, and of Malebranche in his treatise, " Recherche de la Vérité," who, in the epigraph of his works, gloried, like St. Augustine, in listening to that internal master which speaks in the language of eternity, and who professed to behold everything in God.

It is upon this great and potent system of Christian metaphysics that, from the fifth century down to our own times, the totality of modern civilization has hinged. Its action, indeed, remains unrecognized amidst the passions and disorders of the present day; but to the serious and enlightened nations of the modern world metaphysics appear as the essence and the guiding principle of all things, as moulding the public opinion of Christian races, as governing everything, and giving the first reason for the institutions amongst which we live. Dante, on reaching the summit of his Paradise, beheld God as a mathematical point, without length or breadth, but as the centre of the revolving heavens:

Da quel punto Dipende il cielo ed tutta la natura.

Metaphysics, the idea of God, form the point whereupon the whole heaven of our thought, of our nature, of our education, all society, the entirety of the Christian organism, is suspended. So, as long as no one has shaken that point, nor laid violent hands on that Divine idea, there need be no fear for our civilization.

THE INSTITUTIONS OF CHRISTENDOM (THE PAPACY AND MONASTICISM).

In our attempted examination of the philosophy of St. Augustine, we have seen how his great genius, the true representative of Christian eclecticism, reunited the two methods which had, up to his time, under the names of intuition and reasoning, love and intelligence, mysticism and dogmatism, divided the world of thought. We followed him along the ways which lead to the knowledge of God; and on scaling the vast heights of speculation to which he had been our guide, perceived that it was his metaphysical system which enlightened, dominated, and influenced the lofty minds of the Middle Age. For whilst the mysticism of the " Confessions" was to inspire the contemplation of Hugh and Richard of St. Victor, and draw from Bonaventura his "Itinerarium Mentis ad Deum," St. Augustine's demonstration of God's existence was to be rigorously drawn out to its conclusions by St. Anselm, and to become an element in the "Summa Contra Gentes" of St. Thomas Aquinas, in which that great master undertook to prove, without recourse to Holy Writ, three hundred and thirty-six theses upon God, the soul, and their relations one with another.

But the remembrance of St. Augustine could not fill the domain of theology without descending into those arts which the Sacred Science inspired. Legend, as we know, had, as it were, seized upon the great doctor of Hippo, and woven around him an especial glory, as for instance in the vision of the sainted host granted to a monk in ecstasy, whose astonishment at not beholding St. Augustine was dissipated by the intelligence that his place was higher far, on heaven's very summit, and veiled by the rays of that

Divinity which it was the work of his eternity to contemplate. Nor was it surprising that monks should cling to his memory thus, when even the Saracens, encamped on the ruins of Hippo, showed their devotion to its bishop; and considering that in our own day the Bedouins of the neighbourhood of Bona come every Friday to the spot which is marked by the ruins of the Basilica of St. Augustine, to honour a hero whom they call mysteriously *the great Roman*, or the great Christian. Painting, too, found in the history of this Saint an inexhaustible store of subject, and, amongst others, Benozzo Gonzali has depicted the incidents of his life in ten paintings in the church of San Gemignano—that charming town of Tuscany which defies the curiosity of the traveller from its rocky site— paintings which, with touching simplicity, unfold the various epochs in his career, from the day on which he was taken by his parents to school at Tagaste, praying God that he might escape the rod.

Thus did the highest intellects of Christian Italy aim to draw near to that genius of old time. Petrarch, in writing his treatise on Contempt for the World, tormented by a passion that robbed his mind of all repose, imagined that he had St. Augustine for an interrogator, and that the Saint warned him that he was bound by two fetters of diamond, which he mistook for treasures, but which in reality were crippling him —namely, glory and love. Petrarch ardently defended his bonds, declaring that he bore, them with joyful pride, and wished no one to lay hands on that Platonic love which had inspired his whole life, and raised him above the crowd. But the other, with a higher wisdom, derived from his Christian instincts, pointed to the perils of an undefined passion, which, though ostensibly ideal, would never have been conceived by him had not the beauty of his Laura appeared in sensible form. St. Augustine saw in it only a dangerous weakness, and prayed God that he might stay with the poet as a safeguard against himself, while Petrarch, at last yielding to the argument of the holy doctor, exclaimed, " Oh, may thy prayer be granted; may I, too, under Divine protection, come safe and whole from these long wanderings, feel the tempest of my mind subside, feel the world growing silent around me, and the temptations of fortune come to an end ! "

But Christianity had not appeared for the sole purpose of promulgating the doctrine which shone with so vivid a light upon the writings of Augustine, but rather to found a society which might unfold itself, and receive within its ranks those multitudinous hordes of barbarians who for many ages before its advent had been in motion towards the rally-point which had been marked out for them. We must learn if any and what influences were ready to subjugate, to instruct, and to organize them, or whether the great institutions of Catholicism insinuated themselves into the Church, as has been often stated, in a time of congenial barbarism, and as if by stealth, in the deep intellectual darkness under which humanity was labouring.

There are two institutions amongst those which were destined to act with energy on the Middle Age, which arrest us at once, as their incontestable preponderance detaches them from the rest—the Papacy and Monasticism; and it is our duty to seek out their origin, to consider the forces they respectively wielded at the moment when their exercise was called for, and to see whether their powers were exerted for the salvation or the corruption of the human race.

This is no place for renewing a worn-out controversy as to the origin of the Papacy, for the equity of modern criticism has reduced the passionate exaggerations of our predecessors, and no enlightened mind of our own day continues to regard it as a premeditated and wicked usurpation on the part of certain ambitious priests. A more impartial method points it out as an historical labour of the ages, the temporary consequence of a certain development which Christianity was destined to encounter. The religion of Christ, they say, took its rise in the conscience, in the inner solitude of man's personality, and so the Christian of the apostolic age was self-sufficient, was king and priest to his own consciousness. It was later that he felt the want of combination, and with it the need of a common authority and a common rule; and thus towards the end of the first century the clergy was separated and distinguished from the mass of the faithful. It was not until the second century that the episcopal power was seen first to arise, then to dominate, so that in the third age the bishops of the different cities were naturally subordinated to the metropolitans of the provinces, and thus the authority of the bishops and the metropolitan archbishops was formed, by necessary consequence, upon the constitution of the Roman provinces. Lastly, when Europe, Asia, and Africa began, in the fourth century, to aspire to a separate existence, the capitals of these three quarters of the world became the three Patriarchal Sees—Antioch for Asia, Alexandria for Africa, and Rome for Europe; whilst in the two succeeding ages, when the barbarians had severed the West from the East, the Bishop of Rome, the acknowledged Patriarch of the West, became, without usurpation, tyranny, or outrage to humanity, the supreme chief of the Latin Church. Such was the theory in vogue at the opening of the present century—the view which claimed the most "enlightened spirits of Protestantism as disciples, and formed the essence of the theology of its greatest modern writers; a thesis which aroused Planck and Neander, and was the corner-stone of the edifice of ecclesiastical history raised by the respected hands of Guizot; a view remarkable from its moderation, and which we must now examine more closely, to find the claim that it possesses to support a system of opinions which have been widely embraced and even become dominant.

In the first place, Christianity in no way admits of this individualism which is thus laid down as the point of departure for the faith. For it is less a collection of doctrines than a society. It has charity as well as enlightenment for its special characteristic, and even the last-mentioned quality is not communicated to man solely by study and reading, but is the result of the spoken as well as the written word, as in a popular religion destined to make its earliest converts amongst the poor and those who could not read. Enlightenment as well as charity found its medium of communication in the contact of souls. For this reason St. Paul regarded the Faith as being the soul of a vast and single Body, of which Christ was the Head and His followers the members; and as the limbs cannot will except through their chief member, it followed that Christendom must be a living and consequently an organized body, and that from its beginning it must be manifested not as a group of scattered and solitary consciences, but as a true society, possessing a constitution with a chief over all, with obedience and control among its lower orders, and offering to the view all the necessary conditions of a complete organization. And this idea is evidenced by the earliest documents of Christianity, though we need enter into no minute discussion on the texts of the Acts of the Apostles to show how continual witness is borne therein to the action of the Apostolic College under the presidency of Peter, in conferring the episcopal character, in instituting priests and ordaining deacons, surrounded, in the meanwhile by the Christian people, from whom it was not separate indeed, but still perfectly distinct.

Thus from this early period we find that priests existed, and not bishops alone. And this has been often controverted, because as the bishop had of necessity passed through the priesthood, the name of priest was often given to him; but not a single passage can be quoted in which a simple priest, on the other hand, has received the title of bishop, whilst to avoid minute discussions, which only cause a loss of time and light, it is evident that St. Paul, in his epistles to Titus and Timothy, confers upon them the right of judging priests, whom the very fact of their yielding to this jurisdiction proves to have filled a subordinate position. And so from the beginning we have a hierarchy, not only existent, but in strong organization.

We might cite here as evidence for the end of the first century, and the beginning of the second, the epistles of St. Ignatius of Antioch; but from their precise character the adversaries of the opinion we maintain have accused them of being apocryphal, as if unable to conceive the authenticity of documents so expressly condemning their position. So we must refrain from using this contested authority, and turn to others which have never been disputed. We come then to St. Irenaeus, to Tertullian, and St. Cyprian, the most ancient of the writers who have treated of the ecclesiastical organization, who flourished at the end of the second century, and from their positions in the Eastern and Western divisions expressed the opinion of the Universal Church. These three great doctors agreed on all essential points, and amidst the strife of opposing doctrines, the din of heresies which were tearing Christendom asunder and snatching at the pages of Holy Writ, unanimously recognized the necessity of tradition in the interpretation of Scripture, and the presence of that tradition in the corporation named the Church. This corporation seemed to them to have been filled with a light which was universal, as the sun is one object, though it spreads its rays over the face of the earth, to borrow its strength from the Divine authority, to be the habitation of the Holy Spirit, which afforded it a perpetual vitality, " like a precious liquid which perfumes and preserves the vessel in which it is contained." But the Spirit could only be transmitted by the medium of the apostles, and the episcopate was but a continuation of the apostolate; so that in the time of St. Irenaeus, at the end of the second century, each of the great churches maintained the succession of its bishops, but had never more than one at a time. Thus was the distinction between the episcopate and the rest of the priesthood established. But another and greater power was appearing contemporaneously, and as its bishop formed the bond of unity for the particular Church, so all these episcopal churches had need of a common centre. And therefore St. Cyprian, in his treatise " De Unitate Ecclesiâ," professed that the unity of the Church must be visible, and that therefore Christ had founded His Church upon the Apostle Peter, in order that its unity thus personified might be patent. Nor did Cyprian confine this primacy of Peter, or the unity which he represented, and whereby he gave strength to the Church, to the time of the Apostle's life, but prolonged and maintained it in the Petrine See, naming it, in a letter to Pope Cornelius, as the principal Church from whence the unity of the priesthood was derived.

Language nearly identical was used by Tertullian; but it may be objected to these witnesses that they were Africans and Westerns—subject, therefore, to the indirect influence of Rome and of Latin ideas. Let us look, then, to counterbalance them, for evidence emanating from the Eastern Church. We shall find it in the person of St. Irenaeus, who wrote earlier, at the end of the second century, and pointed to the episcopal succession as remounting without break to the Apostles themselves. For the sake of brevity, to save the task of enumerating that succession in every town, he paused before the Church of Rome, with which, he said, on account of its higher primacy, all churches that is to say the faithful, throughout the world, ought to agree. These passages are incontestable, generally recognized and admitted even by Neander and Planck, reducing them to maintain that in the time of St. Cyprian, of Tertullian, and of Irenaeus, the primitive spirit of the Gospel had been lost; that the doctrine of St. Paul was veiled by the Judaizing influence which was dominant, and aimed at organizing the Church after the fashion of the synagogue, with a spiritual chief corresponding to the high priest of the latter. So that we Christians have not only to reply to the objection as to why God waited four thousand years before sending His Son into the world, but to another which would ask why the whole order of the newly-granted revelation was disturbed at the end of the second century, and its believers compelled painfully to grope amidst impenetrable darkness for the witness of those few years during which alone the true doctrine prevailed.

But these theories are wanting in foundation, and science itself demolishes them continually. For the Catacombs of Rome are pregnant with novel proofs of the ancient orthodoxy, and show us, with that rugged symbolism which characterized Christian art in the early centuries, Peter in every place teaching doctrine, and exercising the governing functions, and that not only in the short time that his life comprised, but as it were by anticipation in ages yet to come. We may allude especially to a crystal disk, lately found in the Catacombs, carved with the oft-repeated type of Moses striking the rock, from which the life-giving waters of doctrine flowed, whereat all the people might quench their thirst. But the figure as Moses was vested, not in the costume of the East, but in the traditional robes of the Popes, and bore the name *Petrus*— doubtless representing Peter, the guide, like Moses, of the people of God, who was drawing forth, by his episcopal staff, the waters which were to refresh believing humanity.

Thus, then, was the primitive constitution of the Church established: it possessed an authority founded by the intervention of the Almighty; its origin was divine, as was the consecration of its career; it was also visible, and the order descended from the Apostles to the bishops, from the bishops to their ministers. But yet there was scope for liberty in its organization. The Sovereign Pontiff could do no act without having previously consulted his brethren in the episcopate; the bishop referred to his brethren of the priesthood; and the priest was of no authority at the altar without the concurrence of the entire Church—that is, of the whole body of the faithful, who supported him with their own prayers, and joined with him the intercession which he offered.

Before the close of the second century, in those remote times, the hierarchical constitution of the primitive Church contained, as it were, a sphere allotted to God, and another the privilege of the Christian people, principles of authority and of liberty, and all the essential elements of a newly-ordered society. When she was still menaced by persecution, and hunted down with remorseless perseverance, there was but little reason for her to leave traces of her passage, or of her institutions, which, much as they would have enlightened us in these days, would have then served but to betray her faithful children; but from that time forward, in spite of difficulty and peril still subsisting, the question we have been examining grows bright with an unmistakable clearness, and the Papacy is seen exercising its influence harmoniously with the process of time and the increase of danger.

Such, then, is the nature of the historical development, not of the principle, but in the exercise of that chief authority; and in proof that from the first it asserted itself with singular energy, we find Tertullian reproving a Pope, his contemporary, for having assumed the title of *Episcopus Episcoporum* and *Pontifex Maximus*. Strong expressions no doubt, which—or at least the first of them—have seldom been claimed by Popes of modern days, for they have found a preferable title, and a more powerful guarantee, in being styled the servant of the servants of God. The considerable discussions which arose later in the East, as well as the West, threw a light upon the subject which divested it of all ambiguity. The minds of the faithful were troubled by three great questions: the celebration of Easter, the administration of Baptism by heretics, and the case of Dionysius, the Alexandrian patriarch. As the Churches of Asia persisted in keeping the Paschal-time on the fourteenth day, which was the time chosen by the Jews, instead of on the first Sunday after the anniversary of the Resurrection, they fell under the interdict and excommunication of Pope St. Victor. Later, when the Africans, headed by St. Cyprian, decided that baptism given by heretics was invalid, and must be renewed, Rome maintained its validity if given with the appointed ceremonies, and, therefore, that it could not be repeated, and excommunicated the African Churches, who at once made their submission. And again, when Dionysius of Alexandria, in combating the heresy of Sabellius, let fall the expression that Christ was not the Son, but the work of God, the Bishop of Rome summoned him to explain. Dionysius accordingly did so, justified himself, and withdrew the statement. Thus in three important questions, which nearly touched dogma, the Papacy was seen intervening in the plenitude of a supreme authority. In the midst of the light of that brilliant fourth century, which beheld so many great occupants of the episcopal seat in the Eastern and the Western Church, we find the pontifical authority recognized and proclaimed in far stronger terms by St. Athanasius, the great patriarch of Alexandria, who declared that it was from the See of Peter that the bishops who preceded him had derived alike their orders and their doctrine, by St. Optatus of Milivium, by St. Jerome, by St. Augustine—in a word by the Church's greatest minds. And the exercise of that power continued simultaneously, as when the Popes Julius I. and Damasus deposed or reinstated the patriarchs of Alexandria, of Constantinople, or of Antioch; when the legates of the

Holy See took the chief place at Nicaea, and a.d. 347 at Sardica, where they declared that all episcopal sentences might be carried to the chief see of the Church of Rome; and when in the assembly of Ephesus the reunited bishops of the East, at the zealous instance of St. Cyril, who was supported by the authority of Pope Çelestine, pronounced their decision in the case of Nestorius.

No one can doubt, therefore, that in the fourth century the Papacy was already in possession of its entire authority; nor can we see in this fact the work of the Christianized emperors of Rome, who desired to grant the half of their purple and of their dignity to the bishops of the imperial city. Hardly, in truth, had Constantine embraced the faith than he transferred the seat of his empire to Byzantium, and the interest of his successors lay in enhancing the power of the patriarchs of Constantinople, in elevating their authority over the Church, thus making them docile and obedient to themselves. For this they toiled, and in this they succeeded; but the emperors did not spend their cunning policy on behalf of the Roman pontiff— rather if they extended their care to him it would have been devoted to his humiliation. Nor was it any genius on the part of the Popes which raised their place so high, for not a single great man filled the See of Rome during the first four centuries: they were but martyrs, perhaps wise as men, and capable as administrators—those obscure pontiffs who were destined to found so marvellous a power. Even Julius I. and Damasus were as nothing in comparison with the brilliant intellects which formed the boast of Asia and of Greece; for there was hardly a see in the East that had not been distinguished by some powerful mind. Alexandria had held Athanasius and Cyril; Antioch and Constantinople had seen their respective chairs filled by St. Gregory of Nyssa and St. John Chrysostom: and as authority was seated in the West, genius certainly was the property of the

East.

The first man of genius who appeared at Rome to don the insignia of the pontificate was St. Leo the Great, who was especially destined to contribute to the papal see no new principle of authority, but an example of the novel action which it would be called upon to exercise on the barbarous nations. On the 29th of September, a.d. 440, the clergy of Rome assembled upon the death of Sixtus III., and elected in his place Leo, then archdeacon of the Roman Church. The confidence placed in him by the late pontiff, and by the emperors, had made it a worthy choice; and at the very moment of his election the new Pope was in Gaul, occupied in reconciling Aëtius and Albinus, who had turned their swords against each other. Leo was already eminent for the zeal of his faith, and known as a champion against heretics, as a patron of Christian literature, and the friend of Prosper of Aquitaine and of Cassian. He was a man of learning and culture, and his eloquence had gained him the title of the Christian Demosthenes. When called to assume the time-honoured authority of the Roman pontiffs, he showed prompt appreciation of the majesty of the office, and we still possess the discourse in which he rendered thanks to the people, and which he renewed year by year on the anniversary of his election. He expressed therein his gratitude to the clergy and people who had chosen him, modestly lamented the weight of the burden laid upon his soul, but turned confidently to God and the love of the Church, which would help him to sustain it, and above all trusted in the presence of Peter, who sat motionless and invisible behind his unworthy successors. Throughout he developed a doctrine which was the same as that of St. Cyprian, and without being bolder than the view of St. Athanasius, was more explicitly stated.

" The Saviour accords to St. Peter a share in His authority, and whatever He may will to grant in common with him to the other princes of the Church, it is through Peter that He communicates it, and everything which He does not refuse; but Peter did not give up the government of the Church with his life. As immortal minister of the priesthood he is the foundation of the whole Faith, and it is by him that the Church says daily, Thou art the Christ, Son of the living God, and who can doubt that his care extends to all the Churches ? —for in the prince of the Apostles yet lives that love of God and of men, which neither fetters, nor prisons, nor the fury of the multitude, nor the menaces of tyrants can affright, and that dauntless faith which can perish neither in the conflict nor in the triumph. And he speaks in the acts, in the judgments, and in the prayers of his successor, in whom the episcopate recognizes with one accord not the pastor of one city, but the primate of all the churches."

Doctrine cannot be expressed in terms more formal, nor can ignorance go to a further excess than in the case of those who, not aware of the above statement, think it possible to date the rise of the papal primacy from Gregory the Great or even from Gregory VII.

St. Leo had reached the pontificate late in life, and under the most disastrous circumstances for the Church and the Empire; and Providence in no way lightened the difficulties of his mission. It was his task, moreover, to relieve Christianity from the heresies which were tearing it apart; for as if that form 'of probation was never to be complete, the efforts made by Arianism and Manichaeism to wither its doctrine were reproduced under other forms in the middle of the fifth century. The conflict was then restricted to one point, the dogma of the Incarnation, and the person of Christ. Since the Council of Nice, it had been granted that His person was divine; but the issue now arose on the method of understanding that mystery. In order that His mission might be accomplished, it was necessary that He should be God-Man—man, for otherwise humanity could not expiate its offence in His person; God, that the mystery of redemption might be accomplished. But minds trembled at the depths of this mystery, and divided into two factions, one of which attacked the Divinity, the other cavilled at the Humanity. About a.d. 426, Nestorius, the Patriarch of Constantinople, declared in a sermon preached before the assembled people that it was heretical to call the mother of Christ mother of God, as there were two distinct persons in Christ, one divine and one human; that it was a man in whom the Word resided, as God might abide in a temple, without more union than existed between the sanctuary and the Divinity which inhabited it. It was but a transformation of the doctrine of Arius, an attempt to deny the presence of God in Christ, and to sever what He had united by representing the person of the Saviour as that of a mere sage, a man of higher enlightenment, of more intimate connection with God than His fellows, but distinguished in no other respect from the rest of mankind; and the theory tended from its rationalistic character to a denial of the supernatural, and thence in unforeseen consequence to the destruction of the element of mystery in the faith and in time of religion itself.

But the Eastern Church also was aroused by the teachings of Nestorius: the council held at Ephesus in a.d. 431, at the pressing instance of Pope Celestine, condemned the heresiarch, and the contrary doctrine, that one person and two natures dwelt in Christ, was recognized and defined. A little later Eutyches, the archimandrite of a great monastery at Constantinople, pushing his zeal in the controversy against Nestorius to excess, maintained that in Christ there had been only one person and one nature, that the human had been absorbed in the divine nature, and therefore He had not possessed a body similar to ours, or flesh corresponding in substance to that of man, but that as God Himself and alone had laid aside impassibility, and suffered death upon the cross. By supposing a suffering and dying Divinity, Eutyches made a step towards Paganism, and confounded the attributes of the Deity with those of humanity. This doctrine attracted the, notice of Flavian, Patriarch of Constantinople, who deposed its author, whereupon Eutyches, looking to the spot which every Christian held to be the shrine of all wisdom and justice, appealed to Rome, and for greater surety referred the matter also to the Emperor, with whom the influence of Eudoxia and Chrysaphus was exerted in his behalf. Their interference procured his vindication at the robber-synod of Ephesus, held a.d. 449, which acquitted him on every point. But these intrigues failed to deceive the insight of Leo, who had fixed his attention upon those erring theologians, worthy forerunners of the men who maintained a mad dispute as to the nature of the light of Thabor at the moment in which the Turks were pouring through the breaches of the city of Constantine. The Pope had already intervened. With broad wisdom and true Roman good sense, he had written a letter fixing the truth of the contested proposition, and, dispersing with perseverance every obstacle opposed by intrigue, obtained the convocation of a great council at Chalcedon, a.d. 451. He did not select a spot remote from the Court, but a city of Asia, at the very gates of Constantinople, as he was without dread of any opposition which might be offered, and confident in the influence of his eloquence and talent. And, in fact, the letter written by him on the occasion is still considered as a worthy monument of ecclesiastical antiquity; it took its place at once in the cycle of dogma venerated by the Greek Church, and was translated into the languages of the East. We may give a fragment here to show the wise moderation with which Leo the Great kept to the true course.

"We could not conquer sin and death, had not He who cannot be retained by death, nor touched by sin, taken our nature upon Him, and made it His own. He is God, as it is written, at the beginning was the Word. He is Man, as it is written, the Word was made Flesh."

This firm and luminous exposition of doctrine, which ran with so scrupulous an exactitude within the limits of the truth, so charmed and swayed the minds of the Orientals assembled at Chalcedon, that in the second session, having read the Creed of Nicasa, and the letters of Cyril and Leo, they exclaimed,—

"It is the faith of the Fathers; it is the faith of the Apostles. We all believe thus: anathema to those who do not. Peter has spoken by the mouth of Leo. Leo has taught in accordance with truth and piety. It is the faith of all Catholics; we all think thus."

Thus was the great controversy decided, and Leo had made an act of faith in preserving to Christianity its character of a religion, and not suffering it to degenerate into Paganism, or a system of philosophy. He had made an act of faith in guarding its mysteries, lest it should degenerate into a theory in the hands of Nestorius, a myth with the treatment of Eutyches; for, as a theory, it would only appeal to. reason, as a myth, charm the imagination; but, as a mystery, it engaged belief, for faith plunges into the unknown as a just man yields himself to the shades of death, knowing that in its darkness he will glide into a purer light, and find in dissolution another life. The strong mind of Leo, too, knew that in the obscure region of the faith he would receive the supernatural existence given as a grace from God to those who believe; for as the power of persuasion is accorded as well to those who are strong in trust as to those who reason and dispute, so the confident assertion of that Roman priest silenced for a season the sophists of the East, and the Church retired into the long repose of thought, of reason, and of faith.

At the same time, St. Leo saved civilization in the West from the menaces of the barbarians. The era of invasion had arrived, and small were the resources of the Empire to offer resistance to the formidable hordes which swarmed on the steppes of Asia, and penetrated beyond the Rhine until the Gallic provinces, Spain, and Africa, fell under their dominion. Amidst the confusion, it was seen that the official resources of civilization had, indeed, dwindled away: the Emperor Valentinian III., a feeble and bad prince, remained at Ravenna, under the tutelage of his mother, Placidia. He was served by two eminent warriors, Aëtius and Boniface, but they were traitors capable of sacrificing their master to their mutual detestation. Aëtius was in constant communication with the Huns; Boniface had sold Africa to the Vandals: the former killed the latter with his own hand, and was in return poniarded by Valentinian himself, who again was destined to fall under the dagger of Petronius Maximus, whose wife he had dishonoured. Maximus succeeded to his throne and to his spouse, until the widow of Valentinian, on hearing of the crime committed by her new husband, called Genseric to her aid, and opened to him the gates of Rome. This was the signal for the death of Maximus, who was stoned in attempting to fly. He was succeeded by Avitus, Majorian, and Severus, whose short-lived reigns were lost at the approach of the day of doom which was to sound, a.d. 476, for the Empire of the West.

The enemies of civilization, the double peril from which the world must be saved, were Attila, who, with his following of three hundred thousand strong, struck terror into Germany, Gaul, and the whole world, and Genseric, master of Africa and the South, who was feared even by the warriors of Attila. One day the latter sent a message to the two Caesars of Ravenna and Byzantium, "Make ready your palaces, for I am resolved to visit you;" then, with his multitudinous hordes, he passed like a torrent over

Gaul, lost the battle of Chalons, but neither hope nor fury, and, a.d. 452, crossed the Alps, and appeared before Aquileia. Carried by assault, after a short resistance, the town was given over to pillage and destruction, and Pavia and Milan soon shared its fate. The terrified emperor took refuge in Rome, but found therein neither generals nor legions; his only resource was the presence of a few counsellors, amongst the eloquent of the Senate, and the stronger influence which resided in the person of Leo. The Pope was deputed, in concert with Trygetius, ex-prefect of the city, and Avienus, a man of consular rank, to stop Attila, as swords and legions were lacking, by his eloquence, at the passage of the Mincio. The interview which followed has had no historians, for it did not accord with the nature or with the duty of Leo the Great to recount his own victory, nor with the taste of Trygetius and Avienus to avow their impotence. One thing is certain, that after an interview with Leo, Attila retreated across the Alps into Pannonia, where he died in the following year. Different legends were woven around this fact: one especially related how that Attila had told his officers that their retreat was caused by the presence of another priest of severe mien, who stood behind Leo as he spoke, and signified that a further advance would be followed by his death. This tale, free from criticism, though apparently without authority, has traversed the ages as history, and received an eternal consecration from the hands of Raphael in the chambers of the Vatican. And when, in later times, another horde of barbarians, in the shape of the German Lutherans, entered Rome in the train of the Constable de Bourbon, and set fire to the *Stanze* of Raphael, in order to efface the triumphs of the papacy, name and smoke alike respected the victory of Leo the Great.

Leo thus resisted the danger which proceeded from the North, but that from the South was still imminent. Genseric, half Christian, and half civilized, served by a hierarchy of functionaries formed after the method of the Empire, with a fleet under his orders which could annihilate distance and avenge the old disgrace of Hannibal, was more formidable than Attila. Summoned by the widow of Valentinian, he set sail, and in reply to the inquiry of his pilot, 'bade him direct the prow " Towards those whom the wrath of God was menacing"—a menace which, on that day, was hurled at Rome. Three years had elapsed since the retreat of Attila, and frequently had Leo reminded the Romans, of their deliverance, had bade them attribute it not to the stars or to chance, but to the mercy of God and the prayers of the saints, and had adjured them to celebrate the anniversary in the Christian churches rather than in the circus or the amphitheatres. But his words were in vain, and with the foolhardiness of mariners on the morrow of one tempest, and the eve of another, they had forgotten his warnings, till they learnt that Genseric had just landed at the head of a mighty army, was ascending the Tiber, and approaching the gates. Again did Leo go forth to the barbarians, and obtained that they should content themselves with mere plunder, but spare the lives and respect the persons of the inhabitants; whereupon Genseric entered the city, and remained there a fortnight, historians attesting that he pillaged the town, but refrained from shedding a drop of blood. And surely the second miracle was greater than the first, inasmuch as there was merit and skill, less in arresting the course of the barbarous Attila, struck mayhap by the majestic aspect of an aged Christian, than in restraining for fourteen days and nights that Vandal multitude, partly Arian, partly pagan, bound to the Roman population amongst whom they had fallen by no bond of identical belief, and in keeping them faithful to the letter of a treaty which had been signed on the eve of their entrance into a defenceless town.

It was the intense patriotism inspiring Leo which alone gave him such strength in the presence of the barbarians. This quality distinguished him amongst all the doctors of the "West; it was the knot which bound together antiquity and modern times, perpetuating in the Christian mind the legitimate traditions of old. The Pope felt the passions of Cincinnatus and the Scipios within him, and though he took a different view of Roman greatness, was as devoted as they were to the glory of the city, in which he was citizen as well as bishop. He shows us this feeling in that sermon for the festival of the Apostles Peter and Paul, in which he claims a providential destiny for the city in which he was established as servant of the servants of God.

"In order that Grace and Redemption might spread their effects throughout the world, the Divine Providence prepared the Roman Empire, which pushed to such a point its development, that in its bosom all the nations of the world were united, and seemed to touch one another. For it was part of the plan of the Divine economy that a great number of kingdoms should be confounded in one empire, that preaching, finding ways open to it, might speedily reach all the various nations whom one city held subject to her laws."

This was akin to the doctrine which we have marked in the writings of Claudian, and shall find also in those of Prudentius and Rutilius—a view which will run on from age to age, and cause Dante to repeat that it was with regard to the Christian greatness of Rome that God established the Roman Empire. And thus the Roman idea did not vanish, but was revived, at the presence of barbarism, to resist and combat it; and Leo the Great commenced the glorious strife which Gregory the Great and his successors were to carry on until barbarism, purified, regenerate, victorious over its own nature, was definitely to yield in the person of Charlemagne, and to reconstruct the Empire of the West.

We have now sufficiently proved, that whatever power of the papacy there was, none of it was due to the period of barbarism; that it was constituted in the full light of the ancient order, under the jealous eye of Paganism, the discerning gaze of the Fathers of the Church, and raised in the centuries which were greatest in Christian theology; that it owed nothing to obscurity. It was endowed with its incontestable influence that it might resist the menaces of the barbarians, and begin a struggle, which lulled but for a moment under Charlemagne, to be waged again; for when Gregory VII. inflicted upon Henry IV. that penance which has gained him so much obloquy, he was but continuing the work of Leo against Attila, and saving civilization by driving the barbarian back to his proper domain.

But there was another power, namely, Monasticism, which took its part in the preservation of literature and civilization. "We shall not have to rebut on its behalf the charge of novelty, which has been made against the papacy, for monasticism has been accused of too early rather than of too late an origin; of being born amongst the hoary religions of the East, of being penetrated with their spirit, and of being surreptitiously introduced into the Church to bring to her habits which were not her own, and, therefore, of having been less an aid than a peril, far less a glory than a scandal to the Faith. We have already said that Christianity did not create, but transformed humanity. Man already existed, but under the law of the flesh; the family, but under the law of the stronger; the city, but subject to the law of interest. Then Christianity reformed man by the revival of his spiritual constituent; the family, by protecting the right of the weak; the city, by arousing a public conscience. It found temples, sacrifices, and priests in the old society, and these, according to its maxim of regenerating everything, but abolishing nothing, it preserved and purified. It acted likewise as to monasticism, for every great religion has had its monks; as

India with her ascetics, who abandon everything, bury their existence in deserts, with no possession but a rag upon the shoulder, and a wooden platter in the hand, supporting life on grains or roots dug from the earth, and with huddled limbs spend day and night in contemplating the soul of God captive in their bodies, from which it is seeking release. Side by side with these Brahmin anchorites are the coenobites of Buddhism, for in Tartary, China, and Japan there are no priests, but only monks, who live under the law of their respective communities. These Oriental institutions have but the spirit of the Paganism which inspires them; they are founded on a confusion of the principle of the creature and the Creator; and as the Brahmin supposes himself the lord of the universe, and that all men live by his permission, his contempt for his fellows is supreme; whilst the anchorite thinks that the supreme good is an absorption in the incomprehensible Buddha, so that pride and egoism are of the essence of the Indian asceticism. Monasticism appeared under purer forms amongst the Hebrews in the last days of the old order, for Judaism had its ascetics also in the Essenes and the Therapeutae: the first, residing on the shores of the Dead Sea, were devoted to a life of activity; the second were placed at Alexandria, and gave themselves up to contemplation and prayer; while both classes practised celibacy and a community of goods, but rejected the use of slaves. The hard spirit of Judaism appeared in their hatred of foreigners, and their absolute separation from the remainder of mankind, whom they considered so impure, that the approach of a man who was not an Essene had to be followed by a purification; whilst the sinner amongst them could hope for no reconciliation, his fault was irreparable, and the offering him the hand or breaking bread with him was forbidden. These orders survived the foundation of Christianity, and were known to Pliny the Elder, who instanced them as being a people distinguished from all others, " Living without women, abnegating all pleasure, leading an existence of poverty under the palm-trees …. thus, for thousands of centuries, remarkable fact, has this everlasting nation subsisted, and yet no child is born of its bosom, so profound is its hatred for other modes of life."

It is in this quarter, and amongst the Therapeutae especially, that we must look for the origin of Christian monasticism. Whilst imperilled society was still capable of regeneration, and martyrdom was the condition of the consolidation of the faith, the saints remained in the world to die in the circus or on the pile at the hour appointed by their God. As long as persecution lasted, the men were martyrs who would have been anchorites, and **it** was not till the moment which saw the dissolution of the Roman society that a new order was organized to replace **it,** and the bands were disciplined who, when Rome had fallen, were to assume her task and reconquer the universe. St. Paul, the first hermit, appeared a.d. 251. A little later he was followed by St. Anthony, who formed a Rule, and was succeeded by St. Pacomius, who assembled his disciples into regular communities, governed by a fixed law. Under this new rule they spread rapidly over the entire East, and at length St. Basil became the author of the .ordinance which was soon venerated and adopted by all the Oriental monasteries. Suspicious of a solitary existence, he reduced the scattered ascetics to a life in community, and showed his preference for coenobites rather than anchorites. *"For"* as he said to a hermit, " whose feet wilt thou wash, whom wilt thou serve, how canst thou be the last, if thou art alone ?"

We must now mark the adoption by the West of that monastic life which already flourished in the Eastern Churches. We may probably see the precise period of the propagation in the Latin Church of the coenobitic life, and assign to it a more remote date than that usually given at the foundation of Ligugé. For it was St. Athanasius, the friend and biographer of the hermit St. Anthony, who brought with him into the West the passion of imitating his life. In examining the journeys of Athanasius to the West more closely, we find that, exiled by Constantine, he came first to Treves, a.d. 336, lived there for some time, and doubtless then found leisure for writing his life of Anthony, whilst he saw around him evidence of the superior merit of the coenobitic life, for monasteries had early been founded at Treves which retained the life of St. Anthony as their law and constitution. We have already spoken of the tale, related by St. Augustine, in his " Confessions," as making so deep an impression on his mind, of the two officers of the Court, who, whilst walking apart from their comrades in the suburbs of Treves, came to a house tenanted by monks. Entering, they perceived a book upon the table: it was the "Life of St. Anthony." One of them began to read it, and at the tale of that pure life of the desert, spent in communion with God, and under a cloudless sky, the poor officer, lacerated, doubtless, by the injustice of the Court, was profoundly touched, and, turning to his friend, remarked:—

" ' Whither does all our toil lead us ? What end are we pursuing? What hope have we except that of becoming the friends of the Emperor? And what danger we are incurring ! For it is our main duty to become the friends of God, and from to-day.' He began to read again, and his soul was transformed, and his mind despoiled itself of the world. He read, and the waves of his heart rolled tumultuously. He trembled a moment, judged, decided, and already subdued, said to his friend, ' It is over. I give up my prospects, and resolve to serve God here and at once.' His friend imitated his example, and when their comrades rejoined them, and had learnt their decision, they left them in tears, but weeping for themselves."

This history shows the sudden power and irresistible fascination by which the enthusiasm for a solitary life was propagated in the heart of that dissipated, mournful, and worn-out society of the West, at the doors of which the barbarians were already demanding admittance. The companion of that officer followed his friend into the same monastery, and thus arose the coenobitic life in the Western Church. We need not relate how St. Jerome formed and disciplined from his retreat at Bethlehem the colonies of monks who soon spread over the whole of Italy, nor how St. Augustine, charmed by the Pythagoraean idea of a life in common, t which had been a part of the dreams with his friends at Milan in former days, founded monasteries when raised to the see of Hippo, and prescribed to them rules which bore the impress of the wisdom and tact which characterized his genius. Gaul, however, was the peculiar land of the coenobitic life; since St. Martin, who had been educated in a monastery at Milan, founded a similar institution at Liguge, near Poitiers; and a little later the great house of Marmoutiers, near Tours, where he lived as bishop of the neighbouring town, with some eighty monks, and whence he was borne to his resting-place with an escort of more than two thousand. We see without surprise the foundation, in 410, of the great abbey of Lerins, which was to produce so many illustrious names; of another, also, by St. Victor, at Marseilles, which received from Cassian the traditions of the " Thebaid; " and again in the Island of Barba, near Lyons; whilst Vitrucius peopled with his religious the sandbanks of Flanders. So, from the opening of the fifth century, we see that the frontiers which the warriors of Rome had abandoned were guarded by colonies of different soldiery, by the cohorts of another Rome, who would stop the course of the barbarians, would fix them on the soil they had gained, and thus advance far towards the work of their civilization. We may state, in conclusion, the three points of difference between Monasticism and the Roman world, which gave it power over that old society, poverty in the midst of a world which was dying in its own opulence, chastity in a world which was expiring in orgies, obedience in a world that disorder was decomposing. But between Christian and Indian asceticism lay a deeper difference. Though the pagan hermits were chaste, poor, and submissive, they lacked the labour and prayer of their Christian followers. The ascetics of India spurned work and remained motionless, lest the occupation of their hands should trouble their contemplation, but the recluses of Christendom laboured either manually or mentally. The solitudes of the " Thebaid " had their smiths, carpenters, curriers, and even shipbuilders, whilst mental toil was dominant in the monasteries of the West. St. Augustine established it in the convents of Africa; it flourished at Ligugé, Lerins, and elsewhere; and literature found in the cloister its secret asylum. To labour perseveringly, not for self, nor even for wife or children, but for a community, was no light demand upon human nature; and the founders of the spiritual life had only called for this sacrifice and abnegation of leisure in the name of charity. They had never imagined that men could be united in a perpetual restraint, in a companionship which had mortification and forgetfulness of self as its essence, in the name of a pride which ambitioned ascendancy, or of a sensualism which craved for a gratification. To achieve this wonderful result a degree of self-denial was necessary: it was the work of the humility and charity which Christians laboured to attain through prayer. The sages of Paganism and the anchorites of India did not pray. Why should they do so, in their life of contemplation and absorption, having the Deity within them, or being gods themselves? But the motive to prayer with the recluse of Christianity was, that he recognized a principle which was greater and stronger than himself; his devotion was prompted by love, by aspirations to a better life, and to God Himself. He did not despise his fellow-men, but loved them with passionate effusion. Far from forgetting his aged father or weeping mother at the moment of his leaving them, or from becoming generally dead to humanity, the Christian monk remembered his parents and his fellow-men by day and by night, in the moment of silent contemplation, or of loving communion with the Almighty, and his prayers were a method of doing service to mankind, and of cooperating in the work which aimed at purifying and sanctifying the Church.

CHRISTIAN MANNERS.

It was our task to look for the available forces of the Christian society in the presence of that invasion whose mutterings were, so to speak, already perceived; to know what institutions were ready to receive the first onslaught of barbarism, to withstand it from the first, and finally to overcome it. Amongst these, two merited a nearer study, owing to the great destiny which following ages had in store for them. We have examined into the origin of the Papacy and of Monasticism, and found that the first arose out of the constitution of Christianity, and was the type of its visible unity; we have seen it increase in spite of danger, and as occasion called, until it exercised, in the person of Leo the Great, prerogatives as full as any that might be claimed by Gregory the Great or Gregory VII., and proved that the second was a phenomenon necessary to all great religions; and seen how, following the example of the prophetic colleges, the Essenes, and the Therapeutae, the great monastic colonies arose which were to replace the faltering legions on the imperial frontier, and increase so rapidly as to stud the banks of every river; and how the writings of St. Jerome exhaled that aroma of the desert which was destined to attract countless anchorites towards a solitary life, and drive St. Columba into 'the mountains of the Vosges or the forests of Switzerland. Thus the two institutions which have been represented as the work of the barbarians, the inevitable but irregular result of a period of trouble and of intellectual darkness, preceded the shadows which it was their mission to illumine.

It remains to examine the ecclesiastical legislation in its totality, in the cases especially of the new organization of the family by Christian marriage, of property by the laws relating to Church property, of justice by the procedure in the episcopal courts, and the penitential system of the Church, which embraced in some way all the degrees of human morality. But as time and space would be wanting for so vast an undertaking, we must confine ourselves to marking the origin of the Canon Law, that continuation in a purified form of the Roman traditions. And as the old temples remained standing, and Latin literature assisted to educate the generations of Christians who were thronging into the Church, so also was the ancient legislation most effectually preserved in the canonical institutions, which seemed at first sight to veil and smother it. We must study in the decrees of councils, or the mandates of the series of Popes who had followed the martyrs, all that survived of the traditional legislation of their persecutors, and how Ulpian, the great enemy of Christianity, was assured of living to posterity at the moment when the Church, by an amnesty, caused him to enter her fold, and occupy the highest place amongst her jurisconsults.

Thus the new institutions were full of power, but side by side with law was the prevailing state of manners. Society is seated less upon the large, solid, and perceptible bases called law, than on those other foundations, hidden from the scope of science, which are called manners. Pagan Rome had mighty institutions also, but the progress of her legislation was the result of the decay of her morality. Did, then, the Christian society of the fifth century present the same contrast, or did progressive morality accompany the course of legislation ? We may stop at two points of superiority in Christian manners, and dwell on the dignity of the man, and his respect for woman. The barbarians have been credited with the introduction of these two sentiments into modern civilization, and, in truth, those wandering heroes of the battle and the chase, who scorned to yield to any visible authority, and trusted in nothing but their bows and arrows, did bring to the new order of things—with that haughty humour which trampled underfoot for long any legislative attempt to render them amenable to civil servitude—the feelings of independence, of honour, and of personal inviolability. And those savage men also recognized a certain divine quality in women; they sought oracles from them before the battle, came to them for the healing of their wounds when the conflict was past, and knelt before the soothsaying Velleda. Thus they were rich in a sentiment which was unknown to Roman society, which was to adorn the Middle Age and blossom into chivalry. Such, then, were the innovations of the barbarians upon the old world; but it remains to be seen whether they had not been forestalled— whether their contribution of these two generous instincts, which elevated the man, and surrounded the woman with veneration, had not been anticipated by a power which had already placed them in the category of virtues.

The chief, though deep-lying and secret, support of modern society, lies in the noble feeling termed honour, which is synonymous with the independence and inviolability of the human conscience, in its superiority to all tyranny and external force—in a word, the feeling of personal dignity which, be it understood, antiquity, with all its civic virtues, had suppressed. For, as we know, the citizen was nothing in the presence of the state; conscience was silent before law; the individual had no rights distinct from those of the Commonwealth. This was the general rule, and whilst under the old order the dignity of the man was crushed by the majesty of his country, humanity was debased in the three classes of slaves, the working men, and the poor, who formed its great majority.

We know what legislation had effected for the slave; but we hardly realize what was the practical lot of that human creature, or rather chattel, which was used either as a victim of infamous passions, or, as by Cleopatra, to try the effect of poisons, or, as by Asinius Pollio, as food for lampreys. Yet humanity had never quite lost its rights, and Seneca had dared to give utterance somewhere to the rash opinion that slaves might be men like himself. He had twenty thousand slaves of his own, and his stoicism did not issue in the emancipation of one. Moreover, his philosophy had passed into the writings of the Roman jurisconsults? and yet they laboured to diminish the number of manumissions as being detrimental to the public security. A moiety of the Roman population were held in a servitude withering alike to both mind and body. It was a received proverb that Jupiter deprived those whose liberty was forfeit of a half of their intelligence, and the slaves believed themselves to have been fated to their eternal condemnation, under the weight of which they were crushed; and this resulted in the frenzied passion and gross profligacy to which they were abandoned, and which Latin comedy has so freely treated. Plautus himself had once turned the wheel as a slave, and we can therefore receive his evidence as to the deep corruption of the servile condition.

Christianity found matters thus, and has often been reproached with not immediately liberating the slaves; but it had two reasons for its course—in the first place, its horror for violence and bloodshed, and because the Christ who died upon the Cross had not pointed to the example of Spartacus—secondly, because the slave was not yet capable of liberty, until he had been made a man, with a reconstituted personality, restored self-respect, and a reawakened conscience. This was the work begun by Christ in taking the form of a servant and dying upon the Cross, and every one, after His example, in becoming a Christian, entered upon a voluntary servitude, *Qui liber vocatus est, servus est Christi*. Every martyr who died was truly and legally a slave *servi poenæ*, and so from the earliest time the fetters which had been reddened with the blood of Calvary, were purified and newly consecrated in that of the martyrs, and slaves came spontaneously to steep their irons therein, and disputed with their Christian masters the honour of dying for the inviolability of conscience. Amongst the martyred bands who braved death from the earliest days of the faith, the fallen and accursed section of humanity was amply represented. We have St. Blandina at. Lyons, St. Felicita in Africa, and at Alexandria St. Potamiaena, who, when summoned by her judge to respond to the passions of her master, exclaimed, " God forbid that I should ever find a judge so wicked as to constrain me to yield to the lust of my master." From that time forward the conscience was reorganized, the person of man restored, and the slave had bent under a voluntary service. Henceforth the peril was rather that he should despise his master than himself; and we find St. Ignatius exhorting the slaves not to scorn their owners, nor to suffer themselves to be carried away by a pride in their purified yoke. A little later St. Chrysostom replied to those who inquired why Christianity had not enfranchised all slaves at a blow:—

" It is that you may learn the excellence of liberty. For as it was a greater work to preserve the three children whilst they remained in the furnace, so there is less greatness exhibited in the suppression of slavery than in showing forth liberty even in fetters."

Thus did the enfranchisement of humanity commence, as has ever been the method of Christianity, by action upon the soul, in giving to the slave his moral liberty, and preparing the way for this long laborious straggle for civil freedom; for in proportion as the slave rose in his own, so also did he gain the esteem of his master. The dogma of the native equality of all souls appeared; slavery appeared rooted, not in nature, but in sin; and sin had been vanquished by Redemption. No Christian could believe that he possessed in his slave a being of an inferior nature, upon which he had every right, even to that of life and death; and St. Augustine declared that no Christian master could own a slave by the same title as he owned a horse, and that, being man himself, he was bound to love his man as himself; and another doctor, commenting on the words which gave Noah dominion over the animals, insisted that in giving man the power of terrifying and coercing the beasts of the earth, God refused to grant it over his fellows. Slavery then subsisted amongst Christians, but as absolute power over the person was forever abolished, it lost the half of its rigour, and the slave recovered a right in many things which were held sacred. He had rights in the family, to life, honour, and repose. The " Apostolical Constitution," an apocryphal work, but which certainly originated no later than the fifth century, decided that the slave might rest on Sunday in memory of the Redemption, and also on Saturday in memory of the Creation. The Church was skilful in finding pretexts for granting a respite to the poor people, in favour of whom Christ had said, " Come, all ye that labour, and I will give you rest." The master began, in sight of the Face which still glowed with the aureola of the crown of thorns, to recognize in the wretch whom once he had trampled underfoot the image of his Lord. St. Paulinus, on thanking Sulpicius Severus for the gift of a young slave, took himself to task for having accepted the services of a young man in whom he detected a loftiness of soul.

" He has served me, and been my slave: woe to me who have permitted it, that he who has never been the slave of sin should serve a sinner. And I, unworthy that I am, have suffered a servant of righteousness to be my servant. Every day he washed my feet, and had I permitted it would have cleansed my sandals, ardent to render every service to the body, that he might gain dominion over the soul. It is Jesus Christ Himself whom I venerate in the youth, for every faithful soul cometh from God, and everyone who is humble of heart proceeds from the very heart of Christ."

It is obvious that when respect for the individual was thus established, the very foundations of slavery were sapped; and in truth Christianity had but few blows to deal in order to level successively the walls of the half-ruined edifice. At first entire categories of slaves, as for instance those of the theatre, were suppressed. Before they were closed for ever, the gates of the pagan theatres had to open wide to give forth the crowds attached to their service, the numberless dancers and mimes, and the rest who laboured under the most shameful servitude — that of pleasure. Troops of gladiators also were enfranchised from slavery and slaughter, and although certain Christians still publicly paraded their following of slaves with insolence, it was at the cost of a determined opposition on the part of their faith; whilst St. John Chrysostom waited for them on the days of festival in the Basilica of Constantinople, and with scornful brow and outstretched hands demanded an account of their harshness, their prodigality, and their sloth. " Wherefore so many slaves ? One master should be content with one servant. Nay, more, one servant should suffice for two or three masters; and if that seems a hard doctrine, think of those who have none."

He finally granted two slaves to each, but he could not tolerate the rich men who used to walk in the public places and frequent the baths, driving men in herds before them like shepherds; and if it was objected to him that it was done in order to nourish a number of unfortunates who would die of hunger if they did not win their bread thus, would reply, "If you wish to act out of charity, you should teach them a trade and render them independent, and that is what you refuse to do. I know well," he added, "that my teaching is at your expense, but I am doing my duty and shall not cease to speak." His words had other results than the mere accomplishment of duty, and reconquered a right for oppressed humanity, so that every day beheld the manumissions multiplied which Constantine had authorized on the festival days of the Church; and the proper joyfulness seemed impossible if at the end of the service the hymn for the day was not shouted by a crowd of men as they shook off their fetters and cast them far away.

Thus the number of emancipations, once held so dangerous to the state, was ceaselessly enlarged. But now the Romans were bound to accustom themselves to enfranchise the captive barbarians if they wished to be liberated in their turn. For the barbarians had crept through all the chinks of the Empire, and were carrying away women and children in troops, and selling the senators themselves in the market-places. Christendom roused itself at this new phase of slavery, and threw its energy into the work of liberation, whilst the bishops, treated formerly as madmen when they spoke of the manumission of slaves, begged from the pulpit that subscriptions should be opened and collections made for the enfranchisement of the senators and patricians, who were now the captives of some Sueve or Vandal.

It was on such an occasion St. Ambrose uttered the admirable words in which he advocated the sale of the sacred vessels of the Church for the sake of these prisoners, "for," he said, "the redemption of captives is an ornament to the mysteries."

Such are the texts, and time would fail if more were cited, which must be given in reply to the questionings as to where and when Christianity first formally preached the release of slaves. We may also point to St. Cyprian, who found time during persecution, when tracked by the satellites of the proconsul, to collect money from the faithful, not for himself or his priests, but for some man who had been captured on the frontier by wandering Arabs; and later to St. Gregory the Great, freeing the slaves of his wide domains, and giving the following motive for his procedure:—

"Since our Redeemer, the author of the entire, creation, willed to take the flesh of a man that the power of His Divinity might break the chain of our servitude, and restore our primitive liberty, it is a wholesome act to pity the men whom He made free, but whom the law of nations has reduced to slavery, and to render them, by the benefit of manumission, to the liberty for which they were born."

These maxims were essential to the great labour of the Middle Age for the emancipation of classes, that transformation of slaves into serfs, of serfs into coloni, of coloni into proprietors, of proprietors into the middle class, of the latter into that third estate which was destined one day to dominate the modern nations. These principles animated the illustrious St. Eloi, when escaping from the palace of the Merovingian Kings, whose servant and minister he was, he waited in the public place, impatient for the time of sale of the captives, then bought them and gave them immediate liberty in the Basilica, declaring them freemen at the feet of the Saviour. Later, Snaragdus, writing to King Louis le Débonnaire, made it a case of conscience that he should not suffer slaves to remain on his own domain, and should abolish slavery, by edict, from the land of every Christian. The efforts made for emancipation will be felt in the Christian society to the end; and when, in the thirteenth century, the land of France had no more slaves to set free, it was customary on great festivals to recall these solemn acts of enfranchisement by loosing crowds of caged pigeons in the churches, that captivity might be ended, and prisoners delivered still in honour of the Redeemer.

We must secondly consider what Christianity effected for the working men. Nothing can be more inimical to slavery than free labour, and so antiquity, as it supported the former, trampled upon the latter, and saluted it with the most opprobrious epithets. Even Cicero, that man of ability and common sense, to whom men of our own day so much love to recur, said somewhere that there could be nothing liberal in manual labour— that commerce, if transacted in a small way, should be considered sordid; if of vast and opulent character, could not be sufficiently blamed. Brutus, however, lent money, but at such terrible usury that all Greece, in some manner, was his debtor. Atticus also lent at a high risk, and realized enormous profits. Seneca had successively involved his debtors in such cunningly calculated toils that Britain, unable to free herself, and stung by the exactions of the imperial proconsul, rose in a revolt which was nearly proving fatal, and cost the lives of eighty thousand Romans.

Under burdens of this nature free labour was crippled, and the result of this usury was the *nexi* and other penalties which menaced the insolvent debtor. For under the law of the Twelve Tables the man who failed to satisfy his creditor was given over into his hands to be sold as a slave, or might be cut into as many pieces as there were creditors, that each might claim his share. In the time of Seneca, although it was no longer customary to cut him into morsels, the insolvent was obliged to sell his children in public auction; and till the time of Constantine this mode of discharging debts was in force. But if free labour was thus treated by antiquity, Christianity rehabilitated it, following the example of Christ and His Apostles, especially St. Paul, who chose manual labour, and was a partner with the Jew Aquila, at Corinth, in the trade of tent-making, rather than eat bread which had not been won by the sweat of the brow. The early Christians were generally working men, and Celsus professed great pity for "those woolcarders, fullers, and shoemakers, a coarse and ignorant rabble, who kept silence before the aged and the heads of families, but secretly perverted women and children into a belief in their mysteries yet the Church was proud of that mob of her first children for whom he could not evince a sufficiently profound contempt, and even boasted of having taught some true philosophy to shoemakers, to cowherds, and labourers. Moreover, the labour which was elevated by faith and doctrine, was enhanced still more by the sacred objects to which it was applied. Below the priests and deacons, but respected by all, was placed the order of diggers *(fossores)*, so called from their work in providing beneath the quarries of puzzolane which old Rome had dug in the hidden recesses of the Catacombs, the retreats which sheltered the Christian community. They laboured with pickaxe and lantern, as pioneers of the new society, in clearing the way along which we are marching now, and were comprised in the ecclesiastical hierarchy as being the first order among the inferior clergy, " charged after the example of Tobias with the task of burying the dead, that their attention to things visible might lead their thoughts to those which are invisible;" and their condition is attested by numerous inscriptions and paintings which show us the *fossor,* with the instruments of his humble calling. Christianity, therefore, regenerated labour by the force of example; and as it was not sufficient to honour toil, it reorganized it by adding an unselfish element, and teaching men to work in common one for another. This aim appeared in the monastic communities, and from the first St. Basil prescribed manual labour to his monks, and bade them, " if fasting made labour impossible, to live more generously, as being the soldiers of Christ." St. Augustine, too, replied in his work, "De Origine Monachorum," to those haughty monks who, once in the cloister, held themselves discharged from the burdens imposed upon the first man, and argued that Christ had bade them to act like the birds of the air, which toiled not, or the lilies of the field, which did not spin, and yet were not less gloriously clothed than Solomon himself, by pointing out the dignity and majesty of manual work, how supremely excellent it was, in that it did not absorb the whole being, but left scope for meditation. " True that the birds do not sow nor reap," said he, " but as they do not possess your palaces, your granaries, your servants, why should you have them ? " He added that if a multitude of slaves should come and demand admission to the monastery, its doors should be opened wide to them, for such hardy people assured prosperity to a Christian community, but that the men who entered upon the monastic life must not think that they were thus to escape their daily and accustomed toil, nor that peasants were to look for a life of delicacy and repose in the places in which senators buried themselves, that they might labour with their hands.

It was thus, then, that labour was organized in the early days of the Church. Roman antiquity had established industrial institutions; corporations *(collegia),* formed from the association of the working class; and Roman legislation bore plentiful witness to the existence of numbers of these societies for the use of workmen in wood, in marble, gold, iron, and wool. Their colleges appeared early to be in possession of common property with their *ordo,* their *curies* and especial magistrates, who were named *duumviri,* but they were feeble, crushed by the dominant legislation, oppressed by heavy imposts, and corroded by the corruptions of Paganism. Many of these institutions which have been so immoderately belauded were, in fact, only constituted for the purpose of mutual feasting and pleasure-seeking upon fixed days, so lofty was the essential idea of the corporations of labour in the times of heathenism. But Christianity undertook and succeeded in the task of regenerating them by an infusion of novel principles; and when the Empire succumbed the *collegia* and *scholæ* multiplied. Warlike corporations rose speedily in Rome, in Ravenna, and all the cities of the Exarchate and the Pentapolis, broke the power of the

Eastern emperors, saved the Papacy from the perils which menaced it at the commencement of the eighth century, and paved the way for those powerful commonwealths which were destined to so glorious a career. And the devotion which impelled their members to die in battle when the aggressions of Germany had to be resisted and the Guelph liberties, which were also the liberties of religion, had to be defended, was a true sign that Christianity was on their side, and a better idea than that of enjoyment was inspiring their deliberations; whilst in the passion of the Florentine and the other Italian corporations for the arts and for poetry, for all that is lovely and elevating, we may recognize at a later date the mark of the Christian and civilizing mission with which they were stamped—for it was by the hands of associated workmen that the Church of San Michele was reared at Florence, to be a noble monument of republican greatness.

In the third place, we must treat of poverty. Under the old order the poor had been trampled on consistently with the genius of an antiquity which regarded them as stricken with the reprobation of God, and even in the time of St. Ambrose Pagans and bad Christians were accustomed to say, " We care not to give to people whom God must have cursed, since He has left them in sorrow and want." Poverty had first to be treated as honourable, and this was effected by giving to the poor the first place in the Church and in the Christian community; and St. John Chrysostom said of them: "As fountains flow near the place of prayer that the hands that are about to be raised to heaven may be washed, so were the poor placed by our fathers near to the door of the Church, that our hands might be consecrated by benevolence before they are raised to God."

Thus the poor were not only respected but necessary to Christendom, and this explains the saying so often misunderstood and so often perverted: " There always will be poor men." No word has been said as to the perpetuity of the rich, but poverty must always exist in voluntary if not compulsory form, the reason of the institutions in which every member abnegates his own possessions, and vows himself to destitution; and so poverty has taken its proper rank in the divine economy, and become the mainspring of Christian society. Yet this was not enough, and want must also be succoured and consoled. Antiquity could boast of a system of public almsgiving, and could point to the corn laws of Caesar, and the imperial largesses. Aurelian had had kindly feelings towards the people, and desired that the distributions should be daily made to the poor of a loaf of bread of two pounds weight, of lard and of wine, till the praetorian prefect had remarked to him, if he proceeded on thus, there could be no reason for not presenting them with chickens and geese. And the functionary was right; for the paupers of Rome fattened at the cost of their brethren of the provinces, and the Gauls, our ancestors, gave their blood and their sweat to nourish the starving rabble inscribed on the register of the census.

At Rome, almsgiving was not the duty of the individual but the right of all. But Christianity inverted the rule, and in its economy charity was not the right of any person, but the duty of the whole community. Benevolence became a sacred duty, a precept and not merely a counsel, and St. Ambrose addressed the wealthy amongst the faithful in these terms:—

" You say, I shall not give, but mark, if you do give alms to the poor, you give not what is your own, but his. You pay a debt instead of giving a voluntary largesse, and therefore the Scripture bids you to incline your soul towards the poor man and render to him his due."

But if Christianity made almsgiving a duty towards the poor, it was towards that nameless and universal poverty which was in fact Christ Himself in the persons of the destitute. He was the sole Creditor and Judge of the tribunal to which the rich would be summoned who had abused their trust; and the Church conferred no personal right on the individual of reclaiming the share which might be rightly his. St. Augustine said:—"Surplus wealth is the competency of the poor, and the possession of what is superfluous is an usurpation of the rights of others. Give, then, to your brother who is in need, and in giving to him give to Christ." The Almighty, then, as the sole master of everything, was the sole, the invisible, but long-suffering creditor of the rich man, who was but his steward; the judge as to the wants of his fellows; disposing of his wealth and ruling its distribution on his own responsibility. St. Ambrose desired that the wealthy should discriminate those who were able-bodied and could dispense with relief, as well as the rogues and vagabonds, and the men who pretended that they had been pillaged by thieves or ruined by creditors, whilst they made a scrupulous search for hidden misery, elicited complaints that had hitherto kept silence, visited the pallet of unrepining agony, and brought to light the hiding-places which had no echo for the voice of sorrow.

Upon such conditions as these did the charities of the Church proceed; but besides what was done in private she possessed a public system of relief. We need not enter upon the organization of the various societies for almsgiving which were initiated by the collections made by the Thessalonians upon the advice of St. Paul, on the first day of every week. The writings of St. Justin show us that the faithful never separated on the Sunday till a collection had been made for the poor, and we have it on the authority of St. Cyprian and others, down to the time of St. Leo, that these subscriptions were of regular continuance until the establishment of the Roman diaconates. Thereupon a vast system of public benevolence arose, as each one of these deacons was bound to visit two quarters of the great city and to inscribe the names of the poor therein upon a register, mentioning their claims to relief and taking all the precautions of a regular administration. We may give as one example that beautiful story which tells how St. Laurence, when charged to surrender the treasures of the Church to the prefect of the city, promised to do so within three days, and how when the time had elapsed the functionary came to the appointed spot and found ranged under the colonnades a multitude of maimed and miserable paupers, whom Laurence presented to him as forming the wealth and the sacred vessels of the Roman Church.

Moreover, Christianity instituted communities of benevolence, as, for instance, the hospitals which arose everywhere as open asylums for the miseries and infirmities of humanity. These establishments were mentioned as of long foundation in one of the laws of Justinian, and the same idea is expressed in a canon which finds its place ordinarily at the end of those passed at the Council of Nicaea, and shows us the condition of legislation and manners in the East from the earliest days of Christianity:—

" Let houses be selected in every town to serve as retreats for strangers, for the poor and for the sick. If the goods of the Church suffice not for this expenditure, let the bishop cause alms to be continually collected through the agency of the deacons, and let the faithful give according to their ability. And thus let him provide for the poor, the sick, and the stranger among our brethren, for he is their mandatary and their steward. That work obtains the remission of many sins, and of all others is the one which brings man nearest to God."

Hospitals, accordingly, were opened from one end to the other of the Roman Empire, and as they multiplied in the East, the West was not wanting in the work. Two illustrious personages—a Roman lady named Fabiola, a descendant of the Fabii, and Psammachius, the scion of a senatorial family—devoted themselves to God, sold their goods and raised, the one a hospital for the sick at Rome, the other an asylum for the poor at Ostia. On the death of his wife, Psammachius honoured her memory by charity instead of strewing flowers upon her tomb, and St. Jerome, writing from the wilderness in praise of his good works, does not say that they are sufficient:—" I learn that you have founded at the port of Ostia an asylum for destitute travellers, that you have planted a shoot from the tree of Abraham on the coast of Italy, and have raised another Bethlehem, a house of bread, on the spot where Æneas traced his camp. Who would have believed that the great grandson of so many consuls, bred in the senatorial purple, would have dared to appear clothed in the black tunic without reddening at the glance of those who were his equals ? Yet although you, the first amongst patricians, have become a monk for the sake of the poor, find therein no subject for pride. Well may you humble yourself, for you will never be more lowly than Christ. I desire that you walk barefoot, make yourself equal with the poor, knock modestly at the door of the indigent, become an eye for the blind, a hand for the maimed, a foot for the lame, a carrier of water, a cleaver of wood, a lighter of fires; all this I wish for you ; but then—where are the buffetings and spittings, where the scourge, where the cross, where the death?" He lighted upon the secret of Christian benevolence, for it was the memory of its first poor Man, dying upon the cross, which was to impassion those servants of the destitute who were to carry to such a pitch during the Middle Age their enthusiasm for poverty. St. Francis of Assisi was to afford a fresh example, and his devotion, capable of inspiring the poetry of Jacopone da Todi, was to inspire Giotto also to represent in his matchless fresco the marriage of the Saint with Poverty. Neither had the barbarians recognized this sentiment any more than the love of work or pity for the slave. It was true that they felt keenly on the dignity of man, but it was of man when free, and lord of money and the sword. They placed the slave in a happier position than any he had known under the Roman law, but he was still dependent on the caprice of a master who could forfeit the life of a useless servant. And as for poverty, they thought their Valhalla could only open to those whose hands were filled with gold, whilst they scorned labour no less as involving subjection and self-conquest —for the barbarian could conquer everything except himself. Barbarism, indeed, failed to regenerate the states of slavery, poverty, and labour, which antiquity had blighted and dishonoured, and even Christianity only effected little by little, at the cost of many a long struggle, the restoration of their proper dignity to those three types of humanity which had been so long insulted, disowned by the injustice of the old civilization, and trampled in the dust by the scorn of the barbarians. Long ages passed ere some few hospitals were reared in the regions of barbarism. At Lyons, in the sixth century, that great Hôtel Dieu was opened which has never since been closed, and the seventh age beheld the commencement of the hospitals of Clermont, of Autun, and of Paris. Speedily they were multiplied everywhere with a grand prodigality, till the time came when every Christian township had, beside its church, an asylum open to misfortune. St. Gregory of Nazianzum, in relating the foundation of the great hospital at Caesaraea, raised by St. Basil, exclaimed that he was witness to marvels surpassing those of antiquity, excelling the walls of Thebes or Babylon with its hanging gardens, the Monument of Mausolus or the Pyramids of Egypt, those magnificent tombs which could not give life back to one of their regal occupants, and reflected but a gleam of empty glory upon their founders. And he was right, for the old time had excelled us in raising monuments for pleasure, and when we look at our cities of dirt and squalor, with their houses crowded one against another, and the hard and joyless existence meted out to those who are imprisoned within their walls, we may well think that could the ancients return they would think us simply barbarous; and did we show them our theatres, those small and smoky rooms in which we are pressed together, they would retire in contempt and disgust. For they understood the art of enjoyment far better than we do; no sum was too great if spent in rearing their coliseums, those theatres and circuses in which an audience of eighty thousand came and sat with ease; but we can crush them with the monuments we have raised to sorrow and to weakness, by pointing to the numberless hospitals that our fathers consecrated to suffering. Yes, the ancients could methodize pleasure, but ours is a different science: they, too, knew how to die—but let us avow it, the pangs of death are short, we have the secret of true human dignity, our service is long—as long as life itself —and it consists in suffering and in toil.

THE WOMEN OF CHRISTENDOM.

"We have been seeking to know to what degree the Christian society was prepared to receive the barbarians and subject them to its institutions and its customs; how far, also, it excelled them in surpassing the generous instincts that those youthful races had preserved, far away from Roman corruption, under the favouring shade of their forests and their icy sky; and we paused to contemplate the two feelings, as to the dignity of man and the respect due to woman, with the introduction of which the savage tribes have been credited, and which form the essence of modern manners. But we perceived that if the barbarians preserved these sentiments as instincts, Christianity had raised them to the category of virtues. The former had recognized a dignity proper to man, but to the man who was free and armed, who scorned both obedience and labour; they owned, in fact, that chivalrous sentiment of honour which was destined to replace the old military discipline of the Roman legions. But they knew nothing, for the Gospel alone could read them the lesson, of the dignity of that great majority of the human race which was bound' by servitude, by labour, and by poverty, to obey, to work, and to suffer. In woman also they recognized, side by side with the qualities of weakness, an element of divinity. The power of delicately swaying the strong is the chief weapon of the weak, and the gauntlet of iron does not pluck a flower as it crushes a sword so the barbarians beheld in their females the necessary companions of their adventures and of their perils, and could boast of warriors, virgins, and prophetesses amongst them. But their renown was dissipated when the danger that produced it had past; and, on the other hand, classic antiquity was absolutely ignorant of the delicate influence of female tact.

As for the East, the laws of Manou contain exquisite passages on the destiny of woman; but side by side with these they tell us that " women have long hair, but narrow minds; " and the Greeks pronounce that as the gods had given strength to the lion, wings to the bird, and reasoning faculties to man, having nothing left for woman, they gave her beauty. As famous amongst their women they can only cite the courtesans Phryne and Aspasia, and the highest eulogium the Roman passed on the female sex was in praise of their fecundity. Such was the term allotted to female virtue and greatness by the sole nation of antiquity which honoured them at all. Yet we must remember that Rome did admire Lucretia, Veturia, and Cornelia, for she recognized the merit of domestic virtues and family traditions.

Let us confess, in justice to Roman law, that it gave a sublime definition of marriage. It is, it said, the union of male and female on the condition of a common life and a complete sharing in all rights, divine and human—*Nuptiœ sunt conjunctio maris et feminœ et consortium omnis vitœ, divini et humani juris communication.* A law which was grandly expressed, but was daily belied, not only by the prevailing manners, but by other enactments, till, instead of the professed equality, a Roman marriage presented an aspect of extreme inequality. And, firstly, an inequality in respect to its duties; for although there were modesty and virtue of old, and Rome, in fencing them about with oaths, the Divine Majesty, and the terrible image of. the domestic tribunal, had spared nothing to place these qualities out of danger, yet she had neglected male chastity, the surest guardian of the modesty of woman. She had divided its duties unequally, and though she required of the wife virginity before, fidelity and constant purity during, marriage, these were mere virtues of the gynaeceum, which the husband need not recognize. And society undertook to give to women different and most dangerous lessons in admitting them to the ceremonies of the pagan worship, and the mysteries of the Bona Dea. Marriage also brought about a difference in social condition. The best position afforded by the Roman law to the wife on the day whereupon the pair were united by the ceremonies of the confarreation, under the auspices and with the consent of all the gods, was that of being treated as the daughter of her husband, and of having a child's portion on the day on which his property was divided.' This was the utmost the majesty of man could afford to concede to woman—to treat her as a child, and indulge her with infantile pleasures, with playthings, and the luxurious living which was fitted to charm an uncultured imagination; and thence proceeded the complaints of philosophers as to the insolent luxury of the Roman ladies, as to those feeble creatures whose foot could not touch the ground, who could only move a step unless carried in the arms of eunuchs, and dangled from their ears the value of many an estate: all this because the woman was principally but a mere instrument of pleasure.

But she was also a means of perpetuating the family. . A Roman of position always married for the sake of getting children, *liberorum quærendorum causa,* and law itself favoured paternity and maternity by giving privileges to those who had given three children to the State, *jus trium liberorum.* But it was only on the two conditions of pleasing her husband and propagating his race that the wife held her place at the domestic hearth, for if she became old and barren, or wrinkles appeared on her forehead, the gates of the conjugal domicile instantly opened, and the freedman came to bid her go forth: *Collige sarcinulas, dicet libertus, et exi.*

So unequal an union could hardly be lasting, and divorce was introduced into the Roman legislation, and practised under every form and upon every motive. There was the favourite divorce of men of position, on account of weariness, practised by those who changed their wives yearly. Another kind proceeded from calculation, as proved by Cicero, who repudiated Terentia, not because she had caused trouble to his soul, but because a new dowry was a necessity for the satisfaction of his creditors; and, lastly, divorce might have generosity for its motive, as in the case of Cato, who, when he found that his wife Marcia had taken the fancy of Hortensius, transferred her to him, under the title of spouse. But if this was the position conferred upon wives at their marriage, woman found her revenge in the iniquity of the law itself, and made, in her turn, divorce her weapon to serve her interests and her calculations. This occasioned the notorious immodesty of the Roman matrons, who, in the time of Seneca, reckoned their years by the number of their husbands, instead of the number of consuls. They also suffered divorce in order to remarry, and married with a view to divorce; and St. Jerome related how he had been present at the funeral of a woman who had possessed seventeen husbands. Women found the equality in vice which their husbands refused them in virtue, and were to be seen, like men, seated at orgies, passing whole nights in glutting themselves with wine; like them, vomiting that they might feast anew, and multiplying their adulteries, till continence was but a synonym for ugliness. They had a place of honour in the amphitheatre, and gave the signal for the butchery of the last gladiator as he fell wallowing at their feet, and imploring their mercy. When, at last, the passion for the fights of the circus had taken possession of the whole Roman people, women followed the knights and senators as they descended into the arena, and the populace had the pleasure of gazing at combats between nude matrons. And thus Seneca could say with force—for the horrors of the time and the degradation of human nature favoured the illusion— " Woman is but a shameless animal, and unless she is given plenty of education and much learning, I can see in her nothing but a savage creature, incapable of restraining its passions." Yet this proud philosopher was ungrateful, for he was the spouse of that Paulina who desired to share her husband's fate, and caused her veins to be opened with his.

Such was the history of marriage with the wisest, most upright, and most practical nation of antiquity. It was from this degraded state that Christianity had to raise the sex, and at first sight it seems as if the memory of original sin, as due to the first woman, would have added to its bitterness. But St. Ambrose did not thus regard it, and applied all his genius to the task of proving that, in the Fall, woman was more excusable than man, for the latter had suffered himself to be led away by his sister, and his equal, whereas the former was deceived by a fallen angel, a being superior to mankind; that- her repentance also had been more prompt, and her excuse more generous, in merely laying the blame upon the serpent, whereas man had replied to God, " It was the woman that thou gavest me!" And what, again, were memories such as these, compared with those thoughts which surrounded the work of Redemption; for if woman had been the cause of the first offence, had she not made due reparation in giving birth to the Redeemer ?—and, as the saint continued with eloquence, " Approach then, O Eve, henceforth to be called Mary, thou who hast given us an example of virginity, who hast given us a God, a God who has thus visited but one, but who calls all to Himself."

It was theology, then, which rehabilitated woman for Christianity, and the worship of the Virgin, speedily introduced, wrought the same effect in practical manners as in dogma. That this worship commenced in the Catacombs has been established by discoveries made up to the present day; and the Virgin and Child figure in frescoes, of which, from the nature of the cement on which they are painted, the third century must be given as the latest date. Thus did the radiant image which was calculated to gild with its rays the weaknesses of women, illumine the shades of that primitive and subterranean Christendom, and emerged thence surrounded by a galaxy of those virgins and martyrs to whom places were assigned on the altars of the Church. It was supremely necessary that faith in female virtue should be restored, and this Christianity effected by founding the public profession of virginity, and giving the veil and golden chaplet to those maidens who remained in the bosom of their respective families, but honoured by an open adhesion the virtue to which antiquity had refused belief. It was needful, also, that women should rival men in the stern qualities which had been thought their monopoly, in the courage that courted martyrdom, and the honour of dying frequently the last of all. Such was the example given in the earliest days by Thecla and Perpetua, and it is supremely touching to note the respect with which the martyrs in their prisons environed these nursing mothers of Christendom, our mothers in the faith, who showed them the way to glory, as angels from heaven, wingless indeed, but excelling the angels by their tears. The early ages of the Church afford many a like spectacle, but nothing chronicled in the acts of martyrs excels in beauty the reverence showed to St. Perpetua by her brethren in suffering up to the moment when she fell beneath the hand of the gladiator, in the presence of the Roman people yelling with delight.

But we must refrain from top near an approach to the sanctuary, and rather than treat of women in their privileged and exceptional positions as deaconess, virgin, or widow, let us consider the place assigned by Christianity to daughters of Eve, whom it had redeemed from their ancient curse, in the ordinary walks of life. It was incumbent upon the Church, in order to regain for woman her proper place in the family, to remould from head to foot the institution of marriage, and add to it all that Paganism had rejected. Under the Christian order the propagation of children was no longer the principal end of marriage, and St. Augustine says beautifully— and it is also the teaching of Tertullian—that its chief object is to set forth the example, type, and primitive consecration of human society in that love which is its bond. And as that type of all society must needs be a perfect unity, an unity consequently in which every part is equal and indissoluble, therefore it follows that in Christian matrimony everything is equally divided but nothing broken; the condition and duties of life are equally shared by the two contracting parties; each is bound to bring the same hope, a heart in due subservience to the ties which are to unite them forever, as St. Jerome says, with his rough and energetic language—" The laws of Caesar are one thing, the precept of Christ another; one thing the decisions of Papinian, another the commands of Paul. The pagans give free scope to the impurity of men, and content themselves with for: bidding them to commit adultery with married women, or to violate freeborn maidens; but they allow them their slaves and the lupanar. But with us what is forbidden to women is not permitted to men, and under a common duty there must be equal obedience."

Such teaching made Christianity burdensome to the pagan world as well as to the Jews and the barbarians; and may we not add that it renders it distasteful to men of our own day ? It was the magnificent equity manifested in the voluntary humiliation of the mighty, the spectacle of strength and weakness subjected to a common yoke, which caused the world to shrink from submitting to the "faith. This appears even in the Gospels, when the Apostles replied to Christ when He used such language, " If it be thus it were better never to marry;" and therefore the Fathers, from the first days of the Church, laboured in instilling these stern maxims into the rebellious hearts even of Christians, and acted, so to speak, the office of police in those Christian families into which concubinage was ever stealthily creeping to banish the wife whom they desired to install as queen over the domestic hearth, unsatisfied till they were assured that henceforth the house would recognize but one ruler, and that no stranger would usurp the place marked out by God for the wife. And as Christian morality was labouring to establish an equality in duty between each married couple, it was also necessary to maintain an equality in their conditions; for woman, destined formerly to serve the pleasures, to please the senses, and to multiply the posterity of her husband, was to be entrusted henceforth with a graver task. So the Church did not shrink from raising her dignity by an austere method, by despoiling her of all superfluous ornament, and stripping off the wretched finery which was of no use in winning the heart of her husband. Tertullian wrote whole books against the attire of women, reproached them with being loaded with jewels, and expressed fear lest on the day of martyrdom the neck which was covered with emeralds should leave no room for the axe of the executioner. The early time of Christianity was no golden time, but rather an age of iron, and therefore the Church assigned such lofty' duties to its daughters, and entrusted them with the majestic ministrations of charity. In his writings to his wife, Tertullian shows us the Christian woman fasting, praying with her husband, rising by night to attend the religious assemblies, visiting the poorer brethren in their hovels, haunting the prisons, and throwing herself at the gaoler's feet to obtain the privilege of kissing the martyr's chain. It was through these severe exercises, these austerities and perils, that the dignity of the wife was tempered, that she shared with her husband the honours of life.

But this was not all, and when unity in duty and condition had been established, it was necessary to make it lasting. The Roman law admitted of divorce without limit, and subject to no condition, by the simple consent of the parties; and so great was the strength of the prevailing habit, the influence of the manners in vogue, that the Christianized emperors dared not touch the law of divorce, or rather did so with cautious timidity, and then quickly withdrew the reforming hand. An institution, enacted by Constantine in the year 331, restricted it to three cases between the husband and wife, but transgression was only punishable by fine. Yet even this legislation seemed too rigorous, for Honorius, in 421, narrowed certain of these provisions, whilst Theodosius the Younger went so far as to restore divorce by mutual consent, in which aspect it passed into the legislation of Justinian, who did not dare to efface it entirely from his codes. But the Christian doctrine could not relax its inflexibility, although the wisdom of the emperors hesitated: it was the occasion then or never to declare that Christianity had its laws as well as Caesar, and St. Chrysostom exclaimed, " Do not cite to me the laws which ordain you to notify your repudiation; for God will not judge you according to the laws of men, but according to His own."

In the year 416, the Council of Milevium forbade parties who had been divorced to contract other marriages, and thus forever changed divorce into a simple separation of body. This expressed the entire Christian theory as to marriage, the doctrine which has ever since subsisted, and has resisted all the opposition afforded it by the advancing centuries.

Marriage, includes something more than a contract, for it involves a sacrifice, or rather a double sacrifice. The woman sacrifices an irreparable gift, which was the gift of God, and has called forth the solicitude of her mother, her first beauty, frequently her health, and that faculty of loving which women have but once; whilst the man in his turn surrenders the liberty of his youth, those incomparable years which can never return, the power of devoting himself for the being whom he loves, that is only found at the opening of life, and the love-inspired effort for the creation of a glorious and happy future. All this man can effect but once between the age of twenty and thirty years—a **little** earlier or a little later—perhaps never;

and therefore Christian marriage is a double oblation, offered in two chalices, one containing virtue, modesty, and innocence, the other a pure love, devotion, the eternal consecration of a manhood to a feebler being, whom yesterday he knew not, and with whom to-day he thinks himself happy to pass his existence: and the cups must be equally full, that the union may be a holy alliance and blessed of Heaven.

It was only by thus making over to woman an absolute dominion over the heart of man, and giving her an undivided rule in domestic matters, that Christianity could consent to open to her the gates of the house, permit her to cross the limits of that **gynaeceum** to which the ancients had delegated her, and advance into the city now disposed to reach her with respectful veneration. For, when during the space of three centuries mankind, Christian and pagan, had become accustomed to seeing women standing as martyrs before the praetorium, as virgins in the churches, speeding in every direction to visit the poor, and hunting out misery for relief, they suffered them to pass free from injury and insult, as heavenly messengers who went through the world only to do good; and there was thus no longer any danger for them in the streets of those tumultuous towns along which formerly the matrons of Rome used to be carried in their litters, borne in the vigorous arms of German or of Gallic slaves, who protected them from insult. Respect was now assured them, and they availed themselves of it to exercise that magistracy over charity which they have preserved to our own day; and not the deaconesses alone, but simple Christian women, devoted their lives, or the part which was left free from the exigencies of family duties, to the service of the poor and suffering, who had never yet had their tears wiped away by hands so tender and benevolent.

St. Jerome relates how Fabiola, the descendant of the Fabii, who in her ignorance of the principles of Christianity had unhappily availed herself of the right of divorce, when touched by the death of her second husband, resolved to do public penance, and presented herself one day at the Lateran basilica with ashes upon her head, in the ranks of the avowed sinners, imploring, amidst the tears of the people, the clergy, and the bishop himself, that she might be permitted to expiate her fault; and how, upon receiving absolution, she sold all her goods and raised out of the proceeds a hospital for the poor, which she served in person. The daughter of consuls and dictators dressed the wounds of the maimed and miserable, of slaves whom their owners had discarded, carried the epileptic sufferers upon her own shoulders, staunched the blood of sores, and in fine, as St. Jerome said, performed all the services which wealthy and charitable Christians, who were ready to give alms of their money, but not to sacrifice their repugnances, were accustomed to transact by the hands of their slaves. But a stronger faith conquered all natural disgust, and therefore popular veneration attached itself to the woman who had so scorned and trampled upon her hereditary grandeur, that she might become the serving-maid of misfortune; and when Fabiola died, St. Jerome related her triumphant obsequies as forming a worthy parallel to the ovations which old Rome had lavished on her great ones. "No," said he, " Camillus did not triumph so gloriously over the Gauls, or Scipio over Numantia, or Pompey over the nations of Pontus. They have told me of the crowd which preceded the procession, and the torrents of the people who came to swell it. Neither the squares, nor the porticoes, nor the terraces of the houses sufficed to contain the multitude. Rome saw all her diverse constituent races reunited into one body, and crowds of enemies found themselves in agreement for the glory of a penitent." We see the female sex already in possession of that tender empire of charity which they have never suffered since to escape from their hands. And a few years ago the spectacle offered by an entire people accompanying the funeral procession of Fabiola, was again to be witnessed, when the same populace hurried to the obsequies of the young Princess Borghese, and the horses of the bier were unharnessed by the crowd, which insisted on carrying the corpse of its benefactress to its last resting-place. This was a pointy upon which the manners of our day touch the usages of antiquity. Scarcely, in spite of the ages which divide them, can we discover the least distance between them, for all the differences of time vanish as they enter the bosom of the Church, the domain of eternity. Armed with the influences of benevolence, women soon acquired a power over the tone of manners, an empire more puissant than that of law. Soon they had their share in swaying legislation itself, as appeared in the fifth century in the case of Pulcheria, the daughter of Arcadius, who being a little older than her young brother Theodosius II., felt forcibly the difficulty of the epoch in which he was called to reign. Therefore, devoting her youth and her virginity to God, she undertook the guardianship of her brother, and thus afforded the spectacle of a girlish princess of sixteen years, grand-daughter certainly, and sole inheritress of the genius and courage of Theodosius, governing the Empires of the East and West, which had no opposition to offer to her influence and her talent, and struggling during a whole reign against the intrigues of a court of eunuchs, and, notably, against that eunuch Chrysaphus, who seemed to be raised up as the evil genius of the Byzantine Empire. On the death of Theodosius, the praetorians made over the purple to Pulcheria herself, and she was proclaimed Augusta, Imperatrix, and mistress of the world. But she soon, in mistrust of her solitary greatness, gave her hand, charged henceforth with the burden of empire, to Marcián, an aged soldier, from whom she obtained a promise of sisterly respect; and the Roman world enjoyed some years of greatness and glory under the united sway of Marcián and Pulcheria. For when Attila, thinking it was still the time when eunuchs governed the court, demanded the accustomed tribute from the Empire of the West, he received as the answer of the

Empress, " I have only gold for my friends, but for my foes iron;" and it was necessary to attain the respect of the barbarian that the throne of Constantine should be occupied by a woman, who was at once a Christian and a saint. We insist upon the workings of Christianity in the manners of the fifth century, because then, as ever, the Church was labouring not for the present only, but for the ages which were to follow. It was essential that the idea of the Christian family should be founded before the barbarians came to trouble it with their disorders. For the instinct which they brought might easily have perished had it not encountered examples which might develop and enlarge it. Nor did they always show respect towards women, for history relates that the Thuringians, who had invaded Gaul in the commencement of the sixth century, and had carried off three hundred young girls, fastened them with stakes to the ground, and then drove their chariots over their bodies. Moreover, as Tacitus informs us, the barbarians practised polygamy, and their chiefs gloried in the number of their wives. Amongst the Germans it was customary to buy and sell concubines, and the dying chief often caused the women who had shared his couch to attend him on his funeral pyre.

Therefore Christianity had to teach the barbarians a constant respect for women, and if it found some succour it encountered more dangers in their native instincts. Theodoric and Gondebald, too, hastened to borrow from the Theodosian code that constitution concerning divorce which had been enacted by Constantine, and by the help of such texts the barbarian monarchs hoped to introduce, if not simultaneous, at least successive polygamy. It was this instinct which caused the Merovingian kings to indulge in a number of wives, and it is well known how St. Columba, having reproached Brunehault with her care in furnishing her son's seraglio, was exiled and forced to find a resting-place amongst the solitudes of

Switzerland, in company with bears and wild beasts, who were more amenable than his fellow-men to his wonder-working hands. And the same question which was mooted during all the dark ages was renewed in the time of King Lothaire, who desired to repudiate his wife Teutberge, but was resisted by Nicholas I. declaring as a sole answer to all his importunities that he would never suffer such an irregularity to gain ground, and encourage men who grew weary of their wives. It also reappeared in the struggle between Pope Gregory VII. and the Emperor Henry IV., whose real aim in laying his hands on the right of investiture was to annul his marriage with Bertha, the daughter of the Margrave of Saxony; again between Innocent III. and Philip Augustus; and finally, in the sixteenth century, between Henry VIII. and Clement VII., affording the remarkable spectacle of the Papacy consenting to see the schism of the former rather than assent to his adultery, to lose a province of the Christian empire rather than outrage the dogma which had regenerated the Christian family. It was the work of twelve centuries to struggle against the violent instincts of the sons of the North, who had abjured none of the passions of the flesh; so long was the strife needed in order to bring out in their full bloom those delicate feelings which had existed indeed deep in the bosom of the Christian society, destined to a momentary eclipse, but to a later reappearance, and which constitute in our own day all the purity and all the charm of modern civilization.

It was, then, upon the condition of their exalted place in the family life that women undertook so large a share in the task of civilization, and therefore were these honoured beings able to bring their barbarous husbands one after, another, and with them the people they ruled, to the faith of Christ. It is enough to name Clotilda and Clovis, Bertha and Ethelbert, Theodolinda and Lothaire, appearing as conductors of their respective nations, whom they drew, as if by enchantment, after the sweep of their royal robes, and tracing out the way in which their descendants were to march. And so great was the confidence with which these queenly women inspired these half-barbarous races, that the Germans, Franks, Saxons, and Spaniards, who gloried in spurning the idea of obedience, yet did not shrink from submitting to a female sovereign.

Yet these premises must not lead us to conclude that Christianity threw down the · barriers of nature, by desiring to plunge women into public life, and so establish that absolute equality which has been dreamed of by the materialism of our own epoch. Not thus did the Church understand the matter, for Christianity is too spiritualistic for such an idea. The part to be played by its women was in some sort to be analogous to that of the guardian angels. They were to guide the world, but to remain invisible. The angels became rarely visible, and then only at moments of supreme danger, as the angel Raphael appeared to the young Tobias, and so it is only on certain long predestined occasions that the empire of women can be seen, and the saving angels of Christian society are manifest under the names of a Blanche of Castille or of a Joan of Arc.

But we have paused to mark the rehabilitation of woman in the prevailing order of manners, in order the better to study her rank and influence in the world of letters; and pursuing this our proper sphere and duty, we shall find ourselves in new paths, and so quit, to return no more to it, the hackneyed theme of the restoration of woman under Christian influences. As the Church had every hope of female intelligence, and was bound to refuse nothing that could tend to its improvement, she took great care of their education. And we possess some striking documents on this very point amongst the correspondence of St. Jerome. He showed in the two letters which he wrote to Laeta and Gaudentius on the education of their two daughters, that, like all great minds, he had no contempt for small things, and bade them commence their educational cares from the nurse's arms; and following the Roman who attributed the earliest corruption of eloquence to the bad lessons of nurses and pedagogues, so St. Jerome wished for a modest and grave nurse, who had often the name of God upon her lips. He desired that they should refrain from piercing the ears of children, or staining their faces with carmine and ochre, or giving to their hair that red hue which was but a first reflexion of hell, and begged that they should speedily be taught to clear their intellects, and that letters of ivory should be placed in their hands that they might learn the formation of words; that a number of Greek verses should be committed to their memory first, to be followed by Latin studies; and especially that they should not be left ignorant of Holy Writ; nor, lastly, of the writings of the Fathers.

Such was the severe and solid system of education laid down by St. Jerome for the use of the daughters of the Church; nor need it surprise us to find him offering his own services towards instruction, and writing thus to Laeta from his desert retreat. " I will carry her on my own shoulders, and will confirm her stammering lips; my task will be more glorious than that of Aristotle, for he trained a king who was destined to perish by the poison of the Babylonians, while I shall raise a servant and spouse for Christ, an inheritress of heaven." After this it may seem surprising that the women of the early ages of Christianity have left such scanty writings, for we can only cite a few excellent letters, which, however, will always do them credit; and some verses, like those of Faltonia Proba, who composed a canto in honour of the faith. These are the sole and feeble claims put forth by these Christian women of primitive times to literary distinction; or rather they gloried more in understanding that in the world of letters, as in that of politics, their influence was to be invisible—their mission to inspire far rather than to shine.

We never find that women inspired any serious works in classic time: if we run through the familiar letters of Cicero we see few, amongst those of Symmachus none, addressed to females. Seneca, indeed, wrote in a consoling strain to his mother and to Helvia; that haughty spirit which so utterly disdained the other sex, was once moved by their tears. But Christianity brought with it an imitation of the example given by the Saviour in teaching the woman of Samaria. St. John corresponded with Electa, and all the Fathers of the Church wrote for women. Tertullian composed two books " Ad Uxorem Suam," and the treatises " De Cultu Faeminarum " and " De Velandis Virginibus; " that proud and captious mind bent before the handmaids of Christ, and declared himself the last and the least of their servants. Similar language was used by St. Cyprian in his work " De Habitu Virginum," while St. Ambrose composed three works upon virginity, and addressing himself to the destined readers of his books, said:—" If you find some flowers herein, they are those of your virtues, and from you proceeds all the perfume of the book."

Courtesy proper to so great a soul, but destined to be even excelled by that of St. Augustine. Augustine was especially the work of his mother, St. Monica, who had twice, as it were, given birth to him—once in the sufferings of the body, the second time in the agonies of the spirit; and in the latter she had borne him for eternity. We remember the tears she shed over the errors of her son, and the joy she had experienced from the bishops prophesying that the child of so much weeping could not perish; how her joy was the chiefest on his conversion; her place the highest at the philosophical discussions of Cassiciaçum; and how, to his good mother's question whether philosophizing women had ever been read of in the books, Augustine asked, in reply, whether philosophy was anything else than the love of wisdom. Monica, who had long loved her God, was far nearer philosophy than many. "For after all, my mother," he said, " do you not fear death far less than many would-be sages ?" adding that he would willingly become her disciple. He also, instead of repelling, drew her on to take a .part in their discussions, declaring that if his books fell into any hands in the future, no reader should reproach him for giving to his mother the expression of her opinion. Whilst they were treating of the Supreme Good, Monica ventured the proposition that the soul had no natural aliment but science, the intelligence but truth, which was in accord with sentiments in the " Hortensius " of Cicero. Delighted with the coincidence, St. Augustine declared that his mother had carried off the palm in philosophy; that he owed to her his thought for truth, his desire to know nothing besides truth, and referred to the inspiration which he had drawn from her his entire vocation as a thinker. And, in fact, he justified this idea in that ever memorable passage of his " Confessions," in which he relates how that a few days before the death of Monica, he was standing with her near to a window at Ostia, discoursing of the future life, of God and of eternity, and touched by a momentary effort of the soul the things of which they were speaking. Monica ended the interview by declaring that no more work remained for her on earth; and she died shortly afterwards, with her task accomplished, for she had moulded her son according to the method which God had appointed to her. St. Augustine many a time in after life trod again the road' which he had followed with his mother in that last conversation; he came back again and again to God, and reached a high point in the knowledge of Him; but it was always by the same track, repassing the same places, into which, then but an inexperienced neophyte, he had first adventured himself under his mother's care.

But St. Augustine, as a genius, **was** of tender nature, and he might well one day have been carried onwards by a mother's hand. The case of St. Jerome seemed different, and it is a marvel how that man of fiery and untamed spirit, of ardent and undisciplined imagination, then conquered by Christianity, was only developed under the same influences by Christian women. We have already noticed St. Jerome at Rome, but the fact is less known that at that time he was fifty-two years of age and had written little—merely two or three letters and some treatises of mediocre importance. These represented the entire produce of that long life which had ripened in the desert. But his reputation brought around him in numbers the most illustrious Christian matrons of Rome, such as Paula and her two daughters Eustochia and Blaesilla, Felicitas, Albina, Marcellina, the widow Laea, and the virgin Asella Marcella, at whose house the others assembled to listen to the great doctor. She had a passionate love of the Scriptures, and never could see Jerome without plying him with questions, multiplying objections, and never leaving him till her view was clear. When he had left Rome she became the soul of that little society of Christian women, answered their questions with the tact and delicacy which is the special attribute of women, and saying always that such and such was the doctrine of St. Jerome or some other doctor —never speaking in her own name. After his return to Bethlehem, St. Jerome was still pursued by the questionings of these noble matrons, and, moreover, some of them came and joined him, that they might recover the light which they could not surrender. They followed him into his desert solitude, and thus we see Fabiola crossing the seas, ostensibly to visit the Holy Places, but in fact to read the Book of Numbers again with Jerome, and to receive his explanation of chapters which she could not comprehend. Paula then also become a widow, and her daughter Eustochia, renouncing theglory and fortune which surrounded them, also crossed the Mediterranean and arrived at Antioch, from which city these women, of the class which once required the support of their eunuchs' arms for a journey into the streets of Rome, mounted upon asses, and set out for Jerusalem over the rugged passes of Lebanon. On their arrival at Bethlehem they founded a monastery and three convents, and the rule of the latter made a study of Holy Writ incumbent upon every nun. These institutions were in fact schools of theology and language, since the interpretation of Scripture was necessarily founded upon the study of foreign tongues; and these Roman ladies were adepts in Latin, in Greek, and in Hebrew. Paula, in fact, used to chant the Psalms in Hebrew, and on her deathbed answered St. Jerome, when he asked if she suffered, in Greek. They left him no peace, these two women, and pressed him to read the whole Bible from end to end with them, and to comment on its details. For long he refused, and when at last he acceded, found that he had undertaken a burdensome task, as they would not permit him to ignore anything, and answered his plea of want of personal knowledge by a demand for the most probable opinion. It was for them that he undertook his great work in the translation of the Scripture, which not only redounded then to his glory and influence, but made him the master of Christian prose for succeeding generations. The Vulgate was begun simply to satisfy the keen impatience of Paula and Eustochia; it was to them that he dedicated the books of Joshua, Judges, Kings, Ruth, Esther, the Psalms, Isaiah, and the twelve minor Prophets, declaring in his preface that to them was owing the influence which caused him again totake up the plough and trace so laborious a furrow, to remove the brambles which ceaselessly germinate in the field of Holy Scripture, and that to them must lie his appeal from all who would doubt the exactness of the version. "You are," he said, "competent judges in controversies as to texts upon the original Hebrew; compare it with my translation, and see if I have risked a single word." Whilst as he was the object of every kind of accusation, as his translation troubled some as being a novelty, and reduced to despair all the priests who possessed magnificent copies, parchments lettered in gold, to whom he said in fact that newer ones were required, and who preferred cavilling at the exactness of the fresh translation to admitting so mortifying a truth, he found a resource and comfort in the prayers of Paula and Eustochia, and begged them to take up his defence against the tongues of his revilers.

Thus did these women of Christendom emulate the example of their German sisters; like them they were present at the conflict, but it was a struggle of the mind; they also predicted its sequel, assured it a happy issue, and tended the wounds dealt in the controversy. And in this manner was a Christian school of women constituted which was destined to continue through many centuries, and be the exemplar of that sight of many persons of moral and social excellence who also did not shrink from growing pale over the holy books and writings of the great doctors of the Church, which was the wonder of the seventeenth century; for the women of the Church had already taken possession of that double work of inspiring and of conciliating which will be theirs until the end.

But if they gained every advantage in the order of knowledge, there was danger of their losing ground in that of art and that of poetry. For it seemed that as women had been sources of frequent and perilous inspiration to the sculptors and poets of Paganism, so Christianity might seek to efface forever the images which appealed too forcibly to the imagination and the awakened passions. Yet this was not the case, and a visit to the Catacombs, those rugged homes of the most austere Christianity, will show us, amidst the relics of persecution and memories of the menacing guards, who were perhaps then at the entrance, on the point of laying hands upon the priest at the altar and the faithful who surrounded him, in the light of torches and lamps, a certain number of paintings decorating the sanctuaries, and developing into garlands around the altars. Of the subject of these pictures we shall treat in another place; but may remark that the most frequent after the Good Shepherd is that of the figure of a woman at prayer, alone, with arms crossed, the head often veiled, dressed in the simple fashion preached by Tertullian and St. Cyprian. In other places, it appears as a martyr at the place of execution, dressed like Felicitas and Perpetua, when they stood in the arena, without veil or ornaments, despoiled of those necklaces and emeralds which would have balked the sword of the headsman, covered only with the *stola,* a simple white robe, with a girdle of purple descending to the feet as her sole adornment, the eyes and hands alike raised towards heaven. It was thus under the features of a woman that Prayer was symbolized by the Christians, as if persuaded that the orisons, which were accompanied by the humility and gentleness of so holy a being, would move the Almighty more easily. She was again represented in the company of two aged men, who stood on each side, and supported her uplifted arms; and sometimes two names were written underneath the painting. The two elders were named Peter and Paul; and the woman who stood between them praying, with outstretched hands, was named Mary. So this figure, which appeared always side by side with that of Christ, was the first representation of the Madonna, of that long course of Byzantine Virgins which were destined to inspire the painters of the Middle Age, the regenerated woman who was to recreate art for the modern world.

But it was not sufficient for Christian womanhood to take up with a reforming hand painting and the plastic arts; it was also to enter the domain of poetry, then overflowing with the ardours of Sappho and Alcaeus, burning with the passion which had been kindled by the women of old time—poetry which was to be purified by being sprinkled with the blood of those virgin martyrs who were to be for the future the heroines and inspirers of the Christian bards. And it is a touching fact, that the first woman who moved and drew forth new accents from poetry for the Church, was a young girl, St. Agnes, who was martyred at Rome at the close of the persecution under Diocletian, a.d. 310. A sort of preeminence was attached to her, as the youngest born of the numerous family of martyrs. All the efforts of the imagination of the time, added to love, respect, and enthusiasm, were united, as it were, to compose her crown. A short time after her death, one of the most beautiful of Christian legends was related as to her. It told low, as her parents, some little time after her martyrdom, were spending a vigil in prayer at her tomb, the virgin Agnes appeared in the brightest light, amidst a multitude of virgins clothed like herself in long robes of gold, and having a snow-white lamb at her side, she addressed her weeping parents, and said, " "Weep not, for you see that I have been admitted into this company in the abodes of light, and that I am united now with those whom I have ever loved."

Her life seemed to have attracted the notice and charmed the respect of all the men of her age, and no sacred topic has been more often celebrated in the discourses of the eloquent, or the verses of poets. Three times did St. Ambrose return to it, and at the beginning of his work "De Virginitate," took pleasure in honouring the action of the maiden who had braved her executioners, and had advanced to the place of slaughter with a more triumphant step than if she had been about to bestow her hand on the most illustrious scion of the consular houses. But the poets, especially, claimed it as their own, and the Pope St. Damasus, in the first place, who lived at the end of the fourth century, sang in a short but forcible poem of the martyrdom and glory of St. Agnes. " How, at the mournful signal given by the trumpet, she rushed from the arms of her nurse, trampled underfoot the tyrant's menace; and how, when her noble body was given over to the flames, her young soul conquered their great terror, and how she covered herself with her long hair for fear lest her eyes, then about to perish, should not behold the temple of God."

Viribus immensum parvis superasse timorem,

Nudam profusum crinem per membra dedisse

Ne Domini templum facies peritura videret.

And those beautiful verses are equalled by the hymn composed by Prudentius, a poet of the beginning of the fifth century, in honour of St. Agnes, in which he narrates at length the history of the martyr, and crowns her by the following invocation:—

" O happy Virgin, O new-born glory, noble dweller in the heavenly palace, lower towards our mire your brow, now girt with a double diadem. The light of your favouring countenance, if it penetrates therein, will purify my heart. For every place on which you deign to cast your eyes becomes pure; every place on which your foot, so brilliant in its whiteness, has alighted." Surely this poetry has recovered the ancient fire, but the path along which it journeys is one which leads to heaven.

And yet another breath was to proceed from the lips of women, to penetrate the depths of Christian poesy, and reveal therein a fertility, of which succeeding ages would reap the fruits, in the shape of Platonic love. This sentiment only just began with Plato to free itself from the obscurity and depravity of the Greek idea of love; but when a Christian, who had been touched by its inspiring influence, wrote for the first time in prose, a prose instinct with poetry, when Hermas composed his wonderful

"Shepherd," Platonic love found place in its pages, but suffered no surroundings which were not chaste. He related that in his youth he had loved, for her beauty and her virtue, a young Christian slave, the property of his tutor, and often had said, "Happy should I he had I such a wife." But sometime after he wandered into the country, alone with his thoughts, honouring the creatures of God which seemed so fair; and at last, falling asleep, dreamed that he was on his knees at prayer in a wild spot, and as he prayed the sky opened, showing to him the maiden he had loved, who said to him,—

" Hail, Hermas !" " My lady, what do you there?" " I have been called hither to accuse you before God." " My lady, if I have sinned against you, when was it, and where ? Have I not always regarded you as my mistress, and respected you as my sister?" " An evil desire has found its way into your heart; pray to God, and He will pardon you your sin." And the heaven closed again. Thus commenced the love which questions even the legitimate object of marriage, which desires nothing in its own interest, but is consistent in its sacrifice and devotion, and becomes faulty in the moment that it ceases to forget itself.

However, we soon recognize this as the essential principle of Christian literature in the future. The barbarians came, but Christendom had already secured their daughters. Frank and Saxon virgins filled the cloisters, and the saints of time wrote for them as the Fathers had done for their sisters of the primitive ages. Fortunatus, during his long sojourn at Poitiers, composed poetry for St. Radagonde, the wife of King Clotaire, and St. Boniface, in the midst of his great apostolic labours, addressed verses to the beautiful Lioba, abbess of an English cloister, who was destined later to follow in his steps, continue his missionary work, and raise convents in the forests of Germany to serve for the education of the young barbarians. Alcuin also was to number amongst his disciples the daughters and nieces of Charlemagne, who demanded from him a commentary on St. John, and did not neglect to remind him that St. Jerome had not despised the entreaties of noble ladies, but had written them long letters in explanation of the obscure passages of prophecy, adding that there was less distance between Tours and Paris than between Bethlehem and Rome. And so he was unable to resist them; and from that time we see posterity carried away by his example, and Christian women gradually taking rank in theology and literature. In the tenth century Hroswitha, in the twelfth St. Hildegard, in later times St. Catherine of Siena, shared the glory of the greatest writers, and, lastly, St. Theresa, who stands on the threshold of modern times, and at whose genius the world is still wondering.

And thus their influence showed itself in continuance, when amidst the light of the sixteenth century some of the greatest minds appeared canvassing the respect of a certain number of superior women, such as Jacqueline Pascal, who shared her brother's toil, and thereby was associated in his fame; Madame de Longueville, who lent so favouring an influence to the genius of Nicole; Madame de Sévigné, Madame de la Fayette, Madame de Maintenon, and the other illustrious females who were destined to consummate the intellectual education of the world's most polished race.

If it effected so much for prose and for science, respect for women was the generating principle of poetry, the very soul of chivalry. Without the idea of sacrifice, the whole essence of that poetry must have vanished; the knight was bound to serve his mistress disinterestedly, and the poet of chivalry was only suffered to sing of her upon the same condition. The worship which effected a purification in the minds of its votaries, became the dominating influence of all the poetry of the twelfth and thirteenth centuries; it enkindled the first troubadours, the first minnesinger, the early

Italian poets, and was, the presiding genius of Dante and Petrarch. For what, in fact, was Beatrice but a living personification of the divine intelligence, a symbolical representation, but at the same time a perfect and fascinating reality ? What was Beatrice but an influence destined to purify the soul of Dante, and to free it from all its earthly constituents. The mere smile of the maiden as she passed sufficed to flood the poet's heart with joy, to give him peace, to lower his pride, to blot out his offences, and dispose him to virtue. Doubtless, Dante attributed too great a power to Beatrice; but, at least, it was a power that he had experienced. When he found her once more, as she appeared to him on the topmost point of purgatory, in the terrestrial paradise which he had reconstructed, it was not to receive flattery and empty praise, but blame for not having vowed to her a love that was pure enough, for having suffered his soul to be weighed down towards the perilous atmosphere of earth; and as the beautiful slave accused Hermas, so did Beatrice accuse Dante; and thus the unknown slave, whom Hermas had casually loved, stood, as it were, in the place of elder sister to Beatrice, to Laura, and the noble women whose task it was to strike the most brilliant chords of modern poetry.

We have before us, then, a spectacle which is rare in the annals of literature. Ages there are like the spring time of the year, when the human intellect flourishes throughout, but to reach down to the lowest roots, to the earliest germs of these flowers of the mind, to know from whence their life and sap may flow, is a pleasure but seldom tasted. But this is what we have just attained, and therefore we need pause no more to contemplate the blossoms which poetry put forth in the days of chivalry, the roots of which lay hidden deep in primitive Christendom.

In studying Christian manners, during the fifth century, we have witnessed the greatest intellectual revolution that has ever taken place. For literature is governed by intellect, but the mission of intellect is to instruct or to charm. It is his audience which moulds the orator; the crowd for whom he sings inspires and kindles the poet. Under the old order philosophers only spoke for a handful of select spirits, of the initiated, and of adepts; though the orator harangued the crowd which covered the market-places, that crowd was only composed of citizens. At Athens, the poets composed for the theatre, but it was only frequented by men who were free. The women of Rome attended the theatres, but the Latin poetry was scarcely intelligible to the vulgar, and could only be enjoyed by the cultured minority. Horace complained of this, knowing that, like Virgil, he could only be appreciated by, at most, the knights, and that his genius could never make itself felt in the lower ranks of the sovereign people. The literature of antiquity had appealed to but few, but Christian culture, on the other hand, was addressed to all. The Fathers composed for slaves and for women, and St. John Chrysostom boasted, in the forcible language which we have cited, that the Church taught shoemakers and fullers to philosophize. They mounted the pulpit, not merely to address those who had the freedom of the city, but to all the freedmen, slaves, women, and children who were assembled in the same Basilica.

The invasion and settlement of the barbarians has been considered a grave event in the history of the human mind: and it was so, for they appeared to recreate the intelligence of humanity in affording to all who could speak or write a new crowd of auditors, bringing no wearied ears or dulled intellects, but ready to open hearts free till then, and disposed to shudder at and respond to everything that was truly worthy of admiration. It was a grave event, for the rush of that wave of fallow minds could not but modify the intellectual conditions of the world. But still not sufficient attention has been paid to a greater and more important inroad accomplished before that of the barbarians had begun—the invasion of the world of intellect by slaves, workmen, paupers, and women—the vast majority, in fact, of humanity—who came, not to demand empire, goods, or property, as did the barbarians later, but their rightful share in the enjoyment of truth, of the good and of the beautiful, which has been promised to and is the just due of all.

HOW THE LATIN LANGUAGE BECAME CHRISTIAN.

We have found that, at the moment in which the barbarians stormed the gates of the Empire, two kinds of civilization existed face to face. On the one side stood the civilization of Paganism, powerless to receive into itself, to enlighten, and, above all, to soften the terrible guests whom Providence had sent; condemned, in consequence, to perish, though not entirely and without a struggle, nor without leaving to religion, legislation, and literature dangers and advantages which the following ages would reap; whilst, on the other, Christian dogma, then strong enough to proceed in victory from the debates of theology, and to produce, in the writings of St. Augustine, a philosophy of its own, was capable of building up an entirely new society. And the elements of this already existed in that hierarchy whose antiquity we have demonstrated, and in that code of manners which had been the means of receiving slaves, the poor, and women into the life of the spirit; whilst it was the case that this , inroad of those whom the old world had disowned, whom the ancient society had despised, paved the way for, preceded, and surpassed in its proportions that other invasion of the barbarians; for it had already enlarged the audience to whom human eloquence could address itself, and in so doing had renewed the inspiration innate in literature.

We will now study the early efforts of the Christian literature, and search out the method whereby the regenerating principle, descending all the degrees of thought, took possession of eloquence, of history, and of poetry, and moulded them from the fifth century into those very forms which, in the Middle Age, appeared expanding with such vigour and brilliancy. But it was necessary, first, that Christian literature should find its proper language, and enter upon the still more difficult task of composing it out of existing but opposing elements. Latin was, of necessity, the language of the Western Church, as being the natural tongue of the dying society whose last moments she was called upon to console, and the borrowed language of that host of Germans, of Franks, and of Vandals, who were already making their way on to the lands of the frontier, into the ranks' of the army, and even the high offices of the Empire. But it remains to us to discover the miracle whereby Latin, the old pagan tongue, which preserved the names of its thirty thousand deities, which was also tainted with the indecencies of Petronius and of Martial, became not only Christian, but the language of the Church and of the Middle Age; how the idiom which seemed destined to perish with that world from whose side it had proceeded, remained a living language upon the tomb of an extinct society, so that, throughout the mediaeval period, it was continually used in preaching, in oratory, and in teaching; and noble races, even in our own day, have refused to abjure the Latin language, as forming a certain portion of their liberties. It is this transformation, then—one without parallel in the history of the human mind—which we will now take into account, as it amply deserves some measure of our attention; and our thorny task has been facilitated and smoothed by the work of a contemporary historian, who has shown how the same revolution was accomplished at Alexandria in the language of Greece.

Nothing, indeed, could seem, at first sight, worse adapted for the ideas of Christianity than that old Latin tongue which in its primitive harshness seemed only fitted for war, for agriculture, and for litigation. Mark its harsh, terse, and monosyllabic forms, befitting the idiom of a people who had no leisure to lose themselves, like the Greeks, in long discussions, nor to waste their time upon the marble steps of the Parthenon, or beneath the porticoes of the Agora. It points, on the contrary, to men of business, less greedy of ideas than of pelf, meeting each other by chance on a dusty road, scorched by the rays of the sun, and exchanging briefly, in the tersest and most elliptical language, words expressive of their rights, of their longings, and of their hopes. Thus, if war were in the question, all the expressions referring to it were short and forcible: *Mars, vis*—war, strength; *æs*, the iron from which weapons were forged. If they talked of the country, we must not expect its beauties to be celebrated in harmonious and ear-filling expressions, but in monosyllables: *flos, frux, bos*—flower, fruit, ox; everything which appertained to the agriculturist was ended by a short sound, as contracted as the moment which was allotted to him for the sowing or reaping of his crops. And the language of business had its germ in those compressed expressions which seemed to concentrate the whole energy of a litigious and law-making race: *jus, fas, lex, res*—right, justice, law, thing; the essential roots, in fine, of the language of law.

Doubtless on a closer view one can discover the affinity of Latin to the Æolian dialect, and see traces of a remote parentage amongst the languages of the East; as, for instance, Sanscrit. But, on setting aside these useful and luminous theories of science, in order to consider that alone which characterizes the genius of the people, it is impossible not to recognize in the speakers of that harsh and concise idiom the same men whom Plautus, at the opening of his "Amphitryon," caused the god Mercury to address, and for whom he wished no soft and fascinating day-dreams beneath cool shades, nor delights of wit or of imagination, but a speedy enrichment through a solid and enduring gain. So vulgar was the character of the people whose language was destined to be the universal dialect of civilization.

But as soon as the manners of Greece had invaded Rome, her orators set themselves to model the Latin tongue after Grecian forms. Thus an artificial culture arose which, though confined to a small number of enlightened minds, was pushed to an incredible pitch of ardour and of perfection. Cicero trained himself to declaim in the Greek language, as offering greater wealth than his own in resource and ornament. Nay, more, not content with stealing the figures, reasonings, and hardy flights of the oratorical compositions of Demosthenes and of Æschines, he sought also for the secrets of their eloquence and the mysteries of the harmony whereby the speakers of Greece used to flatter the itching ears of its multitudes. So we see Cicero making research with infinite art and prodigious subtlety in the works of Aristotle, of Ephorus, and of Theopompus, for the diverse measures which could be introduced into an oratorical period, to render it richer and more satisfying to the ear. Nor must we believe that he suffered his speeches to be composed of long and short syllables at haphazard: a certain number of trochees, paeans, and other feet was indispensable, and he continually expatiated on a speech which he had heard in his youth, when Carbo, tribune of the people, in the peroration to a fierce invective against his political adversaries, won the popular applause by a phrase which was crowned by the most harmonious ditrochee that had ever been heard—*Patris dictum sapiens temeritas filii comprobavit.* The word *comprobavit,* with its two long alternated by two short syllables, had so ravished the ear of the audience that the orator was surrounded by one long murmur of approbation. To such a point were the refinements of euphony insisted upon by this people, who also expected that a flute-player would always accompany the orator in the tribune, and keep his voice to the proper level.

A like measure of care, zeal, and laborious application, was also bestowed upon poetry. The metres of Greece had passed in succession, first into the epic, and then into the dramatic poetry of the Latins; and finally Catullus and Horace had borrowed from the

lyric poets of the Æolian school the most subtle and delicate combinations that were permitted by the harmony of their beautiful language.

Thus a time came when Greece possessed no treasure upon which Rome had not laid her hand; and the hour, though it was but a brief one, arrived which saw the perfect maturity of the Latin language, capable then of pursuing with Cicero the loftiest flight vouchsafed to the intellect of man, as far as the threshold of the infinite; capable also of diving with the jurisconsults into the lowest depths, the most delicate subtleties, and the remotest windings of human affairs; and capable, moreover, with Virgil, of drawing from syllables, till then harsh and inharmonious, sounds which were destined to charm the ears of a long posterity, to charm them even now; poetic lamentations which caused Octavia to faint away in the arms of Augustus.

Such was the grandeur and beauty of that Latin tongue, to which too high a tribute cannot be paid, ip that incomparable but fugitive period which we have noticed. But this artificial culture could not be of long duration, for languages contain an inherent law of decomposition which wills that, on arriving at a certain stage of maturity, like the fruits, they should fall, open out, and render to the world seeds from which newer languages might germinate. Whilst Roman society, in its most elegant and polished portion, clung to all the delicate perfections of an exquisite language, the people were without the capacity of raising themselves to so high a level, without the patience necessary to a respect for the exigencies of patrician ears. For, in fact, two kinds of rules exist in a literary language, those rules of euphony which regard art, and those of logic which look towards science; and the people, pressed with business, articulating carelessly and without regard to purity, spoke as the occasion called, and thereby violated the laws of euphony, whilst they outraged the rules of logic by erroneous constructions.

So it followed of necessity, that in a short time a popular and imperfect language—a dialect, in fact, of some coarseness—was formed beneath the learned Latin, and circulated amongst the mighty multitude which thronged in Rome and her provinces. Nor are traces wanting of the colloquial diction which prevailed in the streets of the city, and which the comedians employed as a means of bringing themselves within the sympathies of their audiences; for it appears in the works of Plautus, and in the inscriptions we may find still stranger instances wherein the rules of grammar were incredibly violated. For instance, *cum conjugem suam, pietatem causâ, templum quod est in palatium,* with numerous other expressions of like nature.

Thus the Latin language was in process of decomposition as early as the time of Cicero, who used to point to the age of Scipio Africanus as its golden era. To Cicero, as to many others, the century in which he lived gave him a sad impression, as being smitten with decay; and so he placed the apogee in a time remote from his own. It was, he said, the privilege of the age of Scipio to speak as well as to live with purity; but since then speech had been corrupted by a host of foreigners. Quintilian again said, later, that the whole language had altered, and bears witness that more than once, when a tragic spectacle had roused the emotions of the audience, the exclamations which burst from all sides of the theatre had comprised some barbarous elements, which, as it were, belied the purity of the language which the poet had designed.

Accordingly, from the earliest days of the Empire corruption had set in, the Latin language was perishing, and far from its desolation being the work of Christianity, it was only through the Church that it was destined to revive.

Antiquity had been divided by three influences, the genius of the East, namely, that of contemplation and of symbolism, which led through the observation of Nature to a discovery of the language of the Creator, and that of true poetry—for poetry is nothing but a divine contemplation of things of earth, an ideal conception of the real; secondly, the genius of Greece, specially adapted to speculation and to philosophy, with the capacity of adapting expressions of refined accuracy to all the shades of human thought, which sufficed for all the wants of the past—may we not say, also, for all those of our own time?—for it is from that language that we ask for words to designate the discoveries of the age; and, lastly, the Latin genius, which was that of action, of law, and of empire. In order that these three influences should subsist, it was necessary that the triple spirit of the East, of Greece, and of Rome, should in some measure form the soul of the nascent nations. The Latin tongue offered to the Church a marvellous engine of legislation and government, fitted for the administration of her vast society; but it was also required that the language of action should become that of speculation, that its stiff and pedantic nature should be made supple and popular, that it should be endowed with the qualities which it wanted in order to satisfy the reason with a regularity and exactitude cognate to that of the Greek terminology, and to charm the imagination with splendours kindred to those of the Oriental symbolism. This end Christianity effected by a work which, though humble at first sight, like everything which is truly humble, concealed one of the boldest and grandest ideas that have ever been conceived, by the translation of the Bible called the Vulgate. A certain man, who was perfectly versed in Latin literature, steeped in all the culture, and nearly all the passions, of the Roman world, after having for some time mastered all the enlightenment and gazed, though from some distance, at the pleasures of that debased society, came to his senses and fled in terror into the desert. He sought an asylum at Bethlehem, amidst its solitudes, which were but beginning to be peopled by the first monks; and therein Jerome forced himself to repel the memories which he had carried from Rome, and the voluptuous images which troubled his thoughts even in the place of his meditation and fasting. The works of Cicero and of Plato were never absent from his hands, and yet they recalled and echoed too loudly the sounds of that old world which he longed to forget. To subdue himself, and conquer the flesh, as he tells us, he undertook the study of Hebrew, and put himself under the tuition, and even at the service, of a monk, a converted Jew, who, greedy of interpretation, taught him, in a quarry and by night—for fear lest his countrymen should detect him—the secrets of the sacred language. "And I," said he, " all nourished as I still was with the flower of Cicero's eloquence, with the sweetness of Pliny and Fronto, and the charm of Virgil, began to stammer harsh and breath-disturbing words, *stridentia anhelantiaque verba*. I tied myself down to that difficult language, like a slave to a millstone, buried myself in the darkness of that barbarous idiom like a miner in a cavern, in which, after a long time, he at last perceives a gleam of light; so in its obscure depths I began to find unknown joys, and later, from the bitter seedtime of my study I gathered in the fruits of an infinite sweetness."

Such was the language of St. Jerome—we may recognize it by the savage energy of its eloquence. The harvest which he desired to reap, the fruits of his bitter study, were the sacred books which he proposed to translate from the Hebrew, and thus to rectify whatever errors might have crept into the visions framed upon the Septuagint, as well as to deprive the Jews of all subterfuge, and cut from under their feet the objections upon which they stood as to the supposed discrepancy between the Hebrew original and the Greek version. It was this motive that impelled St. Jerome to undertake the translation of the Bible, and nothing less than an inspiration of faith, a strong conviction of duty, was necessary to enable him to brave the intrinsic difficulty of the work, and the opposition offered by certain Christians who possessed the older translations, and were quite content to keep them; for, as Jerome said, there were people who prided themselves on having fine manuscripts, without caring for their accuracy. But his native genius and enthusiasm was hardly sufficient to carry him through all the difficulties and disgusts of his long labours. He was sustained by the friendship and the docility of St. Paula, of Eustochia, and the other Roman ladies who shared in his toil; and with their encouragement and help he advanced in his work, following a system of translation which he arranged himself, and which consisted in the continued practice of two rules. The first and the most common was to preserve, as far as was possible, without injuring, the sense, the elegance, and euphony of the language into which the translation was made. For thus, he said, had Cicero translated Plato, Xenophon, and Demosthenes; thus the Greek comedians had passed on to the Latin stage under the auspices of Plautus, Terence, and Catullus; and in this manner did he propose to transfer the beauties of the Hebrew language into the Latin text without marring the grammatical purity of the latter. But the second rule, to which he sacrificed the former, was to the effect that when it was a question of preserving the sense in translating an obscure passage, nothing besides should be considered, and that the language used in translating must be violated rather than that any of the energy of the original should be lost, for the Divine text must be correctly rendered at any cost. This, then, St. Jerome desired, proposed to himself, and pursued with a marvellous boldness. He did not ignore the barbarisms that of necessity crept into his style, and entreated Paulinus not to suffer himself to be repelled by the rude and simple language of Scripture. In another place he begged that his reader should not demand of him an elegance which he had lost through contact with the Hebrews.

Thus was produced the translation of the Old Testament into Latin, named the Vulgate, which was one of the greatest achievements of the human mind, and has not been sufficiently studied under that point of view. Through its means the whole current of the Eastern genius entered, so to speak, into the Roman civilization; and yet not so much by the small number of untranslatable Hebrew words, which St. Jerome preserved, and which need not be taken much into account. For it was not by a mere adoption of the Alleluia and the Amen that the Latin tongue was enriched, but by the bold constructions which it appropriated, the unexpected alliance of words, the wonderful abundance of images, by that Scriptural symbolism in which events and persons are figures of other events and of other persons; in which Noah, Abraham, and Jacob have their chief value as types and foreshadowings of Christianity; in which the solemn nuptials of Solomon represented the nuptials that were to be between the Messiah and the Church; in which, finally, every image of the past had reference to the future. And this gave rise to a phenomenon which has somewhat escaped observation in the depths of the Hebrew genius —the parallelism which is of its essence, and which was now added to the newly gained riches of the language of Christendom.

The Greeks nearly always founded their compositions upon the number three. Thus their odes were formed of a strophe, an antistrophe, and an epode; and the Greek grammar comprised three tenses—the past, the present, and the future. But the Hebrew arrangement was different, and we find the verses of their psalms always divided into two nearly equal parts, counterbalancing and responding to one another. That language, with the peculiarity which was also common to the other Semitic languages, possessed only two tenses.

Hebrew has in it no present, and rightly, for what is the present but an invisible point of intersection between the past and the future, which can always be divided between the one and the other, and is, therefore, non-existent as the present. It comprised only a past and a future tense, like the Hebrew people itself, which has no present destiny, and recognizes only that of the past, which it calls tradition, and that which is yet to come, which it knows as prophecy. Hence, in its language and its poetry, the novel characteristic of the people effected that the two periods of time, tradition which had been, and prophecy which would be fulfilled, stood face to face, calling and responding the one to the other; and that the idea of the present was effaced by these two tenses, which were continually changing their names and positions between themselves. For often did the prophets make use of the past to express futurity; Isaiah related the passion of Christ as an accomplished event, whilst, on the other hand, Moses speaking of the alliance concluded between the people of Israel and its God, placed his facts in the future. This predestined peculiarity of the Hebrew language, which, as it were, effaced time, and produced that sentiment of unity which was at *the* root of Eastern ideas, entered with it into the Latin tongue, and imprinted on it a stamp, which was to mark the whole literature of the Middle Age, for it was the notion of eternity which came into the Latin at the time of which we are treating, penetrated it thoroughly, and remained rooted in its soil.

We come to a second point. Only a portion of the Old Testament had been written in and translated from the Hebrew; but the remainder, with the whole New Testament—those Apostolic epistles which contained the most essential analysis of Christian theology, and the works of the early Fathers—was in Greek. It had been of necessity translated in primitive times into Latin, for the purposes of religion; but now it also passed beneath the hand of St. Jerome, as the Pope Damasus required that he should completely revise the Scriptures of the New as well as those of the Ancient Covenant. Consequently, the theological treasures of Greek Christianity passed in their turn into the Latin language; and here again we may take small notice of the new words, which must, perforce, have been borrowed from the Greek—as, for instance, all that related to the liturgy and to the hierarchy—*episcopus, presbyter, diaconus*, the name of *Christ*, the *Paraclete*, the words *baptism, anathema*, and many others; for such gains cannot be counted as conquests to a language, and merely resemble the stone which the avalanche gathers up in its course, but which is no part of itself.

The lesson gathered by the Latin tongue from the school of the Greek Christianity did not consist either in those oratorical artifices and tricks of number and rhythm which had struck Cicero, but rather in supplying from its stores the insufficiency of her own philosophic terms, an insufficiency which Cicero himself had lamented, when, in his attempts at translating the writings of Plato, and endowing his own language with the treasures of Greek thought, he found himself occasionally conquered and despairing. But Christianity did not feel his despair, nor accept the defeat; and when once the Latin tongue had been bold enough to translate the epistles of St.

Paul, which contained the most difficult propositions and the boldest flights of Christian metaphysics, there was nothing thenceforth that it could not attempt. The Church created certain words which were necessary to Christian theology— *spiritualis, carnalis, sensualis*—as designating states referring respectively to the soul, the flesh, or the senses; and also verbs expressive of certain ideas which had been unknown to the ancients, as, for instance, the verb *salvare*. Cicero himself having somewhere said that no word existed to render the Greek σωτήρ, to express the idea of a Saviour, therefore a Christian innovation was necessary to coin *salvator;* and thus *justificare, mortificare, jejunare,* and many new verbs were in time produced.

But this was not sufficient, and a deeper descent than any that the ancients had dared, into the delicacies of the human heart, was needed. Seneca had doubtless pushed his scrupulous analysis far; but Christianity transcended it, and discovered virtues in the deep recesses of feeling with which the ancients had never credited humanity. Christians were the first to use the term *compassio,* which had been unknown to the Romans, though it is true that they were unable sometimes to frame Latin words, and often confined themselves to a mere translation of the Greek, as in the case of *eleemosyna,* alms. They were bound to prosecute vigorously the work of creating resources before unknown to their language, and were not hindered by a fear of forming new expressions.

The Latin language had always preserved a concrete character; it had no love for abstract expressions, and no means of extracting them from its own resources. Thus the ancients expressed gratitude by *gratus animus,* and used for ingratitude the words *ingratus animus,* but Christianity was bolder, and coined the word *ingratitude.* Facilities appeared for the construction of many analogous terms, for multiplying and filling the Latin dictionary with names for abstract ideas, and thus appeared the words *sensualitas, gratiositas, dubietas.* But these expressions were not merely superfluous and adapted to encumber with vain redundancies a language which already sufficed for itself; they rendered what before had been expressed by a periphrasis, or, owing to the unwillingness of men to denounce anything that is not comprised in a single word, had not been expressed at all. Through their aid close reasonings and subtle distinctions could be sustained in Latin, now the language of Christianity, which in following the thorny disputes on Arianism had been obliged to mould itself after the supple delicacy of the Greek, and 'to acquire the same readiness in serving the intellect by providing it instantly with the word which it required to express a definite thought. And thus Latin gained the richness which had been peculiar to the Greek, and the power of creating words to meet its requirements.

But Christianity only achieved this revolution in the Latin tongue on condition of doing great violence to the beautiful idiom of Cicero and of Quintilian, in forcing upon it the unheard-of expressions which we have just noticed, and making *sensualitas, impassibilitas,* and the other words required by the oecumenical discussions, possible in a language formerly so exquisite. The Bible had commenced and been chiefly instrumental to the change by introducing into Latin the poetic wealth of the Hebrew on the one hand, and the philosophic wealth of Greek on the other. But in this task the Bible and the Church itself had two auxiliaries, firstly in the Africans, and secondly in the populace, who, in the epoch of which we are treating, were semi-barbarians.

Let us mark the fact, which has been too little studied, of the invasion by the Africans of Latin, and especially of Christian, literature in the time which we are discussing. It has been often remarked that Latin literature made in some measure the tour of the Mediterranean; going forth from its cradle in Etruria and Magna Graecia, it crossed the Alps, and found in Gaul writers of the class of Cornelius Gallus, Trochius Pompeius, and their contemporaries. It then passed into Spain, to find there poets and historians, though of a less pure taste, and finally a little later into Africa, where it gave birth to the latest, but not least laborious generation of its children, who brought to the study of letters all the fire of their climate. Amongst the latter may be numbered Cornutus, the disciple of Seneca, who flourished in the time of Nero; Fronto, the tutor of Marcus Aurelius, the poet Nemesianus, and many others, and finally that Martianus Capella, whose learned allegory on the marriage of Philologia and Mercury we have already noticed. The speciality of African genius was, however, manifested by Apuleius, who showed strikingly, in his romance of the Golden Ass, a taste for obscure metaphors, archaic expressions, and daring hyperboles. He loaded his poetry with adornments proper to prose, and filled his prose with poetical turns, thus trampling remorselessly upon all the rules of Latin taste. It seemed in truth as if these writers of Africa had bound themselves to avenge the misfortunes of Hannibal upon the language of his conquerors; and yet we must recognize amidst all the irregularities of their style a certain fire which smacked of the heat of their sun and of the sand of their deserts. And this was still more apparent when the African School had become Christian, and had produced the first and most illustrious of the Fathers, such as Tertullian, called always by St. Cyprian *the Master*, St. Cyprian himself, Arnobius, and above all St. Augustine.

Thus we see that Christian literature of the primitive ages was African by origin and in character, and Tertullian, the chief of the school, showed all the failings of the African genius. He was wanting in repose—a cardinal fault in the presence of the calmness which is generally the marked characteristic of the literary works of antiquity. His impetuous thought always snatched, *not* at the most accurate, but the most forcible expression.

Had he a truth to present, he was certain to present not its most attractive but its most wounding side. Rash and aggressive, he defied the intellects which were to follow him; but still the darkness of his style only veiled its brilliance, and the pomp of his verbiage never served to cloak poverty of idea. He broke the ancient moulds only because they could no longer contain the fast-flowing lava. His energetic expressions, which seemed so many challenges, often obliged unwilling reason to own its defeat; and the man who argued so barbarously achieved in the end the highest triumph of human eloquence, in saying what he meant, rudely perhaps, but thoroughly and without compromise, after a method alike forcible and enduring. Thus on one occasion, in order to express the totality of the Roman civilization, he coined the monstrous but pregnant word *Romanitas,* and again, in defining the Church, said in a jargon which assuredly no Roman would have owned, ' ' *Corpus sumus de conscientia religionis et disciplines divinitate et spei foedere.* " (The Church is a mighty body resulting from the consciousness of the same religion, from the divinity of the same discipline, from the bonds of the same hope.) Wishing again to pursue to the last details the decomposition of the human organization, he used the following strong expressions: *Cadit in originem terram, et cadaveris nomen, ex isto jam nomine peritura in nullum inde jam nomen et omnis vocabuli mortem,* and bequeathed to Bossuet the following immortal phrase: *Ce je ne sais quoi qui n'a de nom dans aucune langue.* These Africans, therefore, if barbarians, were at least gifted with eloquence, and if they broke down the edifice of polished Latinity which had been reared by the ancients, it was because they knew that they could build up a grander fabric from the ruins.

However, it was not the Africans alone who lent their aid to Christianity in the great work of destruction and reconstruction; for they only formed the vanguard of the advancing columns which now formed in truth the bulk of the Roman people, and which had been recruited from all the barbarous nations. From the remotest time, long before Goths or Vandals came in question, the mission of Rome began and accomplished itself day by day. When in the fifth century of its existence, for example, the slave Herdonius, with a multitude of his fellows, found himself master of the Capitol, the city was already in the power of the barbarians. Her population was composed of slaves, freedmen, and mercenaries, strangers who took liberties with her language; and Scipio himself, the man whom Cicero placed at its golden age, said to the people from the tribune, with the audacity of a dauntless warrior :—" I see that you are all Numidians, Spaniards, and barbarians of other kinds, whom I brought hither with your hands bound behind your backs, freedmen but of yesterday, and voters of to-day." Thus the mass which was named the Roman people was but a great and increasing ingathering of barbarism, and it was also recruited by Christianity; for the religion which did not despise the mean and ignorant, which had been the first to approach them, opened widely its doors for their entrance, showed no repugnance at their coarseness, and permitted her Catacombs to be covered with inscriptions which bristled with barbarisms and solecisms: " *Quam stabilis tibi hæc vita est—Refrigero deus animo hominis—Irene da Cálda*"

We see, then, that the language of the inscriptions of the Catacombs was identical with the language of that people whom we have before noticed as taking no heed of rules of euphony or of logic, and using a very different pronunciation from that of the chosen and elegant few who used the idiom of Cicero and of Horace. They even corrupted the popular Latin of the Psalms, and St. Augustine tells us that in the churches of Africa the clergy were unable to bring their congregation to chant *Super ipsum efflorebit sanctificatio mea.* They persisted in saying *floriet*, nor could all their Christian docility uproot the solecism. The same authority also tells us that in order to be understood by the people, it was necessary to say, *"Non est absconditum a te ossummeum,"* instead of *"os meum"* and that

he preferred that rendering, as it was more essential to be understood than to use good Latin; and even St. Jerome, fond as he still was of the beautiful diction of the poets and the classic memories of Cicero and of Plautus, granted that the Scriptures ought to be in a simpler style, which would put them within the grasp of an assembly of the unlearned.

But it was in the domain of poetry especially that the intervention of the people became marked and fertile. Side by side with that learned versification which only the minority could justly appreciate, stood another poetry; and whilst the cultivated courtiers of Augustus were delighting in the dactyls and spondees which fell from the lips of Virgil, the Roman populace, too rude for such mental pleasures, possessed their own popular verses in those atellans and old Saturnine rhythms of which we -now know so little. We are certain of but one peculiarity in the poetic taste of the ancient Romans, but that is a most interesting fact, namely, that they delighted in seeing their verses in rhyme. Of this traces appear in the works of Ennius, the poetical writings of Cicero, and even in the measures of Virgil, the hemistich often rhyming with the end of the verse; and we find it used with care and a certain affectation in the pentameters of Ovid, who seemed to take delight in bringing the consonant terminations of his lines into apposition, as if it were a certain method of extracting applause. So that this taste, which could be not entirely suppressed in the elaborate poetry of the Augustan age, seemed to proceed from the instincts of the people, who formed a species of poetry which was germane to the rude qualities of their language, as we find many rhyming couplets amongst the ancient relics of the popular Latin melodies, for instance in the Roman war song,—

Mille, mille Sarmatas occidimus!

Mille, mille Persas quaerimus !

Christianity, always considerate of popular tastes, had no need to outrage this one, and we find even in the poetic attempts which first fell from Christian hands that the rhyme was developed to a point which reminds us of modern habits. We will cite here, for the first time, a poem which is scarcely known, but which seems decisive on this point—a poem bearing the authorship of St. Cyprian, but which can hardly be his, though certainly dating from his era, which was also that of the persecutions. Its subject is the Resurrection from the Dead, and the first fourteen verses form a singular train of monorhymes:—

Qui mihi ruricolas optavi carmine musas,

Et vernis roseas titulari floribus auras,

Æstivasque graves maturavi messis aristas

Succidi tumidas autumni vitibus uvas, &c.

After fourteen lines which rhyme in *as,* follow five in *o,* and six in *is,* as if the Christian poet, seeking to impress their meaning upon his auditors, could find no method surer than this reiterated rhyme to lay hold of the memory and charm the imagination.

A little later the Christian Commodianus, who also lived during the persecutions, composed eighty chapters, *Adversus Gentium Deos,* which aspired to be in verse. But they were not equal to those which we have just quoted, and had nothing in common with the old heroic verse except the number of the syllables, which the author, in order to obtain the necessary dactyls and spondees, made long or short arbitrarily. The last twenty-six lines formed a long succession upon a single rhyme,—

Incolas cœlorum futuri cum Deo Christo,

Tenente princípium, vidente cuncta de cœlo,

Simplicitas, bonitas habitet in corpore vestro.

"Wretched lines intrinsically, but yet curious as showing the prominence given to the rhyme, which, from being a mere accessory to the poems of the age of Augustus, formed the sole object of the new poetry, in which the imitation of the old heroic verse was but a discredited tradition.

But St. Augustine entirely discarded the methods of the ancient poetic art and the harmony of the Latin metres, upon which he had formerly composed a treatise in five books; and for the sake of his flock, in order to fix in their minds the principles of the controversy against the Donatists which had so long troubled the African Church, composed a psalm *Contra Donatistas* of not less than two hundred and eighty-four verses, divided into twenty couplets of twelve verses each, accompanied by a refrain, and not including the epilogue. These verses were all composed of sixteen or seventeen syllables divided in the middle by a caesura, and all ending with the same rhyme,—

Omnes qui gaudetis de pace modo verum judicate.

Abundantia peccatorum solet fratres conturbare.

Propter hoc Dominus noster voluit nos praemonere,

Comparans regnum cœlorum reticulo misso in mare.

From this we may see that all the artifices of the ancient poetry had disappeared; all that referred to quantity, dactyls, or spondees, was effaced, leaving only the two constituents of all modern popular poetry—the number of its syllables and rhyme.

Moreover, it is a striking fact that the plan of following the same rhyme for twenty, thirty, or forty verses, until it was fairly exhausted, was precisely the earliest method adopted for the chivalrous poems of the Middle Age, for the poems and romances of the Carlovingian period. In them also the same assonance returned over and over again, until the patience of both the orator and the audience was wearied, as if the human mind found a singular charm in the novel artifice which had taken the place of the canons of the ancient poetry. And to look closer, it appears as if the attractions of rhyme consisted in the expectation which it roused and satisfied, in the experience which it produced, and the memory which it recalled, in the return of an agreeable consonance, the reawakening of a pleasure once enjoyed when most pleasures pass by to return, no more. Such was perhaps the psychological principle of that new art which was introduced with the popular element into the Latin tongue, and became the ruling canon of all modern versification.

These, therefore, were the achievements of Christianity, with the Bible for her instrument, with Africans, barbarians, and the populace, who were recruited from the latter, for her servants. Nothing less than this great transformation of the Latin language was needed in order to mould from it the classic tongue of the Middle Age, and to reunite the scattered elements of the ancient civilization.

For, in the first place, the Middle Age was a period of contemplation, full of that ascetic and coenobitic life which was already flourishing on every hand, and which could only find adequate expression in a language which sparkled with the fires which had lightened the anchorites of the East. And the Middle Age had to find in the idiom which it used a vehicle for that symbolism which had become its want; for no epoch has striven more to represent ideas by figures, and to discover in every being the mark of a divine thought; and thus throughout, in its poetry and its architecture, in its works by brush or by chisel, did the Middle Age preserve a character of allegory, and the chant of the Psalms alone could give to its Gothic cathedrals a worthy voice. Latin was the necessary language of the Liturgy, which formed the poetic song of the mediaeval period.

And, secondly, the Middle Age was rich in the genius of speculation, in an activity of mind which never ceased to analyze and to distinguish. It produced those legions of logicians and controversialists whose dauntless subtlety never wearied in fathoming the regions of the intellect; and as to render their thoughts a supple language like that of the Greek metaphysic was required, so the mediaeval Latin became the language of the schools.

In the third place, the Middle Age possessed the genius of action; it was pressed upon by the idea of law, so that the majority of its great wars began, so to speak, by lawsuits. It was filled with Pleadings for and against the priesthood, or the Empire, or divorce. Litigation lay at the root of all its armed quarrels; it was a juridical epoch, and produced the Canon Law; and as it required a language adapted to the rendering of all the subtleties and the satisfaction of all the needs of the jurisconsults, therefore the Latin of the Middle Age became the language of the law courts. And most of all, those ages represented the childhood of the Christian nations; therefore their common infancy called for one language as the instrument of its education, and demanded that it should be simple, expressive, and familiar, capable of lending itself to the meagre intellects of the Saxons, Goths, and Franks, who then formed tho bulk of the Christian world. For this reason the Church, with reason, preferred the idiom of the people to the idiom of the learned few, and prepared in advance a language which would be accessible to those sons of the barbarians who soon were to throng her schools.

Thus all the modern languages, one after another, were destined to gather energy and fertility from the ancient Latin; and not only those of them which have been styled Neo-Latin, such as Italian, Provençal, and Spanish, but the Teutonic dialects also were not free from the tutorship exercised by the language of the Romans. Long were they subject to its happy influence, and the English, which amongst all the languages of the North preserved the most of its effect, was also the tongue which acquired a peculiar clearness, energy, and popularity.

But the Latin which thus moulded our modern languages was not that of Cicero, nor even that of Virgil, deeply studied as these authors were in the Middle Age, but the Latin of the Church and of the Bible, the religious and popular idiom whose course we have been tracing. It was the Bible— the first book that the new languages essayed to translate, that was taken up by the French in the twelfth, by the Teutonic tongues in the eighth and ninth centuries— which, with its beautiful narrative, with the simplicity of its Genesis and its pictures of the infancy of the human race, was found speaking the very language which was needed by the infant races who were about to enter upon civilized and intellectual life. Our fathers were accustomed to cover the volume of Holy Writ with gold and precious stones. They did more, for when a council assembled, the Scriptures were placed upon the altar in the midst of the conference, over which they were to preside, and whose deliberations they were to conduct. And when processions marched under the open sky, amid their ranks, as Alcuin tells us, the Bible was ever borne triumphantly in a golden shrine. Assuredly our ancestors were right when they covered it with gold and carried it in triumph, for the first of the books of antiquity is also the chief book of modern times; it is, in fact, the author of all our literature, for from its pages proceeded all the languages, and all the eloquence, poetry, and civilization of the later ages.

CHRISTIAN ELOQUENCE.

The Latin language perished by the dissolving process which sooner or later awaits every learned idiom, which begins by sapping its principles and ends by resolving it into a number of popular dialects. But the decaying language was in this case to subsist for the use of Western Christendom. We have glanced at the extraordinary transformation whereby the Latin tongue was adapted to its new destiny, and seen how the living forces of the Bible entered into the ancient idiom of Cicero to add to it breadth, the boldness of the Eastern symbolism, and the wealth of the Greek metaphysic ; how the great work was seconded even by barbarous influences, by those African writers who remorselessly violated the ancient forms, as well as by the various crowd of foreigners who outraged the laws of language as unscrupulously as the frontiers of the Empire, who, in debasing the purity of the idiom, reduced it to their own rude level, and rendered it accessible to the multitude of Goths, Franks, and Saxons, whose speech it was one day destined to become. Thus was formed the Latin of the Church, a curious idiom which, though at once old and new, was frequently sublime in its very rudeness, which also possessed a native grace, ornaments, and great writers of its own, was sufficient for all the requirements of the liturgy, of the schools, and of the feudal and canon law; popular enough to serve for all matters of business as well as for the teaching and education of the barbarians, and gifted with a fecundity which brought forth the whole modern family of the Latin languages.

Christian civilization, therefore, had found its proper tongue, and we now must examine its production of the three constituents of all literature—eloquence, history, and poetry. We will treat firstly of Christian eloquence. Antiquity had loved to excess the pleasures of speech, pleasures we may call them, for under its order eloquence was bound to charm the senses and not merely to satisfy the intellect. To the Greeks and Romans a speech was a spectacle, and the tribune a stage. As the Greek theatre was a species of temple, wherein the actor, clothed in majestic and ennobling costume, represented the gods and heroes of old, and was bound to preserve a kind of statuesque dignity, so was the Greek and Roman orator expected to manifest on the tribune, by the taste of his dress and his whole attitude and adornment of person, the correctness of a figure by Praxiteles or Phidias. His voice was raised and carefully sustained by the flute-player, who was his constant companion, whilst the exacting ear of his audience forbade his allowing it to rise or fall beyond a certain number of tones selected to satisfy the musical craving of their fastidious and sensual organizations. Therefore, although it was customary to divide rhetoric into the five provinces of invention, disposition, elocution, action, and memory, Demosthenes, that great master of the art, declared that action, comprised the whole matter, and that an audience was conquered at once if the eye and ear were won. If such was the case with the sensual Greeks, equally must it have been so with the Romans, the most essentially materialistic race that has ever existed.

But the time came when the political interest, which had been the sustaining influence of these great displays, failed, and as the Greek stage had refused to produce any great tragedians when inspiration had , departed from a conquered patriotism, so did eloquence wither on the disappearance of the mighty topics which had been provided by the centuries of liberty. At the time of which we are speaking only three roads were open to eloquence; the first of which was that afforded by the Bar, which had, under

Valentinian, reconquered the right of public speaking. This was one of the benefits conferred by the Christian emperors, and the forums of the great cities, such as Milan, Rome, and Carthage, could show a certain number of orators famed for their skill in pleading. But the Bar was not the path to fortune. Martianus Capella, who was the boast of his contemporaries, and remarkable alike for the extent of his erudition and the suppleness of his style, confessed that the Bar of Carthage had never enriched him, and that he was dying of hunger whilst surrounded by applauding crowds at the tribunal of the proconsul.

The second employment open to eloquence lay in panegyric of the emperors, of their ministers and favourites, and even of the favourites of their ministers. But the talent was degraded by thus crouching at the feet of the degenerate and contemptible greatness of that period, and in danger of losing the nobility of heart, the *pectus quod disertos facit,* which provided its healthiest inspiration. For what could he hoped for from men who could only praise Maximian, the colleague of Diocletian, by comparing him to Hercules, scorning a parallel with Alexander as far too weak; who, if Providence sent them a man of mark, could in the degradation which a course of miserable flatteries had brought upon their intellects and imaginations, find nothing new to say in praise of him; like Pacatus, who, in celebrating the merits of Theodosius, could only remark that Spain in giving him birth had excelled Delos, the cradle of Apollo, or Crete, the country of Jupiter.

It is elsewhere, then, that we must seek for the last remnants of the ancient eloquence, and, perhaps, it may be found in another form less known, but, perhaps, more in use amongst the ancients, namely, in the declamatory discourses pronounced by itinerant rhetoricians, who were in the habit of strolling from city to city with speeches prepared to serve for exordium or for peroration, or of extorting the applause of their audience by improvisations made at the request of a town, and with certain precautions. This was an ancient usage, and showed how devoted Greece had been to those pleasures of the ear for which her poetry alone was not sufficient; and we find men like Hippia s and Gorgias, in the early days of Athenian history, making it their business to teach methods of proving the just or the unjust, and advertising their art in sustaining a thesis or maintaining a declamation as a means of drawing attention to their school.

Therefore, although liberty, and with her the serious motives of eloquence, had disappeared, this occupation still remained. We see, for instance, Dion Chrysostom, the rhetorician, pursued by the hatred of the Emperor Domitian, taking refuge in an exile more remote than that of Ovid, in the town of Olbia on the shores of the Black Sea, inhabited partly by Greeks, partly by Scythians, and, on his arrival, being surrounded by a crowd of men who spoke a language which was barely Greek, inhabited the ruins, and were ceaselessly menaced by Scythian invasion, but who pressed round the orator who had appeared amongst them, led him to the temple of Jupiter, assembled in masses on the steps, and conjured him to address them until Dion was obliged to discuss some common subject, and mingle with his oration the praises of their native town. And this passion, so strong in the East, was not less so in the West. Of this Africa, in the second and, perhaps, the third century, affords a notable instance in the person of Apuleius, who used to travel throughout the towns of Numidia and Mauritania with a collection of various discourses ready to be delivered upon emergency, which he called his " Florida." Once; on arriving at Carthage, he congratulated himself in his speech on the immense audience which had assembled to hear him, and begged them not to confound him with those miserable strolling orators who veiled the hand of a mendicant under the cloak of a philosopher. He went on to compare himself with the rhetorician Hippias; and although he was unable to make his garments, his wig, and his pot of oil with his own hands, " Still," said he, " I do profess to be able to turn the same pen to every description of poem, whether those whose cadence is marked by the lyre, or those which are recited by the wearers of the sock or the buskin; as well as satires, enigmas, stories of every class, discourses which men of eloquence would praise, and dialogues approved by philosophers, all in either Greek or Latin, with the same application and the same style."

To such a pitch had the effrontery and, at the same time, the degradation of the art of speech been pushed that this man, finding out that he had flattered himself too grossly, excused himself on the plea that his self-praise was merely a device to fix the attention of the proconsul, with whose eulogium his oration was to terminate, and thus fell into a double obloquy from his vanity and his meanness.

If eloquence was thus lost, it mattered little whether lessons in rhetoric were still given in the schools, or if the youth of the time continually repeated the same exercises, composed the same harangues, or renewed the laments of Thetis or the death of Achilles, or those of Dido on the departure of Æneas. These themes, preserved throughout the times of barbarism, are to be found in the writings of Ennodius, who composed many of them, and later in those of Alcuin, who recommended and used them himself in tuition. But it was evident that they contained no intellectual vitality.

But Christianity could not suffer eloquence to perish. She more than any system was bound to hold it in honour, as representing the Word, the creative spirit of the universe, which had also redeemed and was one day to judge His work. That same divine eloquence was to be perpetuated in the Christian Church by means of preaching, and no form of outward respect was too honourable for its enshrinement. The ancients had given a truly magnificent pedestal to human eloquence. They had raised for it a tribune in the midst of the Agora or Forum; thence it might preside over those intelligent and passionate cities the conquest of which was the guerdon of victorious oratory. It was difficult to find a more honourable post for a mere human thing; but Christianity effected this by planting her eloquence, not on a tribune, but within her temples, side by side with her altars. The Church raised for it a pulpit, a second altar, as it were, hard by the sanctuary, and offered a spectacle, unseen by Paganism, of an oratory, prosaic in form and simple in matter, delivered in the pause of her mysteries. It was true that thereby the conditions of eloquence were changed; it ceased to be a means of enjoyment, and became a medium of instruction. Its end was no longer to enchain the senses, but to enlighten the mind and to touch the heart, and, therefore, action disappeared almost entirely from Christian oratory; for who could expect it from those bishops who sat motionless on their pontifical seats, in the depth of the apses, to address a multitude composed of paupers, slaves, and women, little skilled in the antique delicacies of Greek and Roman declamation?

And, secondly, elocution was doomed to lose much of its importance. Disposition of the subject was to be neglected, for the Christian art was to be entirely devoted to invention and to a profound and exhaustive grasp of the subject-matter. But as art diminished so did inspiration increase; and as in the fifth century inspiration had quitted rhetoric and left only a phantom of art, so, if art was absent, inspiration had returned to the eloquence of the Church, and method was soon to follow it, attracted sooner or later by the presence of the inspiring influence, as the sun on his rising calls all the harmonious voices of creation to salute him.

From the first appearance of a Christian school of eloquence we may trace in it an inherent and profound separation from the theories and methods of that of antiquity, and also an element of originality which touched mankind and was its true secret. St. Paul came into the midst of those intensely refined Greeks only to trample on the base resources of human oratory, to hold cheap the sublimities of speech, and to profess the knowledge of a single thing, Christ and Christ crucified. Yet we, like St. Jerome, cannot fail to perceive that the man who even thus appears uncultured had resources within himself of which his auditors of Areopagus were ignorant, and that his harsh, unexpected, and unpolished words struck home like thunderbolts. But as the Christian society was enlarged, the system of preaching was extended, and a want of organization was felt. A ministry of such scope and continuity soon found its laws, and St. Ambrose, in his work "De Officiis Ministrorum," founded, in some measure, on the "De Officiis" of Cicero, traced out the various functions of the priesthood, including that of preaching. Ambrose has been erroneously placed in the category of the Fathers who were estranged from art and inimical to literature, whereas he had so well preserved the tone of the masterpieces of antiquity upon which his mind had fed, that he sought for artistic rules in Holy Scripture itself, and laboured to prove, in a letter written to a certain Justus, that it was possible to find throughout a respect shown to the three points considered by the old rhetoricians essential to a complete discourse, namely, a cause, a matter, and a conclusion. Moreover, his esteem for the canons and graces of the ancient eloquence appeared to some extent in the rules he laid down for the Christian orator. They were as follows:—" Let your discourse be correct, simple, clear, lucid, full of dignity and gravity, with no affectation of elegance, but tempered by a certain grace. "What shall I say of the voice? It suffices, in my opinion, that it should be pure and distinct; for its harmony must depend rather upon nature than our own efforts. The pronunciation should be articulate and strong, free from the rude and coarse intonation of the country, without assuming the emphatic rhythm of the stage, but always preserving the accent of piety." This shows that St. Ambrose was no mean authority, but a member still of the school which took into account not merely the thought and the expression of the orator, but also his gestures and the disposition of his drapery.

But the true founder of Christian rhetoric was St. Augustine, to whom the function appertained, especially in the capacity of his former profession as a rhetorician. This is evidenced by the fourth book of one of his most important treatises, " De Doctrina Christiana et de Catechizandis Budibus." Having devoted the first three books to an exposition of the method and spirit in which the Scriptures ought to be studied, he showed in the fourth the proper manner of communicating to others the science which had been mastered, and thus collected in bis theory of Christian preaching all the precepts of a novel rhetoric: " And in the first place, he declared that he knew well the rhetoric of the schools, but did not propose to relate or to discredit its precepts—for as it had for its object persuasion of what was true and what was false, who would dare to affirm that truth should remain unarmed against falsehood?" But he did innovate in adding, what the ancients had not dared to say, that eloquence could exist without rhetoric, and could be achieved by listening, by reading the works of eloquent authors, and exercising the mind in dictation and composition. On these conditions the subtleties of the schools could be dispensed with, and by this path a man could attain to the ineffable gift of persuasion and of eloquence.

But having made this just division between eloquence and rhetoric, St.

Augustine suddenly returned to the precepts of the ancients, and selected from them, leaving aside whatever was unnecessary for the simplicity of the new era. He gave the principal share to invention, as befitted a Christian epoch in which the empire over mere form had been assured to ideas, and, adapting from the beautiful treatise of Cicero, " De Inventione," insisted that wisdom was the very foundation of eloquence, and of far surpassing value; for that whereas wisdom, without eloquence, had founded states, eloquence, deprived of wisdom, had more than once brought them to destruction. Applying these precepts, he continued, that though it was better that preachers should speak eloquently, it sufficed if they spoke words of wisdom, precepts admissible alike in their liberality and their fitness; for had the Church been as severe as antiquity in matter of art, had she given the right of speech only to the eloquent, few indeed would have been entitled to spread her doctrines, few able to receive them, and thus the teaching of Christianity, instead of being the light and consolation of all, would have remained the pleasure and privilege but of a few. Great, therefore, and pregnant in consequences, was the fiat which opened the pulpit not only to the man who had been exercised during » long years in oratorical struggles, like Demosthenes and Cicero, but to the humblest priest who had the faith which could inspire him, and -the good sense which would keep him in the right track.

St. Augustine preserved, like Cicero, the distinction between the three parts of oratorical invention, for, said he, it is an eternal truth that a speaker is bound to convince, to please, and to touch. Nor can we wonder that he wished to retain for the Christian orator his mission of convincing, of stirring, and touching the rebellious will, nor especially that he permitted him to please; for we know the insight of St. Augustine, that finished expert in the mystery of the human heart; and we know also that the secret of pleasing is the secret by which souls are won. But even in this case he calls only for what is essential, declaring that if the key will really open, it matters little whether its substance be of gold, of lead, or of wood, only that it must be efficient to unlock the barriers of the heart to all the light of truth and the gentle evidence of the divine influence.

In elocution also he preserved, as being founded upon nature, a distinction of three styles—the simple, the temperate, and the sublime. The subject of Christian oratory must ever be sublime, but it was not so with the style of the orator. A simple style, said Augustine, is the one which the auditor can listen to for the longest time; and more than once in his long career he remarked that admiration for a brilliant period 'sometimes extracted less applause from the audience than the pleasure of having clearly and easily grasped a difficult verity which a simple sentence had brought down to its level. Such were his recommendations in the matter of elocution. With regard to oratorical rhythm, he declared that although he aimed at preserving it without affectation in his own discourses, yet he really held it in slight esteem, and rejoiced at not finding it in the sacred books, delighting rather on the frank, uncultured, and highly spiritual beauties of Scripture, which was, as it were, released from these usages of a sensuous antiquity.

However, there was a certain danger in the contempt evinced by Augustine for the delicacies of style, some traces of the Decline, and of the vicious taste of his age. But however deficient he might be in his views upon elocution, and though his rules as to invention were but a repetition of the canons of the Ciceronian rhetoric, he recovered himself singularly when he entered into the hidden depths of the philosophy of eloquence, and promulgated the true mystery of the new school which he was about to found. This he effected in another work, which is interesting both from the circumstances which produced it, and as giving us an insight into the soul of its author. A deacon, named Deo-Gratias, who had been entrusted with the instruction of the catechumens, wrote him a letter relating the disgust, trouble, and discouragement encountered in his difficult duty; and the saint endeavoured to raise his courage by representing, in masterly analysis, all the trials which must befall the man whose duty it was to expound the word to his brethren, and pointing at the method by which he might vanquish his difficulties, and triumph, sooner or later, over the repugnance shown by his own heart or by his hearers. The two secrets of the eloquence, which had its essence in the study of the human heart, were love towards the men who had to be instructed, and the love of that truth which was nothing less than God Himself. For St. Augustine found in charity the craving to communicate to our fellows the truth which has convinced ourselves, and in the impulse which causes us to open to others the hand which we deem to be filled with the stores of truth, beauty, and righteousness, a provocative to eloquence which had been unknown to the ancients: "For," said he, "like as a father delights in becoming childish with his child, and stammering out with it its first words—not that there is an intrinsic attraction in thus murmuring confused utterances, though it is a happiness looked for by all young fathers—so it should be a pleasure for us, as fathers of souls, to make ourselves little with the little ones, to murmur with them the first words of truth, and to imitate the bird in the gospel which gathers her young under her wings, and is only happy when she is warmed by their warmth, and can warm them by her own." And, in fact, no one could better understand than Augustine that mysterious sympathy between the speaker and his audience, by means of which the one enlightens, sustains, and guides the other, whilst both work at the same time, and by the same effort, to discover and to glorify the same verity.

But if the love of humanity was one principle of the new kind of eloquence, there was also that real sacred love of truth, of the supreme ideal, which ought to fill the whole mind of the orator, never perhaps to be grasped in its full perfection, sometimes lost to view, but capable when seen from time to time of sustaining and quickening his zeal. And this influence, better known to Augustine perhaps than to any of the eloquent ones of classic time, is thus described by him:—" For my own part, my discourse generally displeases me, as I covet a better rendering, which I often seem to hold in my mind before I begin to express by myself in the sound of words; and so, when all my efforts remain inferior to my conception, I grieve at finding that my tongue is not sufficient for my heart. An idea flashes through my mind with the rapidity of lightning, but not so language, which is slow and tardy, and permits the thought to return into mystery whilst it is unfolding itself. Yet as the flying thought has left some fair traces imprinted upon the memory, which last long enough to lend themselves to the sluggishness of the syllables, upon them do we form the words that are named the Latin, Greek, Hebrew, or any other tongue; for these same traces of the idea are neither Latin, Greek, Hebrew, nor of any other nation, but as the features are marked upon the face so is the idea in the mind. . . . Hence it is easy to conjecture the distance of the sounds which escape from the mouth from that first glimpse of thought. . . . But in our eager desire for the welfare of our hearts, we long to speak as we feel. . . . And because we do not succeed we torment ourselves, and, as if our labour was useless, are devoured by discouragement, which withers our speech and renders it more impotent than it was when, from a feeling of futility, discouragement first came upon us." We need not insist upon the merit of this, for eloquence was certainly renovated when not only the influences which could inspire it, but all the accompanying discouragements and melancholy were thus appreciated; and this was the method used by the chief Christian orators in reconstructing the theory of eloquence. It would now remain to us to observe the practical working of the new rules in their discourses, but this matter has already been treated by M. Villemain with a superiority which forbids a further analysis, and our subject simply demands an examination of the chief features of the changes gradually produced by the action of these rules, and the adaptation of eloquence from the shapes it had assumed in the classic period to the form which prevailed in the Middle Age.

The Christian eloquence of Greece seemed to have been born from the scoff hurled by Julian at Christianity, when in a moment of passionate contempt he bade the Galilseans go to study Luke and Matthew in their churches. It was then that Gregory of Nazian-zum replied to him:—" I abandon to you everything else, riches, authority, birth, glory, and all the good things of this life, of which the memory passes like a dream, but I lay my hand upon eloquence and regret not the labours and journeyings over land and sea which it has cost me to acquire it." The Christians were far from wishing to abandon their share in the empire of eloquence, and then in fact arose the great school in which, side by side with St. Gregory of Nyssa, flourished St. Basil and St. Chrysostom, whose conversion caused constant regret to the rhetorician Libanius, who lamented daily that he, Chrysostom, had been stolen from him to whom he had intended to bequeath his school; but from our point of view, Chrysostom was no great loser.

The Latins were not, like the Greeks, masters in the art of disposition, or gifted with their brilliancy and grace of elocution, nor ready with those comparisons which, though old enough, were always fresh drawn from the sea, the port, the theatre, and the palaestra. They had not the same pure instinct in the choice of expressions, and a certain barbarism was apparent in their subtleties and coarseness, as well as in the laboured refinement which was the offspring of bad taste. The fact was that the Latin Fathers did not address so polished an audience, but a variously mixed multitude; whereas the Greek Fathers at Antioch, Caesarea, and Constantinople, had before them a select remnant of the ancient society. The congregation which crowded around the chair of the Bishop of Hippo was principally composed of fishermen and of peasants; and the multitudes of Milan even and Rome comprised a vast number of freedmen and mercenaries, who by the guttural sound of their voices recalled the forest from which they had sprung. Therefore other methods of conquest were necessary for these mingled populations upon whose rude natures the external graces of speech would have been wasted, and as the eloquence which moved them must be familiar, plain, and pathetic, these three qualities generally formed the dominant characteristics of the oratory of the Latin Fathers.

But we see in the eloquence of St. Ambrose a more faithful adhesion to the traditions, and a kind of lingering perfume, as it were, derived from the ancient art. Whereas in his teaching he gave a large share to grace of form and even of costume; so also did his language contain a spice of the Attic honey. It is told how, when still an infant, as he was one day sleeping in his cradle in the court of the praetorium at Treves, a swarm of bees settled upon his lips, as of old upon the lips of Plato. The tale gained credit with the growing fame of his eloquence; an eloquence which kept the people of Milan at once in perseverance and in duty, in firmness and in submission, whilst for two days the soldiery of the Empress Justina besieged the basilica, in order to make it over to the Arians; an eloquence .which was of so winning a nature that mothers hid their daughters when St. Ambrose glorified virginity; and the power of which was able to arrest the guilty Theodosius upon the threshold of the sanctuary; its sweetness to ravish St. Augustine, still half Manichaean, still undecided, but more than half gained by the spells of so skilled a speaker.

But although the character of the oratory of St. Ambrose stood so high, we pass it over to come to that of St. Augustine, which filled a higher place in the opinion of posterity. It was true that the latter was less ornate, less antique in form, less moulded upon Greek models, and its author had not, like St. Ambrose, translated from their original Greek many of the writings of the Fathers. Augustine has left us about three hundred and ninety-eight sermons, not including several treatises, which were preached before being written, and they show the characteristics which we have noticed as recommended by the saint himself, and which gave to preaching a novel form, by their familiar, simple, and attractive style. For, in fact, the discourse of the Bishop of Hippo was simply a discussion with his people, who often interrupted him, and to whom he replied. Often, also, he related his most private and domestic affairs, as, for instance, in two sermons he described to his audience the life in community which he led with his clergy; how their union was in imitation of the primitive community at Jerusalem; how none amongst them possessed any property of his own; and the bishop himself combatted any objection that might be raised against it. It was a common complaint at Hippo that the Church was poor because the bishop refused to receive either donations or legacies, and that nobody cared to offer more. To this Augustine replied that he had, in fact, refused heritages and legacies from certain fathers who had disinherited their children in order to enrich the Church: " For with what excuse could I, who, if both were living, would be bound to labour for their reconciliation, receive an inheritance which was in itself evidence of a passion which refused to pardon ? But let a father who has nine children count Christ for a tenth, then I will accept the portion. When a father disinherits a son to enrich the Church, he must find someone else than Augustine to receive the legacy, or rather may God grant that he finds nobody." Still, these minute explanations of even his household expenses did not hinder his expounding to his people the hardest passages of Holy Writ, of initiating them into the mysteries of allegorical explanation, of relating the history of its persons and its events, of showing the figurative which underlay the apparent sense, and refuting the opposition made by the Manichaeans between the Old and the New Testaments. He kept up also the struggle against Arianism, and, in the presence of his rude people, handled all the difficulties and objections, penetrated and dispersed the mists of controversy, and compressed into his rustic and simple sermons, with an admirable art, the momentous considerations and mighty views which were spread throughout those theological treatises which he had composed for the whole Christian Church. He succeeded in teaching his humble hearers how the Trinity was imaged in the triple unity of the memory, the intellect, and the will, and thus the idea which was exhaustively developed in his philosophical writings' was laid in summary before fishermen and peasants. He led them into the domain of psychology, and the inner details of human thought, in asking, " Have you a memory? but if not, how do you retain the words which I speak to you ?" " Have you an intellect ? but if not, how do you comprehend what I say?" "Have you a will? but if not, how can you answer me?" And then, having caused them to disengage from the chaos of their coarse perceptions the three constituent faculties of the soul, he showed to them their co-existent unity and variety; and, little by little, that crowd understood, followed, and anticipated him, until he exclaimed in delight at their appreciation, " I say it sincerely to your charity, that I feared to delight the subtle minds of the skilful, and to discourage the slow, but now I see that, by your application in listening and your promptness in understanding, you have not only grasped my words, but have forestalled them. I render thanks to God."

It was indeed an achievement to elevate to the regions of metaphysic, and endow with intellectual power, those rough and uncultured minds, and, as Plato had inscribed on the door, "None but geometers enter here," it was a glorious contradiction to write, in the words of Christ, *Venite ad me omnes*—" All you who labour, who dig the earth, who fish in the sea, who carry burdens, or slowly and painfully construct the barks in which your brothers will dare the waves, all enter here, and I will explain to you not only the *γνῶθι σεαυτον* of Socrates, but the profoundest of mysteries, the Trinity." And this was the secret of that simple eloquence.

At other times he delighted in giving more polish to his discourse, and some place to the ancient art (though always using the same form of a familiar discussion), in unrolling before his hearers the greatest memories of Holy Writ in succession, and using also those literary reminiscences which would appeal to the minds of the small number of cultivated men to be found among his flock. As one instance of these discourses, we may cite the homily on prayer, spoken on the occasion of hearing the news of the capture of Rome by Alaric, one of the most curious, if not the most eloquent, of his sermons. We must mark the echoes awakened throughout the world, at Hippo as at Bethlehem, by that tremendous catastrophe, whilst crowds of fugitives were landing for refuge upon every coast, who had purchased their hare lives by the abandonment of gold, silver, and treasure. Hearts began to quail before such disasters, and even the fishermen and peasants of Africa began to say, like Symmachus and his followers, that everything was collapsing in that Christian age, and that the new religion had ruined that greatness of Rome which the old divinities had guarded so well. St. Augustine, provoked by these complaints, answered with a mixture of irony, playfulness, and sternness, " You say, behold how all things are perishing in these Christian times. "Why do you murmur ? God has never promised that these things of earth should not perish, nor did Christ promise it. The Eternal One has promised eternal things. Is the city which gave us temporal birth still standing ? Let us thank God and pray that, regenerated by the spirit, she may pass on with us to eternity. But if the city which gave us temporal life is no more, that city is standing which engendered us spiritually ! . . . What city ? The holy city, the faithful city, the city which has its pilgrimage upon earth, but its foundations in heaven. Christians, let not your hope perish, nor your charity be lost; gird your reins. Why do you fear if the empires of earth fail ? The promise has been given you from on high that you should not perish with them, for their ruin has been predicted. And those who have promised eternity to the empires of this earth have but lived to flatter men. One of their poets makes Jupiter to speak and say to the Romans,—

' His ego nec metas rerum, nec tempora pono;

Impérium sine fine dedi.'

"Truth has answered ill to these promises. That endless empire which thou givest them, O Jupiter, thou who hast never given them anything, is it in heaven or on earth? Doubtless on earth, but were it even in heaven, has it not been written that heaven and earth will pass away? If that which God has made is to depart, how much more quickly that which Romulus founded? Perhaps, if we had found fault with Virgil about these lines, he would have taken us aside and said, ' I know it as well as you do, but what could I say when bound to charm the ears of the Romans? ' and yet I took the precaution of putting these words in the mouth of their Jupiter—'a false god could be but a lying oracle '—whilst in another place, speaking in my own name, I said—' for see I then affirmed that their empire would perish.'

" It is plain that St. Augustine only quoted Virgil here in order to oppose the poet in one place to the poet in another, and thus to shake the extravagant respect still shown to him by the cultivated minority.

Knowing, moreover, that a certain number of his hearers lamented his severe treatment of the calamities of Rome, and murmured when he spoke of the recent events—for there were two parties in Africa, one Roman faction, and one opposed to Rome, to the latter of which St. Augustine stood in the relation of chief—he at once forestalled their objections: " I know that some say of me, if he would only say nothing about Rome. As if I came to insult others and not to move the Almighty, and to exhort you to the best of my power. God forbid that I should insult Rome.

Had we not many brothers therein, can we not still count many there? Has not a great part of the city of God which is sojourning on earth its place there? What can I say, then, when I do not wish to be silent, except that it is false that our Christ has lost Rome, and that she was better guarded by her gods of wood or stone? Do you speak of more precious ones? Then by her gods of iron, add to them those of silver and gold, and mark to whom learned men have committed the guardianship of Rome. How could those gods who failed to preserve their own images have saved your houses? Long ago did Alexandria lose her false deities, long ago did Constantinople give up hers, and nevertheless, reconstructed by a Christian emperor, she has increased and still increases. She stands and will stand as long as God has determined,' for even to that Christian city we can promise no eternal existence."

This last fragment has much grandeur, whilst the opposition of the new destinies of Constantinople to those of the elder Rome, and the view of a mighty but perishable empire attached to the former city, shows the accuracy of the glance flung by St. Augustine down the stream of history, and would make us conclude that he saw in ages to come another horde of barbarians, led by a second Alaric, announcing to Constantinople that her day had arrived.

We may find many equally eloquent passages in the sermons of this saint, and entire fragments gleaming with beauties analogous to those which are so common in the writings of St. John Chrysostom and of St. Basil, of which the following extract from a sermon on the Resurrection may form an example:—

" You are sad at having carried a beloved one to his sepulchre, sad because suddenly you have ceased to hear his voice. He lived and is dead; he ate and eats no more; mingles no more in the joys and pleasures of the living. Do you weep, then, for the seed which you cast into the furrow ? If a man was so utterly ignorant as to mourn for the grain which is brought into the field, placed in the earth, and buried beneath the broken clod; if he said to himself, ' Why then have they hidden this wheat which was gathered with such care, threshed, cleansed, and preserved in its granary ? We beheld it, and its beauty caused us joy: but now it has vanished from our eyes ! ' Did he weep thus, would they not say to him, ' Be not afflicted, this hidden corn is truly no longer in the granary, no longer in our hands; but we will come again and visit this field, and you will then rejoice at beholding the richness of the crop standing in the furrows whose aridity you now deplore. . . . These harvests may be seen year by year, but that of the human race will only be seen once at the end of the ages. . . In awaiting it, we, creatures as we are, unless we are dull, will speak of the resurrection. Sleep and awakening are daily occurrences; the moon disappears, and is renewed month by month. Why do the leaves of the trees go and come again? Behold it is winter, assuredly these withered leaves will bud forth again in spring. Will it be the first time, or did you see it last year? You have seen it. Autumn brought winter, spring brings summer. The year begins again in its appointed time, and do those men that are made in the image of God die to rise no more?"

We will show in conclusion how St. Augustine could raise himself to that third degree of eloquence which was called the sublime; and how, after traversing the region of simple and familiar language, and using a style which was rich in ornament and condition, he had a method still by which he could assure himself of victory in the depths of the heart. For this purpose we will cite two facts, recounted by the saint himself by necessity, and in no way to vaunt his eloquence. From time immemorial there had existed at Caesarea, in Mauritania, a custom called the Caterva, a small, but serious and bloody encounter, which took place yearly, and in which the inhabitants of the city were divided into two armed bands, fathers against sons, or brothers against brothers, and fought to the death for five or six days, until the town flowed with blood. No imperial edict had availed to uproot the hateful custom, which- fact will not surprise those who recollect that mediaeval Italy knew several similar usages which it required persevering efforts to repress. St. Augustine attempted to abolish a practice against which the edicts of emperors had been directed in vain; he harangued the people, and was deafened by their applause, but not thinking the victory gained as long as he merely heard applause, he spoke till tears began to flow, and then felt that he had conquered. In fact, he said, "I have spoken on it for eight years, and it is now eight years since the annual custom was celebrated."

Another time a less dangerous custom, but one which it was less easy to uproot, was in question. At Hippo semi-pagan banquets had been instituted, which were called Laetitia, and were celebrated in the church.

The inhabitants seemed little disposed to abandon the custom, when the ancient bishop, Valerius, called Augustine to share with him the burden of the episcopate and the ministry of the word, and charged him to attack the profane usage against which his own efforts had been useless. It was the occasion of another triumph for Augustine. As soon as it became known that he would preach on the subject, the townspeople agreed to pay no heed to his discourse. However, some came to hear him from curiosity. He spoke on it three times on three different days, and on that which saw him in possession of the field, he appeared so to speak in his full panoply, for he sent for all the books of Holy Scripture, read out the passage in the Gospel as to the Saviour casting the merchants out of the temple, that in the Exodus which told of the Jews adoring false gods, and lastly the passages of the Epistle of St. Paul to the Ephesians, in which the Apostle condemned banqueting and drunkenness, and then, having returned the volumes to their guardian, " I began," he said, " to represent to them the peril which was common to the flock which had been committed to us and to ourselves who would have to render an account to the Prince of Pastors, and implored them by the sufferings of Christ, by the crown of thorns, His cross and His blood, that if they wished to destroy themselves they would at least have pity on us, and would consider the charity of their old and venerable bishop, Valerius, who had out of love for them imposed upon me the formidable task of preaching the word of truth. And it happened that whilst I reproached them thus the Master of Souls gave me inspiration according to the want and peril. My tears did not provoke theirs, but whilst I spoke I own that, anticipated by their weeping, I was unable to restrain my own, and when we had wept in company, I finished my discourse with a firm hope of their conversion."

These are worthy examples of the victories of speech, and humble and obscure as their subjects may have been, every spiritual conquest begins from humility and obscurity, and the eloquence which vanquished the inhabitants of Caesarea and of Hippo was destined to conquer on wider battle-fields.

Christian orators of the school of St. Ambrose and of St. Augustine were numerous in the fourth and fifth centuries, and we need only point to St. Leo, so eloquent in unfolding the destinies of Christian Rome and in inviting St. Peter to take possession of that capital of every system of Paganism; St. Zeno of Verona, whose sermons are both interesting ano) instructive, being addressed to catechumens at the moment of their admission to baptism; St. Peter Chrysologus of Ravenna, Gaudentius of Brescia, and Maximus of Turin. But that the discourses of St. Augustine with those of Gregory the Great remained as the principal and favourite models of the Christian oratory during the Middle Age is proved by the fact of the sermons of St. **Caesarius** of Aries being confounded with those of Augustine himself, and by their still being placed in the appendices to the works of the latter, from the close resemblances of their minds and the close adherence of the disciple to the master. And in its turn the collection of the discourses of St. Caesarius became the manual of all who were incapable of original preaching, and were moulded into the *homiliana* or homily-books which served as repertories for the numberless missioners who were sent to all the extremities of the world to win the barbarians to the faith.

The new era, therefore, was in possession of the eloquence which it wanted, which could be simple, to meet the requirements of St. Eloi, St. Gall, and St. Boniface in touching the souls of neophytes, who were still filled with the memories of their coarse Paganism and of the bloody deities of the Valhalla. It could be familiar and rustic in the mouths of the preachers of the Carlovingian period, who had to instruct and enlighten the swineherds and shepherds, for whom they so carefully procured the Sunday rest, that one day at least might be free for an advance in a knowledge of their religion. And it was bound to remain in sufficient loftiness and power to preserve the high thought of the Christian metaphysic, to render all its delicacies and subtle details, and impress them one after another upon intellects which seemed the least fitted to grasp them, and able also at a given moment to stir the blood of nations. We do not wonder, after our study of the divine marvels of eloquence, at the work achieved by it in the eighth and the ninth centuries, for it is harder to create societies than to guide and to arm them when made. And when we find Christian preaching able to rescue whole nations from Paganism, to bring them into new ways and uproot their most inveterate passions, it is hardly strange that it should have the power in later times of reconciling the Lombard cities and John of Vicenza on the field of Verona, or of driving with St. Bernard the whole assembly of Vézelay under the banner of the Cross.

CHRISTIAN HISTORY.

We have seen how exhausted eloquence was freshened at the springs of Christianity. History was, after eloquence, the chief occupation of the genius of the ancients. Amongst those nations who through their uncertainty of a future life sought for an immortality here on earth, sculptors and historians became powerful to give glory, to rescue heroes from the lapse of time, and to cause them to survive for eternity in living marble or on the ineffaceable page of history. But as history thus became, like sculpture, an art to the ancients, so also it possessed the characteristic of an art, seeking beauty rather than truth; aspiring rather to please than instruct mankind, and imitating the methods of poetry or of eloquence. Herodotus, in describing the strife between Asia and Greece, was ever mindful of Homer; the names of the Muses were conferred on his books, and they were read at the Olympic Games amidst the acclamations of assembled Greece. Thucydides witnessed the spectacle, and seeing the impossibility of competing with such a rival upon his own ground, inserted in his work on the Peloponnesian war thirty-nine harangues of his own composition, which continued to be the admiration of his contemporaries and the principal object of the study and imitation of Demosthenes. And the same influence was at work amongst the Latin writers. Livy celebrated the epopee of Rome in his first books, and devoted the later ones to relating the chief instances of political eloquence; Sallust and Tacitus used the same licence; and all alike manipulated the events of the past with the freedom of Praxiteles or of Phidias, in chiselling the marble into form. History thus was especially poetical and oratorical in its nature; and it was not till later that it strove to become critical and gave rise to men like

Dionysius of Halicarnassus, or Diodorus Siculus, who, though obscure in comparison with their predecessors, dived into the recesses of antiquity and the hidden causes which they had neglected, but always to be confronted by an insurmountable obstacle. For all the efforts of the old historians, confined as they were by a narrow spirit of nationality, issued, even while like Diodorus Siculus they aimed at a general view, in the apotheosis of a single people; they invariably appealed to secondary causes, whether political or military, and therefore Polybius, one of the most gifted with insight amongst them, gives us indeed an admirable idea of the warlike superiority of Rome, but goes no farther, and does not raise a corner of the veil which would open out the general advance of humanity. Ancient history had, in short, two defects; it did not love truth sufficiently, and carried away by national egotism, it failed to compass universal destinies.

Moreover, in the fifth century, history properly so called was no more; the " Scriptores rei Augustse" had succeeded amidst the general decline to the biographer Suetonius, and the last historical pages of the Latin tongue were scarcely read. History only lived under the pen of a soldier, Ammianus Marcellinus, who, being a pagan and a man of slender learning, could only follow the course of events with a troubled eye, but who wrote from the heart, and forced the Roman patriciate, who had summoned him to read his composition, to applaud the withering description of their vices. Such was the last echo of the plaudits of Olympia, the last imitation of the triumphs of the historians of old. Herodotus and Thucydides had as their successor an obscure and uncultured soldier, whose chief honour in that evil age lay in the possession of a shred of probity.

But history was of necessity to be regenerated by Christianity, for the new religion was historical as opposed to the religions of fable, and was impelled to re-establish and to rearrange history on those motives, in order to dissipate the myths which the nations had woven round their cradle, and which charmed them still; to refute the charge of novelty which was hurled every day against its children, by attaching the New to the Old Testament, and thus reascending with Moses to the origin of the world; and, lastly, to resume the broken links of human society and bring to light the providential designs of God, which were to issue not in the inevitable and imperishable superiority of a single nation, but in the common salvation of the whole human race. Thus the history that Christianity desired, unlike that favoured by antiquity,' which erred in its leaning to what was beautiful, and in fixing itself in the narrow limits of nationality, aimed at being true, and also as far as possible universal, and these characteristics we shall find marked in the different forms taken by history with the Christian writers of the fifth century.

It is the fashion to throw doubt upon Christian antiquity, and to represent it as without books and monuments, and possessing only uncertain traditions. Doubtless Christianity is a religion of tradition, but it is also a religion of scripture. The Apostles and their disciples wrote; the bishops of the first three centuries followed their example, and each Church had its archives, which it could not always save from its persecutors. The acts of martyrs and canons of councils were the sources which supplied the ecclesiastical history at the period of which we are treating. At this time, then, we find history decomposed and reduced to its elements, but a reconstruction was imminent in the midst of the decay, and the separate constituents were but waiting for the breath which would quicken and reunite them. We find amongst distinct and differing writers three forms of historical work—firstly chronicles, which re-established the order of time; secondly, the acts of saints, which gave life to the foremost figures of the new era; thirdly, the first essays of that philosophy of history which unrolls the whole order of the divine economy, penetrates deeper than life itself, and arrives at the idea presiding over the succession of ages and of men, embracing and sustaining the totality of passing things, which would be unworthy of the attention given to following them, or the effort of memory in retaining them, was there not beyond the crowd of years which press upon us behind or before the idea of an invariable agency which impels and sustains, advances and causes to advance.

We find, firstly, chronicles, and this was a new fact. Doubtless the ancients had possessed some chronicles— as, for instance, the works of Eratosthenes and Apollodorus, but they had found the task tardy and unsatisfactory; and the calculation of time and the art of verifying dates, as historical criticism was never a dominant feature of the genius of antiquity, had not been thoroughly cultivated. Certain efforts had been made to fix the time and place of particular events—those made, for instance, by Polybius, or to arrive at a particular study of certain causes, but they had never been extended to the universality of human destiny.

The early Christian apologists, Justin, Clement, and Tatius insisted at once, and not without sufficient motives, on the antiquity of Moses and the superiority of his wisdom to that of the sages and heroes of Greece. Julius Africanus wrote a chronography from the commencement of the world to the time of the Emperor Heliogabalus; St. Hippolytus, in his work upon Easter, gave a chronology down to the first year of Alexander Severus, and a paschal cycle for the celebration of the feast calculated for sixteen years. And the same idea occupied Eusebius, who undertook an universal history, which was translated and augmented by St. Jerome, and applied himself to placing side by side and harmonizing the profane and sacred chronologies. To effect this, he skilfully chose as a fixed point of departure the fifth year of the reign of Tiberius, which was the date of the advent of Christianity, and going back to the Olympiads and the Assyrian era, counted two thousand and forty-four years as the time back to Ninus. Then, by the aid of the sacred books, he also reckoned two thousand and forty-four years between the fifth year of the reign of Tiberius and the time of Abraham, and thus found points common to the two antiquities, and a possibility of agreement between those two pasts which had seemed eternally estranged. Eusebius, or rather St. Jerome, who translated, corrected, and completed his work, carefully collected complete lists of the kings of Assyria, Egypt, Lydia, and the different cities of Greece; of kings, dictators, and emperors of Rome, as well as of the Jewish patriarchs, judges, and kings, and fixed accurately the length of their respective reigns. This first part of his book was merely introductory, and contained little besides names and numbers; but when he had, as it were, laid down the mathematical elements of history, and taken his vast domain into possession, the synchronical tables were unfolded, in which he marked by periods of ten years the succession of kings and chiefs in different nations, from Ninus and Abraham to Constantine. This, by the side of the shapeless attempts of antiquity, was a bold and able array indeed. It confronted, in the first place, the Assyrians and Hebrews with the kings of Sicyon and of Egypt, then gradually the picture was enlarged as the Argives, Macedonians, Athenians, Lydians, Persians, and lastly the Romans struggled forward into light and life. But the advent of the last was a signal for the retreat of the rest; and whereas at first his tables showed the Hebrews and Greeks side by side with the Romans, gradually the Greeks disappeared when Corinth lost her liberty, the Hebrews on the destruction of Jerusalem by Titus, until Rome occupied the page alone, invading and devouring the space once held by other nations. And thus the rise of Christianity was entangled in the history of Rome, and amongst the annals of the latter were placed the story of the persecutions, of the martyrs, and of the rise and succession of heresies, for the plan of

Eusebius and St. Jerome did not neglect the history of human thought, but carefully placed side by side with the memories of kings and the mention of the events which marked the destinies of the nations, those of poets, philosophers, and all who devoted their mind or their blood to the service of humanity. So that the two great aims of history, verity and universality, were achieved as far as was possible in the first attempt at founding a science which all the Benedictine erudition of the seventeenth and eighteenth centuries has not sufficed to complete.

An example of such brilliancy called forth imitators, and St. Jerome continued the chronicle of Eusebius from 325 to 328. Prosper of Aquitaine, a theologian and poet, took up the history until 444; and the Spanish bishop Idatius, in his retreat in the depths of Galicia, amidst barbarians, and at the world's extremity, brought it down to the year 469. The latter writer mingled with it in terse but moving terms his sad experience of that time of universal ruin, and tremblingly pointed to the last blows which were being dealt to the perishing empires, under which, for a moment, the Church also seemed to totter; and told, with the brevity as it were of a funeral hymn, how, after the barbarians had ravaged the provinces of Spain, and famine and pestilence had followed to complete the work, the wild beasts came forth from their dens, penetrated into the towns, and gaining ferocity from their feasts upon the unburied corpses, engaged the living whom they met in bloody and mortal combat.

The very precision of these chronicles gave them interest, but their dominant characteristics were brevity and dryness. They simply registered events, without thinking of the tears which their narration would force from the eyes of men; and being written upon papyrus, which was destined to become so rare, they possessed a monumental character as if they had been written upon marble or upon iron. Yet the world had reached an epoch in which history, as known to the ancients, was impossible. No hand, then, was bold enough to wield the pen of Tacitus or of Livy; that of Prosper of Aquitaine or of Idatius must have seemed lighter, and there was no monastery so wanting in intelligent men as not to hold at least one monk who would write year by year of the events which had brought joy or mourning to the neighbourhood. It was done briefly, with a strange admixture of the particular griefs of the compiling monk and of the general sorrows of humanity. And thus we find, in some Frankish annals of the year 710, the entry, "Brother Martin is dead," the brother, probably, of the poor writer; whilst some years afterwards the great victory of Charles Martel over the Saracens, on the plains of Poitiers, was inscribed in the same annals with a similar terseness, as if in fact it was only by compressing itself that history could survive those difficult times, like the seed which always finds a breeze, strong enough to carry it to the place which God has fixed.

Such, then, was the first form of history, of such nature the benefits which flowed from it. But it is certain that had the chronicle alone survived, all the beauty, all art and vitality of history would have been extinguished. This was not for the interest of Christianity, which had every reason for showing the living forces of humanity, the combat of the spirit with the flesh, the strife of the passions, and the ideal life in the persons of her saints; and therefore her children laboured with respect and love to describe in full the career of those amongst them who had cast into the world the seed of an elevating eloquence or a faith-bearing death. For this reason the acts of martyrs early became a portion of the offices in their honour, and were read publicly upon their feast-days; and from the primitive times we find in the Roman Church, under the Popes St. Clement, St. Antherius, and St. Fabian, "notarii," who were charged to collect reports of the martyrs' acts, which they drew sometimes from their indictments purchased from the recorders. These were solid foundations for the Christian hagiography, as the indictments, which were really authentic, left no place for interpolation, and the brevity, simplicity, and sobriety of their details attested the good faith of their compilers. It is to this category that the acts of the martyr St. Perpetua, the letter of the Church of Lyons upon its martyrs, and the admirable letter from the Asian Church which related the death of St. Polycarp and the acts of St. Cyprian, respectively belonged. The latter was a legal document, which might well, from the absence of comment and of any expression of personal commiseration, have been the report of the pagan official attached to the tribunal of the proconsul. However, the fidelity with which the greatness of the martyrdom and the emotion and pity of the bystanders are depicted, point to a Christian hand, faithful and incorruptible, but neglecting no means of making his narration vivid, and giving to it the colour and beauty that one might have thought it had lost forever. It was in the following terms that the editor of the *Acta* related the interrogation of St, Cyprian: " Galerius Maximus, proconsul, says to the Bishop Cyprian, 'You are Thascius Cyprianus ? ' Cyprian answers, ' I am he.' Galerius Maximus replies, ' It is you who have made yourself bishop of those sacrilegiously-minded men?'—'It is I.' The proconsul says, 'The most sacred Emperors have commanded you to sacrifice.' The Bishop Cyprian answers, ' I will not do it.' Galerius Maximus says, ' Think of your safety !' The Bishop Cyprian responds, 'Do what you have been commanded, there is no room for deliberation in so just a cause.' "

Every one might suppose these words to have been written under the very dictation of their utterers; nothing was added to give scope to the feelings of their chronicler. Their freedom from abuse of the proconsul or the emperor, which might have been expected from a hagiographer of the barbarous epoch, points to the austere and dignified period of primitive Christendom. The judge pronounced sentence with unction, and the crowd of the brethren who surrounded the bishop exclaimed, " Let them behold us also with him," and he was then conducted to the place of execution with such a following of his deacons and the faithful as almost made his persecutors tremble. It was necessary that he should undergo his sentence, but they left him surrounded by those who had always looked upon him as a father, and. now a saint. Putting off his tunic and dalmatic, he ordered that twenty-five pieces of gold should be given to his executioner. Then the brethren brought him the pieces of linen, and as he could not bandage his own eyes, this last office was performed by a priest and a sub-deacon, after which he suffered with the majestic dignity of a prince surrounded by his people. When night came he was carried to his resting-place with lights and music and all the pomp of a triumph. Such was the energetic life of that ancient and powerful Church of Carthage which even in the third century had become formidable to Paganism.

Up' to this period, then, we have absolute certainty, and these recitals were followed by others which offered the same guarantees, namely, the lives of certain men of ever illustrious name, such as St. Ambrose, St. Augustine, and St. Martin of Tours, which were written by their disciples, friends, and fellow-labourers, St. Paulinus, Possidius, and Sulpicius Severus. But to the epoch of the martyrs and the Fathers succeeded that of the anchorites. The distance of their desert retreats, the remoteness of the period, and the transmission of their histories from mouth to mouth left room for the introduction of an imaginative and poetical element. These stories of solitude fascinated the soul of St. Jerome, who undertook to collect them and so form a series of Christian pictures. It is not known whether his design was carried out, but three of these lives, namely, those of St. Paul, St. Hilarion, and Malchas, have come down to us. We will pause at the first to gain an idea of the tales which were peopling the Thebaid, were to be repeated throughout the East and West, and were destined to stir all souls which longed for peace and repose in self-sacrifice.

St. Jerome tells the wonderful story thus: That a young Christian of sixteen, living under his sister's roof in a town of the Lower Thebaid, during the reign and persecution of Valerian, and dreading the fanaticism of his pagan brother-in-law which threatened him daily, determined on quitting the hospitable roof and finding a retreat in the mountains. After a long wandering he at last reached a spot wherein an almost inaccessible precipice offered a single opening into a somewhat spacious chamber hollowed in the rock and open to the sky; a vast palm-tree stretched its branches over the cavern and formed a roof, whilst a clear and refreshing stream flowed at the foot of the tree. Paul halted and took up his abode there, and lived—no surprising fact with his sobriety of manners, and considering the manners of the East—till the age of a hundred and thirteen years. As his last hour was approaching, the anchorite Antony, who was then ninety years of age, and had served God in the same desert for many long years, fell under the temptation of crediting himself with being probably the oldest and most perfect monk in the world. But the following night he was warned from on high to seek for an older and more perfect anchorite than himself, and the road which he was to take was indicated. So on the morrow he set forth; and the old man, already bent double with age, tottered painfully on his staff under the burning heat, until at the end of four days and four nights he fell exhausted at the entrance of a rock-hewn cave and cried so loudly that Paul, its inmate, heard him and appeared on the threshold. Paul, after some hesitation at breaking the impassable barrier which had up to that time guarded his solitude, brought the anchorite Antony into his home, and asked the first man whom he had seen for so long whether they still built roof by roof in the cities, whether the old empires subsisted, and the idolatrous altars still smoked. When Antony had satisfied him on all these points and had become hungry, a raven alighted on the palm-tree hearing a loaf baked upon coals, and Paul said to Antony, " Behold the providence of God ! Daily, until this day, I received half a loaf, but to-day Providence perceived that we should be two to break bread, and He has sent me an entire loaf !" Paul then informed Antony that he had expected his arrival, "for the hour of my departure from this world has arrived, and thou art only come to provide for my burial." And he asked him to wrap his body in the cloak which had been given him by 'St. Athanasius. Antony returned to his own cell to fetch the garment, saying to himself: " Wretch that I was, I have seen Elias; I have seen John in the desert; I have seen Paul in Paradise." But on returning to the abode of Paul with the garment of St. Athanasius, he found that the hermit had just expired, his lifeless corpse in the attitude of prayer, in which death had surprised him. Antony then took thought as to burying him; but how could he open the ground? He sat down in despair, resolved rather to die than resign the corpse as a prey to wild beasts. Then two lions appeared, and Antony took no more notice of them than if they had been doves. They dug a trench and then came to lick Antony's feet, and taking pity upon them he exclaimed, " O Lord, without whose will the leaf is not severed from the tree, nor does the sparrow fall to the earth, give these Thy creatures what Thou knowest to be good for them." Having then blessed the lions he dismissed them and departed, carrying with him the tunic of palm-fibre which Paul had made for himself, and which he wore from that time forth upon the days of great festival, such as Easter and Pentecost.

We need not wonder at the artlessness of the narrative, for even the great mind of St. Jerome could believe in the superiority over creation which manhood regained, in the re-establishment of the empire over every creature given to our first parents in that primitive order wherein whatever lived in the world was made to serve the wants of the world's masters, and in the reconciliation of all things through Christianity. We are now in the Middle Age, surrounded by the ideas and influences which gave to the men of that barbarous epoch their courage, their zeal, and their power, and the achievement of St. Paul in the desert was to be related of St. Gall, whom the legend makes to appease the bears of the Alps, or of St. Columba, who attracted about his steps the wild beasts of the Vosges, or of St. Francis of Assisi, who, as he crossed the plains of Umbria, was followed by the lambs and swallows as if they wished to gather up his words, whilst the wolves fled away from him. Truly, the conviction was necessary for the men who had to conquer nations which were fiercer than wolves, and we must feel less surprise at beholding the docility of the lions who came to dig the grave of the anchorite Paul than at seeing the most independent and implacable of men, accustomed to serve no master, to pardon no injury, to seek no counsel but that of the sword, learn at the voice of these monks and missioners, not only to obey, but to pardon.

Such was the commencement of a method peculiar to the Middle Age, and destined to form for the future the two parts of every historical work—on the one hand chronology, or the simple truth bare and dry in form; on the other, legend, containing the life, colour, and movement of history, but often touched by the licence of poetry.

But, to analyze more deeply, if the ancients had been content with obtaining an approximative verity in facts and a certain beauty of colour and movement, the times of Christianity had a higher ambition, for they panted to know causes, with the longing which besets both great souls and those which are feeble but spiritual. For first causes are immaterial, and therefore the periods of materialism aim at nothing but a knowledge of facts, whilst, the periods of spiritualism seek to arrive at causes which move in a higher sphere than facts, in the region of spirit. Nothing similar to this had been known to the ancients. Content with collecting facts and visible causes, they had never risen to the superior and invisible causes which rule the universe, and therefore their efforts in constructing a philosophy of history had been scanty. Doubtless the wont of referring every phenomenon to a superior principle had not entirely abandoned them, and Herodotus himself, in describing the fall of empires, showed a certain mysterious power, which he called το θείον, which nourished a secret jealousy against everything which elevated itself, and sooner or later overthrew that earthly greatness which had risen too high; but this was the whole of his philosophy of history. His successors explained the succession of events even more insufficiently, and therefore Christianity had an effort to make, and then, as ever, great facts were needed to produce a potent inspiration. For surely no mighty event has ever happened in the world without producing an imperishable book, though not always one of the sort that might have been expected; and thus in our opinion it was the Battle of Actium which inspired the " Æneid," and drew it like Venus from the waves in her shining beauty.

And now another event, the greatest since the day of Actium, had just happened in the world: Alaric had entered Rome with his barbarians, and had encamped for three days within its walls. It was the most formidable event ever chronicled in the annals of-the world, yet there was no elegy ready to be poured forth over the watch fires kindled by the barbarians at the foot of the Capitol; no orator was there to protest, at least on the third day when Alaric had departed, that the danger had passed; there was no disciple of Symmachus or Macrobius, no successor of those pagan rhetoricians who had been so excellent in the craft of eloquence, to make the world echo with his ardent protestation. No, the cry wrung from humanity by that great and terrible spectacle was to proceed from Africa, and the book produced by the sack of Rome under Alaric was " The City of God," the first real effort to produce a philosophy of history. Nothing less than that mighty collapse was required to turn the attention of the world to the Supreme Hand which could shake it thus.

The Goths, on entering Rome, had set fire to the gardens of Sallust and a large portion of the city, but had halted in terror and respect—for they were Christians, although Arians—before the Basilica of the Apostles. They had respected the keepers of the sacred vessels, and the crowd of the faithful and of the unbelieving who had sought for life and liberty under the aegis of the sacred relics. Yet the humiliations of the Eternal City had unloosed the passions of the pagans, and many of those who owed their safety to the tombs of Peter and Paul reproached Christianity with the ruin of Rome, and asked the Christians where their God was; why He had not protected them, but had suffered the good and the evil to be confounded; why He had not rescued the just from spoliation, death, and captivity, but had abandoned their very virgins to the mercy of the barbarians. These lamentations came in the mouths of a multitude of fugitives to trouble Augustine in the repose of Hippo, and to them in an inspired moment did he resolve to reply. He did this by pointing out to the pagans that the troubles of Rome were the necessary consequence of war, and how the intervention of Christianity was manifested in the power that had conquered the barbarians on the moment of their victory, and triumphed over their unshackled liberty. To the question as to why the same ills had befallen the righteous and the sinners, he answered that they were sent as a probation to the one, but as a punishment to the other, like mud and balm stirred by the same hand, the one of which exhales a fetid odour, the other an excellent perfume. Moreover, it mattered little to know who it was that suffered, but much to understand the manner in which the misfortune was borne—*non quis sed quails*. For the Christian knew of no other evil but sin, and the captivity which did not dishonour Regulus could not disgrace a brow which had been marked with the character of Christ. Many, doubtless, had died, but who was to escape death? And when the resurrection day arrived the eye of God would discover those bodies which had remained unburied. He had consolation also for the outraged virgins, and then turning upon the pagans, said, " What you really regret is, not that peace in which you could enjoy your temporal goods with sobriety, piety, and temperance, but a tranquillity which you laboured for at the cost of a profusion of unheard-of luxuries, and which tended to produce from the corruption of your manners evils worse than the utmost fury of your enemies."

After this triumphant invective against the friends and defenders of those false gods which the pagans of all times have ever regretted and re-demanded, Augustine entered upon the discussion, and confuting those doctrines of the pagan world, and of Rome in particular, which accounted for the destinies of a state by the power of its deities, he undertook to prove that those gods could effect nothing, either for the present life or for that of eternity. The gods of Rome had spared her neither crimes nor misfortunes; plentiful were the examples they had given her of the first, for was not mythology filled with recitals of their scandalous doings, and had not the infamies of Olympus taken their place in its worship? Had not Rome followed these examples in the rape of the Sabines, the ruin of Alba, the fratricidal strife of the two orders, the civil wars, proscriptions, and frightful corruption of manners? The gods who had left Troy to perish could not have saved Rome? Had not she honoured them, indeed, when she was taken by the Gauls, humbled at the Caudine Forks, conquered at Cannes? Sylla put to death more senators than the Goths had pillaged, and still the altars smoked with Arabian incense; the temples had their sacrifices, the games their delirious audience, and the blood of the citizens flowed at the very feet of those deities who were so powerless to save them. He then maintained, upon the authority of Cicero, that Rome had never known the republican idea, which, according to the definition of the latter, was nothing else but the association of a people for the furtherance of justice, and the satisfactions of its legitimate wants.

We wonder at the boldness with which the African reconstructed the history of Rome in the light of its failures and chastisements; yet his enlightenment could not but show him also its value and its glory, and he explained the greatness of Rome by its place in the divine economy; for the true and supreme God, who had ordered not only the heaven and the earth, but the organs of the minutest insect, the plumage of the bird, and the flowers of the field, could not exclude the guidance of the nations and the destiny of empires from the laws of Providence. His justice shone forth in the government of the world, and especially in the career of Rome. The Romans of old only existed for glory, which they loved with a boundless attachment: "For it they wished to live; **for it** they did not hesitate to die, and by that all-absorbing passion they stifled all the rest. Finding it shameful to serve and glorious to rule, they strained to render their country free, and then to make her mistress of the world." Therefore God, desiring to found a mighty Empire in the West, that all the nations, being subject to one law, might end by forming a single city, having need of a people strong enough to vanquish the martial races of the West, selected the Romans, and thus recompensed their imperfect virtues by a terrestrial prize. '' They had spurned their own interest for the public welfare, and provided for the safety of their country with a mind which was free, and exempt from the crimes which their laws condemned, seeking by every method honour, power,' and glory. Therefore God, who could not grant them eternal life, willed that they should be honoured by all nations; they subjected to their rule a vast concourse of nations; their glory, perpetuated by history and literature, filled the whole earth; they have no cause to complain of the divine justice, for they have received their reward."

The pagan deities could effect nothing for eternity, and every explanation of the things of time must have some reference to eternity. A summary of political and military events is not the sole function of history, but to collect ideas, and teach the revolutions of the human mind; and this St. Augustine bore in mind in his examination of the principles and transformations of Paganism. Following Varro in his poetical, civil, and physical theologies, he refuted all the attempts at saving the false gods by means of an allegorical interpretation which could not justify an obscene and sanguinary symbolism. Socrates, Plato, and the Neoplatonists, amongst the philosophers, had gained a glimpse of the truth, but had not glorified it; they had rehabilitated the plurality of gods, theurgy, and magic, whilst every system of error had found its proselytes amongst the disciples of the school of Alexandria, who, vanquished at last by a consciousness of their own impotence, had avowed with Porphyry that no sect had yet found the universal way of deliverance for the souls of men.

Having thus established the inefficiency of Paganism, he continued by unfolding the novel philosophy imported into history by Christianity. God desires that His creatures should he intelligent, associated in community and good; but He foresees that some of them will be evil, which He does not effect but merely permits, as subserving alternately the well-being of the good and manifesting the beauty of the scheme of the universe, as in a poem, by contrast. Hence arose the two cities, " built by two principles of love—the city of earth by that self-love which tended to a scorn of God; the city of heaven by the divine love which issued in the abnegation of self;" both being so interlaced and confounded in the present life that the pilgrims of the heavenly state journeyed through the city of men. The city of God was represented by the patriarchs, the Jewish people, the righteous generally; but that of earth was forced to attach itself to things of earth. Cain built the first city, Babylon, and Romulus, like Cain a fratricide, built the second, Rome. Babylon was the first Rome, and Rome the second Babylon; the end of the one empire was confounded with the rise of the other. Both enjoyed a similar duration and the same power, and showed the same forgetfulness of God. St. Augustine summarized history in a synchronical table, at the head of which he placed the Assyrians, the Jews, and the kings of Sicyon and of Argos, and continued it to the advent of Christ and the progress of the Gospel. The city of God was still increasing, and had not finished at the fatal period of three hundred and sixty-five years which the pagans had assigned for its duration, a period that ended in 339, the very year in which the pagan temples had been closed at Carthage. The problem as to the end of man had divided the philosophers into two hundred and eighty-eight sects, all of whom had looked for it in the present life, whilst Christianity placed it in a future existence. It proved the emptiness of earthly pleasures against the Epicureans, and confuted Stoicism through the insufficiency of human virtues. Man was born for society, but social justice can never be fully realized on earth; therefore a judgment was necessary which would ultimately sever the two cities and assign the one to ruin and the other to salvation; and although the Almighty had reserved the secret of its happening, yet we may compare the world's duration to that of a week, upon the sixth day of which it had already entered, and was thus approaching the eternal Sabbath, which would be a season of repose, brightened by intelligence and love.

This is a rapid *and* incomplete sketch of that astonishing but ill-arranged work which at first sight shocks us by its repetitions and omissions, which cost St. Augustine eighteen years of toil amidst the labours of his episcopate, and which, as its author composed the last twelve books after the first ten had passed from under his hand, was of necessity full of redundancies. Yet the toil of penetrating its apparent obscurities will be rewarded by finding a real arrangement and a wealth of insight and enlightenment. It shattered the pagan solution of the destinies of the world, imported philosophy into the realm of history by its novel doctrine, and sought for the secret of human affairs, not in the aberration of the passions, but in the mysteries of metaphysic, and the hard questions of Providence, of liberty, of prescience, and .the natural end of things. It showed us ourselves in the sphere we had thought our own, no longer as filling the world, but as small and hardly visible, absorbed by the Divinity which was ever enveloping and moulding His creatures, and taught mankind that, struggle as it might, it must be moved by God.

But great as was his achievement, St. Augustine was not content, and wished to undertake a completer treatise of universal history; and as he was unable to accomplish his design, he bequeathed it to the Spanish priest Orosius. We cannot stay to analyze his work, which gained celebrity, showed much talent, and an occasional flash of the true Spanish genius. But Paulus Orosius showed little of the. prudent moderation and sustained firmness of his predecessor, and many were the illusions to which he succumbed. He maintained, for instance, that as Christianity extended, so would the empire of death diminish in the world; that the era of blood would close when the Gospel had mastered Europe; and prophesied an eternal duration to the brief peace which the Empire was then enjoying, in which the Goths and Vandals would consent to become the chief soldiers of Caesar. However, his views were occasionally remarkable for their happy temerity, as when he spoke of the vocation of the barbarians to the Church, and, although more intensely Roman than St. Augustine, declared that if at the price of invasion and its attendant horrors, captivity, famine, and outrage, he could see the Burgundians, Huns, Alans, and Vandals saved for eternity, he would thank God that he had been suffered to live in those days. The Christian feeling thus prevailed over the Roman national sentiment in his desire to initiate the barbarians into the sacred mysteries in the midst of the fall of the Empire, an auspicious event if it made a breach through which his brother might enter.

Several years passed, and in 455 Salvian wrote his work " De Gubernatione Dei." But circumstances had changed; there was no room then for illusion, for Rome had actually fallen, and the invincible barbarians had devoted seventeen days to the pillage of the world's capital. "Who could speak of the eternity of the Empire then ? The pagans, amidst their cries of terror and despair, asked where was the God of the Christians, and Salvian replied by showing the causes, natural and supernatural, of the ruin of Rome. He pointed to them in the corruptions of a society which was dying through the disorder of its institutions, and in the degradation of manners fostered by the Roman laws, insisting upon the superiority of the barbarians in this respect. " The Franks are perfidious but hospitable; the Alans are impure but sincere; the Saxons are cruel but upright; whereas we combine all their vices." He maintained that the Vandals had been sent into Africa to sweep away the filth with which the Romans had defiled it, and declared that their legislation was superior to that of Rome in not recognizing either prostitution or divorce; whilst he applauded the conduct of those conquered Romans who preferred becoming Germans to remaining subjects of the Empire, for Salvian had taken the last step and passed over to the side of the barbarians. Thus may we trace the progress of the philosophy of history; the new science which in the last years of the fifth century had lost none of its force. In the difficult time which was about to follow infinite popularity was to surround the name of Augustine. Charlemagne himself, in his leisure moments, sought for lessons in the " City of God;" Alfred the Great translated the work of Paulus Orosius into Anglo-Saxon; and the mind of Dante had been so nourished that a canto of his " Purgatory" was simply a paraphrase of a chapter of the " City of God;" and Orosius had a place amongst the five or six authors who formed the companions of his solitude.

Thus the whole mediaeval period was trained in the doctrines of these great men, and we must instance among the many historians who imitated them the celebrated German writer of the twelfth century, Otto of Freysingen, uncle of the great emperor, Frederic Barbarossa. That ancient bishop, although weighed down by the number of his years, was not content with writing the history of his own times, but extended his views to the composition of an universal history, and followed the scheme of St. Augustine in opposing the City of God to the City of Man. Writing with a thorough and somewhat severe freedom, he paused occasionally to vindicate his authority as uncle, and to warn his imperial kinsman in the words of the Psalmist —*Et nunc reges intelligite; erudimini qui judicatis terram.* And so the precursors of Bossuet were found, and so numerous were the links of the chain which bound his work to St. Augustine, that the connection never for an instant escaped out of sight.

These, then, formed the three constituents of history: the chronicle, which brought to it bare facts; legend, which afforded it colour and life; and philosophy, which formed its soul, gave to it a coherent explanation, and referred it ultimately to God as its First cause. Henceforth it was necessary to the production of veritable history that the three elements should unite and grow beneath the fostering wing of the modern genius into a single organism capable of explaining and containing every fact. But to have prepared the minds of their successors was not the sole achievement of the men of whom we have treated, for they did more by preparing the way for events. We must insist upon this, for it is morally profitable to show to writers and to thinkers the point to which they may act, not only upon the sentiments, but on the events of the future. Two things might have occurred had the Christian writers of this time thought, and written otherwise than they did. Augustine, Paulus Orosius, and Salvian might have taken the side of Rome absolutely as against the barbarians, or have ranged themselves in the ranks of the latter without pity for Rome. Had they taken the course which seemed the most natural one, and abandoned themselves to that despair which is so common in our day, and in which certain minds seem to find some excellence, they would by their example have so discouraged the Church of the West that the entire Christian population of its component nations would have declared an unreserved hostility against the barbarians. They would have made the seeming enmity of the latter to God and the human race a reality, and have brought upon Rome, upon the Christian civilization, and upon humanity, a series of incalculable calamities. On the other hand, had they taken up the second position, and given a precipitate adhesion to the cause of the barbarians, they would have made themselves judges in the place of God, condemned Rome as the second Babylon to an eternal ruin, and brought such a chastisement upon her that hardly one stone would have remained upon another; and thus they would have lent their aid to elimination of the central point of the world, displaced the rally-point of Christian life in the Middle Age, and disturbed the whole economy of the succeeding ages. They would have quenched the spark of light of which Rome was the sole preserver up to the time of Charlemagne, and consequently would have deprived humanity of the civilizing influences which had been thus treasured up for its benefit. But with a happier inspiration they evinced the courage, branded by those who knew it not with the name of optimism, which enabled them to regard those difficult and menacing times with a firm and calm glance, and could wisely distinguish the real property of the past amidst, the trembling destinies of the future. Without committing themselves to the side of the barbarians, they met them half way, and applauded the Goths for the clemency which had spared the Basilica of St. Peter and St. Paul; nor shall we find a single Christian writer of the period who did not celebrate this generous action of a conquering and success-maddened people. By this means they conciliated the barbarians, half won from that moment, and thrust their swords back into the scabbards, so that every chief amongst them envied the glory of Alaric, and respected the altars which had been blessed by the aged bishop or priest. And as defeat was thus made more tolerable to the vanquished, so did courageous zeal reinspire the Christians, who perceived that after all their conquerors were not devourers of men, and that as the work of their conversion might be undertaken and accomplished, a lasting spirit of despair was not necessary. They might enter as pilgrims into the city of God, and the wild-beast skin which covered the barbarian might vest a future citizen of the Eternal State.

Moreover, in taking the part of Rome in a certain measure, and recalling its virtues and glory, they showed that the city was still worthy of respect, and that if she had merited a punishment for her crimes, God had but stricken in order to warn, and that the time for her consolation had arrived. They so worked upon the barbarian mind by their pictures of her ancient might that they produced the result described by Jornandes, and caused Rome to reign through the imagination, if not by force of arms; and well has she shown that her new method of empire was a thousandfold more powerful than that of old; for she entered thereby on her novel destiny, and founded that spiritual sovereignty of which she was always to remain the centre. Those who had undertaken her defence against the weapons and the invectives of the barbarians formed, as it were, a circle round the tomb of St. Peter, and, extolling it as the spot selected by God for the centre of enlightenment, compelled the barbarians who had encamped around the Capitol firstly to respect and then to submit; and thus arose the mediaeval economy wherein antiquity, regenerated in Rome, enlightened and disciplined the barbarism of a new era. Such was one of the greatest examples of the influence of literature, not merely over minds, but over events; such the nature of one of those glorious delegations of power made occasionally by Providence to the genius of mankind.

POETRY.

In commencing our study of the Christian literature with its prose, and placing eloquence and history before its epopee, we have reversed, in some measure, the commonly established order. Had it been our object to examine an ancient literature such as that of the Greeks, we should have found that for many ages poetry alone was produced, and that it was only gradually that prose emerged from its golden mists, for the civilization of Paganism was cradled amidst fables. The nations then, like children, understood no language but that of the imagination, and the lapse of seven ages, from the time of Homer to that of Herodotus, was necessary in order that reason might gain courage to address mankind in its natural language.

Christianity, on the contrary, could not suffer its origin to be veiled by fiction, for it proposed facts and dogmas which were defined verities, to the reason and not merely to the imagination of the nations; and therefore during three centuries it spoke to them in prose and prose alone. It was at the end of that period that Christian poetry took its first and feeble rise. And yet nothing seemed wanting to inspire it in the greatness of passing events and the revolution which was sweeping over the world, or in the emotions of the soul and the inward agony which was upheaving the depths of the conscience; but the spectacle was still too near at hand, and, as M. St. Marc Girardin has admirably expressed it, the truth of that era was too powerful to create poets, and could still only make martyrs; for an interval must ever lie between deep emotion and poetical inspiration; and we shall find that those silent ages were not too long for their work of ripening the rich harvest of Christian art.

We may pass by the small band of unknown poets who wrote at the time of the persecutions, and omit several compositions, attributed sometimes to Tertullian, and at others to St. Cyprian, but which were certainly of contemporary date with those great men. The peace of the Church was like a day-dawn, calling forth harmonies from every side, and Christianity seemed as she assumed in the person of Constantine the crown of the Caesars to inherit also, so numerous were the Christian versifiers, the laurel wreath of Virgil. Their great number already calls for a division, and we, adopting the great classification of the ancients, may divide them into epic and lyric poets, for the Church had not at that time reopened the theatre.

Thus the two orders in poetry were already existent, and to the epic order we may assign, as did the ancients, the didactic poetry, such as the instructions given by the poet Commodianus against Paganism, or the poem against the Semipelagians which was written by Prosper of Aquitaine, and has since become so famous through its imitation by Louis Racine. But the principal tendency and the chief effort of Christian poetry from that era was to reduce the narratives of its religion to its own laws. Its dominant idea was to lend to the Biblical traditions, which were the very foundations of the faith, the brilliancy of the Latin versification and some of the ornament which had been borrowed from the pagan authors. We see some poets, like Dracontius, St. Hilary of Aries, and Marius Victor, turning their minds to the earliest narrations of the Bible, to the scenes of Genesis *and the lovable simplicity of an infant world;* whilst others, as Juvencus and Sedulius, confining .themselves to the evangelical history, laboured solely towards the reproduction, with harmony and accuracy and a certain amount of poetical adornment, of the text of the Gospel. However, the common characteristic of all these poets and translators of Holy Scripture into verse was a scrupulous and exact fidelity, and thence followed on the one hand a remarkable gravity and sobriety, a renunciation of that wealth of epithet and hyperbole which had formerly roused the emotions, so that even the sufferings of the Saviour, the ingratitude of the Jews, and the coldness of the Disciples, extracted no bitter epithet which had not already fallen from the sacred writer himself, and the general effect of the poems presented a certain solemnity and grandeur. But, on the other hand, it must be confessed that their sobriety often verged upon dryness; that they contained neither episodes nor descriptions, and hardly any paraphrases or commentaries, but simply the text itself, adapted to the hexameter measure, which was kept as close as was possible to the ancient form.

We can understand the motives which inspired these labourers by the explanations given by the authors themselves; for Sedulius, one of the most popular amongst them, has accounted in his dedicatory epistle to the Bishop Macedonius, for the influence which guided his pen. He declared that he desired to devote to the service of the faith those studies which had been commenced with a different aim, and to consecrate to the truth the predestined instruments of vanity. "For," said he, "I know that many spirits will not accept the truth, nor willingly retain it, unless it be presented to them beneath the flowers of poetry; and I thought that people of such a disposition should not be repelled, but should be treated in accordance with their natural wants, in order that each man might become the voluntary captive of God according to his own genius!" Light is thrown upon this by our previous knowledge of the Roman schools: the whole order of instruction was founded by the ancients—and this was most wisely preserved during the Middle Age—upon the exercise of the memory and the study of the poets. In Greece it was commenced by Homer, and in the West by Virgil; but under the auspices of Virgil, the Christians and the pagans of the fifth century learned by heart, and imprinted upon their recollection, all the ideas, doctrines, and images of Paganism, and it was against these that the early Christian poets strained every nerve. They wrote under the idea of polemical controversy, and made it their aim to dethrone the false gods from the envied place which had been given them in the memory and the hearts of children, and to enthrone thereon a worthier deity. For this reason they laboured to retain the pure and classic forms of Virgil, whilst they cast their novel ideas into the ancient mould, at the risk of beholding them burst through the form into which they had been compressed, and finally destroy the mould which had received them.

Some of them went so far as to reduce the Gospel into cantos, and to make, like Faltonia Proba, a history of the Saviour in three hundred hexameters, each composed of two or more fragments of Virgil. But Sedulius and Juvencus, without proceeding to this extremity, aimed at preserving the language of antiquity, in which they succeeded in many respects, and were not inferior to any of the pagan poets of their day. We recognize in their writings a constant imitation of Virgil, of Ovid, and of Lucretius. It is, doubtless, often without meaning, as for instance where the verse in which Virgil represents Cassandra as raising her eyes in supplication when her hands were bound, is made to express the action of the good thief upon the cross in turning his eyes to Christ because his hands were nailed to the wood of torture. More than once is this copy of antiquity wanting in taste and accuracy; but still the poets who used it attained their object, and obtained from it the result they desired, and another of which they had never dreamed. They caused the verities of Christianity under this poetic form to penetrate more easily and more thoroughly the cultured classes of the Roman world; this was their object, and to this they attained. But that which they had never desired, and of which they had never dreamed, but which they nevertheless effected in a marvellous manner, was the laying hold later of a society which was no longer Roman, which although Christian was barbarous, and by the means of their Christian poetry penetrating it with the taste, and to a certain point with the genius and traditions, of the literature of antiquity. In fact, Sedulius and Juvencus, those two Virgilian Christians so to speak, were destined to become the favourite instructors of the youth of the barbarous ages; their evangelic poems were to be placed in the hands of all, and to begin the education of infancy. Having thus gathered disciples, they also found imitators, not only in the Latin but also in all the new languages which were being framed upon Latin models; and it was after their example that the Anglo-Saxon Caedmon, that priest who one day by divine grace found himself inspired and became a poet, undertook to sing of the origin of the world and the fall of the first man; whilst later, about the time of Charlemagne, the monk Ottfried did not shrink from writing a great poem on the Harmony of the Gospels, and was the first who forced the glorious language of the Franks to resound with the praises of Christianity.

Yet these frequent and long-sustained efforts did not result in moulding the Christian epopee into the form which might have seemed proper to it. For on seeing Juvencus and Sedulius labouring, even in the fifth century, to sing of the birth, the life, and the sufferings of Christ; on seeing the whole Christian world filled with the same idea, and every art, from painting to architecture, occupied in reproducing it under a thousand forms; and, lastly, on beholding the entire manhood of the Church rushing, at the cry of the crusades, to deliver the sepulchre of the Saviour, does it not seem that the whole poetic effort must have tended to realize the type of which it dreamed, and to treat in glorious and immortal narrative of the advent and the mission of Christ ? Yet it is this that Christian poetry will never achieve. Doubtless it is true that poetry calls for the intervention of the Divinity, but not of the Divinity alone, for it is especially necessary to it that humanity should fill the scene. Poetry attaches itself in preference tó that which is human, because she finds therein elements of passion, of nobility, of pathos, of changefulness, and, consequently, a plenitude of diverse and contrary emotions. And therefore the Christian poetry found its principal resources in the events, the temporal, warlike, political, and military developments of Christendom. The conquests of Charlemagne, chivalry as symbolized under the myth of the Round Table, and the recovery of the 'Holy Places, brought forth the chivalric romances and resulted in the epopee of Tasso. The discovery by Christians of an unbelieving world was to inspire the admirable author of the "Lusiades." Thus it is always from humanity that even Christian poetry seeks its principal inspiration; though it seeks also to bury itself in the depths of the faith, and to return, as far as possible, to that divine epopee which has for its three points the Fall, Redemption, and Judgment. Yet even when it has reached that subject which has never ceased to torment mankind, it succeeds only in grasping the two human extremities, for the Divine mean still escapes it. "We see Milton, indeed, after the lapse of many ages, when the Bible itself had felt the influence of the Protestant controversy, using the boldest interpretation, that he might turn the first pages of Genesis into a poem; but the hero that he took was a mortal man capable of supreme misery—the man who from the beginning to the end of things is ever disquieting us by his weakness and reassuring us by the impulse which bears him back to God. Dante, likewise, causes us to explore the three kingdoms of hell, of purgatory, and of paradise; but he peopled them with men of like nature to himself, and it was from their conversation that he evoked the floods of poetry with which his century was inundated. On the other hand, when Christian poetry sought to touch the mysteries of redemption—the knot of the divine epopee—it shrunk hack ; and however great might he the genius of those who ventured on it, it found itself always arrested, floating vaguely amidst its own conceptions; and whether it brought to the task the piety which breathed through the writings in which Hroswitha celebrated the infancy of the Saviour, or was evinced by Gerson in his charming poem, " Josephina," which was devoted to the same subject; or through the learned and elegant methods of the Revival, as employed by Sannazar, in his work "De Partu Virginis," or Vida in his " Christiad;" or, lastly, was strong in the boldness of the modern spirit, in the charms of a dreamy imagination, and of a richly endowed mind, like that of Klopstock, it still has always failed. And the reason is, that the Christian world has still too much faith, and that the august figure of Christ still inspires so much respect that the hands which approach it tremble. Painters have traced that Form because there was no authentic image; but poets were unable to lend to it speech and action, for they were crushed by the reality of the Gospel. Providence has willed that nothing akin to poetry or to fiction should envelop that fundamental dogma upon which the whole economy of the world's civilization is reposing.

But side by side with Christian hymnody, which surmounted with so much labour the difficulties of its origin, stood that lyric poetry, the free outpouring of the soul, which was only moulded into verse that it might be established and perpetuated. The production of a lyric poetry was predestined from the earliest times of Christianity. St. Paul himself exhorted the faithful to sing hymns of praise, and we can mark traces of them in the letter from Pliny to Trajan, or that in which St. Justin described the liturgy used by the Christians of his day. Again, an ancient legend prevailed in the East to the effect that St. Ignatius, the Bishop of Antioch, had beheld in vision the heaven opened, and had heard the angels singing in double choir the praises of the Holy Trinity: he had therefore introduced the double chant into the Churches of the East. It was a graceful and majestic idea that caused the music of the Church to originate in heaven itself.

But although the East had adopted the Christian hymnody from the beginning of the fifth century, the same was not the case in the West. It was in the time of St. Ambrose, and owing to a remarkable circumstance in his life, that church music was definitively adopted in Italy. St. Augustine relates the fact thus:—the Empress Justina was persecuting St. Ambrose, and the people of .Milan watched day and night around their bishop in order to protect him from her fury. And he, touched by their fidelity and the long nights passed in guarding his person, bethought himself of beguiling their interminable vigils by an introduction into his Church of the Eastern method of chanting the psalms and hymns. It spread gradually thence over the whole of the Church, and St. Augustine does not neglect to convey to us the profound impression which those sacred songs exercised over him; for he says, in speaking of the day of his baptism, " Thy hymns and canticles, O my God, and the sweet chant of Thy Church stirred and penetrated my being. These voices streamed upon my ears and caused the truth to flow into my heart; the emotions gushed up therein; lastly my tears poured forth, and, I rejoiced in them." However, this man, who had such a profound appreciation of music, perhaps from its very intensity felt doubts as to its fitness, and asked himself whether the pleasure given by the music did not injure the meditation of the soul, and whether he did not give too much attention to those harmonious modulations which were so charming to the ear. Happily, however, the scruples of Augustine did not survive in his own mind nor in the Church, and so the cause of religious music was gained.

St. Ambrose not only introduced the chant, but was himself the composer of hymns to be sung in his own Church. Numbers of these have been collected under his name, which were more probably the work of his disciples, or of later times, but which were composed in conformity to his spirit and the rules which he had laid down. Twelve only can, with certainty, be attributed to him; but they are full of grace and beauty, thoroughly Roman in the gravity of their character, and of a certain peculiar manliness amidst the tender effusions of Christian piety, as if still animated by the tone of primitive times. We may cite the following as an instance:—

Deus creator omnium

Polique rector, vestiens

Diem decoro lumine,

Noctem soporis gratia.

St. Ambrose himself acknowledged the authorship of this. Whilst its language was ancient, its versification had something of the modern form, in that little strophe of four iambic verses of eight syllables, which lends itself so easily to replacing the quantity by the accent, and thus paving a way for the rhyme, which, as we have seen, was introduced early into Christian versification,-was used by St. Augustine himself in his psalm against the Donatists, and recurred for twenty-four verses, every two of which rhymed, in the hymn addressed by Pope Damasus to St. Agatha. Thus the sequence of the Middle Age had already appeared, nearly all of which are thus cut into strophes of four verses, each containing eight syllables, with this difference, that in the mediaeval poetry quantity was replaced by the rhyme, which was to afford to the ear the satisfaction which the ancient prosody would henceforth be unable to offer. It was a strange fact that it was only upon the condition of breaking loose once and for ever from the ancient forms, that the poetry of Christianity was at last to attain that liberty without which it must lack inspiration, which was to endow it with the abundant wealth and strength which it possessed in the thirteenth century, and, finally, with the majesty of the *Dies Iræ* and the inexpressible grace of the *Stabat Mater*.

Such, then, was the general aspect of Christian poetry in its commencement. We must now demand whether the century which has shown us so many men of eloquence did not also produce some few who were really touched by the beams of poetry; whether we are only to observe in them the obscure beginning of that which was destined to become illustrious, or if they did not already manifest some inspiration? We may answer the question by separating from the mass two men, St. Paulinus and Prudentius, who deserve to be placed side by side and to be known by us.

If poetry could be found anywhere, it was surely in those disquieted souls which came for refuge to the Christian life, bruised by the long resistance of the flesh and the passions. It was an age of tormented consciences; feeble minds were hesitating, stronger natures were deciding, and found in the shock inspiration, eloquence, and poetry. Such was the state of Ambrose, Augustine, and the many others whom we have seen by their side. Those great souls had the courage to break with the past, and in the effort they found that which has always been its recompense, the strength which comes from on high to aid the will. That strength was, to some, the courage to act," to others the courage to speak; it came to some as eloquence, to certain as philosophy, and to others, lastly, in the shape of poetry.

Paulinus, who bore the surnames Pontius Meropius, came of a great Roman family, of senatorial rank. He was born in the environs of Bordeaux, and received his first education at the schools of Gaul, which then possessed the most illustrious masters in the West. The poet Ausonius had been the first tutor of Paulinus's youth, and had communicated to him that versifying art which he had himself carried to a point of such marvellous subtlety. Paulinus was rich from his own patrimony and the demesne of his wife, and was covered with every honour; he had already reached the consulate, and there was nothing to which at the age of twenty-six years he might not have aspired; for who amidst the continual revolutions which shook the throne of the Caesars could know that the descendant of so many illustrious men might not one day he called to sit thereon ? However, at that epoch, in 398, the news reached Bordeaux that Paulinus had clandestinely, and without the knowledge of that' Roman aristocracy to the whole of which he was related or allied, been initiated into Christianity and had received baptism. On his becoming a Christian he had retired to his Spanish property, where he lived with his wife in retirement, but not in penitence, detached from the grandeurs of life, but not from its sweetness and illusion, as far as we can perceive from the following prayer in verse, which from that time he addressed to God:—" O Supreme Master of all things, grant my wishes if they are righteous. Let none of my days be sad, and no anxiety trouble the repose of my nights. Let the good things of another never tempt me, and may my own suffice to those who ask my aid. Let joy dwell in my house. Let the slave born on my hearth enjoy the abundance of my stores. May I live surrounded by faithful servants, by a cherished wife, and by the children which she will bring me." These are the wishes of a Christian, but not those of an anchorite. Paulinus shortly after had a child born to him which he lost at the end of eight days. This severed tie broke all those which bound Therasia and himself to the things of earth, and they both agreed to sell their goods and distribute them to the poor, to lead thenceforth a monastic life, and moreover to live in that state of simple fraternity which was authorized by the ancient customs of Christianity, and which caused many a saint after his conversion to keep his wife in the position of sister, as a sharer of his prayers and almsdeeds. Therasia also became the companion of the retreat of Paulinus, and their letter to the magnates of the Church was signed *Paulinus et Therasia peccatores.* They left Spain and retired into the depth of Italy, to Nola in Campania, near the tomb of the martyr St. Felix, for whom Paulinus had conceived a singular devotion, and lived there in poverty and penitence.

This secession had at first surprised and then enraged the Roman aristocracy. What frenzy could have driven a man of such name and birth, clothed with so many honours, and endowed with so much genius, to abandon his hopes and break the succession of a patrician house ? His relations did not forgive him, his brothers disowned him, and the members of his family who happened to come near him passed like a torrent, without stopping. But when temporal society rejected him, religious society received him with open arms, and Jerome, Augustine, and Ambrose congratulated one another on counting another great doctor in their ranks. Paulinus became, in fact, a considerable theologian; but he had another talent within him, for a poetic soul had gradually formed and revealed itself amidst the interior agonies which his conversion had cost him. Ausonius, on learning the change in his disciple, had been at first smitten with despair, and had written him a powerful letter, in which he begged him no longer to afflict his master, thus: " Disdain not the father of thy spirit. It was I who was thy earliest master, the first to guide thy feet into the path of honour. It was I who introduced thee into the society of the Muses. O Muses, divinities of Greece, hear my prayer and restore a poet to Latium." St. Paulinus answered from his remote retreat, in verse, and in the following terms:—' ' Why my father, dost thou recall in my favour the Muses, whom I have renounced? This heart, henceforth dedicated to God, has no more room for Apollo nor for the Muses. Formerly I was one with you in invoking, not with the same genius, but the same ardour, a deaf Apollo from his Delphian cave, in calling the Muses divinities, and demanding from the woods and from the mountains that gift of speech which is given by God alone. But now a greater Deity enthralls my soul." "Nothing," wrote Paulinus again to his friend, " will tear you from my remembrance, during the entire span of that age which is granted to mortals. As long as I am captive in this body, and at whatever may be the distance which severs us, I will guard thee in the depth of my heart. Present everywhere for me, I shall behold you in thought, and embrace you in soul; and when delivered from the prison of this body I shall fly from earth into whatever star the common Father may place me, thither shall carry thee in spirit, and the last moment which will release me from earth shall not deprive me of my tenderness for you; for that soul which survives our organs which have perished and is sustained by its celestial origin must of necessity preserve the affections, as it retains its existence. Filled with life and with memory, it cannot forget, as it cannot die."

These were measures which Ausonius, with all his wit and learning, never found. His wit had taught him the artifices of the poetry of a decaying society which excelled in acrostics, in playing upon words, and every kind of subtlety, but had never taught him the secret of that heartfelt poetry which gushed forth in Paulinus and made him so greatly to surpass his master. Paulinus repudiated indeed the inspiration of the pagan muses, but he knew of an influence which was more powerful. He did not abjure poetry in his solitude at Nola, but still shared all the joys and sorrows of his friends, and his verses reached every place in which there was a tear to be dried or happiness to be partaken. We find amongst his writings accordingly an Epithalamium composed for the wedding of a Christian couple named Julian and Ya, in which he saluted charmingly the virgin spouses whom Christ was about to unite like two well-paired doves to the light yoke of His chariot. He removed far away the divinities who had formerly profaned marriage, Juno and Venus, and dwelt upon the just, true, and touching maxims of Christian matrimony, the necessary and. fertile equality of the spouses before God, the affranchisement of woman from her former state of slavery, the conditions upon which he promised the presence of the Saviour at their wedding :—

Tali conjugio cessavit servitus Evse,

Æquavitque suum libera Sara virum;

Tali lege suis nubentibus adstat Jesus

Pronubus, et vini nectare mutat aquam:

Thoughts which have nothing in them of the classic tone, and through which a thoroughly new spirit was already breathing.

We find the same characteristic in the consolation afforded by him to Christian parents upon the death of a child, in which, borrowing the most charming images of the Faith, he represented the same child as playing in heaven with the one whom he had himself lost, the remembrance of whom had never been effaced from his heart, although he had sat so many years as a penitent at the tomb of Nola. "Live, young brothers, a happy couple in that eternal participation, inhabit those joyous dwellings, prevail both of you through your innocence, and may your prayers be more powerful than the transgressions of your parents."

Vivite participes œternum vivite fratres,

Et lœtos dignum par habitate locos;

Innocuisque pares meritis peccata parentum,

Infantes, castis vincite sufiragiis.

This is far superior in charm to all the idyls of Ausonius or the panegyrics of Claudian, and nowhere before have we found such pathos, such life, and such inspiration. We could instance many other religious compositions, for the works of Paulinus are abundant, but those in which the inexhaustible effusion of his loving soul is especially manifested are the eighteen pieces composed for the anniversary of the feast of St. Felix. That martyr, to the service of whom Paulinus was consecrated, had bound the soul of the latter by the tie which the Scripture mentions as attaching the soul of David to that of Jonathan; and he never wearied in relating the life, the miracles, the festivals, the honours of St. Felix; the pilgrimages which were made to his tomb, the church raised above it, the homage paid to him from every quarter of Italy, and especially, as a theme which constantly recurred to his pen, the description of the popular festival which was celebrated in bis memory. " The people filled the roads with their motley swarms. Pilgrims arrived from Lucania, Apulia, and Calabria, and others from sea-bound Latium. Even the Samnites descended from their mountains. Piety conquered the difficulty of the journey; there was no pause, and, unable to wait for day, the pilgrims marched, by the light of torches. Not only did they bear their children in their bags, but they often brought with them their ailing cattle. Moreover, the walls' of Nola seemed to expand till it equalled the royal city which enshrines the tombs of Peter and Paul. The church was bright with the light of lamps and tapers. White veils were hung over the gilded doors, the precinct was strewn with flowers, the porch was crowned with fresh garlands, and spring blossomed forth in the midst of winter." The poet then addressed in self-recollection the following invocation to the martyr. ' ' Suffer me to remain seated at thy gates; let me cleanse thy courts every morning, and watch every night for their protection. Suffer me to end my days amid the employments which I love. We take our refuge within your hallowed pale, and make our nest in your bosom. It is therein that we are cherished and expand into a better life, and, casting off the earthly burden, we feel something divine springing up within us, and the unfolding of the wings which are to make us equal to the angels."

Et tuus est nido sinus. Hoc bene foti,

Crescimus, inque aliam mutantes corpora formam

Terrena ejcuimur sorde, et subeuntibus alis

Vertimur in volucres divino semine verbi.

These, again, are fine verses, but they are more, for they were the chrysalis from which proceeded those still more striking lines of Dante:

Non voccorgete voi que noi siam vermi

Nati a formar l'angelica Farfalla?

The idea is similar, and Dante's often-cited comparison was first roughly sketched by a poet who sang long before him.

We may have long studied the poets and have sought in history for the true nature of poetry. After many years of search we know what poetry is, but cannot define it; it is impossible for us to grasp and examine, so to speak, face to face, that unknown thing which is veiled from our eyes like Love in the tale of Psyche, which only remained whilst invisible, the presence of which was evidenced by its voice, its accent, and the charm which surrounded it, but which evaporated on being perceived. So when we encounter anywhere the graces of imagination and an infinite tenderness of heart, the indefinable charm which no art can give, and. the alternations of divine smiles and equally divine tears, we declare without a moment's doubt that poetry is there.

This man, then, was a Christian poet—an undeniable poet—but he did not stand alone. By his side we find a fellow, less tender perhaps, and less imbued with the spirit of Petrarch, but even more truly a poet through the abundance and richness of his compositions, and this was Prudentius. Paulinus, in fact, was essentially a bishop and a Father of the Church to whom poetry and grace had been given in addition; but the principal function, the sole vocation and glory of Prudentius, lay in his being the poet of the Christians.

Born in Spain at about the same time as Paulinus had been born in Gaul, about a.d. 348, he had passed through its schools, in which he had learnt eloquence, the art, as he said, of deceiving in sonorous words. After a striking success at the bar, after having governed two cities of his native country in succession, and having, lastly, been raised to some of the higher dignities in the imperial hierarchy, of which he does not define the nature, Prudentius, when fifty-seven years of age, and at the summit of all the honour which was open to a provincial advocate, grew weary of his dignities and occupations, and resolved to return to , God; for his already whitening hair had warned him, as he tells us in a kind of little preface to his works, that it was time to consecrate what remained of his voice to Him. Some of the different compositions which flowed from his pen were devoted to theology and controversy; others to the inspiration of the lyric muse. However, in spite of his intention of serving the Catholic faith by discussion, as he boldly expressed it, he did not exaggerate the force of the arms which he was about to carry in the service of a holy cause, but spoke of them with a humility which was not without grace. "It is time to devote to God the remnant of the voice. Let hymns accompany the hours of the day, and let not the night be silent. Let heresies be com-batted, the Catholic faith discussed, insults cast upon the idols, glorious verses rendered to martyrs, and praise to apostles. In the mansions of the wealthy, rich services of plate are spread out, the golden goblet gleams there, and yet the iron boiler is not wanting. We see therein the vessel of clay and the broad and heavy platter of silver, massy vessels of ivory, and others hewn from the elm or the oak. So does Christ employ me as a valueless vessel for humble occupations, and permits me to remain in a corner of my Father's palace."

Hic paterno in atrio

Ut obsoletum vasculum caducis

Christus aptat usibus,

Sinitque parte in anguli manere.

We see that Prudentius announced himself at once as a poet, theologian, and controversialist armed for the fray; but he was not about to undertake the part in order to confine himself to turning theological treatises into verse, and to express thoughts which were not his own, with a fidelity which was often servile. He, on the contrary, found his inspiration and his fire in himself alone, and the accents of the poet betray more than once, especially in the two books composed against Symmachus, the habits of the orator. We have noticed how Symmachus had petitioned Valentinian for the restoration of the altar of Victory, and how, after an eloquent reply from St. Ambrose, he had encountered the refusal of the emperor. But his request survived in spite of this; it passed from hand to hand as the eloquent protest of Paganism against those who were overthrowing its altars, and it was on account of the power which it had retained over the minds of men that Prudentius felt bound to reply to it in two books of verse.

In the first of these he undertook to combat the worship of the false gods by the ordinary arguments, and then to celebrate, id triumphant accents, the defection of the nobility and populace of Rome, who had gradually passed from the service of these fictitious divinities to that of Christ. He delighted in counting all the families, the descendants of the Manlii and of Brutus, who rallied one by one around the Labarum. The idols remained abandoned, but the poet did not ask for their destruction, but rather that, as the deities had disappeared, their statues should be saved, and should remain standing as immortal monuments to witness to the past. He used the following expressions, which are curious as showing us one of the usages of Paganism, which archaeology has never perfectly accounted for; the old statues are often found covered with a crust, the quality of which cannot always be determined, and which changes their colour. Prudentius said, in addressing the Roman senators—

Marmora tabenti respergine tincta lavate,

O proceres ! liceat statuas consistere puras,

Artificum magnorum opera hœc pulcherrima nostras

Ornamenta fiant patriœ, nec decolor usus,

In vitium versre monumenta coinquinet artis

They used to rub the statues of the gods with the blood of the victims as a means of slaking the thirst of Jupiter with the blood which he loved. These lines, which have not been often cited, are very remarkable, and we may notice generally in the works of this poet a passion for art which caused a mind which was thoroughly hostile to Paganism to demand, when once the old religion had been suppressed, the preservation of its statues, and to open widely to them the asylums built and guarded by Rome for many centuries, which were to receive, under the name of museums, all the trophies of vanquished Paganism.

He replied, in his second book, to the arguments of those who found the cause of the victories of. Rome in her piety towards the false gods, and sought for and pointed to the real cause in the designs of Providence, which used the Romans for the purpose of reconciling, ruling, and civilizing all the nations of the West, that a way might be laid open for Christianity, and her task made more easy **when** the whole universe was subject to the same law. Here his patriotic feeling broke out, and he triumphed in the name of Roman greatness at the refusal of Valentinian to rebuild the altar of Victory, which had been destroyed forever, to give place to a higher protecting influence, and concluded by an ever-memorable request to Honorius, the son of Theodosius, for the abolition of the gladiatorial combats. He had just depicted the amphitheatre as it rang with the cries of the combatants. "May Rome, the golden city, no longer recognize such crimes as these. For this, I adjure thee, most illustrious chief of the Caesarian Empire, command that so odious a sacrifice should disappear like the rest. This is the merit which the tenderness of thy father desired to leave for thee. ' My son,' he said, ' I leave thee thy share; ' and so he made over to thee the honour of this design. Make then thine own, O Prince, the glory which has been reserved for this century. Thy father forbade that the sovereign city should be polluted with the blood of bulls; do thou not permit that hecatombs of human life should be offered therein. Let no one die any more that his agony may form a sport! Let the hateful arena be content with its wild beasts, and no longer afford the bloody spectacle of homicide! And let Rome, devoted to God, worthy of her prince, powerful by her courage, be so also through her innocence." Here was poetry put not only at the service of Christianity, but of that humanity which it had so often betrayed.

It would be more instructive perhaps to examine the. theological poems of Prudentius, which dived into the deepest difficulties of dogma; to analyze the poem styled "Hamartigenia," in which he discussed all the objections levelled against the divinity of Christ, or that entitled " Psychomachia," in which he occupied himself with the origin of evil; to note the boldness with which the man who had up to that time been devoted to the business and the disputes of the bar attacked the highest metaphysical questions, discussed the existence of the two principles of good and evil, explained how the mind could perceive without the assistance of the senses, and traced out the inner struggle between the flesh and the spirit. He grasped and expressed these truths with an energy which he might have borrowed from Lucretius, and which recalled the language of Rome's old philosopher-poet; whilst on the other side the reader might, from the Christian idea which reigned throughout, imagine himself transported into that paradise of Dante wherein the poet, emboldened by the presence of Beatrice, dared to probe the most formidable topics of theology.

But perhaps Prudentius was even greater as a lyric poet. We must look to his two collections styled the " Cathemerinon " and the. " Peristephanon " for these hymns, twelve of which were devoted to the different hours of the day or the different solemnities of the Christian year, and fourteen to a celebration of the anniversaries of the martyrs. It was in these especially that he showed the research and perseverance with which he had mastered all the forms of the ancient versification. Thus all the Horatian metres were to be found in these hymns, used in the same variety if not with the same purity, and often with an attention to rule which is surprising in a century of decline, whilst whole passages might be cited as models of a Latinity which was superior to that of *the* Latin poets at the end of the second and even of the first century. The two characteristics of his poetry were gracefulness and force; the former appeared especially in passages wherein he showed the earth pouring forth her flowers to surround and veil the cradle of the Saviour; or where he described the Holy Innocents as the flowers of martyrdom whom the sword had reaped as the whirlwind reaps the budding roses, and who play as children in heaven, and under the very altar of God, with their palm and their crown. This again was followed by a description of heaven, which in its quaintness foreshadowed the loveliest paintings of Fra Angelico da Fiesole; and, in fact, when we listen to Prudentius as he gracefully depicts the souls of the blessed singing in chorus as they moved, and scarcely brushing the lilies of the field which failed to bend beneath their footsteps, we might well imagine ourselves gazing upon one of his heavenly pictures.

But the power of the poet appeared far more when he described the conflicts of the martyrs; and he caught, as it were, all their fire when he represented St. Fructuosus on the pile, St. Hippolytus at the heels of the untamed horses, or St. Laurence on the gridiron. The latter was one of the dearest memories of the Roman people, for that apostle and martyr of the faith was also the martyr of charity, and had suffered for refusing to give up not only the Christ whom he bore in his heart, but those treasures also of the Church which were hoarded for the nourishment of her poor; and Rome has shown her gratitude by the fact—so popular has the memory of the deacon, who was the servant of the poor, ever remained—that after the Virgin there is no saint, including St. Peter himself, who has had as many churches dedicated to him. Prudentius sang of him, and was led through the enthusiasm inspired by the face of the young saint to put into his mouth the following prayer, which again showed that Christian inspiration which surveyed the destiny of Rome with a glance of assurance:—" Christ, only name beneath the sun, splendour and virtue of the Father, author of the earth and the sky, and true founder of these walls, Thou who didst place Rome as the supreme head of all things, willing that the entire universe should serve the people who bear the toga and the sword, that the customs, genius, tongues, and worships of the hostile nations might be brought under the same laws, behold how the human race hath passed in its entirety beneath the law of Remus, and opposing manners have approached in the same word and the same thought. O Christ, grant to Thy Romans that their city may be Christian, that city through which Thou hast given a like faith to all the cities of the earth. May all the members of her Empire unite in the same Creed. The world has bowed; may its sovereign city bend in its turn; grant that Romulus may become faithful, and Numa believe in Thee."

Mansuescit orbis subditus, Mansuescat summum caput.

Fiat fidelis Romulus, Et ipse jam credat Numa

But lofty thoughts and strong expressions are the property of all men of eloquence, whilst gracefulness is the distinction and inimitable characteristic of poets, and, therefore, it marked as with a first seal all the compositions of Prudentius. They always returned to

his own person with a great charm, and concluded with thoughts which left a soothing influence upon the mind, whether he showed the white dove escaping from the pile of St. Eulalia, or invited young maidens to bring baskets full of violets to the tomb of the virgin martyrs, reserving to himself, as he said, " the task of weaving garlands of verses, which, though pale and withered, had yet a certain festal air; " or whether, again, the poet concluded his history of the martyrdom of St. Romanus by this touching prayer : "I should wish, ranked as I shall be on the left amongst the goats, to be recognized from afar, and that to the prayers of the martyr the merciful judge might turn and say, ' Romanus has prayed to me; let them bring me that goat, let him stand as a lamb on my right hand, and

let him be vested in the fleece.' "

Vellem sinister inter hœdorum greges

Ut sum futurus, eminus dignoscerer,

Atque, hoc precante, dicerit rex optimus:

Romanus orat; transfer hunc haedum mihi: -

Sit dexter agnus, induatur vellere.

This man, whose verses we are now admiring, was destined not to remain without admirers. The Middle Age rendered him a homage which was equal to that received by the most illustrious teachers, Boethius, Bede, and St. Boniface. All the writers of the seventh century loved to borrow his verses and place them as examples by the side of the finest rhythms of antiquity. In later times he was cited as the first and the most famous of Christian poets. At last we find St. Bruno, one of the most learned men of that learned Germany of an epoch that is but little known, one of the men of that Teutonic revival which we have not studied yet, but may examine one day in company, placing in the library of his Church a copy of Prudentius, which thenceforth was scarcely ever out of his hands. This poet held his post of honour up to the Revival. The Revival entered the Christian school and found therein Christian poets, ranked beneath those pagan bards to whom, as befitted the most eloquent, the first place had been granted. Virgil and Horace still retained the honour which antiquity had bestowed, but as for the poets of Christianity, since their language was not of Ciceronian purity, since Prudentius had been convicted of using seventy-five words which had no precedent amongst earlier writers, they were swept away and put to flight forthwith as a barbarous crew which had been introduced into the school under the pretext of their Christianity, that the pagans might remain sole masters of the ground.

There were also some accessory reasons for the step. Prudentius had become somewhat irksome with his passionate devotion towards the martyrs, and these numberless acts of homage to the saints were so many damaging testimonies which must be suppressed or silenced. In vain did some men of taste and learning, as for instance Louis Vivès, one of the most famous and zealous adherents of the Revival, complain courageously of this, and demand a resting-place for the instructors of our fathers; it was necessary that they should disappear.

Let us he more equitable, let our admiration be wide enough to render to the poets of the first centuries of Christianity the justice which for so long a time was not refused them; and as Prudentius, fervent convert and penitent as he was, tolerantly wished that even the statues of the false gods should remain standing in the Forum, so let us reclaim for the early Christian poets their standing-place before the school. There would be no rashness in the act; and yet, in spite of all the poetry to which we have been bound to point in the works of these writers, which we have just traced in a perhaps too lengthy analysis, we must at length affirm that the true Christian poetry, and its very basis, was not there, but in a quarter which we shall now proceed to examine.

CHRISTIAN ART.

We ought to have closed our history of the Christian literature of the fifth century with that of poetry; and yet when we sought for that poetical inspiration which seemed to spring forth with such abundant life from the great scenes of Christianity, it was with difficulty that we found it. It did not lurk in those numerous epic and dialectic compositions in which so many writers laboured, with more exactness than originality, to bend the stories of Scripture or the hard points of dogma to the metres of Virgil and of Ovid. It is true that we perceived the poetic ray upon the brow of two men of different genius and destiny, St. Paulinus and Prudentius, the former of whom renounced honour, fortune, and the whole world in order to consume his days at the tomb of St. Felix of Nola, though he never gave up those sweet rhythms which flowed as naturally as tears, and served, like tears, as an outflow of his feelings; whilst the latter devoted his last days to the service of the faith, and employed himself in defending its doctrines and its glory. We saw how power and grace combined to weave his verses into so many crowns, which, as he said himself, he used to hang amongst the fresh garlands with which the faithful decked the sepulchres of the saints. Poetry doubtless existed therein, but not entirely; certainly not in such a measure as might have been expected after three centuries of persecution, after Constantine and the Nicene Council, in the times of the Fathers, and in the days in which the heroic anchorites flourished like so many plants of the desert. Then if poetry cannot be found complete there, it must have existed elsewhere. There must have been some source whence it sprang in abundance to flow on and spread abroad over the succeeding ages.

Symbolism is the common fount of all Christian poetry. Symbolism is at once a law of nature and a law of the human mind. It is a law of nature: for what, after all, is creation but a magnificent language which is speaking to us by night and by day? The heavens tell us of their author; and all created beings speak not only of Him who made them, but of each other, the meanest and most obscure unfolding the history of the sons of light and glory. What is the returning bird of passage but the sign of the spring which, it brings with it, and of stars which have been coursing on for months? And does not the fragile reed which casts its shadow on the sand serve to register the height of the sun on the horizon? Thus do all existences bear mutual witness, arouse and summon one another from one end of immensity to the other, and thus do their continual combinations, their numberless symbols and harmonies, form the poetry of the world which we inhabit.

Thus the Almighty speaks by signs, and man in his turn, when he speaks to God, exhausts the whole series of signs which his intelligence can grasp. What other language could the human intellect speak than that which it has received, and in which it has been formed ? And therefore prayer alone does not satisfy man when he is addressing God; he desires music and those sacred ceremonies which also express in their way, by their development and the choice songs which they contain, by their pauses and their advances, the movements of the soul, its headlong flight towards the infinite, and the want of power which forces it to halt on the way. A sacrifice is wanted, too, to be the symbol of adoration and of human impotence in presence of the Divine Power. Therefore also the temple appears to act as a grand and abiding witness, planted upon the earth in order to mark the fact that intellects are present which desire, after their own fashion, to attest their efforts to reach their Creator. Thus the whole of nature instructs mankind by symbols, and it is by symbols that man replies to nature's Author.

The same idea appears in Christianity, and in Scripture God spoke only in the language of symbol. The entire Old Testament is full of realities, and has, doubtless, an historical value, but, at the same time, all the patriarchs and prophets represented Him who was to come. Joseph and Moses were but the precursors and, at the same time, the signs of Him who was one day to accomplish the law, and in whom every type was to find its reality. The New Testament, in its turn, only addresses us in parables; and Christ Himself, using the familiar language of rustic life, that kind of life which is most natural and most grateful to humanity, said one day, "I am the vine," and on another occasion, " I am the good shepherd." It was the same in the whole ulterior development of the New Testament. St. Paul interpreted Scripture by means of allusions and allegories; the two mountains represented, according to him, the two covenants, and the Red Sea, which the Hebrews had crossed, became in his eyes the symbol of baptism. Again, in the Apocalypse, that especially symbolic book, each figure was produced with a mysterious meaning attached to it; and when St. John represented the new Jerusalem as resplendent with gold and jewels, with its wall of precious stones and its gates of pearl, it was not mere material splendour, nor a flattery of the senses which he offered to the men who were daily dying, braving martyrdom and renouncing every treasure, as the supreme end of their efforts; for in the language of the East every precious stone had a symbolical value, which was admitted according to rule into all the ancient schools, and represented in a mystic manner certain vague virtues of the soul and certain forces of the human understanding or of divine grace.

Therefore, when the Christians had to compose their language we need not wonder that, imitating the Bible, they formed one that was figurative and full of types and symbols; or that when the first apostolic fathers, St. Clement and St. Barnabas, interpreted the Scriptures, allegory superabounded throughout their works and in their interpretations. About the same time a Christian writer named Hermas, whose history has remained unknown, but whose book had preserved a singular character of antiquity and beauty, wishing to instruct the faithful, did so by means of parables, after the fashion of the ancients. His book was divided into three parts; the visions, the precepts, and the parables. In the visions, for instance, the Church was represented to him under the figure of a young girl, of a queen, or of a mother whom age had already marked with its character and endowed also with a sign of authority. The institutions and callings to which God had given the support of His will always appeared to him beneath that living and sensible figure, and when he desired to represent the diversity of human conditions, he employed the following analogy. Hermas, whilst walking one day in the country, saw a vine and an elm, and paused to consider them. Thereupon the shepherd appeared to him: '' That vine," said he, "bears much fruit, and the elm has none; yet if the climbing vine was not supported by it, it would produce but little, and that of scanty value. Therefore, as it can produce no fruit abundantly or of good quality without the support of the elm, the elm is not less fertile than the vine. The man of wealth is generally poor in the eyes of the Lord, because his treasures lead him away from God and his prayer is feeble. But if he gives to the poor, the poor, who is rich in the eyes of the Lord, and whose prayer is powerful, prays for him, and God answers it. Thus, if the rich lean upon the poor man like the vine upon the elm, they both become rich, the one by alms deeds, the other by prayer."

We see that this symbolical language penetrated and even became necessary to Christian manners. After the period of liberty which Christianity enjoyed up to the time of the first persecutions, the rulers of the Church recognized the necessity of veiling its mysteries in the discipline of the Secret, and they were communicated gradually, so as not to be immediately exposed to profanation from the unbelieving. The necessity of keeping the mysteries secret, and also of a mutual recognition among Christians, led to the adoption of rallying signals, intelligible to those alone who had learnt their meaning, and consequently to a symbolic system whereby Christians might interchange ideas without laying them open to sacrilegious minds. The number of these symbols also increased infinitely, and at the end of the third century had become so great that Meliton of Sardis, a father of the Greek Church, wrote a book named the " Key," devoted to an explanation of these symbols, which at that remote period had so multiplied as to render a scientific interpretation of them necessary.

In the fifth century St. Eucher wrote the Book of Formulas for the spiritual understanding of the Scriptures—*Liber formularum spirituális intelligentiæ*— in which he gave precisely the mystic sense of the numbers, flowers, figures of animals, of plants, and precious metals, which had all a meaning, and had puzzled the ancient philosophy by their value and mutual relation. He explained therein, after the manner of a great symbolical dictionary, all the signs then used in the language of theology, the figures of the lion, the stag, the lamb, the dove, the palm, the olive, the pomegranate, and many others. It showed as it were the secret of Christian hieroglyphics, unveiled voluntarily by a priest, when, as the danger of the persecutions and with it the necessity of the discipline of the Secret had vanished, the Church could satisfy her inherent craving to communicate everything, whereby it differed so entirely from the ancient priesthood whose theory and practice had ever been to hide and to obscure.

It is because all religions are necessarily symbolical, that they become the guiding principle and cradle of the arts, for all the arts are born beneath the shadow of a religion. We need not wonder at this, for if man is obliged when he desires to say anything, to employ figures which, precisely because they are material, always remain inferior to his idea, much rather must the same be the case when he undertakes to speak to God, of God, of things invisible, of all the infinite conceptions which the understanding can hardly grasp, of which it catches a hasty glimpse, but which pass in a moment like the lightning, and which, though it longs to arrest them, have disappeared before we have been able to compare the imperfect expression with the very idea which it would render. This is why no sign can satisfy man when he wishes to speak of these eternal things, why all methods are employed, and so to speak come all at once under his hand. All that the chisel, the brush, or stones piled towards the heaven into inaccessible heights can effect, all the harmonious illusions that speech can produce when sustained by music, may be used by man, and yet nothing result to satisfy the just demands of his mind, when once it has been occupied with these mighty and immortal ideas. Yet in spite of that feebleness, the ideal which he pursues suffers itself to be glimpsed at with a sort of transparency; and it is this transparence of the ideal through the forms in which it is clothed that truly constitutes poetry, which in its primitive aspect does not lie only in verse nor in rhymed words, but in every effort of the human will to grasp the ideal and to render it either in colour, or in stone, or by any of the means which have been granted to strike the senses and to communicate to the understanding of another the conceptions of one's own.

We see, then, that Christian art found its destined cradle in those Catacombs which formed the cradle of the Christian faith, and we must descend into them in order to find the origin of the poetry which we have sought in books. But the people who assembled there were too fervent and full of emotion to be satisfied by one or two of the methods whereby man is able to translate his thoughts. They were also too poor and ignorant, too much composed of the lower classes of the Roman society, to be able to carry perfection very far in their use of the arts; so they were obliged at once to essay all the arts and all the methods whereby ideas can be expressed, in order imperfectly to render those emotions with which the glad tidings of the faith had lately filled their hearts. We must picture to ourselves the Catacombs as a vast labyrinth of subterranean galleries, stretching for a considerable distance beneath the suburbs and the Campagna of Rome. No less than sixty of these Christian cemeteries have been counted, and the circumvallations which they formed around the ancient city extended, according to the popular tradition which is repeated by the herdsmen of the Campagna, as far as the sea. But on a descent into these sunless haunts, one is more struck by their depths than by the space over which they spread themselves. The entrance to them lies chiefly through the old quarries of *puzzo-lano,* which doubtless supplied material for the monuments of Rome, and were the work of the ancients. But beneath and beside these quarries the Christians themselves have dug out of the granulated tufa other galleries of a totally different form, which could never have served for the extraction of stone, but only for the object for which they were used. All these galleries descend to two, three, or four stories beneath the surface of the earth, that is to say, to eighty, a hundred feet or more; they branch into countless windings, sometimes ascending and sometimes descending, as if to balk the steps of the persecutors when, engaged in their task, they press upon the crowd of the faithful by whom their approach had been heard. To right and left the face of the wall is pierced by oblong horizontal niches, 'like the shelves of a library, each shelf forming a burial-place, which served, according to its depth, for one or more bodies. As soon as the burial-place was filled, the ledge was closed by blocks of marble, bricks, or whatever material chance threw in the way of these persecuted workmen. Here and there these long corridors opened into chapels, in which the mysteries were celebrated, or upon chambers in which the catechumens received their instruction and penitents made their expiation.

We must give immediate proof that these great works were really those of the early Christian centuries, the ages of persecution. Of this we have evidence in the writings of Prudentius and St. Jerome, who both descended there more than once to honour the sepulchres of the martyrs, and spoke of the place as much with awe as with admiration. St. Jerome, when a young student at Rome, in the zeal of his soul, descended every Sunday into these bowels of the earth, and tells us that these occasions always recalled the word of the prophet, *Descendunt ad infernum viventes*, and the line of Virgil—

Horror ubique animos, simul ipsa silentia terrent;

a mingling of the great traditions of the faith with secular associations which shows the double nature of the education bestowed upon Jerome and his contemporaries.

In fact, at first sight, the works of the Catacombs show traces of the effects of terror and necessity; but on a closer inspection, they appear full of eloquence, and had the monuments of architecture no other object but that of instructing and moving the hearts of men, no construction in the world would afford such mighty and terrible lessons. For when we have penetrated these depths of the earth, we learn perforce that which is life's great lesson—the severance of one's self from what is visible, and even from that light itself whereby all things are visible. The places of burial close in upon the whole, as death envelopes life; and even the oratories which open here and there to right and left are like so many days opening upon immortality to console man in some measure for the night in which he is living here. Thus did architecture achieve there all that it was destined to achieve in after times, in instructing, in moving, and in pervading everything.

Let those then who, when young, wander out on their pilgrimages of travel descend into these vast caverns, and tell us on their return if they did not find emotions there that none of the great constructions of antiquity, neither the remnants of the Coliseum, nor of the Parthenon, nor of any other of the buildings which seemed to have been destined to immortality, could ever produce.

But this was not all, for these oratories were covered with paintings, which were often of the rudest nature.

There were but few great artists amongst the Christians of the early centuries, amongst those poor plebeians whom Christianity preferred. The Apelles and Parrhasius of the time remained in the service of Nero, and decorated his golden horse. It was the poverty-stricken refuse which descended there, and yet something superhuman betrayed itself amidst the weakness and powerlessness of a degraded art. On descending, indeed, into those Catacombs, which appear to have been dug in the remotest centuries, we can recognize the faithfully observed tradition of the arts of antiquity, and find paintings which may be said, without exaggeration, to show some remant of the old beauty, without any evidence of that decline of the Roman art which was not strongly pronounced until the second century. Thus the paintings themselves bear witness to the antiquity of the walls on which they were traced, and to beliefs which they demonstrate; and it was, in fact, impossible for the nascent Christian art not to reproduce, in many respects, the traditions of art as they existed in the classic epoch. Some pagans, like the Scipios, had possessed painted and even subterranean burial-places, in which they were accustomed to bury the dead of the family, after the manner of the Christians. In the tombs of the Scipios, the Nasos, and others, paintings and cheerful designs, such as of flowers, animals, Victories, and genii, have been found spread over the walls, as if to enliven the sadness of death. What wonder if the humble diggers *(fossores)*, as they were called, who were the first to decorate the Christian burial-places and chapels, reproduced in many ways the processes, figures, and subjects of the ancient artists ? It was thus that the same allegorical figures, which often seemed only fit for Paganism, such as Victories, or winged genii, adorned several Christian tombs; as, for instance, the three paintings of the cemetery of St. Callistus, in which we find the figure of Orpheus represented after the ancient manner. But the wisdom of the Church, ever watchful over the simple ignorance of her poor workmen, was careful to develop the symbol, to purify it, and give it a novel significance. She achieved the same for art that she had achieved for language; it was necessary that she should adopt the ancient tongue, but in doing so she had given to the ancient terms a new sense, which was destined to add a fresh fertility to eloquence. Orpheus figured amongst these Christian types; but, according to St. Clement of Alexandria, he figured there as an image of Christ, who also attracted all hearts, and stirred the coldest rocks of the desert, and the fiercest beasts of the field; as he figured later in the Christian art of every century down to the time of Calderon, who gave to one of the most admirable of his *Autos Sacramentelles* the title of the Divine Orpheus. Likewise, archaeologists have good reason in affirming that the figure of the Good Shepherd, which the painters of the Catacombs represented on the archivolt of their oratories, was copied from the antique.

The ancients used often to represent pastoral employments in their places of burial and elsewhere; and amongst those graceful pictures in which the painting and sculpture of antiquity delighted, none was more pleasing than that of the young shepherd bearing a kid on his shoulder. The Christians in their turn adopted for their sepulchres this figure of the shepherd, with the chlamys and the complete details of his costume,

and placed on his shoulder the traditional kid; for the ignorant artist, unfaithful to the text of the Gospel, which speaks of a lamb, generally copied exactly from the ancient picture, without troubling himself as to conformity with Scripture.

This is the account given by the archaeologists, but it is a somewhat exaggerated interpretation, and we shall see how a deeper and more enlightened criticism can throw sudden light upon an obscure point and bring out all the significance and beauty of a symbol.

It happened that at the very moment in which the Christians were digging the Catacombs of St. Callistus at Rome, at the end of the second century, there was a question in the Church as to one of the gravest points which she has ever mooted, as to whether the promise of pardon to the sinner had been made for once or for many times, and whether the lapsed could be admitted to penance. A considerable sect, the Montanists, presided over by the most illustrious of the seceders from orthodoxy, namely Tertullian, maintained that pardon was only extended to him who had sinned once, but not to the man who had fallen again; that the good shepherd bears upon his shoulders the strayed sheep indeed, but not the goat, which at the day of judgment would be placed on the left of the judge, whilst only the sheep would be seen on his right. The Christians pointed, in objection, to the parable of the good shepherd, whereupon he answered, with bitterness, that the shepherd had gone in quest of the sheep, but he could nowhere find that he had sought for the goat; and in his work, " De Pudicitiâ," he reproached the Bishop of Rome with going in search of goats instead of confining his attention to strayed sheep. It was then that the merciful instinct of the Church gave a loving and lofty answer to the pitiless men who refused pardon to the weakness which fell once and had fallen again, and caused the good shepherd to be painted in the Catacombs, no longer with the lamb alone on his shoulders, but with a goat, with that type of the sinner who seemed lost forever, but whom the shepherd notwithstanding brings back in triumph on his shoulders. And thus in the place in which some have only seen an error of a workman, an awkward copy of the antique, is unfolded a charming mystery of grace and mercy.

Around this picture of the good shepherd, which generally fills the keystone of the vault of the Catacombs, are arranged four compartments, separated from one another by arches of flower designs. These generally contain paintings of four sacred subjects, two taken from the Old and two from the New Testament, put in apposition for the purpose of comparison and parallel. These subjects scarcely vary. The most frequently represented have been about twenty in number, and this has been attributed to poverty of genius in the artists of the time, who could never get beyond a small circle of conventional models. Yet, if we examine the subjects, we find that they are not always identical, that they follow no absolute type, but are treated with a certain freedom. Some of the representations, as, for instance, that of the original fall, vary singularly, according to their artists and their dates, and it is evident that the restricted number of subjects is owing to the need of symbolizing thereby a certain number of dogmas, to their symbolical nature, and to their possessing a deeper meaning than that which they express. Thus, the serpent placed between our two first parents expresses sin; the water running from the rocks represents baptism; Moses bringing down manna from heaven symbolizes the Eucharist; the figure of the paralytic healed and bearing his pallet on his back points to penance; that of Lazarus expresses the idea of the resurrection; whilst the three children in the furnace, Jonas cast into the sea, and Daniel in the lions' den, symbolize martyrdom under its three principal forms, by fire, by water, and by wild beasts. But it is remarkable that reference was always made to the triumphant martyrs who had been crowned of God, and never, except in the case of St. Hippolytus, to those who were contemporary. It was not till some age afterwards that the Christians traced some pictures of their martyrs in the Catacombs, but the Christians of the times of persecution, those men whom Tacitus had branded as the horror and shame of the human race, never chose to depict what they had suffered themselves, or the tortures they had seen inflicted upon their fathers, their children, and their wives. This fact surely demands our admiration, that, whilst pagan art was wallowing in the grossest and most odious realism, and whilst, in order to stir the senses of those worn-out men, it was necessary to burn a slave at the close of the tragedy of " Hercules on Mount Æta," or to outrage a woman on the stage in the course of some play by Euripides, whilst this same realism held every Roman theatre, and reigned throughout the triumphant city which queened it over the world, those few poor and detested men, without influence, hidden beneath the earth in places where they could hear, strictly speaking, the yells of the crowd, whose cry was " the Christians to the lions," could only give us as a type the martyrdom of antiquity, but never that which they were suffering themselves, or figures of the resurrection, and other graceful, amiable, and touching symbols, thus affording us at once the finest example of an art which loves not materialism, and of a charity which can pardon and forget.

The Catacombs had not afforded an asylum to architecture and painting alone, although sculpture necessarily found less place there as being the special art of Paganism. The representations of the gods were less often in pictures than statues, and therefore sculpture did not now find such favour as painting. Doubtless we find it employed from the earliest times to help out words in the inscriptions which were placed upon the tombs. Often did a sign, a hieroglyphic, or a symbol, lightly traced with the point of a chisel, tell more than many lines from the hand of the most skilful poet, who would have sought to express the grief of those who were left, or the faith of those who had been taken. Already had the ancients beautifully expressed the frailty of human life by a flower upon the tomb, or the rapidity of the days of man by a ship under sail; and the Christians adopted these signs with that excellent spirit and admirable good sense of the nascent Church, which, as we have already seen from the history of literature and of philosophy, took from antiquity all its beauty and its worth.

And in adapting these signs the Church added new ones, and gave consolation in death after her own manner by placing on the tombs the dove with the branch as a type of hope and of immortality; the ark of Noah instead of the common hark, as the ark which gathers mankind into a place of safety, and bears it over the abyss; and, lastly, the fish, as the mystic sign of Christ, because the Greek word $\textit{ἰχθυς}$ comprised the five initials of the various names by which He was designated. The latter sign had been agreed upon among Christians; had served as a rallying signal and means of mutual recognition; whilst the fish also expressed the believer who had been dipped in the waters of baptism. Thus a certain burial-place, the inscription of which has been preserved, bore no verse, nor even a word in prose, which could in any way point to the dead, but only showed the fish and the five miraculous loaves. Yet it was eloquent, for it said, here lies a man who has been baptized and has tasted the miraculous bread of the eucharist, and afforded thus a forcible and expressive epitaph. Sometimes words came in as an auxiliary, and sometimes with a graceful simplicity, as in the case of that plain inscription, *τόπος Φιλημονος.* Sometimes a word of tenderness and gentleness appeared on the tomb of a child, *Glorentius felix agnellus Dei;* or at others the fear of the judgment of God is expressed with a terrible exclamation, as in the inscription of the father of Benirosus, *Domine, ne quando adumbratur spiritus veneris.*

Lastly, the inscription in verse burst forth and spread over these sepulchres, and the true poetry in rhyme set its seal upon the stones of the Catacombs. The following verses relating to a child of four years old, though of an extreme rudeness, are remarkable from the classic association which they perpetuate:

Hic jacet infelix proprio Cicercula nomen

Innocens, qui vix semper in pace quiescat,

Cui cum bis binos natura ut compleret annos,

Abstulit atra dies et funere mersit acerbo.

Certainly one could not expect to find a line of Virgil at the close of these Christian but barbarous verses. But these tattered memories of antiquity apart, everything then was popular and even coarse. We must not wonder at the multitude of faults in orthography and grammar, nor at the number of Latin words written in Greek characters, nor the many other solecisms and barbarisms of which these inscriptions are so full. It was in this very thing that the glory of that ignorant, coarse, and impoverished people lay; it was thus, moreover, that they were destined to triumph over the rich and powerful class above their heads, who inhabited the gilded places beneath which they dug their burial-places. No doubt, had these Christian stones with their verses been brought to the rhetoricians of Rome, they would have shrugged their shoulders and asked how miserable Galilaeans who wrote so badly could dream of reforming the human race. Yet it was from the depths of those cemeteries and the poetry of those tombs that the new art was to proceed which would change the intellectual aspect of the world.

It would be our proper task to look for the destiny of art at the precise epoch of which we are treating, that is, after the period of the Catacombs, but it was necessary first to trace out its roots. It was, in fact, after Christian art had emerged from the Catacombs, and after the era of persecutions had closed, that it was seen to develop with more liberty and variety; that its branches detached themselves, though still being nourished by the same sap and covered with the same flowers. Sculpture was still supervised and restrained, for it was natural that suspicion should hover round the sculptor at a time when it was so difficult to preserve him from the perilous seduction exercised over his mind by the old images of Jupiter. Yet we must hesitate to believe that this art was forbidden in the early ages of Christendom. We find a statue of St. Hippolytus, in the time of the persecutions, of incontestable authenticity and of as early date as the third century, which is now placed in the library of the Vatican. There are also statues of St. Peter and of the Good Shepherd, which date from the earliest Christian times. But it was especially in bas-relief and the decoration of sarcophagi that sculpture placed its career and found its liberty. It generally represented therein the same subjects from the two Testaments that we have remarked in the Catacombs; and the aim likewise was to render through symbols and figures the chief mysteries of the Christian faith. However, some novel subjects were added, as is shown by the admirable but unfinished studies upon the Christian sarcophagi of the fourth and fifth centuries. A great number of these are to be found in the Vatican; but they should be compared with those at Ravenna, and the fine collection already made of them at Aries; Rome, Ravenna, and Aries being the three great Imperial cities during the fifth century, the latter for some time the capital of the Gauls, having succeeded Treves in that dignity. In each of these towns a different school of Christian sculpture was formed, all possessing common rules, but each claiming a peculiar originality. The same subjects were not equally popular in each place; at Aries, for instance, we find the passage of the Bed Sea treated as often as three times in the sarcophagi of St. Trophimus. The breadth, scope, and life of these point to the skill of a practised chisel, and are imitations of the finest battle-pieces upon the ancient bas-reliefs. At Aries, again, we may find historical subjects which are to be met with nowhere else; as, for instance, two warriors kneeling before Christ like Constantine before, the Labarum, which signified the recognition of religious truth by the temporal power, and the submission to truth by the bearer of the sword; an expressive and simple image of a leading fact of the epoch in which the temporal authority was bending the knee before the truth which it had so often persecuted. "We may content ourselves with pointing to the presence of these great schools of sculpture which found disciples in the other great cities of Italy and Gaul, for we find Christian sarcophagi at Parma, Milan, and on the shores of the Rhine, which, though of not an equal merit, do not the less bear witness to a condition of the art which merits study. We must not, as has been too often the case, hasten to judge of the sculpture of these times by the triumphal arch of Constantine at Rome, or say that, as but four or five bas-reliefs of real merit can be found there, which themselves had been pillaged from earlier monuments, it stands as proof of the impotence of the contemporary artists, who were incapable themselves of producing anything worthy of examination. It is true that the frieze has been covered with the most disproportionate figures, from which all the sculpture of the fourth and fifth centuries has been judged, but was it not a period when court artists might under the favouring caprice of the prince crowd

the place which should have been filled by the works of true merit with their coarse and miserable performances ? Does not every epoch show the same inequality in talent? Is not the temple of Phigalia with its rude carvings exactly contemporaneous with the Parthenon upon which are displayed the unrivalled compositions of Phidias? However, side by side with those trivial works which disgrace the monument which bears them, we possess sarcophagi of incontestable beauty, and there are several amongst those at Ravenna which testify to a great purity of conception. Accordingly we cannot doubt that sculpture had not perished, but was defending itself, preparatory to a difficult journey across the dark ages, and if we lay to the account of this art the capitals of our pillars, the façades and the portals of our cathedrals, we shall gain some idea of what it was destined to achieve.

Following sculpture and enjoying greater favour, came painting, and if some were scandalized at the number not only of sacred but of profane figures with which it was the fashion to embellish the churches, the custom was defended by the greatest minds of the time. It is hard to conceive how it can be stated that the employment of images was a novelty in the Church, when all the writings of the Fathers of the fourth and fifth centuries were filled with witnessing to the religious use of images, and the place they had in the decoration of all the basilicas, whether in the East or West, with the exception of a certain number of provinces, as for instance Judaea, where it was feared they might offend the prejudices of the Jews. But in spite of this, the evidence is unanimous, and in the fifth century we find letters written by the anchorite St. Nilus to Olympiodorus, the praetorian prefect, praising his intention of decorating the basilica which he had just founded with paintings. We have also some letters in verse, a kind of poem, of St. Paulinus, in which he explained the ornament with which he had enriched the church at Nola, and described the pictures which he caused to be drawn upon the porticoes.

Such is the proof and also the justification of the use of painting in the Christian basilicas. This art also was to be perpetuated in times which seemed the most unfavourable to it, as is shown by the innumerable Byzantine Virgins that are to be seen throughout Italy, pictures that are very ancient and often nearly effaced, and which may be recognized still at St. Urbano della Cafarella, near Rome, in the subterranean church of St. Peter, in St. Caecilia, in the church of the Four Crowned Saints, and in that of St. Laurence, which contains a succession of pictures dating from the eighth to the thirteenth century; of the time, that is to say, in which the art was supposed to have been entirely extinct. The genius of painting scarcely appeared, indeed, in these generally coarse attempts; but it was not entirely eclipsed, and reappeared under another form in the mosaics with which the churches were adorned from the fifth to the thirteenth century; for it was in 424 that Pope Celestine I. ornamented in that manner the church of St. Sabina. In 433, Sixtus III. caused those which still, exist, after fourteen hundred years, in the basilica of St. Mary Major, to be executed; and thus that representation of the bloodless Cross decked with precious stones, with the figure of the Virgin beneath, the history of the infancy of Christ around, and the twenty scenes from the history of the Old Testament at its side, dates entirely from the time of that Pope. Little by little this mosaic work crept into all the great Roman basilicas, such as St. Peter and St. Paul; and, at length, in the capital of the Christian world, and in the great cities of

Italy, Milan, Ravenna, Verona, and Venice, the apses of the churches were filled with that imposing and resplendent delineation of Christ and the heavenly Jerusalem which glowed so brightly, as if to reanimate the hopes of the faithful amidst the perils of those ensanguined centuries.

The mosaic filled the whole Romanesque period, survived until the rise of the Gothic, and soon gained possession of the ogival arcades of the churches built by the Normans in Sicily; thus at Monreale and in the Palatine chapel of Palermo, the traditional figures of Christ, the Virgin, and the saints still shine after the conception of the artists who were contemporary with Constantine and Theodosius. So obstinate was the prevalent fidelity to the ancient types that it extended even to borrowing images from antiquity, and we may cite this as one of the knots which bound the time of which we are treating to the Middle Age; in the baptistery of Ravenna, for instance, the Jordan was represented after the pagan fashion, under the form of a river-god, crowned with marine plants, and leaning upon his urn, whence the streams gushed forth which formed the sacred wave in which the Redeemer was plunged. This imitation was so inveterate that it was ceaselessly reproduced. At Venice, again, the four Evangelists were accompanied by the four rivers of the terrestrial paradise, to which they answered in the symbolical language of the Church, the streams being here also covered with, seaweed and leaning upon their urns. Charlemagne was scandalized at this, and lamented in the Caroline works that in the midst of the sacred pictures rivers had been represented under pagan emblems; but Charlemagne could not get rid of them, and we may still, in the cathedral of Autun and the church of Vézelay, see the streams of the earthly paradise depicted under the form of classic deities supported on their recumbent urns.

But painting and sculpture were still only subsidiary to architecture, which, in primitive ages, is always the dominant art. And, in fact, to tell the truth, these bas-reliefs, frescoes, and mosaics could only form the monumental accessories of an edifice which would be capable of sustaining and grouping them into a system which would have a precise and extensive meaning, and would afford them the means of truly instructing and touching the hearts of men. This is hardly the place in which to unfold the history of Christian architecture from its rise in the Catacombs, or to trace out exhaustively the first origin of the basilicas. We may shortly state, however, that that origin seems to have been of a double nature. On the one hand, the first churches seem to have been nothing but a development, and, if we may so express it, a germination of the sepulchral chapels of the Catacombs. Those chapels were square, or round, or polygonal, and nearly always terminated by a vault surmounted by a dome. Gradually they were divided into four compartments. When the persecuted Christians, those glorious members of the Church, escaped from their obscurity, it seemed as if their sepulchres burst through the earth, raised themselves over it, and formed its crown; for the first chapels, the first Christian tombs, and the first baptisteries which were constructed upon the face of the earth, instead of being hidden within its depths, all affected that form. The baptisteries were round, and so were the first Christian burial-places, as, for instance, the baptistery of St. John Lateran at Rome, the tomb of St. Constance, also at Rome, built by Constantine for his sister and other illustrious members of his family, and we may also cite the cathedral of Brescia, which is a rotunda. In the East, that form was destined to prevail and to form the cupola; for already the Church of the Holy Apostles, constructed by Constantine, showed a cupola crowning the intersection of a Greek cross. In the case of St. Sophia, the cupola was developed still more, until it extended on every side, and, in some measure, absorbed the limbs of the cross, thus forming the special Byzantine type which was to remain peculiar to the East.

But another and not less incontestable origin was that derived from the use made by the Christians of the old Roman basilicas. Athens had possessed a portico, named the Kingly Porch, which had served for the audiences of the archon king, and Rome had imitated this architecture. In the arcades wherein justice was administered was comprised a building styled a basilica. This was a vast palace, divided into three naves by colonnades placed tier upon tier, and at the end was the tribunal occupied by the judge and his assessors. When Christianity had expanded and grown powerful, it did not desire to borrow from antiquity its temples, for they were too small; but it borrowed its basilicas. It is thus that the churches of Tyre and Jerusalem, of which we have the description; those of St. Peter and

St. John Lateran, built by Constantine; that of St. Paul, founded by Theodosius; and, lastly, the Basilica of Nola, of which St. Paulinus has given us an account, were all constructed.

But we do not exactly understand all that was signified by a church in these early Christian ages. It was not simply a place to which a hasty visit of a half hour was made once a week for the accomplishment of a pious duty. The church was bound to embrace every portion of the Christian society, and to be the image and representation of the universal Church of the earth in its whole hierarchy from the bishop to the humblest penitent. Thus the bishop's throne was placed in the apse; around it were ranged the benches of his clergy, to right and left; separated in the two naves, lying north and south, were the men and women, who were admitted to participation in the mysteries; at the extreme end of the principal nave was the place for the catechumens and some of the penitents; and, lastly, in the atrium, the vestibule, and the arcaded court which separated the church from the street, were stationed the penitents of lower degree, and another portion of the catechumens. Thus all in their previously assigned positions occupied a similar place in the sacred building to that which they filled in the designs of Providence. Moreover, the Church was bound to instruct men and to attract them, that they might go forth informed and touched, desirous too of returning as to a place in which they had found truth, goodness, and beauty. Accordingly the church was covered with symbolical pictures, with lessons written beneath them in verse; every wall spoke, as in the case of the beautiful frescoes which we have seen painted on those of St. Germain des Prés, and there was no stone there which had not something to teach to mankind. So with that mingling of architecture, of painting, and of inscriptions, multiplied occasionally to such an extent that in St. Mark, at Venice, there is a whole poem of two hundred and fifty verses on the walls. The church contained a theology, a rule, and a sacred poem. It was after this manner that the basilica of the first Christian ages was conceived, and it was thus that it was repeated and reproduced until it became the dominant system of the West.

Nevertheless the East and the West were not without connection, and during the whole period which separated Charlemagne and Constantine, there was no breach between these rival and often jealous sections of the Church. Hence we find many mutual exchanges and adaptations; the Byzantine cupola invaded the West and was annexed in Northern Italy to the ordinary type of the Roman basilicas. The style thus formed, which has been named Romanesque, Lombard, and inaccurately Byzantine, was continued on the banks of the Rhine, and still shows excellent specimens at Spires, Worms, Mayence, and Cologne. Those fine churches of the tenth and eleventh centuries confound us by their grandeur and solemnity. Their form was always that of the Roman basilica, with its body divided into three naves, but with the cupola crowning the centre of the cross, and sometimes the apse itself.

Lastly came the Gothic period, having less to effect than has been supposed, for the Romano-Byzantine architecture had already pushed farther and raised higher than had been dared by the contemporaries of Constantine and Theodosius, every portion of the sacred building, especially in those great buildings of the Rhineland, with their infinite wealth of detail, their belfries which rose towards heaven on every side, and their towers which seemed to defy all that antiquity had told of the giants. Gothic architecture was destined to a last effort, like one rising from the dead who would strive to raise the lid of his sepulchre and end by breaking it. So the Gothic, in labouring to raise the Byzantine arch, broke it in the midst, and the pointed style was formed. With it broke forth that architectural system whose marvels mayhap are yet neither known nor admired enough; for although Rheims and Chartres are at our sides, we seem to ignore them. We now go to the Parthenon and say that we have never seen the like; whereas marvels of a different grandeur and variety, and equally immortal, lie around us. However, this Gothic architecture was still only the development of the Christian basilica as it had been moulded in the fifth century; and a near inspection will show the same disposition and the recurring idea of the keel *(navis)* of the vessel; and, in fact, this nave and this vessel imitated the ark of Noah, of which the Scripture spoke. But the arch of the thirteenth century had so extended the cross that it was necessary to support it by buttresses—things unknown to the ancients. Their weight was concealed by their number; they were multiplied, lightened, and diminished, until they appeared as so many cables extended to bind to the earth the heavenly bark, which otherwise would escape, sail away, and disappear.

Such was the origin of the Gothic architecture, and it points also to the origin of the Revival; but we see that the Revival preferred the rounder form and the cupola which was so dear to the Byzantines. The new St. Peter's, which was then reared upon the ruins of the older church, was but another mighty effort to raise still higher into the air the dome which already swelled over St. Sophia, St. Vitális at Ravenna, and St. Mark at Venice; only the new shrine was to be greater and vaster than had ever been seen. It was to soar higher than had ever been reached; for beneath it was a generating tomb—one of those burial-places that are always full of life; one of those germs that are ever shooting forth—and which, beneath the obscure basilica which had veiled it, had laboured ceaselessly to shape the walls which it found too strait. Above it now is suspended the loftiest dome that has ever been built, nearly equalling the height of Egypt's greatest pyramid, which is, after all, but a masterpiece of materialism, a mass of piled up masonry; whereas great waves of light and life ebb and flow beneath the arches of St. Peter's. Its stones are instinct with spirit, and, borne into the air by the hands of faith, they command the neighbouring mountains. You start from the lowest step of the basilica and your view is cramped; you mount the endless stairs, and, at last, above the church and its cupola, you find the platform and see from thence the hills sink down and disappear on the plain; and over them you may perceive the sea, a sight never gazed upon by Romans in their triumphs from the heights of the Capitol.

THE MATERIAL CIVILIZATION OF THE EMPIRE.

We know How the ideas which formed the spirit of the Roman civilization escaped the ruin of the Empire, traversed the barbaric period, and descended to the mediaeval epoch, of which they became at one time the beacon light, at another the scandal. We have also noticed the marvel of wisdom and accommodation by which Christianity saved the feeble remnants of the ancient worship, the greater part of literature, and the whole legal system. Meanwhile, however, the baneful influences of Paganism subsisted in the popular superstitions and occult sciences, in the policy of the princes who busied themselves in reconstructing the absolutism of the Caesars in their own interests, and those mythological fables which were ever relished, and which tended to propagate the poison of the ancient licentiousness. Thus were perpetuated the two traditions of good and evil; thus a double bond linked the ages which history has vainly separated; and thus was strengthened that wholesome but terrible law of reversibility which causes us to reap the fruit of the merits of our forefathers and to bear the burden of their faults.

But beneath the current of ideas which dispute the empire of the world lies that world itself such as labour has made it, with that treasure of wealth and visible adornment which · render it worthy of being the transient sojourn-place of immortal souls. Beneath the true, the good, and the beautiful, lies the useful, which is brightened by their reflection. No people has ever more keenly appreciated the idea of utility than that of Rome; none has ever laid upon the earth a hand more full of power, or more capable of transforming it, nor more profusely flung the treasures of earth at the feet of humanity. So we must also closely examine what may be styled the material civilization of the Empire, that we may know whether it also perished entirely at the time of the invasions, or, if not, how much of it was stored up for the ages to come.

At the close of the second century, before the barbarians had carried fire and sword across the frontiers, the rhetorician Aristides celebrated, in the following terms, the greatness of the Roman Empire:—·"Romans, the whole world beneath your dominion seems to be keeping a day of festival. From time to time a sound of battle comes to you from the ends of the earth, where you are repelling the Goth, the Moor, or the Arab. But soon that sound is dispersed like a dream. Other are the rivalries and different the conflicts which you excite throughout the universe. They are combats of glory, rivalries in magnificence between provinces and cities. Through you gymnasia, aqueducts, porticoes, temples, and schools are multiplied; the very soil revives, and earth is but one vast garden." Similar also was the language of the stern Tertullian:—" In truth, the world becomes day by day richer and more cultivated; even the islands are no longer solitudes, the rocks have no more terrors for the navigator; everywhere there are habitations, population, law, and life." In fact, we are at once struck by the life which animated every quarter of the Empire, and, therefore, every corner of the world; life which was sustained by commerce, the greatness of which lies in its faculty of thus carrying the sovereignty of man over every sea and every land. The trade of Rome flowed necessarily towards the East and the North, and in the East she had inherited the ideas as well as the conquests of Alexander. The Greeks had penetrated Asia by two great routes—one by land, the other by sea; the first led by the colonies on the Euxine, the Tauric Chersonese, Olbia, and Theodosia. From these places, and from Armenia, they reached Media, Hyrcania, and Bactriana, in which last a Grecian dynasty had sustained itself for a thousand years; and then, traversing the passes of the Imaus, gained Little Bokhara, about the ninety-sixth degree of longitude. Here there was a caravanserai of stone, and to it the Seri brought their silks, furs, and steel in bales, on which the price was marked, deposited them, and departed. The buyers then came, examined the merchandise, and, if it suited them, left the value which the Seri had put upon it. The latter then returned, and, if satisfied with the bargain, they left their goods, and carried off the price. It took the Seri seven months' march, according to Pomponius Mela, to reach their native country of Eastern Thibet, and those dearly-purchased stuffs were handed over to workwomen, who unwove them in order to give them a finer texture: *ut matronæ publice transluceant.*

The principal sea route open to ancient commerce was that by Alexandria. Ptolemy Philadelphus had formed ports upon the Red Sea, and under the Romans 120 ships sailed yearly from Myos Amos, weighing anchor generally at the island of Pattala, at the mouth of the Indus, though a small number pushed their enterprise to the port of Palibothra, at the mouth of the Ganges. They kept close to the shore of the mainland and of the island of Ceylon. The vessels employed in the commerce of the Indus carried there fifty million sesterces every year, but the merchandise they brought back sold for a hundred times as much. It comprised silk, cotton, colouring materials, pearls and jewels, ivory, steel of superior quality, lions, leopards, panthers, and slaves, all this mass of wealth being disembarked at Puteoli.

To the North, however, every facility for trade was the creation of Rome herself. Her legions had constructed the roads which furrowed mountains, leaped over marshes, and crossed so many different provinces with a like solidity, regularity, and uniformity, and the various races were lost in admiration at the mighty works which were attributed in after times to Caesar, to Brunehaut, or to Abelard. There were two routes from Rome to the Danube, one by Aquileium and Lauriacum, another by Verona and Augsburg. Another way ran from the Black Sea along the course of that river and joined Vienna, Passau, Ratisbon, Augsburg, Winterthur, Basle, Strasburg, Bonn, Cologne, Leyden, and Utrecht. The Rhine and the Meuse were linked by a canal; another was destined to reach the Saône, and thus the Black Sea, the Mediterranean, and the Baltic were brought into communication. Beyond, again, lay conquered Britain, divided into five provinces and covered with a network of roads, which ended at the wall of Hadrian. From these northern regions the Roman merchants gained tin, amber, rich furs, and the fair tresses which adorned the heads of patrician matrons. But at length the barbarians came down over all this, and it seemed as if the links which bound the world were snapping. However, a connection was maintained between Italy and Constantinople. The capital of the Eastern Empire formed a place of refuge for the Frankish kings whom their subjects had rejected, or for the chiefs who were persecuted by the kings. Childeric, Gondowald, Gontran Duke of Auvergne found a retreat there; and on the other hand Syrians were found at Orleans, and a Syrian named Eusebius even purchased the episcopal see of Paris. Moreover, the luxury which Roman commerce had produced was not unknown to the West in the Carlovingian period. The Franks found at Pavia silk clothes of every colour, and foreign furs of all sorts, brought thither by the merchants of Venice from the treasures of the East, and the following anecdote, related by the monk of St. Gall, shows that Oriental garments were in fashion even at the court of Charlemagne. "On a certain feast day after mass, Charles took his chief courtiers out hunting. The day was cold and rainy, and the emperor wore a sheepskin coat; but the courtiers who had just come from Pavia, whither the Venetians had recently brought all the riches of the Orient from countries beyond the sea, were clad, after their fashion on holy days, in robes covered with the feathers of Phoenician birds, trimmed with silk and the downy feathers to the neck and tail of the peacock, and adorned with Tyrian purple and fringes of cedar bark; upon some shone embroidered stuffs, upon others the fur of dormice. In this array they rode through the woods, and so they returned torn by the branches of trees, thorns, and brambles, drenched with rain, and stained with the blood of wild beasts and the exhalations from their hides. 'Let none of us,' said the mischievous Charles, ' change our clothes until the time of going to rest, for they will dry quicker upon us.' Immediately every one became more occupied with the body than its covering, and looked about for a fire at which to get warm. But in the evening, when they began to doff the fine furs and delicate stuffs which had shrivelled and shrunk at the fire, these fell to pieces with a sound like the breaking of dry sticks. The poor wretches groaned and lamented at having lost so much money in a single day. But they had been ordered by the emperor to present themselves before him on the following day in the same apparel. They did so; but all, instead of making a brilliant show in their fine new clothes, caused disgust at their dirty and colourless rags. Thereupon Charles said to his groom of the chamber with some irony, ' Just rub my coat a little with your hands, and bring it back to me.' Then taking in his hands the garment which had been brought back to him clean and whole, and showing it to the bystanders, he exclaimed, ' O most foolish of men, which of us now has the most precious and useful attire ? Is it mine, which I bought for a single penny, or yours, which has cost you not only pounds, but even talents of silver?' "

Thus was the tradition of commerce handed down to the Middle Age, when the Church, far from declaring herself hostile, became eminently its protectress. Her councils condemned piracy, and by the mouths of her pontiffs, Gregory VII., Pascal II., Honorius II., and Alexander III., she pronounced against the right of shipwreck. Innocent III., again, obliged a Seigneur de Montfort, who had pillaged some Italian merchantmen, to make restitution. But she more especially infused fresh energy, into commerce by her pilgrimages and crusades. The former were frequent in the barbaric times, and the inhabitants of the commercial town of Amalfi possessed a benefice at Jerusalem. The Crusades had the double effect of drawing the population of France and Germany along the route of the Danube, and of launching on the sea the vessels of Pisa, Genoa, and Venice. Genoa and Venice succeeded to the Oriental commerce of Greece and Rome, and conducted it along the same channels. Their route to the North was by way of Caffa and Tana, upon the Black Sea, from whence the caravans reached Ispahan, Balk, and Bokhara; whilst the way to the South lay by Alexandria, where were stored the cargoes from India. But Christian proselytism was destined to surmount the barriers at which the cupidity of Rome had paused. The mission of Carpinus was to pave the way for the researches of Marco Polo, and Christopher Columbus was to discover America, whilst striving to place the wealth of Asia at the service of a new crusade.

Rome owed the methods by which she gathered in the fruits of the earth to herself alone. Agriculture was indeed the glory of a people which took its dictators from the plough, and whose greatest poem, the " Georgics," was the epopee of the fields. We must not confound that admirable work with the didactic poetry of the literature of the Decline, for it was due to an entirely new inspiration, and Virgil, in the place of a golden era, sang of an age of iron:—

Labor omnia vincit

Improbus, et duris urgens in rebus egestas;

And caused the genius of his country to pass into his verses—

Hanc olim veteres vitam coluere Sabini,

Hanc Remus et frater; sic fortis Etruria crevit,

Scilicet et rerum facta est pulcherrima Roma.

Moreover, the agricultural system, which was their boast at home, was carried by the Romans to the end of that world which the issue of their conflicts had given them: *Romanus sedendo vincit*. In their eyes the frontiers of the Empire were deemed more efficiently protected by a line of harvests than by a wall of stone. Accordingly, military colonies were established by Trajan among the Dacians; by Alexander Severus, Probus, and Valentinian on the German frontier; all of which were provided with cattle and slaves, and exempted from the tribute. Thus the crops which seemed destined to tempt the barbarians really served to ward them off. Roman establishments were placed on the northern coasts of Gaul and on the remotest promontories of Finisterre, and Germany bears witness still to the agriculture of the Empire in the form of the plough now used by the peasantry of Baden, and in the vineyards first planted by Probus on the hills that overhang the Rhine.

Yet it was Rome herself, through the detestable fiscal system of the emperors and the opulence of the aristocracy, that first sapped the foundations of this magnificent system. The immense domains *(latifundia perdidere Italiam)*, entirely abandoned to slaves on the one hand and the exactions of the tribute on the other, were alike fatal to it. The peasant properly so called passed over to the Bagaudes and the barbarians. At length the Northern hordes swept down upon the Empire; half or two-thirds of the land was demanded by the invaders; but they still retained the Roman *coloni*.

Legions of volunteers, however, were formed as time went on, to assist these cultivators in their forced labour. A young man of Latium, named Benedictus, had rallied a certain number of Christians round him, and imposed upon them a rule comprising poverty, chastity, and obedience. These three virtues were placed under the protection of labour, and six hours of manual toil were exacted day by day. One day he embraced his disciple Maurus, and, giving him a certain measure of bread and wine, sent him forth to extend

the system to Gaul. Such was the origin of those monastic colonies whose mission was to push the work of clearing and civilizing into the marshes of Flanders and the depths of the Black Forest, and enlarge the limit of cultivation to the Baltic Sea. Thus the traditions of Rome did not perish, and agriculture, like civilization, generally flourished again under Charlemagne. The following extract, from the "Capitularies," shows the care of that great monarch for husbandry, and its satisfactory condition during his reign:—"We desire that our serfs should be kept in good estate, and that no one should reduce them to poverty; that none of our officers should presume to attach them to their service, to impose forced labour upon them, nor receive from them any gift—neither a horse, an ox, a sheep, a lamb, nor anything But fruits, fowls, and eggs. When the duty of carrying out any work upon our lands falls upon any of our officers, either the ploughing, sowing, reaping, or gathering the vintage, let each of them provide for everything in its proper season, that it all may be done in order. Let them carefully train the vines committed to their charge; let the wine be put into well-seasoned vessels, and let them be careful that nothing be lost. In proportion to the number of farms under the supervision of an intendant shall be the number of men allotted to him to tend the bees. The yards of our chief farms must never produce less than a hundred fowls and thirty geese; and the smaller ones shall nourish, at least, twelve geese and fifty chickens. Let the utmost care be taken that all the produce of our farms—lard, dried meats, wine, beer, butter, cheese, honey, wax, and flour, are prepared with the greatest cleanliness. We also desire that every kind of plant should he cultivated in our gardens, namely, lilies, roses, sage, cucumber, melon, pumpkin, pea, bean, fennel, lettuce, rosemary, mint, poppy, and mallow." We do not smile at the sight of a great mind thus stooping to details; for it is a true mark of genius to embrace the small things which mediocrity despises, as 'the Almighty Himself gives laws to the stars without forgetting the grain of dust, or the hyssop, smallest of plants. Charlemagne counted his chickens as he-scolded the choristers of his chapel or the children in his palace school, and it was thus that he was instrumental in re-establishing both the culture of the fields and the culture of letters.

The face of the earth was transformed by the foundation of cities, which shelter and develop social life. Rome, as a city which had conquered the world, thought that her surest method of preserving her dominion was by covering it with towns like herself. Wherever her legions travelled, they bore with them an emblem of the mother city, *quasi muratam civitatem*. The camp was in fact a military city, and the Roman idea of a town was but an expansion of the permanent camp with its square area, four gates, two intersecting streets, and the praetorium or palace in the midst. There was, moreover, no method by which the soil could be more thoroughly taken in possession than by thus inclosing its space, in forcing its waters to flow through aqueducts, and its stones to rise in porticoes and form temples, thermae, and amphitheatres. The Empire became, therefore, a network of towns, and the itineraries mention one hundred and sixteen in Germany alone. Britain numbered thirty-eight, and Bath and Caerleon amongst them contained theatres, palaces, and magnificent baths. Dorchester possessed an amphitheatre, and St. Paul's and Westminster Abbey, in London, occupy respectively the sites of temples of Apollo and Diana. To these multitudinous and magnificent centres of civilization the invasion of the barbarians was at first most fatal. It was at the outset furious and implacable in character, and Gildas describes how the whole island of Britain was ravaged by fire and sword, and how solid buildings fell on every side beneath the blows of battering rams. The Gothic provinces were invaded by the Suevi, the Alans, and the Vandals; and Spires, Strasburg, Reims, and Mayence fell into heaps of ruins under their hands. The imperial city of Treves, so long the abode of the Court, where the splendours of the banks of the Tiber had been in some measure reproduced on those of the Moselle, became a mere sepulchre. Still greater was the ruin in Italy, and the queen-city of the world was made over to the soldiers of Alaric, who devoted two long days to its pillage. The gardens of Sallust were devoured by flames, and the golden tiles of the Capitol and the bronze plates of the Pantheon were torn off by the invaders.

But when their first fury had passed, the barbarians were touched by the majesty of Rome, and laboured to preserve their edifices. They desired to restore what they had injured, to study the models which they had never surpassed; and the following letter from Cassidorus to the Prefect of Rome on the subject of an architect for the public buildings shows the sincerity of this conservative feeling:—" It is fit," he says, "that the beauty of the Roman monuments should be skilfully guarded, that the admirable thickness of our walls should be preserved by strict diligence. Let your greatness know, therefore, that we have appointed an architect for the buildings of Rome. He will behold works more beautiful than any he has found in books or conceived in thought, statues which still bear the living features of famous men. He will see veins running, muscles strained, and nerves stretched in bronze. He will admire the horses of iron foaming impetuously beneath the motionless metal. What shall be said of columns which shoot forth like reeds; of the lofty constructions which are borne up by light supports; or of those marbles which are so skilfully joined that nature seemed to have cast them in a single piece? The historian of the ages that are passed did but number seven wonders of the world, but who that has seen so many surprising things in a single city can henceforth hold them as marvellous ? It will be merely true if it is said that Rome is one great miracle." The Frankish kings adopted the same policy of reparation, and we find them inhabiting the palace of Julian, whilst Chilperic rebuilt the ruins of Soissons.

But there were other forces at work which prevented the decay of the cities. In the first place their interests were defended by their bishops, who became of great importance in the barbaric period, both from their generally superior culture, and from their using their substantial but ill-defined temporal authority to improve the condition of their episcopal towns. In many cases also respect for the saint who reposed in the cathedral procured immunities. St. Martin became the protector of Tours, St. Aignan of Orleans, and St. Hilary of Poitiers. The Church, in her capacity of a civilizing agency, not only preserved but constructed cities; and her abbeys, as in the case of St. Gall, became germs of new towns to which they gave a name. These cities remained also the cradles of industry. Rome had possessed the nine corporations of Numa and colleges of workmen under the emperors, and there were traces of the system during the barbaric period. The history of St. Eloi, his apprenticeship to Abbon, the overseer of the royal mint at Limoges, and his subsequent career at Paris, shows us the Christian workman with his labour transformed and sanctified by religion. 'We find the workmen among the Franks and Saxons beguiling their toil by singing psalms, and the spirit of piety and brotherhood at last issued in the labour confraternities of the Middle Age. These organizations became a considerable power; throughout France they effected the emancipation of the commons, and in Italy they formed the sinews of the sturdy republics of Lombardy. Labour again was of the essence of the Florentine constitution, and no one could be counted among the citizens until he had been enrolled in one of the twelve arts. Nor did this empire of industry crush the aesthetic sentiment. Far from it; for companies of workmen raised the Duomo of Florence and the church of Or San Michele, and it was for them that the arcades of the old palace were covered by Giotto with his frescoes.

It only remains to us to notice briefly the difference between the cities of Paganism and of Christendom. Christianity had so to speak recovered the true life and affections of humanity. Every man had before been turned as it were to the outer world, had passed his life on the public square, or received his friends and clients in his richly adorned *atrium*, whilst the narrow chambers which opened upon the portico had been thought good enough for the women, children, and slaves. But Christianity had turned the heart of man inwards, had given him the family life, and caused him to find his happiness within his house; so he left it as little as possible, and loved to embellish the spot in which his days were passed in the company of his wife and children with woodwork, tapestry, rich furniture, and skilfully graven plate. Yet the Church preserved the old type of house, but only in her monasteries, where the time was passed in prayer or labour, and it was not needed that the cell should be home-like. Modern towns indeed seem at first sight far inferior to the cities of antiquity. Look for instance at Pompeii, a city of the third order, with its colonnades, porticoes, thermae, theatres, and circus. The pagan city had small temples and gigantic amphitheatres, whilst the Christian town was grouped around its cathedral, and had its hospital and school. The ancients, without question, understood the art of enjoyment far better than ourselves, and we must despair of ever rivalling their pleasure-adapted cities, for our own are built for labour, for suffering, and for prayer, and in this fact does their greatness consist.

THE RISE OF THE NEO-LATIN NATIONS.

We have hitherto studied only that uniform civilization which in the fifth century extended from one end of the Western Empire to the other. Two principals were at issue within it, Paganism and Christianity, but without any distinction of place, under the empire of a common legislation and a common language. Whilst Virgil was solemnly read in the Forum of Trajan at Rome, the grammarians were discussing his works with the utmost zeal in the schools of York, Toulouse, "and Cordova. If St. Augustine, from his retreat at Hippo, dictated a new treatise against the heresies of his time, all the Churches of Italy, of the Gauls, and of Spain listened with attention. Thus at first sight we can only discover one sole Latin literature, which, so to speak, began the education of all the races of the West; a teaching which was to be continued through the barbarous epoch far forward into the Middle Age, until the unity of the Christian society was formed. Yet gradually we perceive differences of genius piercing through the apparent community of the literary tradition. Amongst the crowd of nations subject to the domination of Rome, was there not one which had preserved some remnant of its original character? Could one not discover in their laws, their manners, their dialects, and even in the works of their writers, some distinctive features, some inveterate instincts, some irresistible vocation towards the part which Providence intends them to perform in later times, and which was to constitute their nationality ? This is the question which remains for our discussion.

It has been customary to date the modern nationalities from the invasion of the barbarians and the establishment of the German chiefs in the different provinces of the West. Thus the history of the Franks is made to commence with Clovis, the history of Spain with Wamba, and that of Italy with Odoacer. The history of language has been treated in a similar way to that of nations; and it is to the confusion of the Germanic idioms with the Latin tongue—idioms which, it is said, presented analytical forms, possessed articles, and employed prepositions—that the origin of the languages which were destined to become those of modern Europe has been attributed. We shall separate, in the first place, those countries in which the Germanic wave submerged everything; as, for instance, England, where the British population was driven back to make place for the new Anglo-Saxon race which mastered the soil and imprinted on it the indelible and characteristic mark of language; and, again, Southern Germany, as Rhaetia and Noricum, formerly subject to the Roman civilization, which almost entirely disappeared before the invasion of the Herulan, Lombard, and Vandal races which filled those countries, and handed them down to their descendants. But it was far different in the case of those three great countries, Italy, France, and Spain, over which the barbarians only passed, like the waves of the Nile, to fertilize the land; and it is in them that we may seek to trace out the first features of the national genius, before even the barbaric invasion, and before that mingling of idioms to the intervention of which the birth of the modern languages has for long, but erroneously, been exclusively attributed.

We must here consider those general causes which could preserve a national spirit in each of the great Roman provinces. They are three in number, namely, a political cause; another, which may be called a literary cause; and, lastly, a cause arising from religion. Rome never professed any great respect for her conquered nationalities. She often outraged them; but, in the wisdom of her policy, never more than was necessary for the interests of her domination. She left a shadow of autonomy to the cities of Italy and the great towns of the East and of Greece, and permitted a kind of bond to subsist between the populations of Gaul and Spain. In that organization of the Empire of the West which resulted from the decrees of Diocletian and Maximian, each of the three great dioceses, Italy, Gaul, and Spain, was presided over by a vicar charged to govern and to administer it. This vicar was generally surrounded by a council composed of the notable inhabitants of the province, and thence it followed that each province had, as it were, its representation to defend its own interests and make known its wants; and from that diversity of interests, wants, and resources, resulted the very wealth of the Empire · for every province supplied what was wanting to the others, and thus became an ornament of that mighty Roman society of the time of the Caesars. So true was it that the Roman world derived a certain beauty and grandeur from the very variety which was produced in the midst of its uniformity, that Claudian, the poet of the Decline, in a composition in praise of Stilicho, represented the different provinces of the Empire gathering round the goddess Rome and demanding her aid. They were all personified with their attributes, the expressions of the respective genius of each. Thus Spain, then so peaceful, appeared crowned with branches of olive, and bearing upon her garment the gold of the Tagus; Africa, burnt brown by the sun, had her brow bound with the wheat-ears which she poured into the lap of Rome, as being the feeder of the Roman Empire, and was crowned with a diadem of ivory; Gaul, always warlike, proudly tossed her hair and balanced two darts in her hand; whilst Britain came last, having her cheeks tatooed, her head covered with the hide of a sea-monster, and her shoulders with a long mantle of azure, which imitated, by its flowing folds, the waves of the ocean, as if the poet foresaw that this Britain, then so barbarous, was destined one day to the empire of the seas.

Thus diversity prevailed even in the order which Rome had established in the government of her provinces. And this feature was far more strongly pronounced in the obstinate resistance opposed by these provinces to the Roman administration. In fact, the power of Rome was not established and maintained without much resistance, much passion, and much rebellion. To the horrors of conquest succeeded all the injustice of exaction and all the persecutions of the tribute. In every province, side by side with the prefect, who was at the head of the civil government, stood the proctor of Caesar, charged with the financial administration. At the mere sight of the lictors of the latter, the inhabitants of the country took to flight and the houses of the city were closed; for the Roman fisc was insatiable in its demands. It claimed, firstly, the capitation, which was a personal impost, and the indiction, a tax upon property; and then, in extraordinary cases, the superindiction, or extraordinary impost; then the chrysargyrum, or charge upon industry; lastly, upon the succession of the emperor, the crown tax; which was a gratuitous gift which no one could withhold with impunity. Moreover, these repeated taxes were levied with a cruelty and severity to which contemporary historians bear witness. The tax-gatherers, or comptrollers of the fisc, were spread throughout the rural districts, and in order to evince their zeal and increase their profits, entered the house and made children older and old men younger, that they might bring them upon their lists in the category of those between fifteen and sixty, on whom the payment of the impost was obligatory. When the value of any fortune was hard to discover, they put slaves, wives, and children to the torture, in order to extract the real extent of wealth owned by the father of the family. It could hardly be expected that the provinces should submit with good grace to such unheard-of persecutions; but it was in vain that Constantine issued edicts to stop the cruelties of the fiscal agents, which were pushed to such an extent that after his time the inhabitants of certain provinces emigrated into the territory of the barbarians, that they might find under the shelter of the German tents a life less miserable than that which Rome meted out to them under the roofs of their fathers. At length this profound and bitter hatred broke forth in the words and writings of the eminent men of each province. We have already remarked the existence of an African party in Africa, and perceived the reawakening there of the old spirit of Carthage. This faction had raised a marble tomb to Hannibal, and from his ashes were the avengers to arise who, in their turn, were to go forth and punish Rome, when Genseric weighed anchor in the harbour of Carthage and proceeded to hold to ransom the once proud but now fallen capital. In the meanwhile the African spirit loved to dwell upon its grievances, and it had found in St. Augustine an eloquent interpreter. In spite of the deep charity of that great man, and the love which he extended to Rome, in common with the rest of the universe, the ancient African patriotism showed itself in him frequently; as, for instance, when he reproached Maximus of Medaura for having made a laughing-stock of those African names which were after all those of his maternal language. " You cannot," said he, "be so forgetful of your origin that, though born in Africa and writing for Africans, yet, in contempt of the natal land in which we both were raised, you should proscribe the use of Punic names."

We have seen the same spirit throughout that bold chapter of the " City of God," in which St. Augustine dared to reproach Rome with the glory which was stained with blood and crime, and dashed by weakness and disgrace, and have heard the murmurs which arose around his pulpit when he ascended it to tell of the fall of Rome and her capture by Alaric. "Above all," said many of his audience, " let him not speak of Rome, nor say anything on the subject." And he was obliged

to enter upon the easy task of defending and justifying himself. So true was it that Africa then contained two parties, one in favour of Rome, and another to which St. Augustine was impelled by his patriotic zeal, and this point, which we seem to have been the first to insist upon, has never at least been gainsaid.

In Spain, a similar spirit was manifested in the works of the priest Paulus Orosius. After pointing to the conquests and the grandeur of Rome, he demanded an account of the tears and blood which they had cost. And in those days of supreme felicity for the Roman people, when their triumphant leaders mounted the Capitol, followed by many captives from many nations chained one to another, " how many provinces," said he, "were then lamenting their defeat, their humiliation, and their servitude ! Let Spain say what she thinks of it. Spain, who for two ages watered her fields with her own blood, being at once incapable of repulsing or of bearing with that inveterate foe. Then when hunted from city to city, worn out by hunger and decimated by the sword, the last and miserable effort of her warriors was spent, firstly in massacring their wives and children, and then in mutual slaughter."

The resentment of Saguntum when abandoned by the Romans and obliged to bury itself beneath its ruins, lived again in the bitter words and implacable reproaches of this priestly writer. And if the bands of the Empire were nearly breaking from the very violence with which they had been strained, if political causes were also at work in producing and nourishing a spirit of opposition and isolation in each of the different provinces, we must also recognize the fact that the diversity of their languages also contributed to the same end. Nothing seems more feeble than a language, nothing less formidable to a conqueror than a certain number of obscure words, an unintelligible dialect preserved by a vanquished race. Yet a force lies within those words which skilful conquerors and intelligent despots well understand, and in which they will never let themselves be deceived. We need only point in proof to those who in our own days are suppressing a national idiom and imposing Russ as an obligatory language in the very place in which it has met with an invincible resistance. The Romans likewise had encountered dialects which resisted the sword, and over which the prefect of the province or the proctor of the fisc could exercise no coercion. The Latin tongue was, doubtless, propagated early in many of the countries which the Roman conquest had invaded, as for instance in Narbonensis, in Southern Spain. But the Latin which was established there was the popular idiom spoken by the veteran soldiers who were despatched to the colonies. It soon became corrupted through the fusion of races by mingling with local dialects, and was formed into so many particular idioms, the popular Latin of Gaul being different from that which prevailed beyond the Pyrenees. Moreover, the older languages did not give way, and the Greek survived in the southern provinces of Italy into the heart of the Middle Age. Many districts, entirely Greek in their character, existed in the kingdom of Naples as late as the fifteenth century. In Northern Italy, again, the language of the Ligurians, the inhabitants of the mountains of Genoa, was preserved until the fall of the Empire; whilst the Etruscan still lingered in the times of Aulus Gellius, and was not without effect upon the Latin which was spoken in the neighbouring towns. Moreover, the ancient inscriptions found in the Italic towns are often tainted with that corruption from which the Italian language was one day to proceed. In them were already to be found such entirely modern forms as *cinque, nove, sedice mese,* or such new words as *bramosus* for *cupidus; testa* for *caput; brodium* for *jus.* The declension of words also had completely disappeared, and it was only by the aid of particles that their functions could be determined.

In Gaul, the Celtic language lasted into the fifth century, and St. Jerome heard it still spoken at Treves. In Spain, the old Iberian tongue disputed the ground as it were foot by foot, fell back towards the mountains, within the limits of which it was at last confined, and became the Basque language still spoken there in our own days, and which has left no less than one thousand nine hundred words in modern Spanish. Such then is the resistance which a language is capable of offering. But what influence is that which bestows so much power upon those syllables, which in themselves might seem so ill adapted to neutralize the effects of a conquest ? It is derived from the thoughts, feelings, and recollections which they arouse in man; it is from their containing the sentiments which are most deeply rooted in his heart, from their power of recalling the usages amidst which he was born, the affections in which he has grown and lived. A well-made language—and all languages are well formed when they are developed by themselves and without foreign influences—is but the natural product of that soil which has seen its rise, and of the heavenwhich has shone upon its birth; it is in some measure the very type of fatherland, and therefore as long as its language subsists, the time has not come to despair of a nation.

In the third place, religion itself, that power which seemed destined to bring about unity everywhere, contributed nevertheless to the preservation of the variety and diversity of the provincial spirit. In fact, when the Roman Church was founded, it seemed as if a new power had been granted to Rome, which would thenceforth link to her destinies all the provinces of the "West. But it was no less true that that unity and the power of the Roman authority could only be maintained by respecting in some measure the individuality and originality of national Churches. The wisdom and good sense of the Roman Church was greater in this respect than that of the Roman government, for she knew how to respect the rights, privileges, institutions, and liturgies which were peculiar to the different provinces of the Empire. Accordingly, from the earliest time, we find councils formed in every direction for the religious representation of a whole province. Africa was the first after Italy to afford an example of this, and so numerous were these national assemblies that from 397 to 419 Carthage alone saw fifteen synods. This activity was imitated by the other Churches. In Gaul, the councils followed in quick succession upon that of Aries, in which the right of the Holy See to intervene in the government of the whole of Christendom was so distinctly proclaimed; and in Spain we find, in the year 506, the Council of Illiberis, in which the rule of ecclesiastical celibacy was so stringently laid down, followed by that of

Saragossa, and lastly by the first of those councils of Toledo which were destined in time to mould the civil and public legislation of the nation.

Beside its councils, each province had its schools of theology; such as Marmoutiers and Lerins in Gaul, and Hippo in Africa. Each again of these schools had its doctors to the memory of whom it deferred; and lastly each had its peculiar heresies which in some measure reflected the character of each nation. Thus Spain in the fourth century produced the Priscillianists, Great Britain had her Pelagians, and Gaul gave forth the Semipelagians. Italy alone had no heretics, the reason of which we shall soon see.

Every Church had its saints, its national glory, who also represented it on high. And accordingly the poet Prudentius described the appearance of the Christian nations before Christ the Judge on His descent at the last day, each of them bringing its reliquary, with the remains of those martyrs who would protect and shield it from the divine justice.

Quum Deus dextram quatiens coruscam

Nube subnixus veniet rubente,

Gentibus justam positurus aequo

Pondere libram.

Orbe de magno caput excitata,

Obviam Christo properanter ibit

Civitas quœque pretiosa portans

Dona canistris.

Thus the sentiment which may be balled religious patriotism was of early rise. The Christian nationality differed widely from that of antiquity, which consisted in declaring everything foreign to be hostile: *hospes hostis*. In the economy of the modern world, on the contrary, each nationality is but a function assigned by Providence to a given people, for which end it is developed, made strong, and endowed with glory, but which it can only accomplish in harmony with other races, and in the society of other nations; such is the peculiar property of modern nationalities. Each of them has its social mission in the bosom of that mighty society which is called the human race, and this fact will appear on a review of those centuries of the mediaeval period in which Italy so gloriously fulfilled that duty of teaching which was her function during the eleventh and twelfth centuries, the epoch of her great doctors; in which France formed the right hand of Christendom, and grasped the drawn sword in her defence against all comers; in which Spain and Portugal came, by means of their fleets, under the notice of those backward nations upon whom the light of Christian civilization had not yet shone. Such was the respective destiny and character of these nationalities after their necessary transformation through the hidden workings of Christianity; and thus we see that everything already contributed to the production and development of the individual and original genius of each of the great provinces of the Roman Empire.

But we must now turn our attention to each of those three great provinces in particular which were one day to be, Italy, France, and Spain, and which already, in some measure, bore the marks of their destiny. Italy was the one fitted above all to preserve her historical character; for she was by far the older, had lived longer under the same discipline, and the adverse influences of her social war had had time to abate. Therefore she preserved the impress of those two great characteristics which had shown themselves from the very commencement of her civilization—the presence of the Etruscan and of the Roman element, the genius of religion and the genius of government. The Etruscans, who were especially a religious people, communicated to the Romans their traditions, their ceremonies, the use of auspices, and, in fact, whatever tended to impress upon the Eternal City that theocratic character which she has never put off. Rome has carried into all her works that good sense which made her the mistress of the world, and has marked everything with the seal of that eternal policy of hers, the powerful memory of which has not yet been effaced.

And, therefore, we are not surprised at finding these two principles— the theological and the governing spirit —persistent in the Italian character of modern times. We have already noticed that Italy produced no heresies, and this was one sign of the good sense with which she was deeply imbued, and which preserved her from the subtleties of Greece and the dreams of the East. Every system of error came in turn to find life and popularity at Rome, and only met there with obscurity, impotence, and death. Rome interfered in the great dispute on Arianism; she saved, on that occasion, the faith of the world, and from one end to another of the peninsula illustrious theologians started up in defence of orthodoxy, such as Ambrose of Milan, Eusebius of Vercelli, Gaudentius and Philaster of Brescia, Maximus of Turin, Peter Chrysologus of Ravenna, with many too numerous to mention. Above all this theological agitation the Papacy soared aloft, as the heir of the political spirit of the old Romans, that is to say, of their perseverance, their good sense,

their power, their faculty of comprehending what was great, and their knowledge of the art of triumphing over the mere interests of earth. But it owned one gift in addition to those of old Rome, in that it was unarmed, that it had no she-wolf nor eagle upon its standards, and that it wielded the power of persuasion, which was greater far than that of the sword.

At the moment which saw the government of the world escaping from the feeble hands of the Caesars, in the time of Valentinian III. and Theodosius II., that falling dominion was restored by St. Leo, one of the greatest of the older Popes. We had marked the fresh vigour with which that famous man undertook the direction of all the spiritual and temporal affairs of the West, of the Empire, and of Christendom. On the one hand, he intervened in the East, at Chalcedon, to end the eternal disputes of the Greeks, and fix the dogma of the Incarnation; whilst, on the other, he arrested Attila at the Mincio, and bequeathed to the lasting gratitude of posterity the day whereon he rescued civilization in the West. The patriotism of the Romans of old still lived in his highly tempered spirit, and showed itself in that homily, which he preached on the Feast of St. Peter and St. Paul, in which he celebrated the destiny of the new Rome, and fondly pointed to Providence itself as presiding over the temporal greatness of the queenly city which had paved a way by her conquests for the conversion of the universe.

Thus from the fifth century Rome and Italy, now become Christian, preserved the two great peculiarities of the ancient Italy, and we have proof that they retained it throughout the whole mediaeval period; for at the close of the Carlovingian period, the theological spirit on the one hand was manifest in that succession of famous men, the two Saint Anselms, Peter Lombard, St. Thomas Aquinas, and St. Bonaventura, whilst the political spirit so agitated the peninsula that the humblest artisans of the towns formed corporations whereby they might take part in the government of the commonwealth, and was developed to such a point as to bring forth in due time, in the person of Machiavel, one of the greatest political writers of the world.

And these two elements, which formed the characteristics of the Middle Age in Italy, were united in the persons of such great Popes as St. Gregory the Great, Gregory the Seventh, and Innocent the Third. And they joined also in lending inspiration to the " Divine Comedy," which would have been nothing had it not stood out especially as the poem of theology and politics in Italy, as they had been conceived and produced by the mediaeval epoch.

We must ever carefully distinguish the two periods in the destiny of Italy, and refrain from confounding her mediaeval genius with that of the Revival, or from throwing upon that strong and manly Italy of old, which was ready to suffer and to resist, the responsibility of the actions of that more modern Italy which owned as many tyrants as she had noblemen, ended by degenerating into languor, forgetting her destiny as she knelt at the feet of women, and losing her time in the wretched exercises of an emasculate poetry, or in sensual pleasures; the Italy which still bore her crown of flowers, but beheld all her other diadems trampled underfoot, and all her glories compromised in the dangers of an obscure future. However, mediaeval Italy rigidly preserved the character which she had manifested from the earliest times of the Western Empire.

In the case of Spain, the persistency of the primitive character was still more striking. When the Romans first penetrated that country, they found there the ancient Iberian people mingled with Celts, and remarked their singular gravity of character, which had this especial peculiarity, that they never walked except for the purpose of fighting, otherwise they sat still; their sobriety was equal to their obstinacy; they fought frequently, but in isolated groups, and their women wore black veils. All these traits belong to the Spain of modern times. Roman culture made rapid strides amongst them; Sertorius founded a school at Orca, in the heart of the country, and established there both Greek and Latin masters. Metellus praised the poets of Spain, whose laudation had not been displeasing to himself. A certain foreign element was always observable in that Hispano-Latin school which was destined to such celebrity, and which successively produced Portius Latro, the declaimer, the two Senecas, Lucan, Quintilian, Columella, Martial, and Floras, two-thirds in fact of the great writers of the second age of Roman literature. Yet, with the exception of the faultless Quintilian, they all precisely presented that inflation, elaboration, taste for mock brilliancy, exaggeration in sentiment and idea, and prodigality of metaphor, which make up the defects of the Spanish school. They were all of them represented to a certain point by that rhetorician, of whom Seneca speaks, who was always longing to tell of mighty things, and was so enamoured of size, that he kept bulky servants, bulky furniture, and a bulky wife, for which reason he was nicknamed by his contemporaries *Senecio grandio*. Thus early did Castilian bombast and exaggeration develop.

Neither did the sacred literature of Spain appear capable of greatly modifying these characteristics, for it remained very poor up to the century of which we are treating. It was doubtless a Spanish bishop, Hosius of Cordova, who had presided at Nicaea, yet we do not find either that he had written much, or that his country had produced many doctors. But another province was working for her, and indeed it often happens in the history of literature, that some country seems to labour but to perish, and finally to disappear; then we ask for the reason of such efforts, for the purpose of productions of genius in a land soon destined to be brought under the barbaric yoke, and at last it appears that the genius of the fallen country of that stifled nationality has taken refuge in a neighbouring land. Thus Spain profited by all the labour of Africa, and the spirit of Tertullian, of St. Cyprian, and of St. Augustine was destined one day to cross the strait and inflame the Spanish Church. Where in fact did St. Augustine find his heirs, if not in the country of St. Theresa and of St. John of the Cross ? With a mystic literature as fertile as hers, modern Spain was bound to possess a more abundant poetic literature than had ever yet existed. And in fact we have seen, that if this Christian literature of the fifth century was at all productive in Spain, it was so especially in the shape of poetry, and that with an extraordinary abundance; for all those Christian poets, Juvencus, Damasus, Dracontius, and the inexhaustible Prudentius, were Spaniards. Prudentius was especially the poet of dogma, to which he bent his mind with a singular energy, developing it with all the zeal of a controversialist, and with all the exuberance which afterwards appeared in the poetry of Lope de Vega and of Calderon. But on a further examination we find out the spirit of the poetry of Prudentius; that he was not content with throwing dogma into verse, but that he brought it, as it were, on to the stage, by personifying the human affections and passions, and composing a poem, entitled " Psychomachia," in which he opposed faith to idolatry, chastity to sensuality, humility to pride, and charity to avarice. Nothing assuredly could, at first sight, seem more fanciful than such a composition.

Was it worthwhile deserting that pagan literature, then so charged with heavy allegory, which personified the passions, the fatherland, or war, sometimes Africa, at others Europe, only to create new fictions, and people the field of Christian poetry with unreal personages ? Yet we halt in our condemnation, for the Middle Age was also to be smitten with a love for allegory, and to delight in multiplying in infinite number, and without the least vestige of idolatrous intention, the personification of the human affections; as for instance on the magnificent portal of the cathedral at Chartres, which shows us still the senses, virtues, passions, in a word the whole moral encyclopaedia of man, the " speculum chorale " of Vincent of Beau-vais, represented by human figures, with happily chosen attributes, and we find these allegories carved in stone in every We stern nation.

The Spanish drama effected more, for it placed them in action upon the stage and endowed them with speech. It was the task of Calderon to take up the subjects of Prudentius. In the *Autos Sacramentales* he personified grace, nature, the five senses, the seven capital sins, the synagogue and the Gentile world, until by his marvellous art he endowed with speech that people of statues which had been produced by the Middle Ages. He made them descend from their niches, showed them to the assembled spectators, whom he interested in them as in real personages, and so mixed them with the characters of history that the readers of the dramas of Calderon have to endure a dialogue between Adam and Sin, and to welcome all those other personifications which could only have thus been kept alive by dint of the genius, fire, and inexhaustible spirit which filled these poets of Spain. And this action passed not before a select and lettered audience, nor a handful of courtiers from the court of Philip III. and Philip IY., brought together to enjoy the delicate pleasures of academicians, but before the mighty crowd which filled the great square of Madrid, which pressed together from every quarter to see the allegory from one end to the other, and follow the drama up to its prearranged close, upon which the back of the theatre opened widely and discovered an altar, a priest, and the bread and wine.

Perhaps it is less easy to grasp with the same precision the characteristics of the French genius in the spirit of the Gallo-Romans of the fifth century. For there, in fact, the Germanic impress was stronger, and we cannot forget that the Franks have poured their blood into ours, that their sword passed into the hands of our fathers, that their traditions and language brought aliment to our own. It is certain that on passing the Alps or the Pyrenees, and crossing the rivers of Southern Gaul, and especially the Loire, the German mark is found to be more distinct as the North is approached. Nevertheless, we are above all a Neolatin people, the essence of our civilization came to us from the Roman Conquest, though from no sudden and unresisted invasion, for perhaps no other part of Europe shows so remarkably both the attracting power of the civilization of Rome and the resistance which it encountered.

The conquest of Gaul by Caesar had indeed been rapid, and was quickly consummated by his successors, but as quickly also appeared its impatience against a foreign yoke. In the time of Vespasian, Classicus and Tutor caused themselves to be proclaimed emperors, and forced the vanquished legions to swear allegiance to the new eagles of Gaul. In the third century, and the reign of Julian, Gaul, with Spain and Britain, formed a Transalpine empire, the leadership of which was successively held by Caesars— worthy of a better fate—Posthumus, Victorinus, and Tetricus, who, as warriors, statesmen, and highly-principled men, would assuredly have been capable of founding a durable empire had the season marked out by Providence arrived. Lastly, when in the fifth century Gaul was invaded by the Vandals, and had been forgotten by the Court of Ravenna, a soldier named Constantine, whom the soldiery of Britain had already chosen, and around whose standard they were ranged, was recognized by her as emperor. He remained for five years the master of the Gallic provinces, took possession of several cities, obliged Honorius to send him the purple, and did not die till a.d. 411, after a long succession of treasonable attempts on the part of those around him.

We must not mistake 'the motives which impelled the Gauls thus to rebel against Rome and three times to proclaim a Gallo-Roman empire, nor set it down to their hatred of the Roman civilization, for if they detested the tyranny, they loved the enlightenment of the Imperial city. In fact, they always selected the Roman insignia, and bestowed the purple upon the generals whom they crowned. It was always their desire to preserve the traditions of the Empire, purged from the fiscal exactions and the egoism which sacrificed every interest to the cravings of the Roman populace, in order to provide them with bread and the games of the circus—*φαηβτη et circenses*—and to save Roman literature for their country, whose schools were so flourishing that, from the earliest ages, the rhetoricians of Gaul supplied orators for the nascent cities of Britain.

These schools reached so high a pitch of excellence as to draw from Gratian that decree which conferred such an increase of dignity upon the seminaries of Treves. Ausonius witnesses to the popularity of the crowd of grammarians and rhetoricians who taught at Autun, Lyons, Narbonne, Toulouse, and Bordeaux. In fact, the passion for eloquence and a taste for the art of oratory reappeared everywhere; and whilst we may mark the gradual extinction at Rome of the last embers of the art which had produced Cicero, some remains of it survived in Gaul, and showed themselves in a miserable but still recognizable form in the panegyrists of the emperors. We have already incidentally condemned this custom, and scorned the ignominy of these eulogiums, often addressed, as they were, to bloodstained men by others who were greedy of gold, of dignities, or of patronage; but we must still own that amidst this humiliation and littleness lurked the last traditions of the oratorical art, and that such degenerate men as an Eumenius, a Pacatus, or a Mamertinus bear witness at least to the taste and passion of the Gauls of their day for eloquence and the science of forcible and refined speaking. What Cato said of the Gallic race has always been true—when he defined their character prophetically and with his own admirable terseness in the words " *Rem militarem et argute loqui.* "

There can be no better representative of the Gallo-Roman spirit in this respect than Sidonius Apollinaris, one of the chief writers of the fifth century. He was born at Lyons about the year 430, and was probably of Arvernic race, sprung from one of those wealthy Gothic families which preserved the literary traditions of Rome, and kept alive an hereditary bitterness against her dominion. He had received his education from skilful masters, and studiously guarded the remembrance of them. The name of the man from whom he had received lessons in poetry was Ennius, for the time had come for that usurpation of classic names which soon filled the schools with Ovids, Horaces, and Virgils. His master in philosophy was called Eusebius. Suddenly this young Gaul, who had thus, been trained in the art of eloquence and in philosophical science, found himself called to the highest dignity by the accession of his father-in-law, Avitus, to the Imperial throne. This wealthy Gaul named Avitus had, in fact, just been set over the Roman Empire by the Gothic king Theodoric, and soon after his proclamation fell beneath the hand of an obscure assassin. Sidonius **Apollinaris** had been summoned to Rome to pronounce a public panegyric on his father-in-law in the presence of the senate, and shortly after, on the murder of Avitus, he pronounced at Lyons an eulogium upon his successor

Majorian. A little later, when Majorian had disappeared in his turn, Sidonius, who was too fertile in these eulogies, pronounced the panegyric on Anthemius at Rome. He could not have judged his conduct thus himself, for favours multiplied around him in proportion to the number of his rhymes. He had attained the highest honours in politics and literature, his statue was placed in the Forum of Trajan at Rome amongst the chief poets of the Empire, he had been raised to patrician rank and the dignity of prefect of Rome, and had in a word drained the cup of human delights, when suddenly the weariness of temporal advantage, which is apt to lay hold of higher souls, seized upon him, so that in a short time he was found to have become a convert, to have adopted a severer life, and to have been carried by popular acclamation to the episcopal chair of Clermont. Renouncing thereupon profane poetry and the distractions and wanderings of a worldly life, he assumed the demeanour of a holy bishop. But how could he renounce literature, the first delight of his youth, and how avoid manifesting in all that he wrote the trace of the spirit of the Gallo-Roman schools in which he had been nurtured ? Accordingly, on reading his collected works, upon whatever epoch of his career we may light, whether we have to do with the Roman prefect or the Christian bishop, we always find different sentiments expressed in the same language. For, in fact, Sidonius Apollinaris had desired above all things to gain skill in the art of eloquence, and had gained it. Such, on the authority of Gregory of Tours, was his power in this respect, that he was capable of an immediate improvisation on any given subject, and he himself is careful to inform us, that being charged with the task of providing a bishop for the people of Bourges, who were then divided amongst themselves, he had only two watches of the night, or six hours, in which to dictate the discourse which he had to pronounce on the occasion before the assembled clergy and people. And therefore he begged excuse, if in consequence " an oratorical partition, historical authorities, poetical images, grammatical figures, and the flashes which the rhetoricians strike out of their controversies," could not be found there; his discourse was in fact merely simple and clear, and that idea humiliated him.

But he vindicated himself by his correspondence, in which he aspired to imitate Pliny and Symmachus. In this he seems so far to have succeeded that he was prevailed upon to collect and publish them. All these letters, in fact, show traces of the polish which was bestowed upon them before handing them over to the chances of publicity. But that which put Sidonius Apollinaris most completely at his ease was the power of rivalling his friend throughout the interchange of correspondence in wit, research, refinement, and even obscurity. He was fond of struggling against difficulties, plunging into hazardous descriptions, and laying open to the last details the life of the Romans or the barbarians of his time; details which, though useful for history, were tainted with all the vices of the Decline. He put the finishing stroke to his achievements, and fancied himself at the summit of literary glory, when he succeeded in mingling with his friendly letters some improvised verses and a few distichs which had suddenly occurred to his mind under circumstances which he had not foreseen. It was upon these little poems, composed out of hand at 'the desire of the emperor or some other personage, that he especially prided himself. Having, for instance, one day to pass over a torrent, he stopped to look for a ford, but as he could not easily find a convenient passage, he paused till the water had lowered, and composed a distich which could be read at will from one end or the other.

Praecipiti modo quod decurrit tramite flumen

Tempore consumptum jam cito deficiet.

The superiority of these verses over those of Virgil and Ovid lay in their capability of being thus reversed—

Deficiet cito jam consumptum tempore flumen

Tramite decurrit quod modo praecipiti.

On other occasions he infused a greater measure of grace and gallantry, so that on reading the verses which he made to be inscribed on the goblet which Evodius desired to offer to the Queen Regnahilda, wife of Euric, one might be reminded of the French wit of the seventeenth century. The princess was a thorough barbarian no doubt, but the lines were most refined. The cup which was to be offered to her was in the form of a sea-shell, and in allusion to the shape and the associations attached to it by antiquity, Sidonius said, " The shell whereupon the mighty Triton bore Venus can bear no comparison with this one. Abase a little, we pray thee, thy sovereign majesty, and receive, O powerful patroness, an-humble gift. Happy is the water which, enclosed in the resplendent metal, will touch the more resplendent countenance of a lovely queen. For whenever she deigns to plunge her lips therein, the reflection of her face will whiten the silver cup."

Nothing can be more graceful than this, and the most elaborate madrigals would fail to excel the exquisite gallantry of Sidonius Apollinaris. There is no indication that he had entered ecclesiastical orders at this period, and he perhaps appears in the character of a poet of the world.

Had he no other claim upon the attention of posterity, Sidonius Apollinaris would present himself as a man of wit, and so fulfil the second condition of Cato's sketch of the Gallic character, " *argute loqui;*" but he would be far from the first, and nothing shows that he had the zeal for action—" *rem militarem*" But this was not the case. On becoming a bishop, Sidonius had adopted all the sentiments of his office, and in consequence he was the defender of his episcopal city. We know how the great bishops of the fifth century became, amidst the universal disorganization and the incessant invasions of the barbarians, at once the civil and voluntary magistrates of their respective cities, and how their moral authority often availed to sustain the courage of the citizens and to daunt and divide the barbarians. Sidonius occupied at Clermont the outpost of the Empire, the edge of the remnant of the Roman province, and the frontiers of the kingdom which the emperors had been obliged to make over to the Visigoths; and the Visigoths, discontented with their boundaries, pushed themselves in daily attack upon the walls of Clermont, and obliged Sidonius to struggle to obtain the intervention of the emperor in order to stem the progress of barbarian conquest and spare the episcopal city the horrors of invasion. He had long hoped, and for long excited the bravery of his fellow-citizens, to defend the city walls in despite of all the miseries of famine and pestilence. An imperial deputation at length waited upon the Visigothic monarch and proposed a capitulation, by the terms of which Clermont was to be abandoned to him on the consideration of his respecting the rest of the Empire. Sidonius was suddenly made aware of this treaty. Whilst he had been so energetically defending the walls of his episcopal city the men in whom he had placed his hopes had betrayed him. Thereupon he wrote to one of them the following letter, in which we no longer find the old spirit of refinement, but the energy, warmth, and dash which marked the character of his race. " Such is at present the condition of this unhappy corner of the earth, that it has suffered less from war than from peace. Our servitude has become the price of another's safety. O misery! the slavery of the Arverni, who, if one goes back to their origin, had dared to call themselves the brothers of the Romans, and to number themselves among the races which issued from the blood of Ilion ! If one stops at their modern glory, these are the men

who by their unaided efforts arrested the arms of the public enemy, who from behind their ramparts defied the assaults of the Goths, and struck back terror into the barbarian camp. Behold, then, our reward for starvation, fire, sword, pestilence, spears that have fattened in blood, warriors emaciated by privation! This is the glorious peace for which we have lived upon the herbs plucked from the crevices of our rocks. Employ all your wisdom to break so shameful an agreement. Yes, if needs be, we should rejoice at seeing ourselves again besieged, at again suffering from hunger, if we might fight once more."

In this man the French genius appears with all the urbanity, with the lightness for which it has been so often reproached, but also with that passionate feeling of honour which will never be effaced. The latter characteristic was preserved throughout those long ages of barbarism, upon the threshold of which we are standing. We may observe the remarkable fact that during the whole Merovingian period, a certain number of illustrious personages may be seen who became afterwards bishops, and in time canonized saints, called to the courts of the kings and raised to the highest dignities of the kingdom on account of their skill in the art of speaking—*quia facundus erat*—and because of their possessing the power which from that time forward subjugated the minds of men. And again, if we go farther, and plunge into the depths of the Middle Ages at the time in which the French language first was spoken, we shall notice that the chief characteristic of that nascent literature was that it was military and chivalric, and destined by those qualities to make the tour of Europe; the whole of Europe, nevertheless, confirming that its origin was France, that it was born in the land whose natives love the art of eloquence, but better still the achievement of acts of prowess—*rem militarem.*

We have thus pointed out the origin of the three great Neo-Latin nationalities in Spain, in Italy, and in Gaul; and at the end of our proposed task we find two points established; the first being that the Roman world and its ancient civilization perished far less suddenly than has been supposed; that its resistance to barbarism was long; and that its good and its evil institutions, its vices as well as its virtues, were prolonged into the Middle Age, and explained many of those errors the source of which has been but imperfectly recognized. Thus astrology, and the exaggerations of royal despotism, all the pedantry, and those lingering memories of pagan art which can be detected in the eleventh, twelfth, and thirteenth centuries, are to be traced back to a time-honoured origin, and formed so many links by which the Middle Age clung to antiquity, and which it did not desire to sever.

On the other hand, we have established the position that the Christian civilization contained already, and in greater completeness than has been supposed, those developments which have been generally attributed to the times of barbarism. Thus the Church already possessed the Papacy and monasticism; and in the sphere of manners we have specified the independence of the individual, the popular sentiment of liberty, and the dignity of the woman. In the sphere of letters we have marked how the philosophy of St. Augustine contained in germ the scholastic labours of the mediaeval epoch. We have seen the " City of God " tracing nobler views of history, and, lastly, discovered in the Catacombs all the elements which were developed in the modern basilicas.

And thus Providence employed a singular art and a mighty course of preparation in the work of linking together periods which, from the different spirits which moved them, would seem fated to be forever separate. We see that when the Almighty desires to mould a newer world, He gently and gradually breaks the ancient edifice which must fall, and uses its materials considerably in rearing the modern monument which is to succeed. As in a beleaguered city the defenders begin betimes behind the works which the enemy is attacking to construct the fortification which is to succeed them, and before which all the efforts of the besieging force will fail, so also, while the ancient barrier of Roman civilization was falling stone by stone, the Christian rampart was being formed behind which society might find another entrenchment. And this spectacle should serve us for an example and a lesson. The invasion of the barbarians was without doubt the mightiest and most terrible revolution that has ever occurred; and yet we see the infinite care with which Providence softened the blow in some respects, and broke the fall of the ancient world. Let us also trust that our own epoch will not be more unfortunate; that if our old fortress is fated to fall, new and solid defences will be raised to protect us; and, in fine, that the civilization which has cost so much to God and to man will never perish.

FINIS.

Made in the USA
Las Vegas, NV
07 October 2021